Road to Recovery
Pandemic's Aftermath

Also by Jon Peirce:
  Canadian Industrial Relations (Pearson Education Canada, 1999, 2002, 2006)
  Social Studies: Collected Essays, 1974-2013 (Friesen, 2014)
  Love and Love: A Novella (Amazon, 2018)
  Plague Take It (with Ann McMillan) (Loose Cannon Press, 2021)
  Work Less (Dundurn Press, 2024)
  The Long and the Short of It: Collected Stories (Amazon, 2024).

Also by Ann McMillan:
  Air Quality Management: Canadian Perspectives on a Global Issue, with Eric Taylor (co-editor) (Springer, 2014)
  The New Devil's Dictionary, with Duane Chartier and Irene Agoulnik (Amazon, 2019)
  Naked in Time (with Duane Chartier, co-editor) (Amazon, 2020)
  Plague Take It (with Jon Peirce) (Loose Cannon Press, 2021)

Cover Layout:
  Loose Cannon Designs
Cover Painting:
  Mona LeBlond

Road to Recovery
Pandemic's Aftermath

Jon Peirce
Ann McMillan

LIBRARY AND ARCHIVES CANADA CATALOGUING IN PUBLICATION

Title: Road to recovery : pandemic's aftermath / Jon Peirce, Ann McMillan [editors].
Names: Peirce, Jon (Jonathan Charles), editor. | McMillan, Ann (Ann Constance), editor.
Identifiers: Canadiana 20240465350 | ISBN 9781988657370 (softcover)
Subjects: LCSH: COVID-19 Pandemic, 2020-2023—Literary collections. | LCSH: COVID-19 (Disease)—
Literary collections. | LCSH: Older people's writings, American. | LCSH: American literature—
21st century. | LCSH: Canadian literature—21st century. | CSH: Older people's writings, Canadian
(English) | CSH: Canadian literature (English)—21st century. | LCGFT: Literature.
Classification: LCC PS8237.C69 R63 2025 | DDC C810.8/03561—dc23

Published by
LOOSE CANNON PRESS

www.loosecannonpress.com

PRODUCTION

Ann McMillan: Co-editor
Jon Peirce: Co-editor
Yves Rochon: French Language Coordinator
Robert Barclay: Compositor and Publisher

DEDICATION

To Bob Barclay, our publisher and so much more than that, for once again willingly and (in the main) cheerfully taking on the herding of a large and sometimes ungainly assemblage of literary cats, emerging with a product that delights the eye as well as the mind. Without Bob's impeccable aesthetic sense, neither this book nor its predecessor, *Plague Take It,* would have been what they are.

A.M. & J.P.

ACKNOWLEDGEMENTS

First and foremost, to our many contributors—newcomers and seasoned veterans alike—for providing us with such a splendid collection of material to work with, and for patiently enduring a publication process that, for reasons too complicated to go into here, took far longer than originally anticipated. To Yves Rochon, our indefatigable French language coordinator, for once again recruiting talented Francophone contributors and shepherding their work through to publication. Finally, to the many people whose names may not appear in the book, but who nonetheless provided us with ideas and inspiration that helped the book develop.

A.M. & J.P.
Ottawa, Ontario
September, 2025

CONTENTS

INTRODUCTION

In the introduction to this book's predecessor volume, I asked, 'What kind of world awaits us once most people have been vaccinated against COVID-19, and we're finally able to resume at least some semblance of our previous 'normal' activities?' The present volume is an attempt to answer that question, once again through the medium of a social history exploring how elders and those who work with elders have seen their lives change as a result of the COVID-19 pandemic.[1]

Is the pandemic in fact over? Well, yes and no. The answer to this question probably depends as much on one's perspective on the situation as on the data on number of cases, hospitalizations, and deaths from COVID—data, I would suggest, that's becoming increasingly difficult to locate in our brave new world.

As I started to write this introduction, it was a balmy early September afternoon, just past Labour Day. The kids were back in school again. And once again the internet news was full of stories about how to protect your kids against COVID. But that year, unlike past years, no one was even suggesting that schools impose mask mandates, let alone that they be prepared to close should the number of new cases rise significantly. COVID, it seems, had by this time been normalized and incorporated into our daily lives, much like the common cold and seasonal flu. From being a plague which everyone was prepared to do everything in their power to avoid, COVID seems to have become, officially at least, something hardly worth mentioning.

Perhaps this normalization was inevitable. Our economy, which took a fearsome drubbing during the pandemic's early years, really can't take much more disruption, of the sort that arose from the lockdowns and school and business closures of the pandemic's early days. Nor could people's mental health have withstood much more isolation, of the sort resulting from the earlier lockdowns. Still, it gives one pause to see people throwing all precaution to the winds. Ironically indeed, as I started to write this piece, I myself was recovering from COVID, my second case of it in less than a year, contracted during my most recent visit to New York, in late August. My girlfriend also contracted her second case of COVID at exactly the same time. And a close friend of hers got COVID while vacationing at a summer resort in Maine with family. I, for one, am not prepared to declare COVID a matter of little importance given the apparent rapidity of the new variant's spread. Both my girlfriend and I had our first symptoms within two days of our initial exposure to the virus. And, while both of us managed to make a pretty good recovery, the same has not been true for everyone I know who has had the new variant. Some have remained weak and in low spirits for weeks, or even months.

Perhaps the most surprising thing about this pandemic, and what may, in the end, distinguish it more than anything else from past pandemics, is its sheer perseverance—even in the face of numerous vaccines. It would have been one thing for my girlfriend and me to have contracted COVID a second time in a year had we never been vaccinated, or had we had just one or two shots and not kept up with our boosters. But each of us had had five jabs— that's right, five—in addition to having had the disease itself the previous November. For those of us who have always believed in vaccines, it's a discouraging saga. If five jabs over 18 months won't protect you, then what will? I'm not prepared to say the anti-vaxxers were right, but such a finding, especially given what should have been the combined immunity of the jabs and an actual case of the disease itself, may offer them some ammunition.

Granted, I recognize that Elizabeth's and my COVID cases were likely nowhere near as severe as they would have been without those five jabs apiece. Given what I know about the kinds of effects resulting from COVID in the early, pre-vaccine days, the vaccine appears, in effect, to have done what the old measles modifier shots did—make the disease less serious so as to reduce the risk of hospitalization or death. That said, haven't we a right to expect more in the way of protection, especially after so many jabs? The implications here seem particularly serious for those who, for whatever reason, simply cannot risk getting COVID. Unless or until some vaccine is devised that functions as more than a modifying shot against the disease, such people appear doomed to live the lives of recluses—particularly given how few precautions the vast majority of people are now taking. When I went to the grocery store recently, I saw exactly one person, a cashier, wearing a mask. Granted, the store was far from crowded. On a beautiful Sunday afternoon in mid-summer, most people evidently had better things to do than shop for groceries. Still, Maxi is (as its name suggests) a big store. Even on this very slow day, by the time I had circumambulated its many aisles and emerged with my cartload of food, I had run across at least 50 other people. We can thus establish that the mask-wearing rate in that Maxi was in the vicinity of two percent that day—a fact that hardly augured well for containment of COVID and other respiratory diseases as we approached the fall flu season.

Thus far, then, the pandemic appears to have no end—a fact which may also give the anti-vaxxers some ammunition. Why bother to get vaccinated against a disease which will continue to be with us no matter what we do, individually or collectively? I would suggest that this is not a situation most of us would have predicted three years ago—not even a philosophical pessimist such as yours truly. Granted, the previous Spanish flu [sic] pandemic of the early 20th century also persisted for more than three years after it first broke out, with many areas reporting more cases during the winter of 1921-22 than they had experienced since the pandemic's first year. But this was in a world in which there were no vaccines against the influenza, and also little or nothing in the way of anti-virological medications to treat those who contracted it. There was no Paxlovid to ease the pain and suffering of the flu sufferers of a century ago. The best they could rely on were home remedies or over-the-counter patent medicines such as aspirin which could provide at most a bit of symptomatic relief.[2]

What is it about the COVID-19 virus, or about the world in which it and we live, that has allowed this virus to hang on with such tenacity, despite the existence of a number of different vaccines against the disease? Is it some thing to do with the virus itself, or is it rather that we live in a world where travel, including that of a transatlantic or transpacific variety, is far more common than it was a century ago? Or is it in fact rather the complacency described in the first two pages of this essay, a complacency leading us to normalize COVID-19 as if it were any other kind of seasonal flu? These are questions we will need to be able to answer definitively if we're to have any hope of real long-term containment of the virus.

Whatever the reason, or reasons, COVID seems likely to remain with us, in one form or another, for some time to come. Paradoxically, perhaps, it's this same persistence that makes the present collection not just possible but important. The pieces that Ann McMillan and I collected three years ago for our first volume described people responding to the shock of the first life threatening global pandemic most had ever seen, and to the equally great shock of the first serious restrictions on their personal freedom most had ever known. In the present collection, as I noted earlier, our primary focus is more on how people's lives have changed as a result of the pandemic. Though there remains some uncertainty as to the parameters of our new world, we seem to be moving toward some kind of new norm, even as it is becoming increasingly clear that some of our old norms are gone forever.

Most notably, perhaps, it seems likely that a great many people will never again return to full-time work in an office setting. The hybrid workplace, in which people spend at least part of their working hours working from home or some other remote location, appears to be here to stay, as is suggested by its acceptance for the Canadian federal public service.[3] The healthcare system has also undergone significant change, with pharmacies playing a greater role than before in healthcare delivery, and a big increase in virtual medical consultation even with the acute phase of the pandemic arguably behind us. And, sadly, a fair number of businesses, including some known and beloved for decades, did not survive the pandemic. John Allen captures some of the sense of grief many of us feel at the loss of a favourite bookstore, restaurant,[4] or in his case movie theatre in his moving personal reminiscence, 'Saudade.'

On the other hand, we are again able to enjoy live musical, theatrical, and dance performances, with few restrictions beyond an occasional request that we wear masks. We can again go to restaurants pretty much whenever we want and receive personal care such as haircuts, manicures and pedicures, and massages without restrictions.[5] And we can once again travel freely, albeit subject to the vagaries of a number of airlines that seem to have been either unwilling or unable to have hired sufficient staff to handle the resurgent demand for travel, as Robert Barclay points out in 'Air Canada, We Stand in Line for Thee.'

Two areas in which life does not appear to have improved since the pandemic, and indeed may have deteriorated still more, are long-term care and politics. Two of the book's long-term care pieces, by Ann McMillan and Fred Andayi, suggest that despite grandiose promises by political leaders such as Ontario Premier Doug Ford, many of the problems with the long-term care system that we pointed to in our first volume remain. As for politics, developments occurring during the pandemic appear to have emboldened anti-vaxxers and other conspiracy theorists, making rational discussion of vaccine and mask mandates all but impossible, elevating people holding views previously rated as being on the fringe to something close to respectability, and, in the U.S. at least, allowing for the election of unprincipled charlatans with little or no political experience, such as J.D. Vance, who prior to the pandemic would probably not have received serious consideration for their party's nomination. Worse still, there's a very real chance that Donald Trump, who as our first volume showed bears much of the responsibility for the U.S.'s horrifically inadequate response to the pandemic,[6] will again be elected President of the U.S., a development which would polarize any discussion of COVID even further and likely make any sort of rational government response to the disease all but impossible.

How will this volume proceed? Like its predecessor, it starts with a bit of history—in this case, a close look at the bubonic plague epidemic by Elisabeth Hoffman. From there, given that COVID is still afflicting many people, it seems appropriate to move on to pieces on health and dying, concluding with Teresa Bandrowska's moving piece, 'Death in Time of COVID,' about the loss of a close friend during the pandemic.

Next we turn to personal memoirs in our 'Connecting during COVID' and 'The French Have a Word for It' sections, which feature pieces covering the earlier part of the pandemic. These are followed by a section in which short but pungent humour and creative non-fiction are combined. In one of the section's more pungent offerings, the reader will learn, among other things, all about 'Lemon Pie and Quarantinis,' artfully cooked up by Sharon Hamilton. Elsewhere in the section, a more elegiac note is struck by John Allen in 'Saudade' and Rodney Clough in 'Buying in/Cashing Out.'

Like its predecessor, this volume offers a broad selection of poetry, some written by poets whose work appeared in *Plague Take It*, and some by poets not represented in that earlier collection. We then turn to politics, with Ann McMillan's long essay on Grannies and their role in the pandemic-era domestic economy, and some more general essays of mine on the politics of

COVID. Then it's on to the slightly less traumatic world of travel; here it's our modest hope that our four offerings, including the aforementioned Air Canada piece by Robert Barclay, will make readers laugh as much as it makes them cry.

The book concludes with a fiction section containing stories by Suha Mardelli, Ann McMillan, Robert Barclay and Ralph Smith, a personal essay section, 'Writers on Writing,' featuring pieces by John Allen, Ann McMillan, and yours truly, and, at the very end, my own 'Personal Pandemic Balance Sheet,' which some may think takes a more positive tone than any author has a right to take in the face of such an horrific phase of our history.

Once again, Ann and I hope that this collection will offer readers a certain amount of wisdom, some inspiration, a laugh or two and a goodly amount of hope. Some of the adaptations to the pandemic described within the collection's pages seem to me nothing short of extraordinary. I hope that you will enjoy reading this book as much as we've enjoyed putting it together. Merci et bonne chance—and try to stay healthy.

> J.P.
> Gatineau, Quebec
> November, 2023
> Revised August, 2024 in Ottawa

---

[1] As in our previous volume, the term 'elders' refers to anyone over the age of 60, or with a serious disability.

[2] Information about the [sic] Spanish flu pandemic presented in this paragraph has been drawn from the Wikipedia article on that pandemic.

[3] I describe this change in considerable detail in the 'Hybrid Workplace' chapter of my book on work hours, *Work Less* (Toronto: Dundurn, 2024).

[4] If a Nov. 3, 2022 CBC News story by Pete Evans is at all accurate, there are liable to be a great many diners mourning the loss of their favourite eateries before long. As Evans noted in 'Restaurant Industry Facing Bleak Outlook as Costs Mount Even Faster than Skyrocketing Prices,' more than half of all Canada's restaurants were then losing money.

[5] During the pandemic, many hair stylists in both Gatineau and Halifax refused to work on men's facial hair, citing COVID as the reason for their refusal. I went for nearly two and a half years trimming my own moustache—and it showed.

[6] See in particular my 'Politics and COVID 1' in *Plague Take It,* pp. 183-222.

SECTION 1
Pandemic
History

As was the case with our previous volume, we begin the present one with a look at pandemics from the past, including most notably San Francisco's bubonic plague outbreak at the beginning of the 20th century, with the hope that learning more about those earlier pandemics will better equip us to deal with our current situation today. Regrettably, Elizabeth Hoffman's fascinating study of the San Francisco pandemic along with other plague epidemics from the more distant past suggests that we've learned little or nothing from that earlier history. The same type of racialized response that initially labelled the San Francisco plague as a disease affecting only Chinese, and thus not worthy of serious treatment by public officials, could be seen in some of the early responses to the COVID pandemic. For some time, public officials seemed to be devoting more effort to ensuring that everyone knew the disease had started in China than to coming up with effective strategies for combatting it or even preventing its spread.

When will we ever learn?

Ann McMillan
Jon Peirce

Racism, Anti-scientific Prejudice, and the History of Bubonic Plague:
Two Plagues Separated by 5,000 Years
Elizabeth Hoffman

Introduction

When we wrote 'Lessons from History' for the previous COVID-19 volume (Hoffman et. al. 2021), I had hopes that with the early discovery of a vaccine, the pandemic would be over soon. After all, smallpox and polio had been conquered through vaccination. How wrong I was! I knew about the anti-vax movement with regard to the MMR vaccine for measles, mumps, and rubella, but not the rise of Q-Anon, leading millions of U.S. citizens to believe that Democrats are pedophiles who eat children and use COVID vaccinations to murder innocent people. Moreover, I did not foresee that vaccine and mask mandates would bring out the worst in people around the world, lead to armed protests, and be framed in the U.S. as unconstitutional infringements on individual rights.

Recently, however, I did a deep dive into the records of two plague epidemics not covered in depth in our previous article. (Hoffman et. al., 2021). The 1901-1904/1907 Bubonic Plague epidemic in San Francisco had just been covered in new depth in a PBS special (PBS, 2022) and a book (Randall, 2019). I had not devoted much space to that plague epidemic in our previous article, largely because the details were similar to other plague epidemics in Asia. Often referred to as the Third Plague Epidemic, even though we now know there was one about 3,000 B.C., it started in China in 1855 and spread widely in India. The death toll in India is estimated to have been at least 10 million people, and the total death toll about 15 million. I knew it had spread to San Francisco, but the death rate in San Francisco appeared to be much lower than the death rate in India. What I had thought was notable about the Third Plague Epidemic was the discovery and isolation of the bacterium that causes plague, Yersinia Pestis, named for Swiss-born French bacteriologist Alexandre Yersin, who made the discovery in 1894 in Hong Kong. In addition, there was a vaccine available shortly thereafter (1897). Four million Indian citizens were vaccinated.

While the outline of the story of the San Francisco Plague epidemic has been well known in the historical public health literature for more than a century, the plague in bronze age Europe is little known and is still being explored using modern DNA sequencing techniques. The picture that emerges is forcing us to rethink the story we tell about the settlement of

Europe and who our ancestors were. What ties this prehistorical plague and the San Francisco plague together is the history of racism told by the evidence from both epidemics' histories.

The San Francisco epidemic was first viewed as only affecting the Chinese immigrants who lived in Chinatown. Racism among White San Franciscans frustrated attempts by public health officials to fight the plague with contemporary medical technology. Racism also affected the historical narrative of those who had settled in northern Europe and Scandinavia, leading to the Nazi story of a master race and the need to rid the world of Jews, Gypsies, and dark-skinned people. The new paleogenetic evidence that has emerged from the genomic revolution of the 21st century has forced a complete rethinking of the genetic history of northern Europeans and Scandinavians. A plague pandemic on the contemporary scale of the Black Death likely played a central role.

Unfortunately, racism and anti-scientific bias still poison our responses to the coronavirus epidemic, even as it wanes.

The San Francisco Plague of 1900-1907

When I started reading about the San Francisco plague epidemic, I discovered that the history of the last plague epidemic in the U.S. had many features I had observed during the past three-plus years of the COVID-19 epidemic. Beginning with the first signs in Honolulu in 1899, the bubonic plague first appeared among the Chinese immigrant workers living in Honolulu's Chinatown. The white population believed it was a disease only affecting the Chinese and burned down Chinatown.

The plague arrived in San Francisco's Chinatown in 1900. Dr Joseph J. Kinyoun was a young bacteriologist sent to San Francisco by the U.S. Marine Hospital Service to identify and work to stop the spread of the disease. He quickly identified the tell-tale swollen lymph glands and buboes and confirmed his diagnosis by studying the bacteria under his microscope. He recommended mass immunization with the vaccine, quarantine, and general cleaning of unsanitary conditions. The link to rats and fleas was known but still not widely understood.

Not surprisingly, people were terrified of the vaccine, which was about 50–85% effective (Hawgood, 2007). Their fear was understandable since vaccination entailed being injected with a long needle containing an unknown substance that made those who took it quite sick for a day or two. Who wanted that? Moreover, the white population convinced themselves it was not their problem if they could quarantine Chinatown. The governor of California, Henry Gage, seeing the plague as a menace to the California economy, declared there was no plague, and demonized Dr Kinyoun, who responded by playing the scientist knows more than the average person card.

Californians then turned on Dr Kinyoun, who was quickly demoted and transferred to Detroit.[1]

Dr Kinyoun was replaced by Dr Rupert Blue, who had graduated near the bottom of his medical school class and thus did not have an inflated opinion of his medical skill. Dr Kinyoun had lived on Angel Island, the quarantine island in San Francisco Bay, and only entered the city proper when he had to diagnose a patient or dispose of a body. Dr Blue set up shop in the middle of Chinatown. He also employed a Chinese interpreter, who had assisted a fact-finding committee from the Public Health Service, to help him speak frankly with residents of Chinatown.

As Dr Blue gained the trust of the residents of Chinatown, dead bodies started coming out of the proverbial woodwork. Dr Blue and his assistants were all publicly vaccinated, encouraging residents of Chinatown to also become vaccinated. Moreover, Governor Henry Gage was defeated in 1902 by George Pardee, himself a physician. Governor Pardee worked with Dr Blue to eradicate the plague. Dr Blue observed that plague appeared to follow mass death by rats. Part of his campaign was a campaign to kill as many rats as possible. By 1904, the plague appeared to be over.

Then, at 5:18 a.m., April 18, 1906, the great San Francisco earthquake struck. Estimated more than 30 years later to have been approximately 7.9 on the Richter scale, the quake ran for 500 miles down the San Andreas Fault and lasted 42 seconds, an almost impossibly long time for an earthquake to last. The devastation was unparalleled, with the possible exception of the recent (2023) earthquakes in Turkey and Syria. Much of San Francisco in 1906 was built of wood or masonry and on soft soil. There were no earthquake-resistant building codes such as we have today. The old newsreels we can still watch today show buildings collapsing throughout the city, particularly in the Market Street area, where the soils are particularly soft. Much of the city was completely leveled.

As terrible as the earthquake was, the greatest damage was done by the great fire which followed the earthquake. The fire was caused both by ruptured gas lines catching fire and by the city dynamiting destroyed buildings. It burned for four days and nights, ultimately causing approximately 90% of the damage and creating 300,000 refugees. Some of the refugees fled to Oakland and Berkeley by ferry, but most were housed in hastily constructed tent cities in the Presidio and the outskirts of San Francisco. The crowded and unsanitary conditions of a 1906 tent city were again ripe for the proliferation of rats, and plague reappeared. This time, however, white San Franciscans were vulnerable, as well. They were forced to confront the reality that this disease was not a 'China Plague' but bubonic plague.

Dr Blue, who had been sent back east after the seeming eradication of the plague before the earthquake, returned to wage a second war against rats and plague. By that time, he had read the research on the rat-flea connection and knew the real culprit was not rats but fleas. He also found that other rodents, such as ground squirrels, can spread the disease through their fleas. Today we know that rodents of the Sierra Nevada and Rocky Mountains still spread the plague, and a few humans get sick every year. Thankfully, we also now know that Yersinia Pestis is no match for modern antibiotics!

One final mystery about the San Francisco plague remained. Why were the spread and mortality rates so much lower than in other bubonic plague epidemics? Recent research may have uncovered a fortunate difference between the fleas of California and the fleas that lived on the brown and black rats of Eurasia. Apparently, the Californian fleas did not inject as much plague-infected blood into their human victims as the Eurasian fleas! Who would have thought? As a result, Californian fleas did not make human victims as sick, on average, and a higher proportion survived. This difference, while fortunate, also contributed to the persistence of the fake news that the disease was not bubonic plague. David Randall (2019) writes, 'The slow spread of the disease—a phenomenon that led the city to doubt Dr Kinyoun's warnings and call the epidemic a fake ploy by corrupt health officials—had hinged on the stomach of a flea, a lucky quirk that spared an untold number of lives…'

The Bronze-age Plague

Historians of the Bronze Age (Drews, 1993; Kline, 2021; Norrie 2016) have long known that many of the great civilizations of that age, such as the Hittites[2] and Minoans,[3] collapsed unexpectedly in the second millennium B.C. Robert Drews (1993) gives several possible reasons for the well-docu-mented collapse, including earthquakes, mass migrations, drought, systems collapse, raiders and changes in warfare. Others add: volcanoes, economic factors, climate change, internal social upheaval, invasion from outside the Aegean World, and general systems collapse. In a recent book, Philip Norrie (2016) argues that the real culprit was disease: smallpox and bubonic plague, in particular.

The discovery that there likely was a plague pandemic during the Bronze Age was only possible in the 21st century. The 2003 completion of the human genome project (NIH, 2003) and the technological changes following that initial feat allow inexpensive human genetic sequencing today. First, it was necessary to find out how to detect DNA from bones and teeth left in Bronze Age burial sites and from Egyptian mummies. Second, it was necessary to identify the genetic signatures of diseases left in these burial items. A 2015 article in *Cell* (Rasmussen, *et al.*, 2015) outlines a study of burial sites in central Asia, Anatolia, Poland, and Sweden that show remnants of *Y. Pestis* in the teeth of skeletons dated from the second and third millennia B.C. Moreover, these remnants do not contain a particular genetic marker that allows *Y. Pestis* to be transmitted by fleas. Thus, it is not bubonic plague but must be pneumonic or septicaemic plague, both of which can be spread from human to human. The recent literature on plague during the Bronze Age draws on the research outlined in the *Cell* article.

The story the bones tell is that not only was there a deadly pneumonic/ septicaemic plague pandemic about 3,000 B.C., but also that mass migrations accompanied this pandemic. We know from research on the Justinian and fourteenth-century plague pandemics that plague is endemic in the central Asian steppes and Himalayan foothills. We also know that cooling temperatures can set off conditions conducive to the spread of plague (Green and Symes, 2014). The historians of the Bronze Age did note that there were volcanic eruptions that led to cooler temperatures, crop failures, and mass migrations. They can be excused for not seeing the link to a plague epidemic since genetic research on plague was not possible until the 21st century, and the link between plague and cooling temperatures was also only discovered in the second decade of the 21st century. (Hoffman *et al.*, 2021: Green and Symes, 2014).

Additional pieces of the puzzle of the genetic makeup of northern Europeans from about 3,000 B.C. going forward come from genetic research showing the following disparate events: the migration of homo sapiens from Africa to Eurasia, the extinction of the Neanderthal and the genes they left behind, the origin of blue eyes, the spread of horses and wheels, and the source of Indo-European languages. Taken together, the histories of these events result in nothing less than an upending of the white supremacist view that the Vikings were a blond, blue-eyed master race that took over the known world in the 11th century A.D., spreading their genes throughout northern Europe and as far south as the Black Sea.

One of the first discoveries using mitochondrial DNA is that all Homo Sapiens are descended from Africans who walked north and then east and west when they reached Anatolia. (Fleagle *et al.*, 2010). At some point, they lost the melanin that makes skin black, probably because lighter skin is better at absorbing vitamin D in the short, cold winter days of northern climates. Along the way, Homo Sapiens encountered Neanderthals, a separate human-oid species. The genomic revolution also allowed scientists to sequence Neanderthal DNA and compare it to homo sapiens' DNA. The result is that homo sapiens' DNA contains about 3–4% Neanderthal DNA, but African DNA contains less than 0.5% Neanderthal DNA, indicating interbreeding between homo sapiens and Neanderthal after the African diaspora. We still do not know why the Neanderthals died off, but we do know that modern Eurasians inherit small remnants of Neanderthal DNA (Teague and McRae, 2022).

A recent article in *National Geographic* (Curry, 2019) summarizes the paleogenetic history of modern Europeans. If we follow the migration of homo sapiens north as the glaciers receded, the early settlers in what was to become northern Europe are direct genetic descendants of early Fertile Crescent farmers and Ice Age mammoth hunters of southern Europe. The DNA evidence also tells us that most of the farmers had light skin and dark eyes, while many of the hunter-gatherers had darker skin and lighter eyes. The genetic and graveyard evidence also suggests that these two populations did not comingle but rather maintained their separate lifestyles and diets. These two migrations take us to about 4,000 B.C. Sometime around 3,500 B.C., the paleogenetic evidence indicates a dramatic change in the people living in northern Europe and Scandinavia. First, villages disappear, suggesting a major negative demographic event. Then, about 500 years later, burial mounds dedicated to warriors (Chechushkov and Epimakhov, 2018: Gibbons, 2017: Anthony, 2007) and decorated with 'Corded Ware' pottery appeared all over Europe (Olalde, 2016). The Neolithic farmers and herders they replaced left more egalitarian, less hierarchical grave sites.

Corded Ware burials are so recognizable that archaeologists rarely need to bother with radiocarbon dating. Almost invariably, men were buried lying on their right side and women lying on their left, both with their legs curled up and their faces pointed south. In some of the Halle warehouse's graves, women clutch purses and bags hung with canine teeth from dozens of dogs; men have stone battle axes. In one grave, neatly contained in a wooden crate on the concrete floor of the warehouse, a woman and child are buried together (Curry, 2019).

The genetic evidence indicates the Corded Ware people were distinctly different from the Neolithic farmers and herders. In fact, they are more similar to Native Americans and residents of the Asian steppes than to the previous European populations. We now know they were the Yamnaya (Gibbons, 2017), a population of horseback-riding nomads who used wheeled vehicles and spoke proto-Indo-European languages. They appear to have originated in the Central Asian steppes and spread east to Siberia and across the Bering Strait land bridge to North America, west to Great Britain, south to Spain and Morocco, and north to Scandinavia. By 2500 B.C., 70% to 100% of the skeletons now available contain Yamnaya DNA, but most indicate male Yamnaya and female farmers or herders. The picture that emerges is a migration of male warriors who raped (or married) the farmer and herder women, leaving behind a new population. The fact that they also left language and burial mounds behind suggests that they stayed (Anthony, 2007: Gibbons, 2017: *Big Think*, 2022).

The question still remains, however: How were the Yamnaya able to take over the genetic makeup of Europe in just 500 years? The answer appears to be that they also brought plague but had a level of acquired immunity sufficient to allow their genes to survive. Skeletons dated before 3,000 B.C. in Europe do not show evidence of *Y. Pestis*. Skeletons dated from the 4th millennium B.C. do. Moreover, this is the strain of *Y. Pestis* that lacks the gene allowing flea-born transmission (Calloway, 2015; 2022: Rasmussen, et. al, 2015).

This emerging evidence suggests that the Yamnaya were on the move about 3,000 B.C., bringing pneumonic and septicaemic plague, which decimated populations the Yamnaya encountered, but not before the invading male Yamnaya left their DNA in the children they fathered. The combination of horseback-riding and wheel-using warrior tribes who killed men, raped women, and brought plague would have been sufficient to topple Bronze Age civilizations. Moreover, this picture conforms both to the historical record of the fall of Bronze Age civilizations and the paleogenetic record (Anthony, 2007; Chechushkov and Epimakhov, 2018; Gibbons, 2017). Interestingly, there is no evidence of *Y. Pestis* in Egyptian mummies, providing an answer to the historical puzzle of why the civilization of the Pharaohs did not suffer the fate of the Hittites (Rascovan, et. al, 2018).

The reasons why the Yamnaya left their Central Asian homeland may be the link between the historical evidence of massive volcanic eruptions and earthquakes disturbing the agricultural climate and the genetic evidence of plague. Volcanic eruptions, in particular, can lead to cooling temperatures around the world as the ash moves with the prevailing winds, lowering the amount of solar energy on the ground. Even a minor reduction in temperature may lead to crop failures wherever the ash plume passes. In addition, it may disrupt the delicate balance between *Y. Pestis* and its hosts (Green and Symes, 2014).

The final pieces of the genetic puzzle of the origins of the blue-eyed, blond-haired Aryan who became the Nazi symbol of a master race are the origins of blond hair and blue eyes. The origin of blond hair is similar to the origin of light skin (Norton, et. al, 2007). Blond hair and light skin have less melanin than dark hair and dark skin and allow people living in climates that allow less sunlight over the year to absorb more vitamin D (Reich and Reich, 2018; Carlberg and Hanel, 2020). Blue eyes also have less melanin, but the source of blue eyes appears to be the result of a single sudden mutation that took place about 10,000 years ago in one individual who then passed on a specific gene for blue eyes to all subsequent blue-eyed humans (Eiberg, et. al., 2008). This startling result was discovered by a team of geneticists at the University of Copenhagen who studied a large sample of apparently unrelated Danes who all had pure blue eyes. Their DNA was compared to a sample of apparently unrelated blue-eyed individuals from Jordan and Turkey and a sample of unrelated individuals with brown eyes from the same places. They discovered that all the blue-eyed individuals from Denmark, Jordan, and Turkey had genetically identical eyes. The brown-eyed individuals were genetically distinct (Eiberg, *et al*, 2008). This startling result, combined with the evolutionary fitness of light hair and light skin, shows clearly that the Vikings/Aryans were not from some master race. They evolved in response to environmental pressure, just as Darwin had predicted, and benefitted from a random mutation that added blue eyes to the genetic mix. Moreover, the blue eye mutation appears to have originated in the central Asian or Eurasian steppes, not in Scandinavia (Reich and Reich, 2018).

Some scholars have speculated that Neolithic hunter-gatherer males likely suffered higher mortality than Neolithic hunter-gatherer females because big-game hunting with hand-held spears and stone points was even more dangerous than childbirth. Since a higher adult male mortality would mean a higher proportion of adult females than males, surviving adult males could be more choosy about their mates. Thus, a male preference for blond hair and blue eyes would reinforce the vitamin D benefit of that combination. This was the pre-genomic explanation. Since we cannot interview Neolithic hunter-gatherers and they left only burial grounds and cave paintings, scientists appear now to favor an emphasis on random mutation and natural selection.

Conclusions and Final Thoughts

These two seemingly unrelated plague epidemics share important character-istics despite the differences in time and medical knowledge. They are both parts of international pandemics, both of which originated on the vast, sparsely populated steppes of central Asia. They were both caused by the same bacterium, *Yersinia Pestis*, although the earlier plague still lacked the gene present in the later plague that allowed *Y. Pestis* to be transmitted from rodents to humans by fleas. This bacterium wreaked havoc on Homo Sapiens for millennia, beginning with the Bronze Age and ending in San Francisco in 1907.

What I find most interesting—and disturbing—is the racialized response to both plagues. Why did San Franciscans decide it was only a Chinese disease, despite the knowledge of plagues in Europe? Why would a U.S. president lead his followers to believe they should not get vaccinated against a disease destined to kill a million Americans in two years? Why would people with white skin believe they were better than people with dark skin when their skin colour is a genetic adaptation to winter day length? Moreover, despite their white skin, their genetic ancestors are black Africans and Central Asian nomads whose progeny includes Native Americans. Why would they storm the U.S. Capitol on January 6, 2021, and try to undo a U.S. election because they believed the people who won would allow darker-skinned Homo Sapiens to replace them?

The answers to the above questions are embedded in the racist mindset that still permeates the thinking of many Americans and is having a terrifying resurgence in book bans, laws banning the teaching of 'critical race theory'—which is actually just a ban on teaching uncomfortable truths about African American history—and the demonization of drag queens. Demonizing the Chinese is as embedded in our racist mindset as is demonizing those with dark skin or alternative gender or sexual preferences. This was especially true in the West and was at its height in the 1870s and 1880s, culminating in the U.S. with the Chinese Exclusion Act of 1882. The act banned the immigration of Chinese to the United States for 10 years. Official representatives of the Chinese government had to present papers from the Chinese government. The Chinese Exclusion Act was extended in 1892 by the Geary Act and only partially repealed in 1943. Canada followed with the Chinese Immigration Act of 1923. It was otherwise known as the Chinese Exclusion Act. Only 100 Chinese were admitted to Canada for the next 24 years.

While I hope the stories I tell in this article will help some of our fellow Homo Sapiens rethink their assumptions about our origins, I fear that recent, post-pandemic political developments are taking us in the opposite direction.

References

Anthony, D. 2007. *The Horse, the Wheel, and Language: How Bronze-Age Riders from the Eurasian Steppes Shaped the Modern World.* Princeton, NJ: Princeton University Press.

2022. *Big Think.* September 14. Accessed 2023. *Search*: big think ancient dna

Calloway, E. 2022. 'Ancient DNA traces origin of Black Death.' *Nature.*

Calloway, E. 2015. 'Bronze Age skeletons were earliest plague victim.' *Nature.*

Carlberg, C. and Hanel, A. 2020. 'Skin colour and vitamin D: An update.' *Experimental Dermatology 864-875.*

Chechushkov, I and Epimakhov, A. 2018. 'Eurasian Steppe Chariots and Social Complexity During the Bronze Age.' *Journal of World Prehistory* 435-483.

Curry, A. 2019. 'The first Europeans weren't who you might think: Genetic tests of ancient settlers' remains show that Europe is a melting pot of bloodlines from Africa, the Middle East, and today's Russia, National Geographic.' *National Geographic,* August.

Drews, Robert. 1993. *The End of the Bronze Age: Changes in Warfare and the Catastrophe ca. 1200 B.C.* Princeton, NJ: Princeton University Press.

Eiberg, *et al.* 2008. 'Blue eye color in humans may be caused by a perfectly associated founder mutation in a regulatory element located within the HERC2 gene inhibiting OCA2 expression.' *Human Genetics* 171.

Fleagle, J.G., J.J. Shea, F.E. Grine, A.L. Baden, and R.E Leakey, eds. 2010. *Out of Africa I: The First Hominin Colonization of Eurasia. Vertebrate Paleobiology and Paleoanthropology.* Springer.

Gibbons, A. 2017. 'Thousands of horsemen may have swept into Bronze Age Europe, transforming the local population: Europeans may be descendants of a massive migration of men from the Russian steppe,' *Science,* February 21.

Green, Monica H. and Symes, Carol. 2014. 'Pandemic Disease in the Medieval World: Rethinking the Black Death.' *The Medieval Globe* 1.

Hawgood, Barbara J. 2007. 'Waldemar Mordecai Haffkine, CIE (1860-1930): prophylactic vaccination against cholera and bubonic plague in British India' *Journal of Medical Biography,* 15(1): 9-19.

Hoffman, E., J. Grant, and A. McMillan, A. 2021. 'Lesson from History.' In *Plague Take It*, ed. Jon Peirce and Ann McMillan. Ottawa: Loose Cannon Press.

Kline, Eric H. 2021. *1177 B.C.: The Year Civilization Collapsed*. Princeton, NJ: Princeton University Press.

Lawler, Andrew. 2020. 'When bubonic plague first struck America, officials tried to cover it up.' *National Geographic*, April 24.

NIH. 2003. 2003*: Human Genome Project Completed.*

Norrie, Phillip. 2016. *A History of Disease in Ancient Times*. Palgrave, McMillan.

Norton, H. L., *et al*. 2007. 'Genetic Evidence for the Convergent Evolution of Light Skin in Europeans and East Asians.' *Molecular Biology and Evolution*, 710-722.

Olalde, I. 2016. 'The Beaker phenomenon and the genomic transformation of northwest Europe, Nature.' *Nature*, 190-196.

PBS, 2022. *San Francisco's Chinatown: Plague at the Golden Gate*. Directed by PBS.

Randall, David K. 2019. *Black Death at the Golden Gate: The Race to Save America from the Bubonic Plague*. New York: W.W.W Norton.

Rascovan, N., *et al*. 2018. 'Emergence and Spread of Basal Lineages of Yersinia pestis during the Neolithic Decline.' *Cell.*

Rasmussen, *et al*. 2015. 'Early divergent strains of Yersinia pestis in Eurasia 5,000 years ago.' 571-582.

Reich, D. and Reich, E. 2018. *Who we are and how did we get here? Ancient DNA and the new Science of the Human Past*. Oxford, UK: Oxford University Press.

Teague, R. and McRae, R. 2022. *Ancient DNA and the Neanderthals*. September 29. *Search*: ancient dna neanderthal.

---

[1] It is worth noting the parallel between the treatment of Dr Anthony Fauci during the Coronavirus pandemic and Dr Kinyoun during the San Francisco plague epidemic. Dr Kinyoun is credited as founding the U.S. Hygienic Laboratory, which later became the National Institutes of Health (Lawler 2020). Before his recent retirement, Dr Fauci was the embodiment of the excellence characterizing the NIH today.

[2] Anatolia, now Turkey

[3] Crete

Section 2
Health and
Long-term Care

As we travel the road to recovery from COVID-19, some things have occurred that have changed us forever. The isolation, the pondering of subjects we usually avoid thinking about, the anxiety about health (our own and that of those we are close to), the possibility of death and its proximity, all these perspectives have permeated our consciousness as never before.

In this section Denise Giroux's 'Flash in the Pan' gives us insight into her new preoccupation with death. Aging, the pandemic, and her personal circumstances all play into a new heightened awareness that eventually that fate awaits us all. Ian Johnson ponders his health, comes to terms with his stroke and courageously walks the long road to recovery. Eventually he returns to many of the activities that occupied him throughout his uncommonly busy life, but with the judgement of age modifies his activities to be both more manageable and more satisfying to him.

Then the section turns to long-term care as I interview two dragon boat friends who lost their mothers during the time of COVID, although it wasn't COVID that stole their lives. The deaths of elderly mothers in long-term care during the time of COVID, but not of COVID, are even more haunting than the deaths of elderly COVID patients in care. Then Julie Stashick gives us both her perspective on losing her mother in long-term care before COVID arrived and her perspective as a personal care worker in long-term care in the height of the pandemic. Julie represents the best of PSWs: she is mature, well trained, and life-wise and loves working with seniors. I know she got neither the pay nor the respect she deserved for her work. It is about time people like me who could not do this type of work step back and recognize the value that the Julies of the world bring to the lives of our parents and elders. Who do we want to provide care for us? Fred Andayi, another staff member seeing that side of COVID-19, provides his personal insight into providing infection prevention and control in long-term care during the pandemic.

In 'Death in the Time of COVID,' Teresa Bandrowska provides an intimate portrait of the death of her friend, Daphne. Her intimate and sensitive account provides reassurance that even in our death-denying culture, end of life can be managed to be an intrinsic and beautiful part of life. Finally, John Eaton summarizes what he sees as one of the tragedies of being old, the result of being moved to long term care, where the emphasis in the final years is on being safe, not on living life.

These seven pieces come from very different perspectives, but all are haunted by a depth of feeling which is based in the life/death struggle that eventually enmeshes us all. All the authors of this section have had their lives changed forever by the pandemic, and while they are now living a new normal as a result, it is a different normal for them and those around them.

Ann McMillan

Flash in the Pan
Denise Giroux

Lately I've been thinking a lot about death. And the shortness, fragility, and unpredictability of life. Of course, as human beings, why wouldn't we all be conscious of this? As soon as we experience the first loss of a treasured or important being, even a family pet, we are confronted with the strangeness of this ephemeral state called life. A friend's passing this summer, at age 62, certainly brought the lesson home to me sharply once more, and these last few months, another woman devoted to making this world a better place, with whom I cried during the election campaign as we shared our angst about the planet and her wellbeing, is undergoing a variety of treatments for generally metastasized Stage 4 cancer. My sister had a terrible time throughout 2020 due to her own cancer surgery and chemotherapy and radiation treatments. Several friends are waiting for hip and gall bladder surgeries, and elder parents are living incredibly narrow lives in retirement or long-term care centres, watching those who surround them, bizarrely all of an age, succumb to reduced mobility, falls, or fatal illness. Another friend only in her early 60s, afflicted by a chronic disease and a series of unfortunate accidental injuries, now wonders if she even wants another 20 years living in 'this uncooperative body.'

On the flip side of the same coin, another friend who had for a long period tended to a heavier weight dedicated himself, this past year and a half, to getting and staying more fit by working out at home, riding miles on his bicycle, and eating healthy and calorie-conscious portions, so that he feels and looks better than ever. One can't fault him for doing this, and it is far better to do what he has done than to acquiesce, too soon or too readily, to the ravages of poor self-care, obesity, and bad habits which we can pretend only for so long will not affect us. Still, I can't help seeing in the obsessive quality of my friend's physical regimen a need to stave off death, based on a fear similar to my own new obsession with the precariousness of life.

Still, these thoughts are more than a reflection of watching myself and those around me age; this is a personal, new fear approaching paranoia. I am newly retired, and as I nurse a cold—the first since the start of the pandemic— I wonder if my inability to identify what exactly I want to do with the next 20 or so years (should good luck and a 'normal' life expectancy be mine to experience), will somehow jinx me and thereby settle the issue for me, by illness and even death. Perhaps, somehow, I am due a (fatal) moment of bad luck in the lottery of life.

It's not that I haven't had any bad luck in my life already. My father had a severe alcohol addiction and was abusive to his nuclear family; I loved and lost, and nothing I could do could change that; I invested a significant amount of my hard-earned money in not one but two gone-really-bad real estate deals; and I experienced the pain of several spinal fractures in an accident, a near-fatal case of meningitis while in Nigeria, and a debilitating depression in midlife. But I was also blessed with a mother who was a strong, independent, and capable caregiver, and I have many friends who really care about me and whom I cherish. Moreover, I still managed to stash away some savings and invest for my old age from solid professional earnings over many years, and I'm active and generally fit. So why the fear of death, why the obsession?

When I review my lifetime, I can, like all 'elders,' account for different milestones, stages and phases, benefits and losses, too, from years at school, jobs held, relationships of all kinds, and different places I have lived. But in contrast to the first 40 years of my life, the last 20 seem to have passed in a flash. It scares me to think the next 20, should I have them, will pass even faster. Yet having them would be a gift, a gift not given to those struck down at my age or earlier still. My fear percolates, that I will never get the chance to play a part in my new granddaughter's life, never hike that hill in Scotland or work with elephants in the South African sanctuary I hope to volunteer with for three months, never contribute further to the causes that matter to me, and I will be cut away from the people who matter and for whom I matter. That has been much on my mind these past few weeks.

Camus and Sartre taught me 40 years ago that such fears are part and parcel of the existential condition: we live, we die, we seek purpose when it is unclear that our lives have any actual purpose or that humanity, itself, can be said to exist for any grand ideal. No one will remember any one of us in 50 years, so what is the point of it all? What do we do with our lives and how might we decide how to behave, what to engage in, from decade to decade? We need to hold the absurdity, the unknowing, in mind—in check, really!—to be able to continue to define what is important to each of us, our reason for being in our community, in this world. But... I have it bad.

There's no doubt in my mind that the pandemic and the restrictive conditions which determine, still, how we are allowed to 'be' with people has played a part in this new fear, and how our personal decisions—even just contact—can affect those we meet with. Just last week, I attended Place-des-Arts in Montreal with a friend and experienced the centre's first performance with full attendance since March 2020. Elbow to elbow, in that full house, we all sat silently, still masked, to watch Les Ballets Jazz play out the memories of a woman just advised by her doctor that she has Alzheimer's. In that crowd, placid and still as the dancers ran and leapt across the stage, it felt as though we were doing something illegal, subversive, resistant, and scary. Yes, scary; large assembly, focussed attention, 'en gang.' Wonderful and terrifying.

Perhaps as interaction continues to open up, the fear I feel might abate. Perhaps the fear I feel is entirely the fear that comes with retirement--the rest of your life opening up, the end of an extended, habituated career-focussed stage, the infinite possibilities that it presents, and the strange tendency I have right now to live as through an extended long weekend (reading and sitting for long periods, catching up with e-mail, buying and preparing nutritious food and eating, watching the weeks fly by). In retirement, however welcome it can be, you nevertheless lose your daily mission--even if that mission was simply reporting for duty and doing what you know how to do, well, for seven or eight hours a day. Perhaps what I am feeling is something many new retirees feel, a certain aimlessness that comes with the ending of a significant period of one's life, and the availability of new-found—yet strikingly limited!—time.

I have seen that some people, upon retiring, throw themselves into pottery classes and self-improvement courses, or sign up almost immediately to volunteer for three or four different worthwhile organizations. I have gone quite the opposite way, so far, in this fall season of 2021: I have holed up, anticipating winter, the slowing of the season and shorter days. Still unable to gather with friends indoors in larger groups, I'm strangely wary of signing onto too many causes—there are so many in this code red world—knowing they will require real investments of time and energy but almost all through online engagement, remotely. Though I always bring real commitment to every activity I work on, bringing it to a remote world just isn't motivating for me right now.

Perhaps I'm feeling the planetary angst so many others are feeling, too. This angst is, at times, downright crippling. We know we have to fight the excess and greed which have brought us to this point—it need not always be thus—but it seems that as we all hole up for winter and the endless iterations of this pandemic's brave-new-world, Goliath cannot but continue to prevail. Is it a losing battle? The nuclear industry and its promoters, the fossil fuel and pharma companies have not stopped lobbying the government daily, even if I, and others, feel removed from the world that prompts us to action.

So, I read, real tales of people struggling with their own instances of bad health, bad luck, aging parents, poor judgment, challenging circumstances and… miracles of good luck, serendipity, acquired wisdoms, meeting of minds, loving acts and devotions.

I suppose I can only give myself the time to wait and see, wait for inspiration; meantime, I can still gently prod myself with home projects and new recipes, or call upon and wait for calls from friends. I will simply watch the deer nibbling up the remains of the Halloween pumpkins, silent, on my septic field. I wish them courage and strength, that they may find the sustenance to survive the hard winter.

Resiliency and Renewal in
my Stroke Recovery
Ian Johnson

In *Plague Take It*, I reported how in April 2020, I had an ischemic stroke (better known as a TIA (Transient Ischemic Attack or 'mini-stroke') which affected my left inferior frontal lobe). Now, I would like to report on how much I have achieved in my recovery from that stroke. Overall, I would say I have almost completely recovered.

Looking back, I can see that there were many factors that contributed to my success during my recovery period. I learned that each person's stroke is different, and therefore, each person recovers in their own way at their own speed. I was fortunate in that after my stroke, I was able to walk and I had no paralysis. Prior to my stroke, I had a history of high blood pressure, and had been on medication to help control it for many years. In addition, I had been diagnosed with Sleep Apnea in 2012. I have been using a continuous positive airway pressure (CPAP) machine since that time.

In June 2021, I was one of three and a half million Sleep Apnea machine users who was advised by Philips International about a recall. The issue was a foam used in this product which may degrade and release carcinogenic particles into people's airways. I have since switched to a different type of CPAC machine, and I am now one of the plaintiffs in a class action lawsuit being organized by a Newfoundland and Labrador legal firm.

On a more positive note, I started to walk and run again. With my younger son and sister, we did the 5 km walks for the Bluenose Marathon in Halifax in May 2022 and for the Valley Harvest Marathon in Wolfville in October 2022. For me, this was a major achievement! I did another Bluenose Marathon Walk in May 2023, and also the Valley Harvest Marathon in October 2023. I have also started to do some weight training with a personal trainer.

After undergoing intensive therapy at the Nova Scotia Rehabilitation Centre in June 2020, I started participating in the six-month 'Acquired Brain Injury Outreach Program.' It covered the same range of therapy that I had experienced at the Rehab Centre. At that time, I was working with an Occupational Therapist, a Social Worker, a Recreation Therapist, a Physiotherapist, and a Speech and Language Pathologist. I was very pleased to have their expertise and compassion as I continued to make progress in my recovery. That involvement continued until January 2021 when the Acquired Brain Injury Outreach Program felt I no longer needed their services since I had made a very good recovery.

From the spring of 2021 until the fall of 2022, I participated in the March of Dimes After-Stroke Virtual Activities. Each week, I took part in the discussion periods and I was also part of the monthly 'Ask an Expert' series. I learned a great deal from all these activities.

In January 2021, I also became a member of an Aphasia Communications Group, and then I joined the Aphasia Book Club. With this Club, I was working with a Speech and Language Pathologist at Dalhousie University and her second-year master's students. We used to meet once a week to look at a portion of the book being read, discuss some multiple-choice questions, and then, consider more general discussion questions. As a result, we have worked through several books. They included works by Indigenous, African American, and European writers. I especially enjoyed *The Sun Does Shine: How I found Life and Freedom on Death Row* by Anthony Ray Hinton which told the story of thirty years in solitary confinement for murders that this African American prisoner did not commit.

Olga (my wife) and I have resumed our active volunteer lives from before the pandemic and my stroke. I was once again serving as Secretary for Region 3 (Halifax) for the Nova Scotia Government Retired Employees Association (NSGREA). This work re-started in December 2022. It involved finding a meeting room, going back to the NSGEU office space I had used previously for our meetings, the finalization of speakers for some of the meetings including the CEO and Chief Actuary of the Nova Scotia Public Service Superannuation Plan (PSSP), the arrangement of hearing disability support services for one of our members, and organizing a special Christmas Dinner for our Region. I also had to send out meeting notices, prepare the draft minutes for our meetings, and construct draft resolutions for the Provincial Convention. By the end of May 2023, I decided to step down from this position after serving five years.

My wife and I have both resumed taking non-credit classes with the Seniors College Association of Nova Scotia, and I have also resumed my trombone and theory lessons at the Maritime Conservatory of Performing Arts. Together, we sponsor a yearly scholarship for a joint brass-woodwind instrument program at the Conservatory.

We have also continued to be involved with the ACE Team (Advocates for the Care of the Elderly) in Nova Scotia. As part of that group, we have been seeking systemic changes to the long-term care system in Nova Scotia. Olga has been helping to develop more therapy programs (including music, art, dance, and gardening). I have continued to help with Freedom of Information and Protection of Privacy (FOIPOP) applications, and to write letters for the Team to the Minister of Seniors and Long-Term Care. Our work has led us to have three meetings with the Minister during the last year.

One particularly important part of my recovery was for Olga and me to get involved as post-stroke volunteers with March of Dimes Canada. We worked closely with the Coordinator of Volunteer Engagement and participated in the post-stroke recovery program with March of Dimes Canada. We were assigned by the coordinator to make weekly phone calls to a stroke survivor in Newfoundland and Labrador. As it turns out, we have become close friends with this person with whom we look forward to talking every week.

Overall, Olga, the rest of my family and I have been through a lot in the last four years. They have been amazing in their support. At the same time, I have benefitted greatly from the stroke specialists/therapists and their programs in our community.

Thanks to my sons and my grandson, I had a wonderful trip to Scotland, where none of us had ever been beforehand, in June and July 2023. I am extremely grateful to them for giving me this special opportunity, as well as for all the other ways in which they have helped me during my recovery.

COVID-19: Insidious Impacts on Elders
Who Didn't Catch It
Susan Mills and Wanda Monuk
(as told to Ann McMillan)

Much has been written about the tragedy of elders who found themselves in long-term care settings when COVID hit. And yet, the tragedy does not stop with those who contracted COVID-19 in long term care settings.

I belong to the Prior Chest Nuts, a dragon boat team of breast cancer survivors who paddle on White Lake in Arnprior. While many of us are older, and have lost our moms already, I was staggered to find that at least three out of the thirty-something women who make up the team had lost their moms during COVID.

None of their three mothers died of COVID, but it seemed that their deaths represent another stream of impacts that the emergence of COVID had on older women and their families. Of the three women affected, Jane Coyle wrote up her experience to submit to the Long-Term Care Staffing Study and shared it with me but did not want it used here. Susan Mills wrote up her experience and it is included in *Plague Take It*. I have had the privilege of interviewing Susan and our teammate, Wanda Monuk, about what happened to their families during COVID. Although many months have passed since the deaths, these women remain deeply affected, not only by losing their mothers, but also by the circumstances of their deaths and their own sense of helplessness, desolation, and, yes, rage, at the stupidity, unfairness and lack of treatment their moms received.

Susan Mills shared that her mother passed away at the Grove in Arnprior in February, 2022. She had been in long-term care (LTC) since March, 2019. Barbara Joan Mills (nee Gibb), Susan's mom, was unable to live by herself after her husband passed away. Although she could receive 3 hours per day on 2 days a week of home support, it was not sufficient. She moved from her house to an apartment which was easier to keep up, but it was already too late. She needed showers and meals provided. One day Barbara wandered out of her apartment and got lost in the community. This incident meant that she immediately became a 'crisis placement' in long-term care. The family requested a private LTC room, and that got her into the Grove more quickly.

At first, she was relatively independent, and staff engaged with her. She was able to attend activities, and she was thought to be quite safe. In September 2019, however, she fell and broke her hip. It was then that the staff shortages started to show up in her care. She had no physio, and she required a lot more care: feeding, changing, etc. There just wasn't a sufficient level of staff engagement to provide such care to her.

And then, when COVID-19 hit, families were locked out. Family window visits were organized and the family basically watched their mother deteriorate through the window. At first, they did some light exercises together, but eventually couldn't do anything. All they could do was put their hand on the window to show they were there.

Every morning at 10:30 am family would call Barbara to talk on the phone and have a cup of tea together through the window. After a while the menu changed to pudding, to avoid choking. Eventually, Barbara, normally a brave old soul, told staff she wanted to give up, and was clearly sinking into depression. The isolation from family almost certainly caused faster deterioration in her health and wellbeing.

It became obvious that families had been doing a lot of the care before COVID and that this care was not replaced by staff time. In fact, it was difficult to get information from staff. The family found out that one staff member was responsible for feeding 20 residents in one room. Barbara was identified as having a danger of choking, and eventually she did choke and required CPR.

The ongoing stress of seeing Barbara deteriorate has left what seems like post-traumatic stress disorder (PTSD) in the family. In order to maintain patient quality of life, staff needed to work in close contact with family and involve them in their care, as had been the case before COVID-19 arrived. That just didn't happen. For example, it was some time before Susan and her family found out that because of staff shortages, the night shift was getting Barbara up at 5:30 a.m. because that was the only hour at which they had time to do so.

Things could have been done differently. Family caregivers could have been admitted with personal protective equipment (PPE). This would have lessened the sense of isolation from family and provided better care. Because the homes are so short-staffed it is imperative to allow residents to have family members serve as essential caregivers.

Recently people have been waiting longer for a placement in homes such as the Grove because they either come as crisis placements or directly from hospitals. This means that there are not many 'independent' residents and most residents have complex needs and require a lot more care than in the past. For example, many residents require two-person transfers from bed to chair or vice versa, and if there are no staff available the transfer cannot be made in a timely and appropriate manner.

There are some obvious physical improvements that need to be made to the facilities as well. For instance, ensuring compliance with Infection Prevention and Control (IPAC) and making better use of divisions in facility areas would help considerably. Units can be set up to contain the spread of disease and staff can work in multiple areas if they gown up and take precautions to limit spread. It requires care and an exercise of will to execute staff procedures to minimize cross contact.

In summary, Susan is convinced that Barbara's quality of life decreased much more than necessary because of COVID-19, and she sees that with adequate staffing and more attention to physical measures as well as an appreciation of the importance of family and essential caregivers, such deterioration need not have occurred. She feels that she and her family were robbed of time with her mother and that her mother's last days were unnecessarily unhappy because of the draconian means used to prevent COVID spread. She agrees that not knowing the state of the facilities and shortages of staff might have been an excuse initially, but asks at what point does it become criminal to be aware of such issues and not address them?

Isolation from family is inhumane, and having to isolate sometimes for periods as long as 10 days is cruel, with severe impacts, especially on elders with cognitive decline.

Susan feels that one of the keys to a better future situation is staffing. Staff retention is very important, to allow for a stable base of experienced staff and few newbies. Turnover needs to be reduced to the minimum; this can be done with adequate renumeration and support.

At first when Barbara went into the facility, the staff knew her from the bingo days that she used to run for other seniors and would take a moment to recall those days with her and relate in a human way. But as the pandemic progressed, the facility was always short-staffed and had to be intensely task-oriented to achieve minimum levels of care, so staff had no time to engage with the residents. Along with the exclusion of family this presented a double-whammy.

My second interview was with Wanda Monuk whose mother, Catherine, was 90 when she passed away at a private retirement residence.

Wanda's mom had been in declining physical and mental health for some time before she moved to care. She'd lived independently in her own home and smoked a pack of cigarettes every day for over 30 years. She smoked and drank more as time went on, as she lost her short-term memory and would not remember that she had just smoked a cigarette or had a drink. She didn't remember to eat or bathe or get dressed for the day. She did not have a capable and supportive partner and hence it became very noticeable when she started not being able to care for herself adequately.

In-home care is not easy to find if one lives in a rural or isolated area as Catherine did. Her smoking and the fact that Catherine would cancel in-home help if she could make it impossible to continue in-home help. Getting buy-in for exercise, provision of food, is all difficult. Lack of consistency of staff is a big problem for people with dementia.

When she arrived at the private residence on an assist-level floor, the care seemed good and the family was happy with it. Once Catherine settled in, she became happy and more vibrant and her physical health seemed to improve.

But as time went on and her dementia worsened, the staff were less able to deal with it, and Wanda felt that the residence staff needed more training to understand dementia patients. The personal care service workers (PCSWs) do all the work that families don't want to do or cannot do. As a society, we don't sufficiently value their training. For example, bathroom and shower issues became difficult as her mom regressed.

Wanda came to see that the residences are not set up properly to deal with people with dementia. They needed to provide more stimulating gatherings for the assist level. Many times, Wanda suggested outside help from the Alzheimer's Society, which had programs already set up and ready to implement without a charge, but there was resistance to change on the part of staff.

Wanda's mom was in an expensive private care residence, but still family had to go every day or every other day when COVID started as the dynamics of care changed. The home did not do well during the first few months of COVID-19. Residents were isolated in their rooms; all events were cancelled. The home had to follow Public Health Guidelines which called for isolation. Isolation is not a good thing for the elderly or for anyone suffering with dementia.

The physical situation was not conducive to managing the spread of COVID. Something like a pod system would have allowed better management of the disease spread. Two stories high is plenty with smaller units set up so staff are close by. While it costs more to set up well in the first place, paying more attention would have saved both money and lives as time wore on.

Wanda is very concerned about Ontario's Bill 7, which allows hospitals to move patients to long-term care homes they didn't choose or bill them $400.00 a day if they would rather go elsewhere and prefer to wait in hospital until the home of their choice becomes available, although she understands the need for it. Sending elders up to 150 km away from their family is not a good way to open hospital beds. First, there need to be standards of care set up and supervised so that the care is harmonized across facilities. It is inhumane to move people with dementia away from their friends and contacts. It ends up being expensive both financially and emotionally. Families that visit are exhausted by the visit and end up having to stay over.

The woman who had been running the home left quickly when COVID hit. There seemed to be no political will to stabilize the staff, leaving many people with no support. There were huge differences in care between someone who had family support and someone who didn't. At first, the home continued to take patients from hospital, but they lost that right because they couldn't provide the necessary level of care. As time went on, care became worse as the staff changed. There were fewer staff and their workload shifted such that they could not spend time with residents. Wanda asked the residence to consider hiring 'comfort ambassadors;' people just to be companions to the residents. This request was turned down. Wanda was told that public health would not allow companions.

Wanda's mother had hidden her frailties in her own home and continued to try to do that at the residence. At first, she fought for the ability to make her own decisions. She did not view doctors as experts to serve her, and she viewed sickness as a weakness. As the proportion of very young staff increased, staff could be patronizing and were often not well-trained, which tended to make the situation worse.

Repeated isolation affected her mom's mental ability towards the end of COVID. She was in and out of the hospital and had to isolate for up to 10 days each time when she returned from hospital, regardless of the fact that she'd had numerous COVID tests in the hospital and before her release.

One member of Wanda's family did not want the vaccine and hence could not go into the home at all. Rapid tests helped with access, but they did not happen soon enough.

As the COVID pandemic hit, at first Wanda was not allowed in to see her mother. Then, if she did a polymerase chain reaction (PCR) test every seven days she could go in as a caregiver. So she would be tested Thursday and the results would be available on Monday. She could then drive down for a multi-day visit. Catherine's residence was five hours away from Wanda's home. The system took a while to work out as the rules were ever changing. Eventually each time she went in she would have rapid test results. She noted that there was a huge difference in training of staff who administered the rapid tests.

When Wanda's mother was hospitalized, Wanda was not allowed into the hospital. Fortunately, a speech pathologist who was familiar with her went in and reported on her condition. Wanda's mother became increasingly agitated, and her doctor warned of her impending death and put her in palliative care. When Wanda's mother became a palliative patient, her care became much better, because there was an outside doctor and nursing support 24 hours a day. The palliative care team allowed the family unconditional access. The nurse there was fantastic about managing her mother's discomfort.

Wanda noted that there is little support available for caregivers, unless you really hustle to find it. There is the Alzheimer's Society, for example. They provided virtual trips and armchair travel. While the home didn't want to use these tools because they thought of them as childish, they were perfect for memory-challenged people. Locally, there is a 'you first' program in Pakenham for caregivers. In fact, there are many local programs, but it takes time and energy to find them when time and energy are what caregivers are struggling to maintain.

As we head toward a 'new normal,' Wanda feels that we need to revamp the whole system. The file needs to be put under a team of capable, experienced managers. The close tie to politics in the province makes it difficult to make real progress. That said, there are very good LTC facilities out there which she found very impressive and different. She is convinced that this is because of the manager of the facility, and suggests that someone like that could make a difference to the whole system.

Wanda is concerned about what will happen to her as she ages. She thinks that self-managed collectives are a good idea. She is concerned that too much of the quality is directly related to money. Her mother's care cost on average $6,000.00 to $7,000.00 a month. Wanda's family were fortunate that their mother had financial resources, but so many people do not. It was a five year wait for Catherine to enter a local LTC facility unless she was in crisis. Her family decided not to wait for more of a crisis and so moved her to the residence when they could.

Wanda thinks there are options for the government to do other things, such as providing a tax break like the TFSA or RSP for future care. She suggests that insurance products should be more readily available or explained more easily. The pandemic has revealed what a hugely complex problem elder care is, but there have to be solutions. She believes that the province needs to start right away to avert another disaster in the care of the elderly. Some of the obvious issues need to be sorted out before Bill 7 is passed, because it won't solve the problems.

Even months after her mother's death, Wanda remains too tired to actively lobby for change. She just hopes that we can learn from the COVID-19 experience and so improve the system. Noting that access, transit, care and treatment all cost money, she believes more resources are necessary to improving the system. There needs to be sharing of information and resources across many different groups that deal with the elderly, between general practitioners, specialty doctors, nurses, PSWs, etc., and facilities, retirement residences, Alzheimer's societies, home care and family caregivers and more. A large team to coordinate care! The start for elder care improvement may be to prioritize home care to allow people to be in their homes for as long as possible and to work on improving dementia care and prevention.

There are common threads running through these accounts: lack of staff, lack of training, lack of family access, and inadequacy of physical facilities chief among them. Perhaps the most serious common thread today is the exhaustion and frustration of the daughters, usually elders themselves, who saw their mothers deteriorate before their eyes and who were prevented from providing the needed physical and emotional support because of the rules instituted to manage COVID.

Keep in mind that the Prior Chest Nuts are a breast cancer survivor group who have dealt with the healthcare system and emerged on the other side of one of the major threats to women's health of our time. These women have come to terms with death and dying and uniformly appreciate the opportunity for them and their families to live their best lives. Their determination to be dragon boat participants speaks to their courage and their values.

I believe that these women, who have undergone enormous personal stresses already, and who have been profoundly impacted by watching their mothers' lives deteriorate due to insensitive rule-making and heavy-handed separation of families and isolation of their loved ones, are now suffering from some version of PTSD as a result. They are being left to their own devices to cope with not only the grief of losing their mothers, but also a mixture of physical and emotional exhaustion and guilt brought on by the extreme lack of support during one of the most emotionally taxing times of their lives.

What more could have been done? A lot is written in these woke days about the increasing equality of women in society no matter their colour or their sexual orientation. Equal pay for work of equal value might not yet be a reality but it is on the table. Young women can have careers in traditionally male-oriented fields if they wish. Of course, women do not yet have control of their own bodies, especially in the USA where *Roe vs Wade* has been overturned and Trump rules. And, of course, women do not have the power to impose some of their fundamental values on the business of healthcare, which is run largely by and for men. Post COVID, I am hoping that the nurses and PSWs, most of whom are women, will stand up as never before to help ensure not only that they are fairly treated in pandemics to come, but that patient and family dignity is protected as it was not during COVID. Elder women play a key nurturing role in our society, and that role needs a lot more respect and support than it has recently received.

COVID-19: Before and After

Julie Stashick as told to Ann McMillan

Late in my career, I decided to train to be a PSW (personal support worker). I have been working with the elderly, my favourite patients, in a long-term care facility. The situation changed when COVID-19 hit. I have heard the horror stories, and my sympathies go out to the staff and residents of some of the hardest-hit facilities. Beyond the facilities themselves and staffing, which are always cause for concern, there were issues around PPE (personal protective equipment), family access, testing, and on and on.

I was very fortunate to work at Fairview Manor, where no patients got COVID-19, although several of the staff did. Fairview Manor declared a COVID-19 outbreak on January 6, 2020. On March 17, 2020, Ontario Premier Doug Ford declared a state of emergency due to the COVID-19 outbreak. We were short-staffed from time to time, as were most of the facilities in Ontario, and things were hectic, but we did get through the pandemic. There was no secret to this: it is a very well-run facility in general, and the staff were a team. It is important to mention that the team included others beyond the healthcare providers. The housecleaners, laundry people, and kitchen crew really stepped up their game in order to cope and to ensure that infection control measures were implemented every step of the way for resident care. Leadership had an important role to play in establishing and maintaining standards. The director of care (DOC) and assistant DOC had to make sense of rules that changed almost daily and adapt them to providing the best possible care to real patients without exposing them to COVID-19. The nurses and PSWs worked together to ensure that patients received adequate care based on their needs, even when families were not allowed to participate in providing care. It is important to realize that many residents of these homes do not have families who are involved with day-to-day care, and their situation did not change as much as those who had attentive families.

I retired from Fairview Manor in January, 2023, and I am proud to have worked there for a lot of reasons. Many facilities are not up to the standards maintained there in terms of leadership, staffing and patient-centered care. In general, residents these days are much more dependent when they arrive at long-term care facilities, with more complex health needs than residents in past times who simply couldn't look after themselves adequately. Budgets do not seem to take this greater complexity of patient needs into consideration, so that during COVID-19 these facilities faced double and triple whammies as they tried to manage more difficult patients with the same or fewer staff and the extra demands of COVID-19 measures.

During my career as a PSW, I observed personally many individual situations which I have tried to group into some sort of overall sense of the situation.

Ageism is a systemic form of oppression that is very often experienced by older people. I would like to say it is not present in long-term care, but the reality is that residents are often not able to formulate their thoughts or speak for themselves, leaving them vulnerable, especially if a facility is short-staffed. When there is a shortage of staff along with patients who cannot speak out, it is difficult to avoid ageism.

Many elderly people experience social isolation and loneliness, which reduces their quality of life. Family members need to recognize this and be their voice for them, especially when they are no longer able to express their feelings. When family members are denied access, this situation can worsen rapidly.

Pain in the elderly is often blamed on arthritis, especially when tests have not been performed. In fact, there are many potential causes of pain and the treatment needs to be specific to the cause. It is particularly important to avoid overmedication, since that contributes to residents' inability to think and speak for themselves.

We need to call out any unacceptable treatment we see and always strive to be the voice for our loved ones when they are unable to communicate for themselves any more. The progression of aging from a requirement for simple assistance and care through a need for total support is a story lived out by the majority of seniors. Surely our society should provide continuity of care and respect for these individuals.

The baby boomers are the largest population in Canada now. Some will be admitted to hospitals and possibly long-term care homes as well. I worry what will happen when the baby boomers hit this stage of their lives. Some of them seem to be aging more rapidly than earlier generations. There are many factors potentially contributing to that; perhaps the widespread use of drugs and alcohol has had an impact.

Early indications are that boomers may be more difficult to manage in care. There is a risk of violence with patients and this risk seems to be increasing. While patients should not be overmedicated, it takes skill and time to manage those who do have a violent streak. Clearly, the approach of a PSW has to be careful and watchful. If a patient seems to be having violent thoughts, it is best just to leave them to give them a chance to settle down. Who knows, at that moment your presence could evoke bad memories of times when they were hurt. It surprised me how many older women reacted to past memories of abusive treatment by their partners. As a PSW in these cases it is important to know enough about patients to be able to manage them effectively.

This raises another point. There needs to be a balance between privacy of information and the need to know in order to give the best possible care. Such personal information is often not available to caregivers, at least until an incident occurs.

Finally, we need to talk more about both sides of the story about aging… not just about decline. The important thing has always been to look for learning, change and renewal, which can occur as the healthy elderly have time for themselves. I am confident that will happen more often in the future! COVID times were not the best for seeing this other side of the story.

My experience as a PSW brought back personal memories, and reminded me that the end-of-life time is always emotionally charged, and no matter how well-managed it will have lasting impacts on families. COVID-19 has been painted as a villain in terms of the deaths of thousands of elder-Ontarians, and the situation undoubtedly made a difficult time even worse for many. Still, my memories of my mother's pre-COVID death are with me, and will be always.

My mother, Shirley, had complex health issues but lived independently in an apartment in Arnprior with the assistance of a personal care worker (PSW) who came in three times a week to help her with showering and personal care. She had COPD and required oxygen.

Mom suffered a fall on August 13, 2009, a day my family will never forget. When the PSW arrived, she called my sister Jill, who had a key to Mom's apartment. The dementia doctor came from Ottawa and assessed our mom. She explained that Mom could not return to her apartment and that we would have to choose three long-term care homes for her. All three we chose had long waiting lists even in 2009, years before COVID-19. Mom would stay at Arnprior Regional hospital until a bed came available for her. She was diagnosed with vascular dementia.

I received a call on January 13, 2010. A bed had come available at Groves Park Lodge in Renfrew. My siblings and I had 24 hours to accept or decline this bed. We talked and decided to accept the bed and move Mom to Groves Park. We were relieved to get this call; hospitals are not the best place for people with Alzheimer's and dementia.

My mother continued to decline, physically and mentally, at Groves Park. One day my brother, Jeff, and I visited Mom and she called him Gary. Gary was our mom's husband and our dad!

Another day I and my husband, Brian, visited Mom. She didn't recognize me, but she looked at Brian and said, 'Hi Brian, how are doing?!' The demented brain works in very mysterious ways. You learn quickly to go with the situation so you don't confuse and upset your loved one.

Mom passed away on December 28, 2010 at 1 a.m. I think about my mom every day and I have a chat with her often. I believe she can hear me, and I will always feel her love.

The last year of my mother's life was challenging for the family... these situations will always be so. We were fortunate to be able to visit her without restriction, and those visits did a lot to maintain her connections to reality and to her family. Although she became increasingly confused, her quality of life was as good as it could be under the circumstances.

In summary, I have seen a lot of black and white reporting on long-term care in Ontario during COVID-19. My experience as a daughter and a health provider tells me that is really not the situation... that it is incredibly complex. Some facilities, like the one my mother was in and the one I worked in, are well-run, and residents receive sensitive and supportive end-of-life care. Others are not so good for a whole variety of reasons, some of which I have mentioned. Staff is short at all the facilities and care would be improved with better trained, more consistent staffing. In fact, leadership and staffing are probably the two most important factors differentiating the best homes from the others.

Sometimes the physical facilities themselves have shortcomings and limitations. We need to work to provide better standards for operators to follow and to work facility by facility to make sure they are functioning well, as well as facilities that allow privacy and separation of residents.

We also need more hospices. Hospice is available at any point that a physician deems a person has a life-limiting illness and their life expectancy is six months or less. People live an average of 29 days longer in hospice care than in alternative forms of end-of-life care and often with more comfort, dignity and peace. Ironically, when the focus shifts from length of life to quality of life, length of life improves, too.

I hope that quality of life is what we all want for our loved ones during their final stages.

Pandemic Stories of Infection Prevention in Long-term Care
Fred Andayi

Standing in the middle of a breakfast-busy dining hall, she held me tightly in a loving embrace and gave an appreciative sigh. Marie (not her real name) felt that this was the best gift she could give me in the moment of COVID-19 forsakenness. However, her cordial gesture took longer than I had anticipated: 15 seconds, 30 seconds, 1 minute… now rolling into what seemed like eternity. I felt a bit uncomfortable. I wondered if she had had a dementia attack that she was not aware of. Maybe I reminded her of humanity's goodness or her wonderful youthful past life, or maybe she was just grateful to see this young man taking risks by visiting her long-term care home bi-weekly and inspecting her settings and safeguarding the quality of her care. Whatever the reason, she was all smiles.

Marie must have been in her 60s or 70s. She was strong-willed but soft-spoken, and one of the residents living independently in a retirement home in Eastern Ontario. Not that many years earlier, she'd retired to an empty nest. Now she had chosen to stay with her peers for companionship in a Retirement Living Serviced Apartment. Her roommate, Jane (also not her real name), had grown up on a farm near Regina and become a much-loved high school teacher. Both had travelled the world in their youth, visited all seven continents, and married early in life. Each had a child and was twice divorced, and fate had brought them here for their sunset years. Marie was a financial expert who had in her professional career served what is now Global Affairs Canada. She had grown up in Chicoutimi, Quebec, and had great nostalgia for the Canada of Prime Minister Pierre Trudeau's years. She seemed particularly grateful that we could converse in French and that I could sit down and engage on matters beyond my work. Whenever I was around, she wanted me to sit across a coffee table or beside her on a couch and engage in intellectual banter. I cherished that; it became a ritual I looked forward to. The two women were in good health, with none of the underlying chronic conditions such as senile dementia, Alzheimer's, psychosis, anxiety, and phobia so common among their peers, especially in this Retirement Home Unit (RHU), which was part of the Long-Term Care (LTC) facility, housing individuals with limited mobility and those needing 24-hour monitoring. Marie and Jane often read international journals such as the *Financial Times*, *Time Magazine*, and *The Economist*, and would engage each other in animated discussion that was dear to their souls.

This particular day was the third of our chitchat sessions since I'd taken up my new position at their facility, one of several facilities I supported as the region's 'Infectious Prevention and Control (IPAC) Specialist'-cum-Epidemiologist. In my job, I sought to ensure that despite the pandemic, residents' living spaces were safe from preventable health and environmental hazards through disease control and routine facility hygiene and sanitation inspection, collectively referred to as IPAC or IPAC Measures. In this role, I had to balance between being a 'Pseudo-government inspector' and an 'Angel Gabriel' or a 'Father Christmas marionette,' depending on the circumstances. I had to swing in moods, according to which robe was pulled, from passionate praise for services delivered to the sternness of an angry father with that 'go to your corner kid-look,' to the military precision mode to keep up with the uncompromising disease-free and high sanitation standards expectations within the facilities. Seniors' lives were at stake, which allowed no room for error. I was loved and loathed in equal measure, depending on the individual in question and their role in the facility.

Residents loved my presence, for it brought timely quality service delivery. Some said that on the days of my visits, tasty fresh food was served on time, rooms were cleaned properly, showers were given, and the residents' clothes changed to fresh and clean. Staff, on the other hand, were not always so glad to see me. To them, I brought additional work demands with little orientation time in an already emotionally and physically draining setting, to the point that one staff member confided that, on the days of my facility visit, IPAC adherence was kind of showbiz. Sadly, this was the case, because my weekly routine visits, on alternating Tuesdays and Thursdays, were known ahead of time. It was dark humour but laced with truth. The senior management loved that I was helping to tell their story to the corporate leadership who owned and managed the facilities but felt an equal measure of fear and suspicion that I was on a fault-finding mission that put their work positions at risk. Many staff suffered psychological distress and burnout, with some quitting altogether.

Even in the pre-pandemic period, IPAC measures had often been neglected and unfunded, and most facilities, including ours, across Ontario, Canada [1,2] and the USA [3] struggled with their transition to internationally expected standards. Facility Executive Directors (ED) often pushed back on some core and critical IPAC expectations. Understandably, the lack of funds and staff did not help, at a time when long-term care homes were facing recurring facility-wide COVID-19 outbreaks causing untold suffering and deaths among staff and residents. Additionally, they had to deal with the residents' families' anger at restricted family visits, particularly the supervised compassion visits for seriously ill residents on the verge of death that demanded wearing 'draconian' PPE (personal protection equipment), the generally reduced number of visits and contact time duration, and the lonely deaths of their loved ones. The families with whom, on rare occasions, I crossed paths were mostly full of praise for my contributions; however, some were greatly frustrated. This social and lifestyle disruption was no different from what our ancestors had faced, over 100 years ago, with the 1918 'Spanish' influenza pandemic. [4] But we apparently haven't learnt our lesson from this past horrendous scourge, on the need for advance preparedness and the significance of nonpharmaceutical intervention. [5]

COVID-19 vaccination began in Canada on December 14, 2020. The vaccine's arrival was a great relief to the LTC industry. It meant more interaction among residents and staff, more openings for family visits, and more group activities. Leading the program of vaccine awareness, acceptance, and eventual uptake among staff and hesitant residents' families was equally fulfilling and challenging. The misinformation on social media on vaccine safety and efficacy had become overwhelming and was definitely a factor in some staff members' reluctance to get vaccinated. By instituting vaccine uptake awareness training, both in groups and one-on-one, we managed to convince some, though others remained adamantly opposed. It wasn't until a corporate policy release threatened potential contract termination that some agreed to get the jab at all. Others refused outright, choosing to resign rather than take the vaccine.

During my awareness campaign, it was disturbing to see that some senior facility managers, not infrequently people with a medical background, had conflicted positions on the COVID-19 vaccine and vaccination in general, resulting in their refusal to take the jab and privately discouraging colleagues from getting vaccinated. On the other hand, junior staff, overwhelmingly recent immigrants or Canadians from remote rural areas with personal experiences of 'systems not working for them as envisioned,' felt this jab was mystically supposed to control them remotely through a microchip. As absurd as this might have sounded, I could, to an extent, empathize. Being both an immigrant and a medical scientist, I saw the vaccination campaign as an opportunity to correct the misinformation rapidly spreading through social media with evidence-based facts, that would positively encourage informed discourse and genuine behaviour change to protect the vulnerable elderly.

The discontented staff members' narrative appears to have been based on unaddressed historical and systematic generational injustice meted out by former colonial administrations in their home countries. A quick invest-igation revealed that between 30 and 45 percent of those buying the narrative felt sincere about their course: to speak out against the unjust system and leverage this rare opportunity to be heard and push for change. Most discontented folks had arrived with Medical Doctor (MD) or BS Nursing training qualifications and experience, and with big dreams. However, for the majority, their current employment was not in line with their previous qualifications and experience. The lack of recognition of their previous credentials made their engagement a matter not of choice but of survival. The formal route to gaining an equivalent practicing license is absurdly warped and convoluted—difficult at best. The COVID-19 pandemic offered a platform, and the vaccination awareness protest was a form of non-violent resistance, a hear-me-now session. For those discontented folks, the anti-vax protests offered, or appeared to offer, a relatively safe way to vent their frustrations at a system that had cheated them out of their ambitions and aspirations to a better life, especially for the skilled economic migrants with unmet expectations.

Working with the facility's senior staff was different. Most of them demonstrated an unfailing commitment to the residents' welfare. They had to balance that with managing the needs and expectations of staff, residents' families, local government, and the corporate brand. For example, Justine's (not her real name) dedication was far beyond expectations. She had the super gentle soul of a nun, full of love and peaceful tranquillity. She disliked conflict and would sort issues out as soon as they occurred, prioritizing internal operational harmony and delegating the corporate head office to handle complex problems, such as relations with local health authorities and the media when there was a crisis, Unfortunately, all this care and pandemic forsakenness took a toll on her health. She confided how it was not uncommon for her to spend 50 to 75 percent of her personal time, including weekends, serving at the facility, at times having to postpone her own medical appointments to cover up for acute staff shortage. In the worst period, she found herself working more than eight hours a day or a straight back-to-back day-to-night shift, without a break, due to lack of staff coverage. While doing facility rounds with her, you could feel her pure passion for her work and team, her genuine and open spirit, her willingness to collaborate with and serve seniors. Her focus on quality service delivery was second to none within the organization. Be it in nursing care, foods and dining, PPE signage, cleaning, and disinfection process, the work she did was unfailingly excellent. She was a hands-on person.

Observing Justine working at her desk with Molly, her Corgi canine companion, was a 'lo and behold' movie scenario. Molly, who was around 10 years old, was now part of the facility team, as its unspoken timekeeper. Molly knew when to eat and go pee, and when the end of the shift was, and she would faithfully cajole her master into obeying and serving her needs.

Most remarkable was the rite of passage always conducted when someone died at the facility. Unlike other facilities I had been at before, here at Justine's place, the staff acted and mourned as a family. First, a coded message was pronounced over the facility's speaker. After six hours of waiting time, the coroner's team would arrive to pick up the deceased. The deceased was processed and placed in body bags on a chariot. As the

41

coroner's team left the premises, all staff would line up at a COVID-safe distance to pay their last respects. Given that almost uncountable deaths were happening at that time, such acts were invaluable gestures of humanity.

'How we die remains in the memory of those who live on,' an English nurse, Cicely Saunders (June 22, 1918 – July 14, 2005), once said. This remains true for many today. Jeff and Jude (not their real names) were a lovely couple. When walking into their room for IPAC inspection and a quick chitchat, you would be hit by a calm ambiance of true love and dedication. You could see at a glance a collection of classical family photos, of their wedding and that of their son and daughter, family gatherings and holidays on display. Judy's knitting product samples and Jeff's all-time favourite car collection models were all frozen in time on the shelf. With their mobility gradually fading away, I often found Jude doing her never-ending knitting and Jeff drawing/painting or doing puzzles. These high school sweethearts spoke in a unique love language refined over 80 years of union—a language that included long silences, sighs, gentle touches, and soft whispers. But then, one evening, in the spring of 2020, Jude complained of a low-grade fever and sneezing. Forty-eight hours later, the situation had rapidly progressed to severe pneumonia, and she was pronounced dead from COVID-19 infection complications. Jeff was devastated, and his body gradually shut down. He refused to eat and lost the will to live any longer. Four weeks later, he died— not from COVID-19, but from heartbreak.

As I let go of Marie's hug and headed to the LTC side to attend the District Coroner's onsite meeting, I could not help but look back on my own life, with memories shifting back from childhood to the pandemic, and then to the future. It had been almost a year and a half since the onset of the pandemic. As of December 2020, I had travelled several times across Ontario and Quebec, firefighting the pandemic in LTC homes for the survival of our beloved seniors. I'd slept in nearly empty hotels, with nearly empty streets, often in the remote areas of Ontario where most LTC homes were located. In this period and location, access to catering was limited, the Uber Eats services (i.e. online food purchase and delivery services) or hotel room services, were non-existent in most accommodation facilities, and it was not uncommon for me to sleep on an empty stomach. On Christmas Eve, I'd flown from Montreal to Ottawa to Toronto to Thunder Bay to support a facility overrun by a COVID-19 outbreak. [6] I worked throughout the Christmas and New Year festivity period, returning to lonesome hotels away from loved ones and family. My small suitcase was always packed and ready to go. Memories of sweet, gracefully aging folks living in the countryside popped up. In my thoughts I could see them tending their treasured farms, feeding their backyard fowls, and gently tending to their kitchen gardens while conversing with their next-door neighbours.

Looking at the body bag of Madame Tani (not her real name) on the coroner's chariot made me wonder if her son, who was about two metres away from me, was cherishing such sweet memories of her. 'Doc, is that according to the Managing Resident Deaths in Long-Term Care Protocol?' Jeannette's (not her real name) voice shook me back to the matter at hand. She sought approval to start the handover of the deceased's belongings and conduct the deep cleaning process for the room. I nodded in agreement.

During the pandemic, the Managing Resident Deaths in Long-Term Care Protocol consisted of four phases. In the first phase, the death was confirmed and the family as well as the funeral home were contacted. The contact information of the family's next of kin was shared. If the deceased had no family, the coroner's office was contacted. In the second phase, the Clinical Service Lead completed the Facility Patient Death Record, consulted with the attending clinician to determine the cause of death, and shared the death information with the coroner's office and other relevant government departments. In the third phase, the deceased resident's body was prepared and bagged according to the established aseptic protocol. A brief body handover ceremony from LTC to the funeral home was then conducted and attended by all staff, including those directly serving the residents. Lastly, a thorough cleaning and disinfection of the deceased's room, furniture, and personal effects was conducted before the room was handed over to a new senior tenant.

Jeannette was the facility director of clinical and nursing services; she was quite professional and dedicated to her work and the seniors' wellbeing. I liked working around her; she knew her stuff and was willing to learn and support me. As the coroner's chariot moved down the residence's long hallway to the waiting van in the parking lot, I again remembered the truth in Cicely Saunders's words, 'How we die remains in the memory of those who live on.'

Epilogue

This story is based on real people and on events occurring between November 2019 and November 2021 in Quebec and Ontario; to protect the privacy and confidentiality of individuals and institutions, the author used pseudonyms and did not disclose specific facility locations. The author's goal is to share his first-hand experience in combatting the COVID-19 pandemic in long-term care facilities (LTC), where his expertise contributed to reducing suffering and loss of life. He highlights the crucial roles played by the under-appreciated junior staff and senior management, especially the homes' Executive Directors (EDs), who worked tirelessly in a challenging pandemic situation with limited resources and preparation, often facing criticism from the media and being used as political scapegoats. EDs often struggled to balance conflicting expectations from the residents' families, residents, staff, corporate brands, and the local government. We must not overlook the physical, social, and psychological stress experienced by these staff members and seniors. Overall, the LTC industry requires significant structural and operational reforms. As we all age, we deserve better care than the system currently provides.

---

[1] Halpern, Lisa, Susan D. Phillips, and Nathan J. Grasse (2022). 'Non-Profit Long-Term Care in Ontario: How Financially Robust Is the System?' Canadian Public Policy/Analysedepolitiques 48(S2):6480.

[2] IPAC Canada (2022). 'A Written Submission for the 2022 Federal Budget from Infection Prevention and Control Canada', August 2021.

[3] Krejci, Buffy Lloyd. 'Broken: How the Global Pandemic Uncovered a Nursing Home System in Need of Repair and the Heroic Staff Fighting for Change.' Bolton ON: Houndstooth Press, 2022.

[4] Andayi, Fred, Sandra Chaves, and MacAllain Widdowson (2019). 'Impact of the 1918 Influenza Pandemic in Coastal Kenya.' Trop Med Infect Dis, 4(2). doi: 10.3390/tropicalmed4020091.

[5] Markel, Howard, Harvey B. Lipman, and Alexander Navarro J., et al (2007). 'Nonpharmaceutical interventions implemented by US cities during the 1918-1919 influenza pandemic.' JAMA, 298(6), 644-654. doi:10.1001/jama.298.6.644.

[6] Rinne, Gary (Producer). Jan 6, 2021. 'Thunder Bay MPPs speak out on Southbridge Roseview situation.' TBNewsWatch.com.

Death in the Time of Covid
Teresa Bandrowska

Daphne and I had been friends since our wild teen years. I rocked her babies, and later, her grandbabies, to sleep. I was the midwife both when her youngest son was born, and years later when he had his own son. We navigated together through marriages, motherhood, divorces, and crazy love affairs; we shared tea and tales while nursing our children.

When the kids were grown, we relished our quiet, undisturbed visits. In evenings, on her porch or mine, with gin-and-tonics in hand, 'the Queen Mum's favourite tipple,' as Daphne would say, we watched for the moon to rise, and discussed everything and anything: anthropology, physics, philosophy, politics, myth, and magic.

She was a true homebody. A 'No-Driving Day' was precious and rare, until she finally retired. She loved nothing more than puttering around her beautiful garden by the Gatineau River.

She was also a misanthropic curmudgeon at times, a woman who never suffered fools gladly, or at all. She spoke her mind fiercely and bluntly. Very intelligent, skilled with languages, she often swore a blue streak, and loved political and social debate.

She could be crabby and short-tempered with some, especially with all the foolishness in the world, but to her friends and loved ones she was warm, generous, and welcoming. She was always there to feed me, to offer respite and comfort when the world had dragged me down. She listened without judgment, even if she had heard my laments many times before, and always gave good advice, but only if asked.

I admired her for her courage and tenacity. She threw out her abusive husband when he had beaten her once too often. She then raised her three boys alone, while holding down a full-time job and completing her degree in linguistics; that took her many years, but she was very proud of the accomplishment. She loved languages, and was fluent in four: Latvian, English, French, and German.

In 2016, when Daphne was only 58, we started to notice something amiss… she was getting increasingly forgetful. At first, it was barely noticeable. But within the year, it was clear: she was going to the grocery store without her money, and calling me in confusion, wondering where she was. She was unable to fill out her taxes or any simple forms. She picked unripe tomatoes for a salad, and boiled up a single strand of spaghetti for dinner. We found her cupboards empty, save for pudding cups and melted ice cream. Though she was reluctant as ever to see a doctor, her children and I finally forced her hand. Diagnosis: early-onset temporal dementia.

45

Her son Daryll, his wife Jen, and Jen's sister Sam moved in to help. Daphne had always enjoyed cooking but was soon unable to do so safely. She began to wander outside to the highway, or to enter neighbouring homes. Soon, locks and gates were installed on appliances, doors and stairs. Sam became a full-time caregiver, feeding, dressing, and washing Daphne and keeping her safe.

We joked that the dementia was taking away Daphne's famous curmudgeonliness, as she became increasingly placid and childlike, happy to just sit watching her family, including her brand-new grandson. Her life became filled with the simple pleasures of meals, music, television and picture books. I would take her on little outings: for walks, for lunch, to fitness classes and for treats after.

But despite safety measures and constant care, it soon became increasingly difficult to keep her at home. She became less and less verbal, until she could no longer speak except in confused repetition. This was hard for us to witness, as she had always been an eloquent and articulate speaker, a master of language. She was soon unable to manage any hygiene for herself, and would wake multiple times a night to wander. She was losing her balance and falling.

Daryll reluctantly put her on a waiting list for long-term care, and we had a welcome respite for a couple of weeks in 2019, when she went to a Long-term Care unit in Buckingham Hospital, an hour away. Everyone loved her there, as by then she was totally gentle and smiling, agreeable and seemingly content with anything. No more F-bombs!

A year later, in March 2020, as the Covid pandemic was ramping up, the call came: there was a permanent spot for Daphne in the same unit in Buckingham. We had been hoping for a place closer to us in Wakefield, but we knew we had to take what we could get. She had to go in right away. All packed up and ready to go, Sam, Daryll and Daphne were on the long road to Buckingham when they received the news. Code Orange: the Premier was locking down the province, and no new non-essential admissions would be allowed into hospitals. Daryll called me in a panic: they were almost there, what should they do? I told him, 'Just go, plead ignorance, I don't think they will turn you away.'

Thirty minutes later, he called again, in desperation, 'They won't let us in!' I told him to stand his ground, to refuse to leave, and to ask for the coordinatrice. (This is the chief nursing coordinator, responsible for bed assignments, staffing, and the general smooth operations of the hospital.) He should tell her that Daphne had a bed waiting for her upstairs, that she was due in that morning, and that they could not take her home.

This was early in the pandemic, when the authorities were scrambling to stem the contagion and reduce the risks. Daryll was clad in his own version of Personal Protective Equipment: covered head-to-toe in a big rain slicker with a hood, a mask, dishwashing gloves and rubber boots. Thus attired, he waited inside the hospital for the coordinatrice, while Sam and Daphne stayed in the car.

After a short wait, Daryll managed to speak to the coordinatrice. He explained the situation, pleading for them to take Daphne as planned. Thankfully, she was sympathetic, and Daphne was finally admitted.

But our relief was tinged with sorrow, as no one could visit Daphne, due to the lockdown. The nurses kindly let her family communicate with her by iPad, but she was now totally non-verbal and didn't appear to recognize anybody. The staff assured us repeatedly that she was well and seemed happy, was getting good care, and that there was no COVID on the ward. And so a year passed.

By the spring of 2021, the pandemic restrictions had eased somewhat, and family members were allowed in to see Daphne, one at a time. Daryll told the staff that I was her sister, and I was given the OK to see her. I drove the hour up to Buckingham, with flowers and treats, but when I got up to the floor, the nurses told me another lockdown had just been ordered that morning, and I couldn't go in! I was so disappointed. A lovely nurse overheard, and told me she would wheel Daphne (who could no longer walk) to the door of the lounge, a few metres away, so at least I could wave to her. I was struck by the change in her. She was extremely thin and frail and looked at me blankly. She obviously didn't recognize me, but she smiled nonetheless, and I smiled under my mask, and waved through my tears. It was but a brief glimpse before I was ushered out and told to leave.

All this time, Daphne had been on a waiting list to transfer to the Wakefield Hospital as soon as a bed was available. After hearing no news for over a year, I told Daryll to squeak his wheel and find out where she was on the list, to plead that it would be so much easier for her family to be able to visit and provide care for her if she was closer, as we all lived in Wakefield. Shortly after he did so in early summer 2021, the call came, and finally Daphne was transferred to Wakefield Hospital. She was now just minutes away!

Daryll again put me on the list as Daphne's 'sister,' as visits were still limited to family. I was able to go in! It was wonderful to see her, to help feed her and help with her care, to spend precious time together. I think she recognized me, or at least, she always seemed happy to see me. For a year we had our regular visits every few days, and I got to know the wonderful, caring staff, who just loved her.

Then one day in late May 2022, Daryll got a call from the hospital: Daphne's health had suddenly deteriorated, she was no longer able to eat or drink, and she was not expected to live for long. They suspected an intestinal blockage, but were not going to perform any invasive procedures; they would keep her as comfortable as possible.

I sped to the hospital, fear burning deep in my belly. I was afraid to see her suffering, afraid of the messiness and turmoil of death. I had had some experience with death, as a nurse and midwife for many years, but this felt different.

Once I got there, I relaxed. Despite an IV and a tube in her nose, Daphne seemed quiet and comfortable, and smiled faintly. I was surprised when she gave me a deep, penetrating, knowing look. She inexplicably seemed more like herself than she had in recent past years, as if the old friend I knew was back. Despite her inability to speak, her eyes were lucid, calm and clear. My fear melted. I was filled with an almost unbearable sadness, and yet also with a sense of deep relief that her trials would soon be ended.

We got her oldest son over from England, called up her friends, and prepared for her death as well as we could. Many people could not face seeing her, but said they would pray, and sent blessings.

Death is very much hidden in our society, and, as with anything unknown and unseen, the fear of it is strong and ubiquitous. Once, we were all familiar with the face of death, as most people died at home, among family and friends. Not many now have sat in death's presence. It is not an easy thing to see a person in the last days of life. It is not comfortable to be reminded of our own mortality, of the unavoidable fate that awaits all living things.

Daphne held on longer than expected, true to her stubborn nature. Every day for the next two weeks, as I drove to the hospital with her sons and our dear friend Erica, I both expected and feared to see her death. That icy claw of fear returned each time, with a nauseating dread of what I might find that day, but as soon as I was with her, I felt calm, and peace diffused the anxiety within me. This was where I needed to be.

It felt very much like the final transition into birth, when the child is close. The air is changed, and charged with an electric energy. The molecules are different, dancing in a new way, as a door is about to open, a passage is near. Time becomes elastic, warping from fast to slow. It is so very ordinary and yet so very special.

A momentous event was coming, and it was impossible to know the hour. It was scary, yet achingly beautiful as well. Everything else had ceased to be important. The daily tick-tock world continued around us, but for Daphne and her entourage, all the unimportant hustle and bustle ceased, and we settled into a time out of time, a world between worlds, a liminal space outside of the everyday.

Every day that beautiful late spring, we took Daphne out to the hospital balcony, where she could sit in the sun and look out upon her beloved Gatineau hills. With her sons and her two dearest friends surrounding her, she was loved with sweet tenderness. There was much laughter as we told stories of her life, and many times we held each other, weeping. Daphne would fix her wise, smiling gaze on each of us in turn, and then the hills, and often up to the ceiling, as if she could see something or someone important there. Every day, we would sing her the beautiful Latvian lullaby that her own mother had sung to her, and later taught to her grandsons. That balcony became our enclave, an oasis where we were mostly alone; we could remove our masks, play her favourite music, pray, smudge, reminisce. It was a living wake! The wonderful staff were so lovely and helpful, making sure she was comfortable, letting us know what to expect, and making sure we were okay too.

Then the day came when Daphne was too weak to go outside, and spent more time sleeping. We surrounded her bed instead, continuing our vigil. We each had some time alone with her, to say our farewells. Her eyes, when open, were still lucid. Just once, I saw fear there, and I found myself murmuring reassuringly, as I would to a labouring mother: 'You are safe, all is as it should be, you are not alone, we are with you.' I told her that she need not hold on, that she could let go, into the arms of the Mother. She sighed, closed her eyes, and slept.

Hers was, in the end, a very gentle passing. Early one morning, with one last, peaceful sigh, her spirit was gone. We washed her and dressed her in her favourite regalia, with her amber necklace and rose petals around her head and shoulders. We anointed her with sage, adorning her with flowers from her garden, before saying our final farewells.

Many years earlier Daphne had transplanted a young oak sapling, now grown tall and strong near the grove she had created to celebrate the turning of the Wheel. Later that week, as we gathered in the grove, circling around the fire to honour and to mourn, her three-year-old grandson told us, 'Baba is laughing in her oak tree.'

I still cannot quite believe my dear friend is gone, even though the Daphne I knew was gone years ago. I thank her for showing me the beauty and blessings of death. There truly is nothing to fear. I feel a renewed peace and a sense of rightness, and I am reminded that our time here is fleeting. Life and love are all the more precious for their impermanence. Carpe diem indeed!

I have inherited Daphne's sandals and her winter boots, which fit me perfectly. Summer and winter, I walk in her shoes and remember her.

A Poetic Vision of Long-Term Care
(for Barbara)
John Eaton

Dedication: to my spouse Barbara, forever in my heart

The era of COVID created a world of 'confinements': restrictions mandated on our freedoms to ensure our safety. This is a reality we routinely impose on our seniors with 'incomplete capacities' in long-term care as we restrict them to cocoons of safety.

Have we become more empathetic in recognizing their realities? Are we meeting our true responsibilities as family and friends when in most cases they are still vibrantly alive humans with minor disabilities? Yet we commoditize them as chattels and impose on them the sterile draconian realities of care in the equivalent of 5s'd production process facilities.

The following is a Free Verse poem to depict these realities of loss and sorrow which is the essence of a senior's realities as they close out their lives in a manner that they no longer control despite their capacities or perceived incapacities by supposedly caring loved ones.

Long-Term Care: The Reward of Incomplete Capacity

How do we reconcile
Our care, our love for who they are
With LTC's 5s'd production scape.
A world of sterile uniformity
Sustained: set, shined and sorted
To keep them safe, just SAFE?

There is no freedom or autonomy
And no rights and limited choices
As a chattel in the assembly lines or empty spaces.
The confining room for sleeping
And their personal functioning
Adds in more place for languishing.

There is no purpose here,
No quality of life
Just loneliness without your timely care
But how do brief phone calls
Or short visits deflate despair
Of mind-numbing imprisonment

This monotony of familiarity,
Of faces in their easy chairs,
Tables with place labels
In this locked confining enclosure,
Destructs all remaining capacity
To complete the lobotomy

Why must this be!
Defying our responsibilities!!!
But lock them up?
We must atone, or ever live in grief
For denial and desertion
Of their 'Realities.'

SECTION 3
Connecting During COVID

*O*ne of the most notable changes experienced during the emergence of COVID was towards isolation to thwart the spread of the disease. People's experience of that isolation often led to a deep-seated longing for connection. This section explores that longing and what people did to deal with it from several perspectives.

Lena Samson explicitly examines the world of relationships and beautifully articulates the importance of our basic need to reach out and touch each other even when we do not have close relationships in the classic sense. She makes the case that acknowledging the existence of others in relation to your own interests and activities makes for a worthwhile human connection. This longing for connection is further exemplified by Ruth Hawkins' description of her connection to her new granddaughter which was based on remote contact but enriched by time spent 'in person.' For his part, Rodney Clough explores the connection between place and feelings in 'Buying In/Cashing Out,' a moving memoir about his and his wife Linda Jo's transition from being innkeepers in rural Michigan to being ordinary retired folk in a Chicago condo.

Several of the following stories explore personal growth through exploration of new activities, concepts and relationships in the context of COVID. Deb Bertrand finds a whole new community and focus in 'And the Plague Continues.' I explain my strengthened relationship to dragon boating. Yvon Bernier explores how elders who have already adjusted to aging now adjust to the 'new normal' of COVID. Sally Arsove explores opportunities offered by Zoom technology to support old friendships made new again. Finally, Elizabeth Zimmer describes both the delight and the complexities of COVID romance. In this section, the whole is greater than the sum of the parts. Each of the individual stories offers a glimpse into the life of the author, but the section offers a glimpse into the changes in society triggered by the retreat into isolation demanded by the early COVID pandemic.

Ann McMillan

My Community of Strangers

Lena Samson

When you stop and think about it, relationships ebb and flow throughout our many years on this earth, bringing joy, pain and everything in between. Some friendships are deep and rich and last an entire lifetime, while others may be fleeting. We have family members, childhood friends, work colleagues, drinking buddies, regulars at the stores we frequent, neighbours... the list goes on and on. For long or short periods of time, they all bring something unique to our lives and help us adapt to the challenges we face every day. For we are social creatures, needing the comfort, support and understanding of others to not only enrich our lives, but even survive. As we emerge from the uncertainty of a pandemic that threatened these critical social interactions, we can start to appreciate how precious our relationships really are.

I'm fortunate to live in a neighbourhood criss-crossed by bicycle paths and bordered by greenery. Mothers amble with their strollers, children teeter on training wheels, and others promenade their canine companions daily. Students walk or bike to schools and parks safely without venturing onto busy streets. For the better part of 13 years, I accompanied my beloved Golden Doodle, Alfie, twice daily on these pathways, socializing with other pets and their owners. I befriended some of these people and we often strolled together, chatting about our dogs, our lives, the neighbourhood or world events. Once, a lovely, elderly Indian lady regaled me with the story of the German Shepherd she and her husband had reluctantly left behind during their posting to Australia, and how their beloved dog had died of a broken heart soon afterwards. She was so passionate in her storytelling that I had to give her all the time she needed to spin her tale, relishing this precious moment of connecting with a complete stranger. This story was important to her, and she honoured me by sharing it. Another neighbourhood woman, with her sweet Doodle, became a trusted friend and offered valued support during my divorce, as I listened and offered comfort during hers. However, all good things come to an end, and I didn't realize how important this community was until I lost it with Alfie's death in 2019.

All these wonderful years, Alfie and I met other dog owners in our nearby park every day. The dogs would tear around, greeting each other in excitement, while we doled out water, treats, conversation and laughter. I loved this daily ritual and the camaraderie it built with people I would never have met otherwise. Children squealed with delight visiting the dogs, and we appreciated their excitement at wanting to throw a ball or try their hands at offering a treat, ensuring that little fingers were kept intact. Monty, the Sheepdog, was Alfie's best friend, and they were a joy to see together, wrestling and playing to their hearts' content. Alfie was a big, loving, goofy boy, and I absolutely adored him.

I stopped frequenting the paths after Alfie passed away, avoiding the pain engendered by kind expressions of sympathy. The walkways were full of Alfie memories, and I didn't need more reminders of how deeply I missed him. But when COVID hit, the urge to stretch my legs and see other human beings pulled me back. And to my amazement, there they were—the elderly couple who held hands on their daily walks, the tall Asian fellow out for exercise, the now-elderly gentleman who'd laid a floor for me 25 years ago with his wife, the young man who lived one street over with his husky and retriever. It was surprisingly comforting to see them again! I don't know any of their names and they don't know mine, but we acknowledge each other all the same. I enjoy saying hello to people on the paths, recognizing and respecting them as fellow community members. Some return my greeting, some don't. I remember walking with my son one day when he smirked at me for greeting someone who subsequently ignored me. But I do it anyway; for all I know, mine might be the only smile a passerby receives that day. Maybe my saying hello and exchanging a word about the weather raises their spirits. There is something special to me in giving a smile to a stranger; it doesn't cost a thing and is a reminder that we all share this place together. In that brief moment of encounter, I can bridge the divides of age, skin colour, language or nationality and acknowledge a fellow human being enjoying our community exactly like me.

Recently, I cared for a friend's dog and ventured out to the paths with him (or her), reminiscing fondly on my thousands of walks with Alfie. Several of the daily walkers, whom I never really knew, asked whether I had a new dog and what had happened to Alfie. It warmed my heart greatly that after a year, he was still remembered. One lady said she was glad I had a new dog, and another recalled what a sweet boy my Alfie had been, bringing me to tears. Others commented that they hadn't seen me in forever and asked how I was doing. It felt wonderful that these virtual strangers remembered me after all this time. Nothing spectacular would make me stick out in their minds—we just shared the common experience of passing each other every day during a pleasant, relaxing wander. Like me, they were taking the time to breathe fresh air, enjoy the scenery, relax their minds and get a little exercise.

Experiencing these random reunions, I came to realize that there is community even among strangers. We care about each other and share each other's grief and celebrations in some small way. When my first grand-daughter was born, I was so thrilled that I blurted out my news to someone I'd never seen before on the path! I was just bursting and had to tell someone. Perhaps that was a weird thing to do, but I didn't care. And the person I told was happy for me!

These brief interactions became even more valuable as we rode out the pandemic. I felt less alone as I walked along the paths, exchanging a smile with a stranger, complimenting a cute baby or scratching a furry friend behind the ears. In our normally far-too-busy lives, we can become so self-absorbed that we don't even notice the people who walk by, each with their own stories that they might love to relate to someone who will listen. How interesting when we start to see—really see—the diverse individuals around us and try to remove invisible barriers instead of sustaining them. How much richer the world becomes!

So, when you feel lonely during a challenging time, take a walk, notice the people you encounter and risk saying hello. It just might make you feel better. And if you venture out every day, you'll start to recognize the same faces and begin to feel less isolated. Family, friends and colleagues don't have to be our only communities. If we are open to it, new friends could be just around the corner, even during a pandemic.

Ottawa, 2020

Metaphor for Pandemic Life:
How a Child Embodies the Shift in Connection
Ruth Hawkins

I have been with my granddaughter, in person, four times since she was born in July 2020. These visits have been sandwiched in during lulls in COVID cases when it felt safe enough to travel across the country to Vancouver. I feel blessed to have managed these visits because her other Nana is in Australia and has yet to hold this delicious child in her arms. If my heart aches from not being able to visit her as often as I like, how very hard it must be for her Aussie Nana.

Without technology—especially video calling—I would have missed even more. I am grateful for this; grateful for technology that allows me to peek in on her sleeping via the baby cam above her crib so that I can start my day with a look in on my sleeping angel. It settles my spirit and allows me to tackle the day. However, it is the face to face, touching, hugging, chasing, pushing on the swing, swimming, bathing, reading part of being a grand-mother that I miss. Children need to connect to others with actual face time, if you will pardon the pun. It may be that they have gotten more of it with their parents during the last few years as the rest of us have gotten less, and we are all the worse for it.

My connection with Ruby began the moment I knew she was on the way and grew from there, although mostly this was a remote, yearning, wishing type of connection on my part. I doubt I truly existed for her until her first birthday when she had spent time with me in the flesh, when she was old enough to experience me, and had a better grasp of object permanence (that objects continue to exist even though they can no longer be seen or heard). Now she could connect the voice and face on the phone with someone she had experienced.

This is where the richness lies in all our relationships: in the physical presence, warmth, touch, and shared emotions neither mediated nor distorted by screens, bad connections, or shoulders-up views. I wondered how long Ruby might hold on to this connection to her Nana without it being reinforced by periodic in-person visits? Would she slowly lose interest in engaging with me, as many of us have done with friends and family as we languished during two years of distance and isolation?

Ruby is now 18 months old. She asks to call Nana and then carries the phone around with her as she runs to and fro, jumping on the bed, climbing on the couch, or showing me her toys. She has put 'me' in her doll stroller, and we've taken a dizzying ride around her home. She hugs me to her chest and gives me sloppy kisses. At least that is what my son and daughter-in-law tell me is happening. I see her face come close as she zooms in to kiss me. I see the camera go blank (against her top) when she gives me a hug. I get slightly seasick as she takes me careening around. It's wonderful that I exist for her, even if it is inside a phone.

How I have longed to give my family and friends non-virtual hugs and kisses! How I wish I was beside my dear friends (rather than talking to them in my head) as I go about my day noticing things I would love to share or discuss. This mental dialogue feels like my inner chats with my long-dead father. Don't get me wrong. I'm grateful for the technology that allows some continuation of connection, and I suppose I have learned to carry my friends, in a way, like Ruby: clutched to my heart, as I go about my day, regular virtual coffee chats, occasional glasses of wine, quick texts and sharing of moments. It felt like enough at the start of the pandemic, but soon became a poor substitute that merely served to underscore the loss and disconnection. Enough already! We are all so done and done in by this pandemic. I need—we all need—the physical presence of our dear ones to really feel seen, heard, loved, cherished, and alive.

Buying in/Cashing Out:
Starts and Stops along Recovery
Rodney Clough
Dedicated to my wife and partner, Linda Jo Clough

It's July 2022, and more than a year has elapsed since the pandemic (2020-2021). More than a year since we dreaded losing what we had built in 2007 and maintained over 13 years: a domicile turned into an inn and, in 2014, into a short-term property rental.

That was 2021. Now it's 2022, and we find ourselves in serious retirement groping our way through life before and life to come. In April we sold Rabbit Run, our two-acre property in Sawyer, Michigan, which we had built in 2007 and which had sheltered and supported us. Today, Rabbit Run still exists as the new owners continue to offer the public a family retreat, a vacation property rental, and a short-term getaway destination.

We've 'cashed out.'

Looking backwards, our 'best years' were when we traversed unfamiliar ground. Our 'best years' were when we gave up our reluctance to see what was beyond the next ridge, to give up what had transpired since our last memorable engagement. For us 'The Rabbit,' a moniker our housekeeper/manager adopted, was not a destination but a stage set. We needed players. This encouraged us to navigate our guests' unfamiliarity. As innkeepers, we were 'around,' and 'out of sight,' but present. In 2014 when we remade 'The Rabbit' into a short-term family vacation rental, we became property owners, renting out accommodations. We were absent.

To pick up where we last left off in *Plague Take It*, the 'first pandemic wave' starting in January, 2020 altered our perspective and what we offered as hosts. With the onset of the pandemic, Rabbit Run ceased being a stage set. It was a refuge.

We re-marketed our property, extoling its assets as an 'outside' place. We purchased outdoor all-weather chairs, a new fire pit, and a new BBQ. We brushed off old hiking maps and crowed about our proximity to Lake Michigan's sandy beachfront: 'it's better when you take 15 minutes and hike to the Lake.'

As larger wedding reception venues were closing, wedding party lodging requests at Rabbit Run soared. We picked up additional bookings from the 'outdoors family reunion' market.

At the height of the pandemic, a small cap fund manager moved his operation and 'zooming staff' from downtown Chicago to Rabbit Run's greeting room. To accommodate his temporary operation relocation, we negotiated with our internet provider to boost bandwidth on the property.

We returned a lot of money, trying unsuccessfully to rebook guests who had canceled and, like other small business owners, trying unsuccessfully to get financial relief. Our business hemorrhaged one-third of our average total year earnings in April of 2020. We didn't recover until 10 months later, and then only with help from our families. We were luckier than most.

What complicated matters for us was that we were trying to sell our property while we continued to operate the business. As we explain to friends, we possess a bewildering knack for bad timing. Remember the Lehman Brothers meltdown in August 2008? That's when we *opened* Rabbit Run.

During the 'second pandemic wave' in November-December 2021, we took the property off the market and rebooted our marketing effort. We temporarily removed the listing while we searched for another realtor. We learned that our property, an erstwhile 'B&B inn,' would not be an easy sale. We reached frustration 'bottom' when one prospective buyer commented that the property lacked curb appeal. We asked ourselves: is 'lacks curb appeal' how you would describe our lane bordered by a file of 100-year-old fir trees? Our property was parked in a real estate limbo. Showings dropped, then ceased.

Then, one wintry day, we received a phone call, 'Hi. My name is Frank with so-and-so Realty and I just noticed that your property listing had expired. Just thought I would let you know and ask if you were considering re-listing it and if I can help.' Our new realtor had found us. So began a 15 month relationship which ended in April of 2022 when we transferred property title to the new owners.

The process was not smooth. Selling a property north of $1M required some 'remediation,' such as removing moss from the roof, purchasing industrial-grade sump pumps, reviewing listing disclosures and more. Bottom line, we invested $35K in property enhancements, which, thanks to hungry contractors, were handled expeditiously.

The agonizing part of selling Rabbit Run was that we suffered two aborted closings. At one closing the would-be buyer walked out, yelling that he was going to sue us and our realtor for misrepresenting the property. We later discovered that this was a ploy to intimidate us; *he* was the one who had misrepresented his intentions for the property. When he couldn't convince the township's zoning administrator that the only way he could manage the property was by turning it into multiple Air B&B's, he walked.

The second aborted closing was caused by the buyer attempting to finance the purchase by borrowing based on future earnings.

'Yikes,' we said to ourselves, 'people act weirdly.' Our financial suffering was rather unusual because as we were functioning again as a business—the pandemic was releasing its hold—we were unable to show the property during the summer season, when most people are house-hunting in our resort area. Eventually, our realtor negotiated a deal in the midst of a sudden February snowstorm, which aborted a scheduled visit and left the prospective buyer unable to see the property. The purchase was full cash, with no physical inspection of the property.

We said to ourselves, 'Double yikes!' But we closed 60 days later. After 13 years of operation, Rabbit Run had new owners.

What helped get us through the years of building, operating and then selling our property was a division of labour. Our 'secret for success' was this: Linda Jo managed 'guest happiness.' I managed debt. I was instructed not to get near guests. Linda Jo was instructed not to get near the books. Together, we owned and cleaned toilets

What this adventure brought us, we tried to return to our guests. Post-sale, we can now enjoy a tranquil Friday night, not waiting up for late arrivals. We once complained to a friend about waiting up for late check-ins, and were advised, 'Just leave the keys out.' We said to ourselves, 'That's not being hospitable.'

Now we no longer have to get up at 7:00 a.m. to pour orange juice into mason jars, warm the local bakery blueberry muffins, dice the apples, and pack bananas in wicker breakfast baskets to deposit in front of the four-bedroom suites we managed. We saved our backs.

When we 'transitioned' to a vacation rental in 2014, we foreswore our neighbourhood of 10 years. We cried and were disgusted at the same time, sad to be leaving, but angry that like most resort areas, our 'little corner of Michigan' had opted for a future as gated communities and McMansions posing as vacation property rentals. We were disconsolate that we were part of this transformation. Gone were the B&Bs, gone were the resort inns, the summer camps, the bungalows, the secret fishing places, the crowded break-fast eateries where retired farmers rubbed shoulders with Chicago transplants.

Gone was a thriving local hospitality industry. If you had the money to rent a house, who needed to go out to eat? If you had the wherewithal to swim in an in-ground pool, why hike to the beach? Who needed to pack a beach chair and umbrella? Who needed to go anywhere, savour anything 'local,' respect a fragile, anxious community eager to serve and welcome you? Now you could 'own' leisure; now you could traffic in 'privacy.'

To rent a $1200.00 per night vacation property, we reinforced the 'make memories' theme. We courted short-term rental websites. We picked vrbo.com as our online host. Sidelined was the earlier, friendlier and chattier rabbitruninn.com. Little did we know that we had begun to 'cash out.'

We remodeled a four-bedroom suite inn into a seven-bedroom, six-bath, two-acre 'mini-estate,' accommodating groups of up to 20. We cleansed Rabbit Run of all things personal, funky to the eye, and 'unfamiliar.' We tossed out pots and pans which felt and looked like comfortable old shoes and replaced them with spiffy Teflon-coated cookware. Choice of potholder colours became an hour-long discussion. Closets were cleaned out. Those left unemptied were padlocked. Rickety furniture was carefully disposed of or stored off property. We compiled a property manual and contracted a house-keeper/handyman couple who lived nearby. We made keys. And more keys.

The one personal possession we left, which seemed to go with the place, was a 300-book library stretching across two rooms. Of the furnishings that had survived eight years of strangers occupying Rabbit Run, only the library remained intact.

Whereas the first wave of the pandemic had taught us to look at our property through different eyes, to marvel at what we couldn't possess, the second wave—thanks to Frank, our new realtor—taught us to let go. To be patient and not hurry the inevitable. We were leaving 'the business.' We made the changes I've just described after the summer season of 2014. Thanks-giving loomed. Our first group booking as a property rental arrived to check in as we were removing plastic bags of personal belongings.

And we were dissolving a partnership.

Though we hated the label 'mom and pop,' we knew that 'mom and pop' was the strength and default qualifier of our brand of hostelry. Without Linda Jo's and my partnership, our relationship became something different. We were reinventing 'ourselves,' feeling closeness in a different way. We were learn-ing how to be personal again.

In 2013, we purchased a co-op apartment in Chicago. We were supporting both properties, commuting between them on weekends. During the summer of 2014, Rabbit Run transitioned to a property rental. Fast forward to 2021: grief at losing Rabbit Run had set in before the pandemic. The pandemic hurried the 'grief' along, which luckily for us, worked in our favour.

Frank, our new realtor, was available and dutifully kept us abreast of how the property visits were proceeding. We had one too many 'This is the one (buyer)' moments. Too many, if you have been through this process as we had.

We were divorcing from a partnership and seeking suitors at the same time. What didn't occur to us was that we were leaving what for 13 years (2008 to 2021) had been our mooring. Rabbit Run as a place was quickly becoming a stranger, and we were becoming dispossessed. Add to this the feel-ings of what life was like after COVID, and you've got a toxic mix of exhaustion and unfamiliarity.

Our values were spinning around seeking realignment. Dispossession echoed what surrounded us. 'Why-ness' took over, resulting in mystified looks at our fellow humans who resisted the vaccine, who refused to wear a mask in tight spaces, who threw out their baleful vitriol. Who were trumpet-ing Trump. Why? Who were they? Who were we?

63

In the 'letting go' process, we were also shedding an identity. There was nowhere to hide any more. Taking off the mask, we lacked a vaccine for exposure. It was the bridal party cancellation which brought home for us what we thought we had lost: a memory of the place. Being a 'mom and pop operation,' we handled all enquiries, reservations and bookings ourselves. If you called Rabbit Run, you were talking to one of the owners, not a call center somewhere in Arkansas. Temporal relationships began over the phone, not on the Internet or a phone app. Who you listened to was who was running things.

Familiarity.

During the transition to the new ownership, we returned money so that guests could rebook their dates with the new management, a property internet 'presence' of 30-odd properties and someone named Tiffany on the chat board. In fairness, a prospective guest could also call Tiffany and leave a message. But for one young bride who was crafting a small celebration and needed lodging for her guests at Rabbit Run, the prospect of engaging Tiffany's interest was a reach.

The bride somehow found our personal cell number and called us. Our kind of guest. She brought tears to our eyes.

Us: *We're sorry but Rabbit Run is sold. The new owners and their property manager will be hosting your stay. We can move your booking over to them. They have assured us that they will provide you the same level of service.*

Bride: *Congratulations. I am happy for you. But I am going to cancel.*

Us: *May we ask why? You could miss booking your wedding party for those dates somewhere else.*

Bride: *Look. I know you. I called you and you answered my questions. You have been generous with your time. I know you. I don't know Tiffany. I know you. So I am going to take my chances. I can postpone the wedding until I find a place like Rabbit Run. But thanks for the offer.*

I will take my chances.

To ease the transition from innkeeper to property manager to question mark, I joked to the lady formerly in charge of guest happiness that she had begun casting for the next incarnation of 'guest happiness.'

Spring of 2022 morphed into summer. We are now full-time residents of Chicago. Visible from our bedroom window, 12 stories below, is a street corner patch of city-owned property, neglected and covered with weeds. Only a single, forlorn-looking tomato plant dots the spread. Linda Jo, my partner, stage setter, and caster, surveyed this urban parterre. I could feel her gaze settle on her next creative endeavor. A month later, she and I completed installing an evergreen shrub patch resembling a Japanese garden without the koi, which we missed from our days of their grazing in the pond at Rabbit Run. I think of it as Linda Jo's new project of 'guest happiness.'

The brides of our new world can find her and me, the one holding the shovel, most afternoons-weather permitting-tending the evergreen patch. We talk, we observe, we share. We build.

June, 2024. Though I would not recommend this to a friend, recently I visited our new owner's online Rabbit Run presence. Call this the curse of the morbidly curious. What I encountered was not a mini-estate nor a group vacation property or romantic wedding reception venue, but an ersatz health/rec facility.

Recreation, I have been told, is the practice of leisure. The 'new' Rabbit Run conveys 'leisure on!' One can try out an outdoor jacuzzi, a pickleball court with basketball hoop, a bocci ball sand field, two fire pits – *in-laws can have their own*. The barn has a ping pong table. The pond has been drained and grassed over.

Fortunately, the 'curb appeal' of 100-year-old fir trees has not been tampered with.

Postscript: August, 2025
In February of this year, we abandoned our Chicago apartment and the Midwest to return 'home' to the east coast and a perch in Cambridge, Maryland, along the banks of the Choptank.

Another adventure in 'guest happiness' awaits.

And the Plague Continues
Deb Bertrand

At the start of 2021, I had formed a game plan to keep me sane while COVID continued to claim hundreds of thousands of lives across the world. While I have remained physically healthy, I believe it takes extra care to keep the mind healthy in order to get through this great change in the world.

The year began with a series of opening and closing of businesses, the continuation of social distancing, the precaution of keeping groups small, and, of course, the wearing of masks. Big drug companies all over the world were scrambling to create a vaccine to reduce the risks of people contracting COVID, or at the very least, ease the symptoms and reduce the number of deaths.

I managed to stay as safe as possible through this pandemic by following the rules: wearing masks, social distancing, and receiving vaccines. My biggest regrets were not being able to travel and not being able to pursue dragon boating. Even these losses did not stop me from living a happy and healthy life by expanding my horizons closer to home.

Back in the fall of 2020, my good friend Louise and I formulated a plan to plant a flax garden so we could grow our own flax fibre to spin and weave it into linen. We got this idea from a Spinners and Weavers Guild exhibition and a sub-group of the Guild that did a two-year project on the same idea. Louise and I both have a love for animal fibre arts through knitting, crocheting, embroidery, and weaving and wanted to expand to plant fibres.[1]

This was a year-round project and occupied a lot of our spare time, which was a good thing as it became a way of preserving our sanity in the midst of the pandemic. We started with research on the processing of the flax, and how to spin it into linen. The garden is on Louise's property and, while growing the flax was fairly easy, there were complex processes to be done with the plants. They needed to be pulled and dried, then the seed heads needed to be removed, retted in a water bath until the fibres started to pull away from the stock, and then dried again. The processing to get the fibres from the stock was all new to us. We couldn't find the hand tools needed to do the job. Back in the winter, when we'd bought seed online, we'd also bought drawings/plans for the processing tools. Those tools consisted of a flax brake, scutching board and knife, hackles, and a rippler. We needed someone to build our tools, and we approached our local Men's Shed, a group of retired men looking for a hobby and for a social outlet as well. They were leery at first but got interested in the project fairly quickly after a detailed meeting with us. We had our tools ready by late October. Our dried flax stems were stored in a dry shed waiting to be processed.

We spent our time over the winter months working on the processing until our flax was a large handful of golden fibres. Now we needed to learn how to spin. Louise bought two old spinning wheels[7] and got them in working order. She learned everything online about the machines, and through videos taught herself how to spin animal fibres clockwise. Then she taught me how to spin. We each bought a more modern traveling spinning wheel on which to spin the flax counterclockwise. Once Louise had mastered the animal fibres, she practiced on boughten flax stricks.[8] Then she was ready to spin our flax. I had learned how to spin flax in the late summer and, with tips and tricks from Louise, managed to master flax spinning myself.

Once we had all the fibres spun, it was time to weave and create our first project. We were well on our way to producing linen. Now we had plans to expand and grow a bigger and better flax garden.

You can tell I have a passion for these new fibre processes and skills I have acquired. That passion couldn't have come at a better time. We spent the year focused on those processes instead of on the doom and gloom of COVID, and while we missed travelling, we were busy while we waited. And 2022 was going to be a better year.

That year started with a glimmer of hope, with the belief that there was light at the end of the tunnel. By this time, I had had not two, but three vaccinations. I was ready for travel when the light turned green. My friends and I were finally able to book a trip to Florida. Again, we jumped through hoops and had the ArriveCan app fully loaded with proof of vaccines and passport. We also had to test negative with a letter of proof 24 hours before our flight. While the process was stressful, everything went well and we enjoyed our first travel in two years.

My second wish also came true in 2022. We got the green light to paddle as a team on the dragon boat. Normally we get on the water by mid-May, but Mother Nature was not on our side this year. Many practices were cancelled due to rain and high winds. As a result, I was only able to get in one practice before joining five other members to fly out for the Vancouver Dragon Boat Festival in June. The second trip of the year—got to love it! We joined a composite team from Manitoba, and two teams from New Brunswick helped fill the boat. We only had one practice before the actual race days, but we blended well together. Again, travel went well. We spent five days in Vancouver for the festival and then took the ferry over to the Island and stayed in Victoria for three days. It was a fantastic trip!

Dragon boat practices were in full swing when we got back from Vancouver. I felt strong and energized even after two seasons with no practice. New members had joined our team, so we spent most of the rest of the season practicing. Our sister team in Kingston was lacking in members and they wanted to participate in the Stratford festival in September. Once again there were four of us who signed up to participate—more travelling!

I felt I just had to fit in as many trips as possible in case we got locked down again. I also fit in a trip to New Brunswick in July to visit my son and grandson. It was a grand visit, and I got to see my aunt and uncle as well. I've booked another Florida trip for 2023. I am looking forward to it because, among other things, my good friend Louise is also coming to join my other friends and me for two weeks.

People are still getting COVID, but not so severely. Vaccines and boosters are still available, and children are also receiving the vaccines. Still, this pandemic is not going away, and I believe we have reached a point that we need to build up an immunity to this disease and get on with our lives.

Over the years, I have changed my way of life. I believe those changes have helped me through this pandemic time. When I was diagnosed with breast cancer 20 years ago, I was baffled as to why a great number of women were diagnosed with breast cancer and others were not. At that time, I needed that answer for myself and was glad I pursued it. To me, it all stems from the spiritual part of one's being. For forty years, I had lived my life through others' thoughts and beliefs. It was time to have faith and believe in my inner self.

A number of years ago I started following the Reiki practice and eventually became a Reiki Master and teacher. I started out with the intention of healing my mind and body, and I continue that practice to this day. I have always been a kind and caring person with empathy for others, but lately I've come to realize that my strength starts from within, enabling me to live a happy and healthy life. My spirit, mind, and body are all connected., with the spirit being most important. If it is not healthy, then the mind and body will suffer.

This insight has kept me healthy to date. Mind you, I do fall into sadness and depression from time to time, but I call upon my guides and angels through prayer to give me strength to carry on. I believe that a great many of those people who suffer from COVID are lacking in faith and are looking to others for the answers. Granted, it is not a fast or easy journey to believe in yourself to change your mind, in order to change your physical being and build your immunity to ward off diseases and conditions. It took me many months to switch over one step at a time. You also need to recognize that you can't change other people. They need to want the change and be prepared to take the steps to make it happen.

The pandemic forced me to take my Reiki practice one step further and to apply it to my own life situation. I sought activities to engage my spirit and mind. My adventures with flax and with dragon boating have been two steps toward a happier and more fulfilled post-COVID future for me. But I am not stopping there, I have more to learn from life and I will continue to evolve by bringing my inner self to the surface. Take writing, for example. Before following the Reiki path, I would never have imagined writing stories and having them published. There is no holding me back now! My children want me to write my life story with all my inner thoughts and challenges.

Even though I have not practiced Reiki on others these last few years, I continue to make it a daily practice on myself. There is a Reiki prayer/mantra that I have modified over the years that applies to me:

- Just for today, I will not worry
- Just for today, I will not be angry
- Just for today, I give thanks for all the blessings I have received (and I have received an abundance, and I am truly thankful)
- Just for today, I release all fears and resentments (from this life, from my past lives, and from all my ancestors before me)
- Just for today, I will work hard to live a happy and healthy life (and my highest intention is to help others live a happy and healthy life)
- Just for today, I will be kind to all living creatures, both great and small (even the mice and bats, but I ask that you remove them from my path)
- I thank you all for watching over me, Amen, Namaste.

Arnprior, Ontario,
January, 2021–December, 2022

---

[1] These technical terms describe the preparation of flax for spinning on the following page:
- Retting is a soaking process whereby the flax stalks are submerged in water to allow the individual flax fibres to release from the centre core.
- A flax brake is a set of intersecting wooden blades that force the retted (soaked) flax straw to snap into short sections which then fall away from the fibres. Flax is 'broken' when forced into the shape of a 'W.'
- Scutching boards and wooden knives are used to remove the broken boon by scraping the fibre.
- Hackling is the last of three steps in processing flax, or preparing flax fibres to be spun. It splits and straightens the flax fibres as well as removing the fibrous core and impurities. Flax is pulled through hackling combs, which part the locked fibres and make them straight, clean, and ready to spin.
- Rippling is the process of removing seed heads from the fully dried flax plant. A wooden or metal comb with a single row of teeth works well for this process.
- A spinning wheel is a tool for spinning fibres into yarn or thread, with a spindle driven by a wheel attached to a crank or treadle. The wheel turns clockwise to spin animal fibres, and counter-clockwise to spin plant fibres.
- A flax stick is a measured bundle of long flax fibres after the three processes of braking, scutching, and hackling.

Thriving, Not Just Surviving:
First Breast Cancer, then COVID!
Ann McMillan

I have always been a deep introvert. To me, going to lunch with two girl-friends is a party. My idea of a good day is to stay in my nightie while reading a good book, alone, curled up on the sofa. When I worked full time in management, I was forced to talk to my staff, participate in meetings, and generally 'get out there.' While I was able to do my job, I found this level of interaction emotionally draining and needed alone time to recharge my batteries.

I was 64 years old when my mammogram came back positive. The growth was small, just about one centimeter in diameter, and not very aggressive. It was also right up against my chest wall, underlying my right breast. Without the tell-tale mammogram, it would have silently grown there for years and eventually killed me. As it was, I had surgery to remove the growth and surround-ing breast tissue, followed by radiation to kill any remaining cancer cells that might be hanging around in the breast or on the muscle underlying it. Several months after my treatment was complete, I started massage therapy to help regain the mobility of my right arm, reduce the swelling or lymphedema in my arm due to the removal of lymph nodes, and allow me to start to exercise to rebuild my right upper body.

Because the growth was discovered just after I retired, my cancer and its treatment reaffirmed my solitary way of being. I never felt lonely, but I did feel that the stress caused by interacting with the world was increasing as I let my social skills wither.

Then one day as I was waiting for my massage treatment session, I noticed an announcement on the bulletin board. The breast cancer survivor dragon boat team, The Prior Chest Nuts, was looking for members and offering training to new recruits. I took down the contact number and pondered.

One of the symptoms of my deep introversion is that I hate to use the telephone. After being a professional for years, I could manage a couple of calls per day at work, but privately I almost never called anyone, welcoming wholeheartedly the option to write letters, or use e-mail for communication, or ignore the need to communicate entirely. Still, after a couple of days, I worked up the courage to punch in the number. A woman named Julie answered in a breezy, upbeat way and told me about the team, which had been formed just a few years previously. They paddled on White Lake, in Arnprior, about a 45-minute drive from my home, and they had their own dragon boat, the *Kahlua*. She invited me to come along to a practice, held

Mondays and Thursdays, to see the lake and the boat and meet the people. With great surprise, I heard myself agree to attending a meeting the very next week.

It was August, and when I found the dock, White Lake was almost perfectly calm after a hot summer day. The light breeze was just enough to dapple the water and blow the mosquitoes and black flies away. The *Kahlua*, much longer and narrower than I had pictured her, was tied up to the dock and there were about 20 women chatting and laughing and greeting each other as everyone arrived. At the center of the activity was Susan, apparently the coach. Coach Susan welcomed me warmly, found me a life jacket and a paddle that 'fit' me and introduced me to the whole crew. While I could feel myself blushing and headed toward shyness, I was soon herded towards the boat and helped in. I found myself sitting on a small bench with my lower cheek pressed firmly against that of the lady next to me. There was no way to ignore that level of invasion of your personal space. I was glad I had showered and brushed my teeth before coming. I actually forget, probably due to sensory overload, to which one of the Nuts I was so unceremoniously and intimately introduced in this way, but I'm thankful that whoever she was, she was gentle with me.

After a short briefing session, unintelligible to me, as to what that practice was directed at accomplishing, the ropes were cast off, and the direction was 'Paddles up, take it away.' I'd been given a 30-second briefing on how to hold and move the paddle, along with the advice to just sit and watch for the first little while. The team's exhilaration was palpable as we pulled away from the dock. We turned and headed down the lake and the beauty of the whole setting hit me so hard I almost burst into tears. After too much time spent in medical settings, this felt like a release back in time to a natural and peaceful existence that had almost ceased to exist for me.

There were 20 paddlers, Susan in the front calling the strokes and work- ing the team through their drills, and Diane in the back, standing firm as a rock, steering. The boat lifted out of the water and flew. The strength of these women and their love of what they were doing hit me and I found myself tentatively picking up the paddle, holding it as shown and dipping it in the water in time with the others.

The moment was magical for me. Who knew that I could be part of a team of women who had all conquered cancer in their own ways and who had re-emerged as stronger human beings? Who knew that I could enjoy feeling the energies of the other women around me and appreciate the group motion and group think that would make us able to propel our boat as fast as possible across that smooth lake surface? That night on the lake changed my life.

At the end of the practice, as we stepped out of the boat, several of the team thanked me for coming and said they hoped to see me again. I reassured them that I would be back and back I have been. The Prior Chest Nuts were able to attend the Breast Cancer Survivor World Dragon Boat Regatta in Sarasota, Florida in 2014. I was there and paddled as hard as I could. The team also attended the next Breast Cancer Survivor World Dragon Boat Regatta in Florence, Italy, in 2018.

My partner of over 20 years had passed away in May 2018 of cancer. He had planned to come with me to Italy, and I was deep in mourning. My sister volunteered to take his place and support me and we went. I have never paddled so hard in my life, and the experience helped me to rejoin the world of the living and to truly accept the deep friendship of this amazing group of women.

The next world event in the four-year rotation was to be held in New Zealand in 2022. The Prior Chest Nuts wanted to go and had started preliminary planning for what was to be the biggest trip so far. And then came COVID in 2020. COVID shut us down as a team, with two years off the water. While outdoor activities such as golf became well-accepted as low risk as the pandemic progressed, there was no way to safely sit cheek to cheek with another, breathing heavily as the paddle dipped and swung, jammed in with 10 rows of women in less than 40 feet.

While COVID shut us down as a team, we maintained friendships through activities such as yoga, walking, making wine, and having Zoom calls to continue to share. I didn't retreat into my introverted shell. I even stepped up to lead the production of *Tales from the Boat*, a little book that the members of the team wrote and which was edited by Jon Peirce and published by Bob Barclay of Loose Cannon Press in 2021. While not a *New York Times* best-seller, the book has captured the interest of readers in the Ottawa Valley and beyond and continues to sell.

In May 2022, as the ice melted and the days lengthened, we were back on the Lake! To our great surprise, we were awarded the 'Mayor's Award for community service by a non-profit organization.' The banquet at which the community gathered to celebrate many such awards was an excellent reminder that life after COVID was coming.

Some of us travelled to Vancouver at the end of June 2022, to participate in the Dragon Boat Regatta there. We became part of the 'Waves of Hope,' and we paddled hard as a blended team and did surprisingly well considering our long absence from the lake and the few practices we had attended. Those of us who went connected with a broader dragon boat community with paddlers from across the country.

In the fall of 2022, we decided to change our tradition of a 'Spring Tea' to a 'Fall Tea.' We attracted over 200 people and initiated a few changes to our usual proceedings to increase food safety. For example, instead of having a massive buffet, we brought our contributions to the kitchen where the ladies plated them carefully, with gloves, to delight our guests and respect their food limitations. In addition, we added a few 'men in tuxedos' who helped with the heavy lifting and provided refills of tea and coffee to the multitudes. It was all a huge success.

The winter of 2023 seemed long, but we decided to revert to the 'Spring Tea' and spent time preparing for that. The yoga, walks and team support continued. We had a multitude of small wooden boxes that several local men made for us to support the team. Ola, one of our oldest and most committed members corralled a multitude of very sexy and unusual brassieres from the local 'Op Shop' which sold gently used items. Many of us completed the bra centerpieces with fake flowers, but some went for the real thing. They were spectacular. We maintained our safety-related changes to food handling and what with the fashion show, silent auction and 50/50 draw we made a lot of money to support the team.

In 2024, we plan to focus on having a more normal year and returning to competition as a team. We have selected three events for participation, and we eagerly await the departure of the long winter as well as the worst of the COVID threat. We all look forward to getting back on the water and celebrating survivorship for another year. It has just been announced that the next world event will be held in Aix de Baines, France in August 2026. We have prevailed over both breast cancer and now COVID. Preparations and fundraising have begun. We will be there!

Stittsville, Ontario,
March 2024.

My Experience with COVID
Yvon Bernier

I live with my wife in a seniors' residence (RPA) in Gatineau, Quebec. It is a residence that includes more than 300 units and houses about 400 residents. My wife and I live in an apartment which is relatively large and comfortable. We have a kitchen in our apartment and take the majority of our meals in our apartment. But the residence has a large dining room where it is possible to take lunch or dinner, or both, if we want. We take advantage of this service once or twice a week. The residence also offers several recreational and cultural activities, including a swimming pool and several other sports. In addition, during the summer months, residents can enjoy two outdoor gardens, where it is possible to play various games such as pétanque and shuffleboard.

At the beginning of the pandemic in March 2020, the management of our institution decreed a relatively severe lockdown: closure of the dining room, no going outside except for medical appointments, and the cessation of all sports and other recreational and cultural activities. It was strongly suggested that we stay inside our respective apartments, except for a walk of a few hundred meters around the residence. A service of meal delivery to the apartment was set up for those who had previously eaten their meals in the dining room.

For more than two months, my wife and I didn't go on any car trips. During this time, employees were disinfecting all common areas of the residence. From the beginning, masks were required for all trips within the residence, and the number of people allowed to take the elevator was limited to two at a time.

In our region, most businesses were closed, with the exception of grocery stores, pharmacies, hardware stores, and a few others. As we were not allowed to leave the residence, we had to call on our daughter to do our grocery shopping for us. Some volunteers from our residence, appropriately dressed in protective gear, took care of handing us the bags of groceries after disinfecting the carts used to transport the groceries to our apartment. Even the church we'd formerly attended on Sundays closed its doors for several months, forcing people to watch Mass and other religious services on YouTube or television.

In hindsight, we must recognize that these harsh lockdowns bore fruit because in the first year of the pandemic, a very limited number of cases were reported in our residence and none were fatal, unlike what happened in many other seniors' residences and reception centres in Quebec.

I am a member of two associations that, before the pandemic, held regular face-to-face meetings. In both cases, these face-to-face meetings were replaced by meetings on the ZOOM video conferencing software application. For one of the associations, this proved to be so practical, in fact, that to reach more participants, the use of Zoom for meetings has become permanent. For the other association—in the field of horticulture—in-person activities have resumed but virtual presentations are still programmed from time to time to take advantage of the know-how of foreign experts.

It was a difficult time for everyone, especially those residents living in the RPA. Still, the lockdown period was not without its advantages. In my case, I took advantage of the winter months of 2020 to improve my knowledge of music. A few years ago, my wife gave me at Christmas an introduction to musical literature that included a series of ten discs and an accompanying book. The idea was that you would play the discs, one at a time, and follow the explanations in the book. I had long put off doing this exercise but, for several weeks at the beginning of the pandemic, I was able to finally catch up with it. Meanwhile, my wife, who loves to make puzzles, indulged in her favourite pastime, together with two other enthusiasts with whom she exchanged many puzzles.

Our residence has a private TV channel. To brighten up residents' lives a little in the first months of the pandemic, several concerts were given on this channel, usually by small groups of musicians and singers. With the return of the summer season, this initiative was pushed a little further. Well-known artists such as Gregory Charles and a few others were invited to give concerts in person in the gardens of the residence. In our case, we could attend these concerts from the safety of the balcony of our residence. It was always a wonder to see all the residents from your balcony, each and every one of them dancing and singing to the rhythm of the music.

These are just a few adjustments that we had to make at the height of the pandemic to continue to enjoy life. Later, when vaccines became available, the restrictions were reduced but not eliminated. Eventually, the dining room of the residence was reopened and gradually the sports and cultural activities were able to resume. A few cases of COVID have occurred in the residence in the last 18 months but, with most residents fully vaccinated, no fatal cases were reported. But even today, almost three years into the pandemic, we still need to be careful. In many ways, we've changed our habits: we often wear masks when meeting with several people and we remain vigilant when going out.

For more than 20 years, my wife and I used to meet every Friday morning with a group of friends for lunch at a local restaurant. After the lockdown, the restaurant having closed its doors, a couple who own a large home invited the other members of the group to enjoy their hospitality for Friday morning coffee, while respecting the government's safety instructions. These friendly

Yvon Bernier

meetings were held on the vast porch outside the house. Such a warm atmosphere developed over time, that even today we continue to enjoy the kindness of this couple of friends. And, on tiptoe, we even enter the inside of their home...

COVID and Aging:
Zooming into Friendships
Sally Arsove

This essay is a happy story about something good that came out of COVID for me: a renewal of life long- friendships, with the help of modern video technology. (This is not to minimize the terrible toll that COVID has taken on individuals and society. The list of its negative effects is long and includes death or persistent ill health, anxiety and depression, separation and divorce, job loss and economic hardship, and overwhelming pressures on the medical community and healthcare system).

In early March 2020, when COVID first officially arrived in Canada, there were no vaccinations or special COVID medicines to help save lives. The possibility of getting COVID from others was a potential death sentence, particularly for the elderly. The fear was real. Many of us chose to not only drastically limit our social engagements, but also to keep them to outdoor venues where the chance of contracting the disease was much less. There were also at times limits imposed by Canadian government authorities on the number of people allowed to meet indoors if they were not living together. As a result, social isolation hit hard throughout society.

Many of us felt lonely and isolated from family and friends and in need of human contact. People living alone and the elderly were particularly vulnerable. I began to phone my friends and family more frequently and talk for longer periods. I spent many hours watching the TV news, not only to stay up to date on the news generally and COVID developments in particular, but also just to see human faces and hear human voices. My new best friends became Heather Hiscox of CBC Morning TV, Adrienne Arsenault and Ian Hanomansing of CBC's *The National*, Lisa LaFlamme of CTV, and Anderson Cooper of CNN.

Then one day in April 2020 I remembered the new internet video technology called Zoom. I had learned to use it in late 2019 to participate in work meetings. It occurred to me that I could also use this technology to connect with friends and family during COVID! I decided to give it a try.

Using the Zoom technology is relatively simple:

- The Zoom 'Host' sends out a meeting invitation by email, from the Zoom portal to a group of 'Invitees' identified by their emails.
- The 'invitees' click on a blue link in the invitation to 'Join' the meeting at the start time. Once they join, they can all be seen together in 'Gallery View' (with each in their own small screen).

- Invitees can join by video plus voice or turn off their video cameras to appear by voice only.
- To prevent unwelcome outsiders from joining the meeting, participants may be asked to enter a meeting password, otherwise the Host must accept them individually into the meeting.

I started with my friends from Wayland High School. Prior to COVID, we'd been meeting in person at high school reunions held in the Wayland, Massachusetts area. I thought of one woman in particular to get the ball rolling: Kathy, who had organized the two previous reunions. She was outgoing and friendly and made strong efforts to connect with old friends. When I told her about Zoom and explained how it works, she was very enthusiastic to try it with me! She then reached out to other women in our group to see if they would also like to join us on Zoom. They too were very excited to try, since everyone had been feeling isolated during COVID and was craving connection with others. Some had more computer skills than others, but everyone was willing to give it 'the old school try.'

I'd actually never hosted a Zoom meeting before; I had just joined other Zooms as a participant. But I was confident in my computer skills, so I decided that if others could host, then so could I. Our first meeting was on a Thursday morning in late spring 2020. Around 10 women joined. It was wonderful to hear their voices and see their faces on the computer screen! I was able to start the meeting just fine (was a bit nervous about that) and there were a few technology glitches after. One woman had trouble getting into the meeting, so she called another participant who helped her get in. Another woman could not figure out how to unmute her voice, but from Zoom we were able to help her fix that. We all had a great time, and before we all signed-off we agreed to continue to Zoom on a weekly basis on Thursdays. Kathy stepped up and offered to be meeting host Thursdays on a regular basis.

During that meeting, one of the husbands saw his wife chatting to us on Zoom, and he decided he too would like to see what it was all about. So, he popped into her screen, said hello and chatted for a few minutes, then waved goodbye and went on his merry way. It turned out that he enjoyed the experience so much that he then contacted some of his male friends from our high school group and asked if they would like to start a second Zoom group on Mondays! Like me, he found his high school friends very enthusiastic about the idea. Then they invited the Thursday women Zoomers to attend the Monday mixed session too.

The first meeting of our Monday Mixed Zoom was held shortly thereafter. Bill, who had a regular Zoom account through his online teaching at Berklee School of Music in Boston, became the regular Monday Host. There was a good turnout of a dozen people. Friends clicked in not only from Massachusetts but also from faraway places including New York City, Illinois, Baltimore, Charleston, Philadelphia, Verona, Italy, and Ottawa,

Canada (me). We had a doctor in the group from Johns Hopkins. In the beginning, much of the discussion was about COVID, with people sharing their anxieties and asking him many questions. Over time the topic of US politics crept in, as people had a lot of anxiety about that also. After a year, a conscious decision was taken by the group to avoid talking about stressful stuff like COVID and politics. People felt a strong need to get back to a semblance of normal life as it used to be.

The wonderful news is that these high school Zooms continue weekly to this day. The Zooms clearly helped us all negotiate the COVID years. They deepened our friendships and allowed us to make new friends too. And they have led to other types of gatherings and meet-ups:

- In September 2022, after COVID vaccinations and medicines allowed us to relax a bit more about spending time together in indoor closed spaces, the Zoom Women had an in-person reunion in Burlington, VT. We chose that location because one of our members lives in the area, and the other members were all within four hours' driving distance. The surroundings were beautiful: mountains, lakes, an outdoor museum and good restaurants. Seeing each other in person once again after two years of COVID was magical.
- In October 2022, Zoom Men and Women met in the Wayland area for a relaxed outdoor dinner at a lovely countryside restaurant. Again, as with the Women's reunion in September, being together in person after two years of online Zooming had a magical quality. We had a wonderful evening of reminiscing, laughing, good food and good wine. I was invited to stay each night of my visit with old friends as well as new friends I had made through Zooming.
- On November 9, 2022, the day of the US mid-term elections, I hosted an impromptu Zoom meeting to discuss the results of that critical day. It was an emotional day for Americans worried about the divisions in the country. I felt the need to be in touch with my American roots that day. We had a good talk and agreed that it provided a relief to meet that day on Zoom.

What made it possible for these virtual connections to continue and blossom? I can think of three main reasons. First, our group had close bonds in high school and had been reconnecting in person before COVID. Second, our Zoom hosts were devoted to providing the venue and made the personal sacrifices to be available weekly. Third, we all had some familiarity with computers and Zoom was easy to learn.

I have personally taken my Zoom experience a step further with other people from my past:

- During COVID I reached out to friends in the United Kingdom with whom I had been a volunteer teacher in Ethiopia in 1974. We had stayed in touch through Christmas cards and occasional visits by me to London as well as emails. I emailed my British friends in June of 2020 to tell them about Zoom and ask if they wanted to try it out. The response was a resounding 'Yes' as they all were feeling isolated and had not seen each other since the start of the pandemic. At our first Zoom shortly after, there were four of us. We had a wonderful time. It was interesting to compare what was going on with COVID in the UK versus Canada. We've continued to meet on Zoom every few months, most recently just a few weeks ago. We talked about the healthcare crises in both countries.

- I contacted a good friend from my Harvard University days who is now a businessman in Asheville, North Carolina. We have stayed in touch periodically over the years by mail and occasional phone calls and visits. During the pandemic I emailed him and told him about Zoom. He is not very computer-savvy or interested but saw the benefits of learning to use Zoom so he could host business meetings virtually. So, we started Zooming to catch up personally, he from his business conference room where he had his tech staff to guide him. He practiced hosting and has totally enjoyed the experience. We continue to Zoom every month. I visited him in person in 2022.

I believe that the video technology that helped me and others get through the social isolation of COVID can also help us get through the social isolation that typically comes with aging. The need to connect will grow even stronger as we inevitably lose some of our physical mobility and mental acuity, and as many of our friends and partners pass on. And our children and grandchildren may live far away. A relatively simple technology that allows us to connect virtually with others will be critical to our well-being.

May we remain Zoomers forever. Viva La Zoom!

Playing for Keeps:
A Pandemic Romance
Elizabeth Zimmer

S he'd had her share of erotic adventures—perhaps more than her share. She'd come of age just as the Pill became widely available and was part of the first generation of American women able to negotiate a level sexual playing field with men her age. The possibility of sowing one's wild oats, previously restricted to guys for obvious reasons, was suddenly available to women, at least in theory.

In practice, it was a different story. She'd inconveniently fall in love with people who had no idea what to do with such a notion, who were simply accumulating experiences, notches, seizing the sudden motherlode of possibilities, and who were apparently afraid of her open heart, her eager intelligence. An unplanned pregnancy just before her 22nd birthday derailed her first stab at graduate school. An impulsive marriage two years later interrupted her second try; she and her new husband emigrated to Nova Scotia, where teaching jobs beckoned. She discovered years later that the Mexican abortion she'd undergone had permanently scarred her Fallopian tubes.

Early in her career as a journalist, in a country hundreds of miles from the city of her birth, she met—in a dance class, of all places—a tall young man with curly hair and invited him along to one of the performances her work required her to attend.

She'd learned on the job that attention can be an aphrodisiac; simply listening to a man talk, and writing down what he was saying, might cause him to invite her to his place, or follow her home. At that point she was still married, but beginning to notice other temptations in her social landscape. The young man with the curly hair slipped under her radar.

Decades passed. She left the marriage, left Nova Scotia, spent years in the Pacific Northwest dancing and writing about dancing, including a burgeoning new discipline called contact improvisation. Then she returned to her native New York City to be close to her aging parents, her marrying brothers, and the major engines of the dance world.

She found some success in her chosen field and managed to earn her living doing things she loved. She made a lot of friends. Most of the male ones were gay: smart, funny, stylish, but not candidates to be her life partner. The straight ones tended to be younger than she, seeking mates with whom they could reproduce.

She'd been alone a long time. When questionnaires asked about her status, she took to writing 'celibate.' But the COVID-19 pandemic, which cut her off from all her casual companions, proved a final straw. Against her better judgment, she joined an online dating site. She'd gone that route before and found only disappointment, embarrassment, an utter waste of time. She began spending inordinate amounts of time on Facebook, where she could maintain at least the illusion of a social life.

Facebook brought the man with curly hair back into her orbit, 50 years after she'd last laid eyes on him. As the pandemic dragged into its second year, he messaged her, requesting a contribution to an anthology he was editing. She guessed it wasn't going to pay much of anything, but she hadn't much else to do in those isolated days.

Her curiosity aroused, she agreed to write. He accepted her essay. They exchanged more texts and discovered that in the years since they'd last seen each other, their careers had developed along remarkably parallel paths.

They planned to get together for lunch. Problems included an international border, the ongoing COVID situation, her work commitments, and the fact that neither of them could drive in the dark. Finally, they agreed on dinner in a small Massachusetts town that Amtrak visited once a day; it would be necessary to stay overnight, since the train back didn't leave until the following afternoon.

They met, they shared a meal, they scoped each other out. They were, heaven help them, by then both 76 years old. They spent the night chastely in a motel room's two beds, each in a flannel nightgown.

A few months and many emails later, he took her hand as they wandered through the Montreal Biodome; she was stunned by the electrical charge, the flutter in her loins occasioned by that simple contact. Never one to shy away from the chance at a sexual adventure—the chances had become, in the past quarter-century, increasingly rare—she trod carefully, but tread she did, jumping his bones during a long weekend in Montreal and his hometown of Gatineau. To her delight, they slept together peacefully.

Nevertheless, she awoke to alarm bells going off inside her head. Who was this person she'd been fondling in two cities and on a Canadian train, who even now was murmuring sweet nothings into her one good ear, in French no less, declaring his love?

She got up to use his bathroom. Which, she observed, was a mess.

Of her own feelings she was not sure. They barely knew each other. She didn't think she was in love with him. She wasn't even sure she liked him. But she lusted after his long, strong body, couldn't keep her hands off his compact butt and the delicate penis nestled between his legs.

Days passed. It snowed. She had to return to her city across the Canadian border. He drove her to the airport, his strong hands gripping the steering wheel, one of hers clutching his thigh. He wrangled her suitcase out of his car. Both masked, they fumbled a goodbye kiss outside the terminal.

Weeks went by.

The thrumming, insistent refrain playing in her head—'Marry me. I want you to marry me'—grew not at all from what she was actually feeling. She'd been married, they both had. They knew how rapidly things could go south. What did she really want?

To be back in his bed, or in hers, with nothing to do but give each other pleasure. The bursts of oxytocin, the endorphins galloping in her blood-stream, had relieved every ache and pain in her arthritic, 76-year-old body. She had lost her appetite for food.

Time passed. Living, as they did, in cities hundreds of miles apart, they resorted to electronic communication: emails, video chats. One evening, staring at him on her screen, she felt, in the course of an hour, the whole dreamlike edifice crumbling. Communicating on Zoom, there seemed to be no *there* there. All the clues she had ignored, excused, obscured were suddenly clear. Was it done, then? Was she losing her nerve? Could she pretend nothing had changed, and continue moving forward? If she did nothing, went quiet, what would happen? Did she have the courage to find out?

By morning she felt better. The warm bath of his attention, his obvious pleasure in her company, even virtually, *did* matter, served as insulation against the bizarre circumstances of the pandemic. Did the problem really lie with this person, or was it the artificial, mediated situation of Zoom? She thought it better to stay in the learning environment their odd little dyad had created than to flee.

F. Scott Fitzgerald famously wrote: 'The test of a first-rate intelligence is the ability to hold two opposing ideas in mind at the same time and still retain the ability to function. One should, for example, be able to see that things are hopeless yet be determined to make them otherwise.'

Weeks later, he arrived at the train station near her apartment, wheeling more luggage than he could handle. She met him there and walked him back to her apartment; within an hour they had shed their clothes and taken to her bed, clutching each other, compressing their two large bodies into the same few cubic feet of space.

Days passed. They both turned 77. He drank coffee and cooked for them. She took out the garbage. They went to the theater, to dance and opera performances, to dinner with her friends. They rode the Staten Island ferry and wandered through the Brooklyn Botanical Garden. It snowed; it cleared up. By the end of the second week, it seemed as though they could read each other's minds. They spent hours every day in bed, finding each other's tender places, pushing at each other's strong ones. Dirty pots and dishes piled up in the kitchen sink.

Gravity, she noticed, makes a tremendous difference in the faces of old people. Standing up, his face was furrowed and rumpled, deep creases marking his forehead and running down the sides of his mouth. Lying beside her, he appeared about 30 years younger, rested, peaceful, wrinkle-free.

After 17 days in his constant company, she began to realize that he was both the light of her life and her cross to bear, her lodestar and the bane of her existence. He went home; she felt, simultaneously, relief and desolation, as well as a powerful urge to find her way to his city, to their shared bed, as soon as possible.

On Valentine's Day, he sent her sunflowers. A curious thing began to happen: she started to trust him, and to trust herself. What may have started out as a booty call was morphing into something else entirely, still grounded in what she could only call lust, but clearly also something more. Something that might endure.

He quit drinking; he knew she hated it, but it took severe physical pain to send him to the doctor and get him to listen to the doctor's warning. She felt enormous relief. She traveled to see him again and felt, immediately, that she was home.

His mind, she'd come to realize, was a worry-seeking missile. There was always something. Once he felt safe and comfortable with her, he began to fret about money. He didn't care about money, he said, but needed it to fix his car, to replace clothing that was wearing out, to eat well, to pay for transportation between his place and hers. He wanted them to have a place that was theirs; figuring out how to pay for that, in addition to the homes they already supported, would be another challenge.

Money, curiously, was not her problem. After a lifetime without much of it, she'd arrived in semi-retirement with a comfortable nest egg, accumulated through years of frugal living and the luck of having landed, decades ago, an affordable apartment.

They continue. The world changes, heats up; the political climate stiffens. Where to live? How to live? Each day presents new challenges, new pleasures. The pandemic continues to rage. They make plans, they travel, they get back to work.

This story has no end, as a wheel has none; it swings all ways with equal weight. The trick is to stay, moment to moment, in the present, even as the world around them crumbles, even as they themselves begin to crumble.

They keep looking at each other.

They move in for a kiss.

SECTION 4
The French Have a Word for It

Travaillant en tandem, les quatre auteurs québécois (Guylaine Bélanger, Nancy Gauthier, Chantal Séguin et Martin Gravel) qui sont membres des Collectifs d'écriture de récits de l'Outaouais, nous offrent un témoignage vivace de la vie quotidienne dans l'Ouest du Québec, aux premiers jours de la pandémie.

D'entrée de jeu, Bélanger saisit magnifiquement l'atmosphère du moment, en nous offrant des images percutantes. Par exemple, la jeune femme qui administre le questionnaire de santé obligatoire chez Jean Coutu, affublée d'un masque et d'une visière, n'est pas une simple employée de magasin, mais un chevalier montant au créneau. Remarquant un carnet pour journal intime intitulé 'accrochez vous' en grosses lettres rouges, Bélanger croit recevoir un message de l'univers. C'est dans ce carnet qu'elle consignera ses sentiments face à la pandémie.

Nancy Gauthier commence par se demander: 'Qu'est-ce que la philosophie, au juste?' Jugeant qu'il s'agit de l'art de poser des questions sans réponse, elle conclut qu'elle n'est pas douée pour le pratiquer. Cela dit, elle réussit plutôt bien à adopter une posture philosophique face à la pandémie – autrement dit, à agir en philosophe – quand elle adopte un mode de vie frugal, voire minimaliste, et constate que, contre toute attente, ce mode de vie lui plaît. Le ménage remplace les courses, ce qui lui permet non seulement de se débarrasser d'un bon nombre de livres superflus, mais aussi de perdre du poids de manière significative. La fin de son texte, une visite au potager, fait écho à la morale de Candide, où Voltaire nous invite à cultiver notre jardin.

Chantal Séguin, excédée par les discussions incessantes sur la COVID-19 dans les médias et même au supermarché, déplore l'absence presque totale de notes encourageantes dans les bulletins de nouvelles. Elle nous invite à réfléchir à d'autres tragédies, comme le meurtre récent de George Floyd, causé d'ailleurs par une sorte de virus, le racisme. Cependant, elle se laisse dérider par une Saint-Jean-Baptiste célébrée sans drapeau québécois et par certaines bêtises de Donald Trump. Le 25 juin, au lendemain de la fête nationale du Québec, elle célèbre la fin du confinement provincial. Même s'il faudra rester prudent, il fera bon de pouvoir à nouveau fréquenter ses amis et parler d'autre chose que de la COVID-19.

En réfléchissant à son expérience de confinement, Séguin s'estime chanceuse de ne pas avoir perdu son emploi ni subi de difficultés financières à cause de la pandémie. Néanmoins, elle reconnaît que la vie a changé et qu'il faudra beaucoup de temps avant qu'elle ne revienne à la normale. La COVID, selon elle, nous a tous obligés à ralentir. Elle voit d'ailleurs la pandémie comme un cri de Mère Nature: 'Vous m'avez rendue malade ; je vous rends la pareille.'

Martin Gravel décrit les premiers jours de déconfinement dans la province, quand on a imposé le port du masque dans presque tous les lieux publics, pour la première fois. Commentant avec cynisme la réouverture expéditive des bars – lieux propices à la propagation du virus – Gravel n'est pas impressionné par la mesure que le gouvernement provincial adopte ensuite pour en atténuer les effets : devancer l'heure de leur fermeture.

Même s'il est gêné par l'obligation de porter un masque au travail toute la journée, Gravel considère celle-ci comme un mal nécessaire. Par contre, employé dans un commerce de détail, il n'apprécie pas d'être obligé de surveiller l'application de cette consigne gouvernementale, comme si lui et ses collègues n'avaient pas déjà bien assez à faire. Il doute que ceux qui, au plus fort de la pandémie, visitent l'épicerie quatre fois par semaine sans suivre les flèches affichées au sol aient davantage de respect pour le port du masque.

Guylaine Bélanger, dont le deuxième texte conclut cette chronique collective, nous fait vivre toute une gamme d'émotions. Nous partageons son enthousiasme face à l'arrivée, imminente, d'un vaccin contre la COVID. Nous partageons son dégoût face à la stupidité d'un groupe de jeunes texans participant à une 'fête COVID' dont le but est de propager la maladie au plus grand nombre, le plus rapidement possible, et face à la muflerie des gens qui persistent à tenir d'interminables et bruyantes conversations téléphoniques dans le bus. 'Un bus n'est pas un bureau,' nous rappelle-t-elle avec raison. Enfin, nous partageons sa fierté de voir sa fille s'indigner de l'agression verbale subie par une collègue, à propos d'une bouteille de désinfectant pour les mains.

Le texte de ces quatre auteurs se termine sur une note d'hésitation et de doute. Ayant décliné une invitation à rejoindre des amis proches au restaurant—le genre de sortie qu'elle n'aurait pas hésité à organiser elle-même avant la pandémie—Bélanger attend l'arrivée de sa sœur, qui la conduira à une clinique de dépistage de la COVID. Cette image frappante pourrait bien servir de métaphore pour décrire le sentiment de toute la société pendant l'été 2021, alors que nous attendions de voir où nous mènerait la COVID.

Anne-Marie Valton conclut la section avec un essai intitulé 'Voyage vers ma lumière intérieure.' Dans cet essai, Valton propose un regard plus spirituel sur la pandémie de COVID-19. Lorsque la pandémie a frappé, Valton venait de terminer quatre mois de préparation intense pour le lancement d'une micro-entreprise en mieux-être. L'apparition de la pandémie l'a plongée dans un très profond désarroi.

Au lieu de se concentrer sur ce nouveau projet et afin de garder un bon équilibre mental et une bonne santé physique, Valton a dû faire un virage de cent quatre-vingt degrés et s'est tournée vers sa propre 'Lumière' intérieur là où on se sent bien intérieurement peu importe la 'météo' extérieure. Ceci lui a permis d'entamer un long processus de découverte de Soi. En fin de compte, Valton a acquis de nouvelles habiletés au cours de ce long voyage, lui permettant d'être une nouvelle personne plus résiliente et plus heureuse qu'au début de la pandémie!

Jon Peirce et Anne-Marie Valton

Chroniques qui n'en sont pas

Premières et dernières pages signées Guylaine Bélanger, avec la collaboration et la complicité de Nancy Gauthier, Chantal Séguin et Martin Gravel du collectif Les Cégé Émènes XIIe course à relais, Été 2020. Collectifs d'écriture de récits virtuels de l'Outaouais (CERVO)

J'avoue.

Avec le déconfinement, j'ai ressenti la peur de l'ermite trop longtemps isolé dans sa caverne, mais aussi l'ivresse du prisonnier, le matin de sa libération. Ces comparaisons ne sont purement que télévisuelles, littéraires ou cinématographiques, n'ayant jamais vécu ni l'une ni l'autre de ces situations.

Je me suis senti revivre. Acheteuse un peu compulsive sélective, j'ai enfilé un des masques cousus lors de ma réclusion. Les prisonnières d'Unité 9 cousaient tout le temps d'affreux sous-vêtements pour hommes, moi, j'ai cousu des masques.

100% coton. Double épaisseur. Il m'a fallu beaucoup d'essais avant d'arriver à trouver le modèle parfait, mais cent fois sur le métier... Et puis c'est devenu facile. Répétitif. Ennuyant. Plate. Mais je travaillais pour les miens et ça donnait du sens à ce stakhanovisme.

C'est donc masquée pour la première fois que j'ai réintégré ma liberté.

J'ai pris l'autobus. Ça m'a fait tout drôle de voyager gratuitement. Pour cette première sortie, je suis allée visiter un ami, ce bon vieux Jean Coutu. J'ai répondu à l'interrogatoire en règle mené par une jeune fille portant masque et visière, jeune chevalière au combat...

Je me suis désinfecté les mains et j'ai pu pénétrer dans ce haut lieu de tentations de toutes sortes... Colorant capillaire? Non. Je laisse mes cheveux gris prendre l'air. Savonnettes parfumées? Oui. Nouveau mascara? Pourquoi? Je ne me maquille plus...

Et je ne reconnais plus cette femme qui pèse le pour et le contre devant chaque babiole...

Je n'en déambulais pas moins dans les rangées de cette pharmacie, heureuse comme une enfant dans un magasin de bonbons. Subitement ce fut le coup de foudre! Je suis littéralement tombée en extase devant un carnet vert acide orné de paresseux et de grandes lettres rouges:

HANG IN THERE!

Tiens bon! Tiens le coup! Accroche-toi! Courage!

N'était-ce pas un message qui m'était destiné, directement envoyé de l'Univers? Je n'ai acheté que ce carnet, sachant d'avance qu'il me servirait à raconter mon épopée, mon étrange traversée dans ce tout Nouveau Monde.

'Dans ce si joli petit carnet, je veux consigner mes actions, mes peurs, ma panique, ma honte, ma colère, mes propres mensonges, bref tous ces sentiments qui m'habitent et dont on ne se vante surtout pas à autrui…'

Pour moi tout a commencé par Wuhan. Qui avait jamais entendu parler de cette capitale d'une province chinoise nommée Hubei? Pas moi, en tout cas… Mais c'était le bulletin de nouvelles, c'était en Chine et disons-le, c'était surtout leur problème.

Puis, plus près de moi, un autre jour, au bulletin de nouvelles, on a parlé d'un couple de Gatinois prisonniers du Diamond Princess. Plutôt luxueuse, la prison…

J'avoue m'être plus souciée du sort des employés que de celui des passagers, ne me sentant pas particulièrement concernée par ce problème de 'riches'.

C'était le 5 février 2020.

Dans les jours qui ont suivi, l'OMS a baptisé ce nouveau coronavirus: COVID-19. 'La' COVID-19, pas 'le'… À moins que ce ne soit le contraire? En fait, tout dépend du continent sur lequel on vit.

Cette calamité ne m'a vraiment atteinte que le 16 mars. En plein dans le plexus solaire! Malade… Malade d'inquiétude: du jour au lendemain, je me retrouvais sans emploi. Complètement paniquée!

Je ne veux pas perdre ma maison!

Pire encore, ma fille, l'amour de ma vie, se trouve directement sur la ligne de front… Caissière dans un supermarché. Nerveuse, oui, mais refusant de quitter les rangs: 'Si tout le monde faisait ça, la population aurait des ostie "de gros problèmes".'

Elle est devenue mon héroïne. Même si elle sacre.

En fin de semaine je suis tombée en amour avec un 'portmanteau', un merveilleux mot-valise: COVIDIOTS.

Comme ce mot nous décrit bien, tous autant que nous sommes! Sommes-nous vraiment policés? Civilisés?

De plus en plus difficile à croire quand on regarde nos comportements.

'Me, myself and I.' Petite formule anglaise qui résume tellement bien ce que nous sommes fondamentalement.

Le gouvernement a proposé une équation mathématique peut-être trop complexe pour la majorité d'entre nous: 10 personnes provenant de trois adresses différentes dans une seule cour *extérieure* respectant la distanciation civile de deux mètres.

En très peu de temps, tout un chacun s'est donné le droit de faire une entorse à ce nouveau règlement, l'interprétant comme bon lui semble…

Je fais partie des obéissants, des peureux, de ceux qui ont peur de l'ennemi mais, en toute franchise, suis-je vraiment blanche comme neige?

Deuxième partie: Nancy Gauthier

Voilà une question philosophique à laquelle je préfère croire à une réponse inexistante. En passant, qu'est-ce que la philosophie, exactement? Je comprends que la réponse à cette question est l'art de se poser des questions qui demeurent sans réponse. La philosophie, une autre activité pour laquelle je semble manquer d'aptitude.

Je remarque des comportements bizarres chez mon chien ainsi que chez mon chat… ou plutôt inhabituels. Ils semblent bons amis depuis le début de la pandémie. Ou plutôt, mon chat tolère la présence de mon chien collé sur lui. Je dirais même qu'il le réconforte. Le chien, meilleur ami… du chat?

J'ai trouvé l'explication à cet étrange comportement plus tard dans la journée. Il se trouve que de nature paresseuse, mon chien n'aime pas faire six promenades par jour. Je devrai donc trouver autre chose à faire de mes heures supplémentaires de loisirs, courtoisie pandémie.

Ce matin, j'ouvre ma facture de carte de crédit. Oh surprise! Le montant est si peu élevé que je manque tomber de mon tabouret! Je profite de ce moment de bonheur intense aussi longtemps que je le peux avant de procéder à l'analyse du pourquoi du comment.

Depuis le début de la pandémie et de la perte de mon emploi, j'ai tout naturellement et sans vraiment m'en rendre compte réduit les dépenses au strict nécessaire. Je vais faire mes épiceries à pied plutôt qu'en auto (et maintenant seule plutôt qu'avec mon chien); l'annulation de toutes mes activités sociales a condamné mon auto à purger une peine de stationnement d'une durée indéterminée dans mon garage. Et il n'y a pas qu'à la pharmacie que je réfléchis au besoin versus désir. J'ai ainsi découvert que je n'ai jamais besoin de croustilles ou de biscuits au chocolat ou de ces bonbons éclairs à la vanille au centre mou. J'ai tenté de justifier le besoin de désir ou… le désir de besoin… rien ne va plus, les jeux sont faits, je suis devenue frugale et minimaliste contre mon gré, malgré que maintenant j'agrée.

J'ai résumé cette situation en une équation complexe. Le revenu perdu est-il moins élevé que l'économie que je réalise avec mon nouveau style de dépenses? Statistiquement, il est difficile de conclure avec un seul mois comme référence. Moralement, je continue de célébrer, sans résoudre l'équation!

Je me suis débarrassée de plusieurs livres ces dernières semaines. En effet, plutôt que de magasiner, je fais du gros ménage. Tout cet exercice m'a fait perdre plusieurs kilos, un autre plaisir gracieuseté de la pandémie.

Ma maison est propre, mon chien dort, mon chat observe son environnement pour mieux s'en foutre, j'ai une chronique à écrire. Qu'est-ce qu'une chronique, exactement? Le dictionnaire dit que c'est le récit d'événements. Est-ce que cela signifie que je doive attendre qu'il se passe quelque chose avant de pouvoir écrire? Mais... tout est au neutre! Le dictionnaire ne précise pas une attente quelconque. Il n'interdit donc pas une provocation quelconque. Je reprends le dictionnaire et l'ouvre à une page au hasard, et j'y arrête mon index sur un mot, toujours au hasard: quenouille. En plus d'apprendre que je ne connais pas le nom du végétal que j'ai toujours appelé 'quenouille', je suis allée en ramasser une pelletée que j'ai transplantée dans mon jardin. La suite de cette chronique à suivre.

Troisième partie: Chantal Séguin

Ça y est, je deviens folle. Quand t'es rendue à planter des quenouilles dans ton jardin en sachant pertinemment que ça ne poussera pas, parce qu'on s'entend que ma cour, c'est loin d'être un milieu humide, c'est signe que l'heure est grave. Mais à force de rester enfermée et de n'entendre parler que du coronavirus, c'est assez pour devenir marteau. C'est partout... Dans les journaux, à la télé, à la radio, au supermarché, etc. Je comprends que c'est LE sujet de l'heure mais comme on dit par chez nous, trop c'est comme pas assez. Si au moins les nouvelles étaient un tantinet encourageantes. Pis là, je parle pas du lavage de mains; si ça continue, une visite chez le dermatologue va s'imposer. Pis le Purell, parlons-en. Je suis à la veille de cuisiner avec pis de m'en servir comme gel pour les cheveux.

Petite trêve depuis quelques jours aux bulletins de nouvelles: la COVID-19 a fait place au racisme systémique après la mort de Georges Floyd. Un autre 'virus' qui ne trouvera pas son vaccin avant longtemps. Autre nouvelle... Comique, celle-là: les célébrations de la St-Jean ont eu lieu... sans le drapeau du Québec. Ben oui, quelqu'un a oublié d'installer le fleurdelisé. Ça pas été long que les commentaires ont fusé de toutes parts. Guy Nantel n'a pas manqué de se faire du capital politique avec ça en parlant de 'dépolitisation de la fête nationale' et de la 'victoire du multiculturalisme sur le nationalisme,' bla bla bla. Martine Ouellet et Louise Harel n'ont pas tardé à lui tomber dessus à bras raccourcis.

Heureusement, il y a Trump pour nous faire rire. C'est pas possible les niaiseries qu'il peut dire ou 'tweeter' dans une journée. Comme si ce n'était pas assez qu'il ait dit que la COVID n'était qu'une petite grippe, le v'là maintenant qui affirme que la construction de 'son' mur à la frontière avec le Mexique a empêché le virus de passer. Un bel exemple qui confirme que vaut mieux se taire et laisser les gens penser qu'on est stupide plutôt que de parler et de leur en donner la preuve. Je ne peux toujours pas comprendre après 4

91

ans que ce bouffon ait été élu… Ça me dépasse. Je n'ose même pas penser qu'il pourrait gagner un 2e mandat.

Alléluïa! 25 juin. Le beau Horacio nous annonce que finalement, le Québec est presque complètement déconfiné. Ça fait du bien à entendre… on l'attendait depuis belle lurette cette annonce. En plus des restos qui commençaient tout juste à rouvrir leurs portes, ce sera maintenant au tour des casinos, des gyms, des bars, etc. Bon, y'aura toujours pas de festivals ni de grands rassemblements, mais c'est comprenable: faut rester prudents. Au moins, on va socialiser un peu. J'ai hâte de voir du monde… pis pas juste les gens à l'épicerie qui te regardent de travers si t'es pas à deux mètres d'eux ou si t'as le malheur de passer dans une rangée dans le mauvais sens des flèches. Ce serait juste le fun de pouvoir en profiter sans continuellement entendre parler de 2e vague. On le sait que ça risque d'arriver, pas besoin de nous le rappeler constamment.

On fait ben des farces mais cette pandémie m'a amenée à faire une introspection. Je ne pensais jamais vivre une telle situation. J'ai été étonnée de voir comment du jour au lendemain, tout s'est arrêté. Je n'ai personnellement pas été touchée au sens où je n'ai pas perdu mon emploi, je n'ai pas de problèmes financiers, je n'ai pas de jeunes enfants à la maison ou de parents en CHSLD, Dieu merci. Mais quand même, la vie a changé pis ce n'est pas demain qu'on va revenir à la 'normale.'

On a beau dire que nos grands-parents travaillaient fort et que la vie était dure dans c'temps-là, mais était-ce vraiment le cas? Eux au moins respiraient de l'air frais et mangeaient des aliments sains. Aujourd'hui, ce n'est plus le cas. La technologie a facilité nos vies, mais à quel prix?

Le virus nous a forcés à ralentir. En réalité, c'est la planète qui nous a envoyé un message. On sait tous que les changements climatiques sont une réalité, et même si on fait notre petit bout de chemin en consommant bio ou en recyclant, ce n'est pas suffisant. Pis comme les gouvernements ne prennent pas les mesures nécessaires, ben notre mère la Terre s'en est chargée. C'est comme si elle s'était dit: 'Vous m'avez rendue malade, là c'est à mon tour de vous rendre malades.' Va falloir tirer des leçons de ça.

Quatrième partie: Martin Gravel
Une 2e vague, parlons-en. Serions-nous déjà dedans? Ou elle arrivera seulement à l'automne.

Afin d'éviter certains problèmes sociaux liés au confinement, le gouvernement a eu la bonne idée de laisser ouvrir les bars. Eh ben oui, chose! Y a-t-il une place où un virus se transmet plus rapidement que dans un bar? On a chaud, on danse, on se colle, la musique joue fort, on parle fort, les particules se promènent. Ça pas été long qu'on a eu des cas. On a donc décidé de fermer les bars plus de bonne heure: on va sûrement se coller moins...

Dans le fond je chiale mais je comprends un peu ceux qui chialent sur le confinement, c'est vraiment contre nature pour nous et c'est vrai que tu peux manipuler les statistiques de telle façon que le virus semble bénin. 10 000 tests par jour, 100 nouveaux cas, 1 décès. Si t'étais pas attentif à la situation en mars, avril et mai, et que tu regardes juste les statistiques actuelles, il te manque pas mal d'information et tu te fais un portrait pas vraiment juste de la situation.

Bon, à partir de samedi, c'est le masque pour tous dans tous les lieux publics fermés.

Depuis lundi, je dois porter le masque pour travailler. Ce n'est vraiment pas l'idéal ni confortable, mais je trouve quand même ça moins pire que de courir la chance d'attraper cette merde de virus.

Je n'ai pas hâte d'avoir à apostropher les gens qui ne porteront pas leur masque ou qui le porteront sur le front, le cou ou dans leur poche arrière. Moi, je m'en fous que tu ne portes pas de masque mais le gouvernement a eu la bonne idée de mettre des amendes qui peuvent être assez salées pour les détaillants. Comme si on en avait pas déjà assez à faire.

— Madame, vous devez porter votre masque.
— Non.
— Madame ce n'est pas un choix, vous devez porter votre masque.
— Non.
— Je vais devoir vous demander de quitter le magasin.
— Non.
— Suivez-moi, s'il vous plaît.
— Non.
— ...Sécurité!

Ce n'est pas arrivé encore mais si je me fie aux instructions données au plus fort de la pandémie, quelqu'un qui va à l'épicerie 4 fois par semaine, ne respecte pas le 2 mètres parce qu'il est trop pressé d'acheter du ketchup et est incapable de suivre des flèches... je ne pense pas qu'il va s'en faire beaucoup au sujet du port du masque.

En discutant avec un ami, on jasait du terme distanciation sociale. Je me questionne sur ce terme. Mais dans une société riche comme la nôtre, elle y trouve son compte. Mon ami n'est pas d'accord avec moi. Je tente de lui faire comprendre que pour moi, la distanciation sociale, c'est l'écart entre les classes sociales. Je lui ai donné l'exemple du gars en Ferrari, arrêté à une lumière pendant qu'un mendiant lui offre de laver son pare-brise. Pour moi, c'est un exemple de distanciation sociale. Je prône beaucoup plus l'utilisation du terme distanciation physique. Lui me dit que je cherche les bibittes, que ç'a vraiment pas rapport et que le terme social n'est pas utilisé au niveau des classes comme je le prétends. Mais il a raison sur un point: les bébittes ne sont pas dures à trouver ces temps-ci.

C'est fou comme on est passé vite par-dessus les histoires de racisme. C'était pourtant à grand déploiement, je croyais bien que ça mènerait à quelque chose cette fois-ci. Probablement que la prochaine fois sera la bonne.

On est maintenant dans une vague de dénonciation de comportement sexuel inadéquat. La belle Marie-Pier est allée rejoindre le beau Éric en ligne au chômage et plein de noms sortent ces temps-ci... presque un à chaque jour. Kevin, Alex, Bernard... Pas facile être une vedette. Certains décrient la façon que c'est fait, Instagram est-il vraiment la bonne façon de faire, et on fait quoi de notre système de justice?

Peut-être que quand notre système judiciaire va être capable de protéger voire même de considérer les victimes, on pourra s'y référer. En attendant, malheureusement, les réseaux sociaux sont une façon de le faire pour eux. À ceux qui me disent, 'Ouain, mais ça détruit des carrières, ces affaires là...' je réponds: 'Ben moi, ça ne détruit pas la mienne.'

Je veux qu'ils le retrouvent vivant, cette crapule, pour le faire payer ce qu'il a fait, on peut lire ça pas mal sur Internet cette semaine: un père qui disparaît, on a trouvé ses deux filles décédées... Il doit répondre à nos questions. Moi, je ne le sais pas... Pas sûr que c'est mieux vivant ou mort... Me souviens d'un Turcotte qu'on a trouvé vivant... Ne me souviens pas d'avoir eu de réponses...

Dernière partie: Guylaine Bélanger

Je suis dehors. J'espère la voir. D'abord connue sous l'appellation C/2020 F3 —on dirait le nom d'un vaccin—elle fut renommée Neowise, d'après le nom du télescope qui l'avait découverte. Je trouve ça joli.

Je n'ai pas de télescope, mais on dit pouvoir la distinguer à l'œil nu.

Jadis, certains prêtaient aux comètes une signification mystique, voire un message envoyé par Dieu... D'autres les croyaient annonciatrices de catastrophes, de grandes batailles...

Un peu ce que nous vivons en ce moment, non?

Est-ce elle? Je pense que oui. Plus brillante qu'Halley. Je prends peut-être mes désirs pour la réalité... Une petite photo, pour la postérité.

Pouvoir dire: 'Je l'ai vue.' Et si ce n'est pas elle, j'aurai quand même assisté à un phénomène céleste, le 21 juillet 2020.

Canular ou autres COVIDIOTS?

Faites que ce soit une simple légende urbaine! Mon amie Hélène n'est pas colporteuse de ragots mais ce qu'elle m'a raconté donne froid dans le dos parce que les humains étant ce qu'ils sont, ça pourrait être possible.

COVID-party chez nos amis du Sud, plus précisément à San Antonio, Texas. Se réunir en groupe de jeunes, moyennant cotisation, et faire la fête autour d'un participant atteint du virus. On se gravite autour, les uns les autres, sans savoir qui est le dépositaire... Le 'gagnant' de la cagnotte serait le premier à manifester les symptômes... Fallait y penser!

Mais la Doctor Jane Appleby existe-t-elle vraiment?

Ma fille est en colère, et moi aussi, après son récit...

Une de ses collègues, de celles qui veillent au bien-être collectif en s'assurant de la désinfection de nos petites mains sales de toucher à tout, travaillait entre ses deux portes...

Un homme est venu pour emprunter sa bouteille de désinfectant, on ne sait trop pourquoi. Elle a hésité entre l'aider ou ralentir l'entrée de potentiels clients... Énervé par son hésitation, il s'est mis à l'injurier, la traitant d' 'ostie de grosse chienne.'

Il devait se sentir bien à l'aise, derrière son masque.

Oui, ma fille est en colère et sa colère me remplit de fierté! Tant et aussi longtemps que nous nous indignerons de ce qui arrive aux autres, nous resterons humains...

Je viens de passer dans le camp 'des gens qui regardent les autres de travers,' comme quoi tout le monde change...

Lourdement chargée de sacs d'épicerie, j'ai décidé de profiter du transport en commun. À l'arrêt suivant, deux jeunes femmes montent et s'assoient, pratiquement sur mes genoux, sur les bancs de travers. Lorsque l'une d'elles retire son masque pour parler au téléphone et régler son problème avec Rogers...

Je me suis levée, avec ostentation, j'ai rassemblé mes sacs comme une poule ses petits et j'ai changé de banc, mettant une distance physique (et/ou sociale) avec cette femme sans savoir-vivre: un autobus n'est pas un bureau et un cellulaire n'est en rien une barrière aux virus. Ostie! Parce que, oui, moi aussi, je sacre...

Je n'étais pas certaine que le masque soit obligatoire dans les autobus mais comprendra-t-elle un jour que sa belle jeunesse ne la met pas à l'abri? Il semble même que ce soit la clientèle du moment...

'C'est juste les vieux qui meurent.'

Ah? Et, jeunes et délicats amis, ça stimule vos instincts de tueurs? Avertissement: ceci n'est pas un jeu vidéo. C'est la vraie vie, celle qui est aussi précieuse que fragile.

Les jeunes... Il n'y avait pas qu'eux à manifester devant le parlement de Québec contre le port du masque. Liberté, prônaient-ils! Les USA n'ont donc pas le monopole de la bêtise humaine...

Comment peut-on être aussi nombriliste? Mais, je ne me décourage pas, l'être humain étant un monstre d'habitudes, qui résiste au changement, jusqu'à ce qu'il s'y habitue…

J'ai trouvé le courage de refuser. Je m'en veux mais la couardise l'emporte. La folle du resto n'ose plus s'en approcher! Des amies très chères ont suggéré une rencontre au restaurant. Avant, j'aurais pu initier ce projet mais, maintenant, j'ai peur d'affronter une telle promiscuité…J'espère que mon refus ne sera pas un coup de canif dans notre si belle entente…

Ma réclusion semble avoir évacué ma si merveilleuse gourmandise… Mais hier, quand je me suis vue sur mon écran, à la fin d'une séance sur Zoom, j'ai peiné à reconnaître ce visage aux traits tombants, aux yeux creusés et mornes… Était-ce vraiment moi, cette vieille femme aux traits fatigués, ridiculement amaigris?

Je travaille. Cinq jours/semaine. Il ne se passe rien. Rien que les jours qui passent, tous semblables, tous monotones et pourtant, comme l'eau des fleuves tranquilles, jamais pareils.

Triste nouvelle: le Cinéma 9 ferme temporairement ses portes. J'ai peine à croire au mot 'temporairement'…

J'attends ma sœur. Elle m'amène à la clinique de dépistage…

F I N

Voyage vers ma lumière intérieure
Anne-Marie Valton

Nous sommes fin février 2020, après 4 mois de travail intense, très heureuse et fière de mon accomplissement, je complète mon plan d'affaires pour lancer une microentreprise d'artiste en mieux-être!

En parallèle, on entend parler d'un dangereux coronavirus qui a forcé le confinement de la ville de Wuhan en Chine, puis en Italie. Cela semble bien loin de chez moi, mais tout à coup, lors d'une pratique régulière de chorale on nous avertit que l'activité est suspendue jusqu'à nouvel ordre à cause du début d'une 'pandémie!' Je ne savais pas ce que cela signifiait, je n'ai plus la télévision depuis quelques années, mais je sentais profondément que cela ne goûtait pas bon et, pour une raison obscure, je suis devenue soudainement très anxieuse à l'intérieur… J'étais loin de me douter à ce moment-là de tout l'impact que cet évènement aura sur ma vie. Ainsi, au lieu de lancer une entreprise, j'ai commencé un long voyage intérieur pour m'accrocher à la Vie et j'en ai profité pour bien me reposer, car comme beaucoup de gens nous étions très fatigués de cette course infernale qu'était la vie de nos jours.

Je vivais seule depuis des années, à cause d'une hypersensibilité particulière et de traumatismes liés à mon enfance… afin de garder l'équilibre intérieur, j'avais besoin de mes activités sociales extérieures, elles m'étaient très importantes… ce confinement venait donc complètement me sortir de ma zone de confort et m'a obligé de changer mes plans pour les mois et années à venir!

L'isolement s'est installé, petit à petit, au début pour m'en sortir je me suis accrochée à quelques amies proches que j'avais, puis, chaque sortie à l'épicerie, au magasin était une occasion de socialiser si minuscule soit elle! La nature était devenue une grande alliée, mon refuge, même si l'on a voulu nous empêcher d'y aller!

Petit à petit, plus le confinement devenait sévère, plus je devenais accro à mon écran. Mais quelque chose me grugeait de l'intérieur: la peur d'être abandonnée par la société, pire encore, que les autorités jugent pour moi ce qui est bon pour moi, sans tenir compte de mes propres limites étant hypersensible, donc très différente des autres, cela me terrifiait! De plus, quelques-unes de mes amies proches s'éloignèrent de moi, la peur du virus, les divergences d'opinions étaient nombreuses durant cette crise! Ceci déclencha en moi le sentiment d'être abandonné et nourrit celui de l'isolement.

Toutes ces peurs m'avaient décentrée, j'ai dû apprendre à mettre ma concentration sur mon intérieur et me rassurer moi-même, puis par une méditation particulière, je réussissais à me recentrer et à me donner le défi d'être bien même seule. Cela a donné de bons résultats, car tout au long de la crise je devenais de plus en plus calme intérieurement.

J'avais toujours espoir que cela finirait un jour. Mais, à l'écoute des nouvelles, celui-ci s'effritait, on parlait de distanciation sociale pour très longtemps, je sentais que je ne pourrais y survivre, moi qui promulguais l'effet nourrissant du toucher sur le mieux-être et qui voulais faire des activités de groupes, pour chanter ensemble, etc. Je ne voyais pas quand je pourrai lancer ma microentreprise en mieux-être! Le désespoir m'envahissait. Après six semaines de confinement malgré l'arrivée du printemps je n'en pouvais plus, j'éclatais en larme facilement, presque tous les soirs, sans comprendre. Plus tard, avec de l'aide, j'ai réalisé que j'avais frisé la dépression comme beaucoup d'autres.

Heureusement, je n'étais pas la seule à ne plus en pouvoir, les autorités ont dû arrêter le confinement puis, l'été était à nos portes. J'ai cru que le tout allait s'estomper, mais la distanciation sociale était persistante, de plus, quoique le virus ne fût pas présent au plus chaud de l'été, on avait introduit le port du masque! Je ne trouvais pas cela très logique, je me sentais toute croche à l'intérieur quand je le portais, c'est comme si j'y perdais mon équilibre, je ne pouvais plus voir les sourires des gens et cela ajoutait à ma déprime. De plus, étant une personne fort intelligente et ayant reçu une formation scientifique, je trouvais que les mesures mises en place et les messages des médias encourageaient la protection individuelle et la division dans la communauté, par exemple en incitant la surveillance entre voisins. Cela me chagrinait, car je voyais notre tissu social s'effriter. Où s'en allait notre société? Il y avait de plus en plus de divisions dans ma famille, avec mes amies. N'étions-nous pas assez divisées? Ma joie de vivre était atteinte, les larmes l'ont souvent remplacée.

Je devenais plus consciente de l'effet de nourrir la peur et la méfiance sur ma santé intérieure, je savais aussi que le désespoir pouvait facilement atteindre ma santé physique, étant hypersensible, nourrir la peur pour moi était, en fait, l'inverse de nourrir la vie, la joie et l'amour.

Avant la crise sanitaire, j'avais à mon actif trente ans de cheminement personnel, trente années où je prenais soin de ma santé intérieure tous les jours par le biais de développement personnel, de prises de conscience, de soins de tout genre. J'ai remarqué jusqu'à quel point la vie avait mis sur mon chemin plusieurs défis que je pensais impossibles à surmonter et qu'en fait je les avais tous relevés, dont celui de retourner travailler après cinq ans d'arrêt pour invalidité! J'en conclus maintenant que je peux faire confiance à la Vie devant l'épreuve, que j'ai, à l'intérieur de moi, tous les outils et les ressources pour y faire face, que c'était là que résidait ma Lumière intérieure!

Plus tard, j'ai appris à focaliser mon attention davantage sur cette belle lumière intérieure et au retour d'un deuxième confinement à l'automne j'ai décidé de me centrer davantage sur elle, de la fortifier, de l'agrandir, cela m'a permis de régler certains dossiers financiers épineux. Cela m'a demandé beaucoup de patience, mais j'ai réussi à relever le défi! Ma confiance en moi s'en est trouvée renouvelée.

Ce chemin vers la Lumière m'a aussi appris à mieux m'écouter et entendre mes intuitions, à mieux distinguer mes forces, mes valeurs, mes limites et à les faire respecter; à faire tomber le mur de la peur par le fait même. Il m'a permis d'avoir de l'assurance, ce qui a ajouté de la profondeur à tous mes talents et mes dons; et à prendre conscience que ce que voulait la société pour moi n'était pas nécessairement pour mon plus grand bien. Étant hypersensible, je connaissais bien les bienfaits des soins naturels sur mon mieux-être à tous les niveaux et je savais que ceux-ci fonctionnent très bien pour moi. Je savais aussi que les soins traditionnels pouvaient être trop durs et m'amener dans de sérieux déséquilibres.

J'ai appris et j'apprends encore à accueillir ma différence et celle de l'autre, que d'avoir des opinions différentes, c'est correct, car nous sommes tous et toutes uniques sur cette Terre, nous avons tous une couleur différente dans notre Lumière, cela nous permet d'expérimenter la joie de vivre dans l'entraide, le partage et la solidarité afin de rendre notre Terre plus belle, plus paisible et plus viable pour nous tous!

Les outils acquis durant cet épisode de ma vie influencent positivement ma microentreprise en mieux-être que je voulais lancer en 2020. Elle repart tout doucement, mais une révision de mes objectifs et services offerts est nécessaire, car j'ai beaucoup changé: déjà, j'observe plus de profondeur dans les accompagnements que je fais dans mes activités de groupe et plus de précision dans ma capacité de ressentir l'énergie; ma lumière est plus éclatante qu'avant lorsque je chante avec mon tambour, mon chant atteint davantage le cœur des gens. J'ai hâte de voir l'effet sur mes toiles d'artiste peintre!

Je sors de cette crise mondiale plus forte, plus joyeuse que jamais, tout en retrouvant un nouvel équilibre intérieur! Je me sens aussi mieux centrée sur mon cœur et mieux ancrée à la Vie sur notre Terre! Ma présence devient Lumineuse!

SECTION 5
Humour and Creative Non-fiction

*T*he authors of our section on humour and creative non-fiction run the gamut from those who thumbed their noses at the COVID pandemic to those who found amusement in the changes it provoked in all our lives to those who used the pandemic as, dare I say, an excuse to reexamine their lives. Perhaps this section provides the broadest spectrum of feelings and emotions to be found in this collection.

Many of us have struggled to articulate these emerging feelings provoked by COVID, and this struggle is well-captured in John Allen's 'Saudade' in which I learned a new and useful word. Next, Sharon Hamilton gives us a hilarious look at the new self-help in the time of COVID as we enjoy lemon pie and quarantinis with her. In 'Bathroom Reading,' I take umbrage at my sister's preference for location of my masterpiece but come around to see the bright side. Jack Denny-Brown takes us on his personal tour of Paris. Cathy MacKenzie thumbs her nose at COVID in rhyme in 'Where Edges Meet.' Donna Chateauvert in 'Cabin Fever' takes a slightly frivolous view of the changes we all had to make to adapt to the new rules that came with COVID. Finally, Jack Denny-Brown takes us on a quick tour of popular culture of our generation from graduation from college through to losing and especially finding the acquaintances of our youth in 'The Biochemist.'

These deeply personal views of life during COVID offer us a nuanced retrospective of our shared pandemic experience.

Ann McMillan

Saudade

John Kevin Allen

February 6th, 2021 was cold and gray in our town. For nearly a week, the slate clouds had shown no interest in breaking. That day, my wife and I drove by the empty shell of our local movie theatre. I sighed.

'I'm sad,' I said.

'Yeah?' my wife said with some disinterest. A frozen slush had settled in the streets, making the road unpredictable and in need of her attention at the wheel. Besides, she already knew where our conversation was going. I gazed at the vacant parking lot, the unused glass doors, and the blank 'Coming Soon' movie poster cases.

'I'm sad the movie theatre is closed.' I continued to look until we rounded the corner and drove away from the building that sat lifeless and dark. 'I wonder if it'll ever reopen.'

'Maybe,' she said. 'We'll see, I guess.' She fishtailed just a little and corrected with a small curse, but I was swaddled in melancholy as the tires corrected through the gray slush.

We had this conversation every time we passed the vacant parking lot. My wife was unconcerned with the empty Regal Cinema, which had become another victim of the pandemic. For her, a closed theatre is like a vacant big-box store—too large to repurpose, it sits like an old tortoise shell found in the woods, a vaguely curious relic. I've seen plenty of abandoned big-box stores whose front doors gathered leaves and plastic shopping bags that fly and shudder in the wind. But this shell of a theatre was not like some big-box store where I went to buy laundry detergent or cat litter or a TV. Our theatre was (and is) a place of memories.

It was the theatre where we'd introduced our grandchildren to the ritual of walking from the blazing afternoon sun into a blast of cold air and a cloud of fresh popcorn steam. My wife and I had our first date there, the 2009 reiteration of *Star Trek* where we realized our mutual love of flashy sci-fi and the thrill of spectacle made massive by the enormous surround sound speakers that pounded out the high drama of titanic space battles. Those were the auditoriums where she and I clung to those cloth-covered seats, grinning, waiting for the Marvel movies' mid- and post-credit scenes. Over there was the spot where my youngest granddaughter had nearly dropped her overpriced, oversweetened, overcoloured Slurpee, saved at the last minute by the heroic gymnastics of my older granddaughter. That was the concession counter where my grandson insisted that gummy worms pair nicely with buttered popcorn.

Each time my wife and I drove by the sarcophagus, I tried to convince myself that I was being stupid and nostalgic, but the sadness always returned.

Perhaps I was feeling sorry for the people who'd lost their jobs when this theatre closed. I wondered about the kids in their short-sleeved polo shirts, who'd tried their best to be professional and courteous when all they really wanted to do was chase each other around with buckets of popcorn in a multi-auditorium hide-and-seek food fight. I wondered about the retirees who stood smiling but tired as they took our tickets, some tearing them in half and others just shrugging and nodding. 'Okay, you're good,' one man used to growl, glancing at our tickets with his one good eye. I wondered about the employees in the shadows who stood ready to clean the trash, popcorn and thoughtlessness out of the auditoriums with their brooms and dustpans.

Most of all, I wondered what had happened to the manager, an officious-looking man who always wore a coat and tie. He rarely smiled from behind his glasses and when he did, it was in a way that said this was a business, dammit, not some rock 'em sock 'em free-for-all. He seemed totally out of place in a sea of jeans, tee-shirts and sneakers. I used to think of him as the poor schlub who couldn't find anything else, so he settled for this position until something better came along. I used to joke with myself that maybe he wore the coat and tie in case he got a phone call telling him he needed to drop everything and rush off right now to interview for some other job. He was always polite, but always formal, a counterbalance to the muted shenanigans of the younger employees and rowdier patrons.

When the pandemic hit in the spring of 2020, the Regal closed its doors to retool for social distancing. It reopened weeks later with plexiglass barriers and hand-sanitizing stations to show first-run movies that never came. The theatre attempted a valiant repivot during the summer, showing classic movies for a fraction of the cost of first runs, like *The Maltese Falcon*, *Casablanca*, or the 1977 *Star Wars*. We took the grandkids to see *The Goonies* on the big screen, which magnified the movie's frenetic energy to the 10th power.

The next day, I was still jittery from watching a 25-foot Chunk perform the Truffle Shuffle when I looked online to see the next classic we could throw the kids into. It was *Jaws*.

I told my wife we *had* to introduce the older grandkids to this cultural icon. I'd never seen it in a theatre—I was 11 years old when it came out in 1975 and my parents forbade me from going with my older brother ('you'd crap your pants, it's so scary,' he told me). I bought tickets and we took the older grandkids. I sat next to my grandson, fidgeting with anticipation. God, I hope he loves it, I thought, and then God, I hope *I* love it.

I was not disappointed—it was all there, the ominous 'shark-is-coming' score, the 1970s fashions and hairstyles, and the best line of dialog in all of cinema history: *We're gonna need a bigger boat*. My grandson thought the movie was fun. I thought it was incredible.

I was basking in the ache of nostalgia when we left the auditorium and I saw our manager. He was masked like all of us, but the coat and tie were gone, replaced by a long-sleeved shirt. I waved and thanked him for showing one of my favourite movies. He nodded and appeared to smile from behind his mask. I was glowing from having gone back to my boyhood for just a few hours, but something else was there, a sense of foreboding, maybe. I sensed that these attempts at remaining open were really the death throes of a business—and I was right. The theatre closed not long after. The chain itself nearly went under as it tried to stop the cash hemorrhage brought on by the near collapse of moviegoing.

For months, the front doors remained locked and paper signs in the windows announced the theatre would remain closed until further notice. I entered the lifeless parking lot to peek through the glass doors every now and then, hoping there might be someone in there I could wave at, but the place was dead.

During those months, it seemed silly to me to mourn a theatre that I had attended only sporadically over the years and especially odd that I was so torn up about a manager whose name I didn't even know, but this was a time for displaced grief brought on by the suddenness of the pandemic and all it destroyed. The virus had taken many lives and livelihoods, and loss hung in the air like a haze that refused to evaporate. I couldn't seem to shake the melancholic nostalgia that lay just beneath the surface and caused me to weep without warning. Our theatre became the holding place for the avalanche of loss, grief, and remembrance the pandemic seemed to have provoked in me. As the weeks went on, the melancholy felt both terribly dark and very sweet, my tears both an expression of grief and a celebration of it. It was confusing yet comforting.

One of my friends told me there was a Portuguese word for this: *saudade*. He explained it is the presence of absence, a yearning homesickness for a home that may or may not have existed. It is spiritual and emotional, not necessarily only grief or nostalgia or pining, but rather a deep state of longing that is somehow sweet. There is no exact equivalent to the word in English, which is probably a good thing given the North American penchant for pathologizing discomfort and throwing a cure at it.

'I used to feel it every Passover,' my friend said. 'I'd set two plates out at the Seder for my late mother and father, and I'd cry. I'd tell stories about how I loved and hated them. It drove my wife crazy.'

'Used to?'

'She and I are used to. Now I set out three plates and cry.' He shrugged. 'It's satisfying and sad at the same time. Seems like the right thing to do.'

105

When I'd drive by our theatre, I wondered about the manager, what he looked like now, if he'd finally found the job he always wanted or had done one of the thousand things that people who were thrown out of work did when things went south. The manager was the gatekeeper to nostalgia and memory of better times. God, I missed him.

And then one day in late May 2021, my wife told me she'd read online that the theatre was reopening. She asked if I wanted to go see *A Quiet Place Part II* and I nearly leapt out of my chair. Back to the movies. Back to *our* theatre. Back to *our* manager—perhaps.

Our drive to the show was full of anticipation. Would the manager still be there? What would he look like? Had he changed? What about those kids? The retirees? I felt like I was going to reunite with long-lost family.

When we walked into the Regal and through that cloud of popcorn steam, I felt giddy. This was the movies again. Relief, wonder and gratitude swirled in and through me like hot, liquid butter. The retirees were gone, but the teenagers were there, looking serious and dedicated. I looked at the counter to find the manager. He was there.

He wore a simple, short-sleeved button-down shirt. I guided my wife to his register at the concession counter and he again appeared to smile from behind his mask. He looked rested and relaxed, as though he'd been on vacation. He said it was good to have customers again and he was glad to take our order. I kept thanking him for being there, for opening the gate to nostalgia and the illusion of normalcy. I wanted to leap over the counter and give him a hug. I think he could sense my intensity and nodded nervously, but I couldn't stop looking at him, drinking him in, remembering this experience, the delight of being here. I was so excited that I forgot to ask his name, which was probably for the best given the beatific look in my eyes.

We went and sat in those wonderful, luxurious cloth seats with a handful of other masked people who were risking a return to life in a public space.

'Isn't this great?' I kept asking my wife. Advertisements were playing on the screen, so I had to speak up a little, maybe too much. Our moviegoing companions eight rows down looked up at us.

'Yes, it's wonderful,' she said and shushed me. The lights went down as music swelled all around and through us while a message from the theatre chain filled the screen, welcoming us back to the movies. I wrestled with a stew of emotions—strange disappointment at losing the melancholic sweetness brought on by months of absence, profound gratitude for being back in this place of memory, and a deep sadness that this all might still be an illusion. There were so few of us in the theatre that day, all of us masked, all of us wary of getting too close. Perhaps this refuge from the pandemic was not a refuge at all—it was just an illusion of safety.

I lowered my mask, wiped tears from my eyes and took a sip of overpriced soda. I knew that people were dying of an insidious virus outside these walls while others struggled with the carnage in its wake, but here in my cloth seat, life was comforting and familiar. At least for the next two hours, the colossal spectacle, so much larger than life, would beat back the grief, the apprehension, the sadness, and everything would be fine.

Lemon Pie to Quarantinis:
Tips for Navigating the New Normal from
The Real Self-Help
Sharon Hamilton

'Stop eating this comfort food that you never ate before.'
'Gearing Up for the "New Normal",' *New York Times*

The Real Self-Help understands that while you remain apprehensive about engaging in previously ordinary activities like hanging out with friends, going on trips, working out at your gym, or pretty much anything that made life a really great thing in the 'before times,' you need to be able to enjoy those pleasures to which you still have access. To that end, we are happy to provide some suggestions for gestures and utterances you can employ in everyday situations to assist you in feeling better about your chosen coping techniques without shame.

For example, to offset feelings of self-reproach while enjoying a bottle of vino with your steak frites, tell yourself that the red wine and the iron in the meat are good for your heart and that ingesting these things in combination allows you to focus a bit less on the 'What is this new disease they are telling us we need to avoid now?' brand of panicked thinking that has an unnerving tendency to occupy people's minds. Similarly, while sipping your pre-meal 'quarantini,' we suggest that if your drink contains a citrus element, such as a slice of lemon or lime, you point to this for the benefit of your 'Quarantine Sexual Relief Facilitator' (in pre-pandemic times 'your spouse') and provide a model of upbeat thinking by saying, 'At least we won't get scurvy.' This technique works especially well for enhancing feelings of positivity while imbibing a gin and tonic or a classic gimlet cocktail.

We observe at The Real Self-Help that a noted side benefit of using booze to survive this global apocalypse-type situation is that it can also serve to mark the now-blurry passage of time. For example, you can establish a kind of 'alcohol clock' by determining what you will drink, and when, and on what days. A martini partaken of only on Fridays at 5:00 p.m., for instance, can enable you to better distinguish weekdays from those previously established and in the 'before times' more readily identifiable days set aside for rest and relaxation.

With respect to the pleasure you may be deriving from favorite forms of nourishment, we suggest you respond to such published advice as 'Stop eating this comfort food that you never ate before the pandemic,' by reminding yourself that the lemon pie you recently impulse-bought while making one of your rare forays into the dangerous, infection-filled outside world made you stupidly happy with every bite and that the sour-sweet taste of the pie filling contrasted to the buttery creaminess of the flaky crust momentarily transported you out of your Totally Crappy Existence into a realm of pure bliss.

We at The Real Self-Help fully and responsibly recognize if your pandemic coping habits are resulting in serious negative health consequences, you should contact your medical professional. We also believe, however, that while you should try to avoid damaging your physical wellbeing, you have never lived through something like this before; so, if a bourbon on the rocks or vast handfuls of white cheese popcorn is helping you get by, self-help gurus urging otherwise should, perhaps, Back the F*** Off.

Bathroom Reading
Ann McMillan

When I retired, and then COVID hit, I thought I would try my hand at writing. I'd written and edited a lot of material as part of my work life and had a lifetime's worth of ideas and real incidents that I thought might be story-worthy.

Along the way, I met Jon Peirce and conspired with him to produce an Almanac related to elders and COVID. We did some of the writing. Actually, Jon did a huge amount of it—and we inspired more than 50 other people to contribute their pieces. The final product, published by Loose Cannon Press in the fall of 2021, was something that I was proud of. We did a book launch in November and even got some modest press coverage. While our sales would never get either of us a villa in the south of France, which Jon suggested as a good objective, the book does actually sell. I sent copies to all my friends and relatives for Christmas, with the expectation that they would read and, hopefully, enjoy the book.

In February, 2022 I visited Vancouver for a month. The idea was to have somewhat of a personal reset after the ordeal of completing the Almanac and before the ordeal of producing a sequel, which was something that Jon and I had decided to do. It remained to be seen if the COVID pandemic was actually over, but it was good to pretend that this was in fact the case. As part of that personal reset, I wanted to get more physically fit in preparation for a dragon boat regatta in Vancouver in June (the first for me since COVID), and spend some time with my sister, Jenifer, a professor at SFU, who was in the throes of planning her retirement.

We met up several times. She came to where I was staying for a meal and gave me a tour of her university facilities. She graciously provided coffee and cookies at her home. After some conversation and an admiring look at the stunning view over the Second Narrows Bridge, it was time for me to move along. In preparation for doing that, I made a quick stop in her bathroom, where I was shocked to see my latest pride and joy, the aforementioned COVID Almanac, *Plague Take It*, resting comfortably on the back of the toilet! The book did look slightly dog-eared, as though it had been read, and that was pleasing… but still. Not wanting to create a scene, I decided not to take umbrage and moved on with my day. But I couldn't help feeling just the slightest bit offended that my expectations had been so wrong and my book had so quickly been reduced to bargain basement status.

A week or so later, Jenifer and her husband got reservations for us at the restaurant Published on Main. How appropriate, and how thoughtful, I said to myself. The restaurant was renowned for its exquisitely prepared and presented local food. Over the fantastic small plates, after the veggies but before the fish, and more significantly, after our first bottle of wine, I could not stop myself from asking. 'So,' I said softly, 'Are you enjoying the book I sent you?' She turned an appealing shade of pink, or at least I imagined that she did?

'You noticed it, didn't you, on the back of the toilet?'

I assured her that, yes, indeed, I had noticed that my pride and joy was keeping bad company.

'Well,' she said, 'I like to read, but I am so busy I seldom have the time. That book has some great short contributions that are perfect for bathroom reading.'

In further conversation it became clear that Jenifer had, actually, read parts of the book, so I forgave her, although my ego still feels a bit bruised. The book had not become a mere ornament in her home residing on her coffee table, and as I had expected, she was reading and enjoying it. I realized that misguided expectations had been my weakness in this situation.

I imagine that the producers of books such as those that appear on Goodreads list of Best Bathroom Books must deal with those expectations somehow. Of course, the writer of *Uncle John's Bathroom Books* is probably laughing all the way to the bank.

Well, as Samuel Johnson so famously said, 'A writer's first duty is to be read.' What better way to ensure that a book is read than to put it in the bathroom, where there are so few competing distractions!

Paris During the Pandemic
Jack Denny-Brown

Okay, so there's really not a whole lot going on these days. Life during the pandemic… I stopped working at the High School on March 13th, 2020, and haven't been back for nearly a year. We don't go out. The highlight of the week for me is my trip to get groceries during the senior hour at 6:00 a.m. on Tuesday mornings. I kid you not! Ann and I used to go out to eat once a week. These days we get 'take out' on Saturday nights. And that's it. I cook the meals, which I enjoy. But there is not a lot going on here. I suspect we are not all that different from other couples during the pandemic. But I don't know for sure… How would I? No one's going out.

Now that my writing projects have ended, I'm at loose ends. How loose, you ask? This past week I pulled out a jigsaw puzzle (can you hear me laughing?) No joke. I bought it for Annie as one of her Christmas presents. Fortunately for me, Ann is not someone who takes pleasure in lots of material things. She knows what she likes and she gets it, all while staying within her means. I'm lucky in that respect. But she is not an easy person to find gifts for. So, I thought the jigsaw puzzle was pretty imaginative. I got other stuff of course. Nothing extravagant. But I kind of thought the puzzle was an inspiration. It's a street scene from Paris. Cafes, cobblestones, colourful old stucco apartment buildings and La Tour Eiffel towering in the background. We can't afford to go to Paris, but we can do the jigsaw puzzle. Ann was under-whelmed when she opened her present. It has sat in the living room ever since.

But I kind of liked the idea of the puzzle, so on a Monday when I had nothing to do, I pulled it out and set out the pieces on the dining room table. One thousand pieces. Then I sat down and worked on locating and assembling the edge pieces. Three hours later I was still struggling to finish the edge. Crap! Maybe I should have bought the 500-piece puzzle!

I was beginning to think I was out of my depth. When Annie came home, she was mildly annoyed that the dining room table had been appropriated for my project, so we brought up a folding card table from the basement to help make space. She clearly felt sorry for me, struggling as I was with the edge pieces, and while I took a break making dinner and whatnot, she began working on the upper right-hand corner. I took some pleasure in the know-ledge that she was getting hooked on the thing, but by the time dinner was ready she had completed a massive section in the upper right and was working her way down the teal-coloured apartment building to the cafe beneath. Clearly, she had a knack for this thing.

And so, over the course of the week I would work on the puzzle during the day for bits and pieces of time, and she would get sucked into it for 20 or 30 minutes after dinner. I was a little ashamed at how bad I was at the thing, but secretly pleased that she was so good at it. My purchase wasn't such a bad one after all.

What is it about jigsaw puzzles? They're quiet. They occupy some part of your mind, but allow room for conversation, or listening to the news on NPR, or music or what have you. The scene within the picture grows on you as you work, gradually filling it in. You are drawn into the picture in a way which you are not when you look at it in its entirety. The little details assume an importance which is absent in looking at the scene as a whole. And then there's the pleasure you feel when you find the right piece and it clicks into place. In a 1000-piece puzzle, you experience that pleasure 1000 times. Doing the puzzle together, of course, that number must be shared. When we're done, Ann will have experienced that feeling 700 times, I would imagine. Or more. Annoying, on some level, but nonetheless... I feel like I did good.

Where Edges Meet
Catherine A. MacKenzie

Dear COVID:
Chilling words, with groans, to receive on phones:

> *URGENT message from the*
> *Province of Nova Scotia.*
> *You have tested*
> *positive for COVID-19.*
> *Self-isolate immediately.*

COVID, I've seen you, see you, and no doubt will see you—or some strain of you—in the future as will everyone, but it's not all blue and bleak, and we're not as weak as you presume for we've weathered unsettling uncertainties and stressful situations and been harassed in the past, and the world will bloom again—is blooming!—despite this gloom you've laid upon our feet;

We've suffered anxiety and loneliness and depression that make minds wander and ponder how we can proceed, and if there's a God above so full of love, why He'd be so cross as to toss such uncertainty upon us;

But we've persevered for the past two-plus years, shed tears at many a dreadful demise after you stole last breaths, grieved at swelling numbers of faceless deaths so graceless and baseless, but we've laughed and loved life in spite of strife and look ahead to a more pleasant world even if you've not totally fled, even if you dump another scary strain in your stead to cause more pain, to disturb, to test our limits or curb our usual enthusiasm;

Me? I'm still revelling in hibernation, my new quirky calm of solitary life, existing in a weird sense of intense glee that sets me free from certain responsibilities: not having to waver between 'yes' and 'no,' enjoying makeup-free days that allow my ageing skin to breathe and improve, sitting at the computer in my cubby to compose poems and prose in grubby clothes without threats of interruptions at the door that used to be a chore to answer, and—

Alas! I spout brittle little lies, most of which appear noticeably upon my thighs: all not so dandy within my world of isolation accompanied with too much candy, boozy drink disappearing within a blink, and gorging on food that makes me brood with a silly fear of appearing nude in front of hubby notwithstanding his undying love—for if the glove doesn't fit properly when it should, I must grin and bear it, but oh man, I swear it's hard to win, to remain thin and healthy when there's not much else to do except drink and eat and stew within this new-found span of blue;

And, of course, I'm still missing my children and grands—the highlights of my existence—not much hugging or kissing, most times seen only from a far distance though cellphones and social media and Zoom somewhat brighten a lonely room, and I'm not complaining for we must remain safe and not chafe at what we cannot change;

Soon, vaxxed or not, masks or not, the world will open, allowing us to live in a greater semblance of reality with glee rather than warring and roaring at others with opposing views that light our fuse, or cringing in fear with every twinging of unknowns we hear, and we'll be back to the mundane: stones thrown haphazardly at weather not to our liking when hiking and biking are inconceivable, grieveable, or happiness at finding a velvety feather or a pretty penny—symbols of mourning, messages from the deceased to add to makeshift shrines—signs those grieving yearn for and never spurn after a loved one's leaving;

COVID, alas, you're still here: your presence incessant, a depressant spoken of without love, but we will remain brave and never cave, persevere despite fears, drink beers, wear masks while on tasks and errands, keep our distance, our persistence;

Though words are endless, often friendless and trendless, sometimes hairy and scary and not in rhyme, by the time these words reach readers you'll hopefully be totally gone, having disappeared at long last, as fast as dew upon a lawn or a valuable sought-after jewel left to pawn at a pawnshop as a hot-smoking deal;

Oh, COVID, no one knows your end, when you will quit and split, wend your way to another realm, one unpopulated…

P.S. In the meantime, with or without rhyme, it would be loverly and utterly vulgarly brotherly—desirous!—if you'd infect Putin with your virus, knock him hard, dead to the ground without a sound, discard him like a Joker card…

Cabin Fever
Donna Chateauvert

I am a Prior Chest Nut, a member of the local breast cancer survivor dragon boat team. We paddle regularly from May to September on White Lake in Arnprior packed cheek to cheek in our dragon boat, the Kahlua.

Along came the Coronavirus or COVID-19. Now just look at all the new words we're hearing and using in our day-to-day conversation. Here are some examples: pandemic, quarantine, social distancing and self-isolation. We are also using high-tech to have meetings and social gatherings.

My husband Mike and I are 'self-isolating' and I'm going nuts. Have you ever heard of cabin fever? Well, I have it… and I miss dragon boat paddling. Let me give you an example of my day. I get up every morning between 6:00 and 7:00 a.m. Please don't think I get up early to start my exciting day. I do remember when I could sleep in until 8:00 a.m. I am just a thing of beauty first thing in the morning. My hair is awful and the bags under my eyes don't add to my appeal. I make my way to the kitchen to be greeted by Mike, who has been up for hours and wants to fill me in on all the news he's read on his iPad. (I silently plead, 'At least wait until I've had my first cup of coffee.') I know we're 'self-isolating' but does it have to be like this?

Our church has been closed because of the 'pandemic,' so for the first time in my life I make my way downstairs to watch daily mass in my night-gown. (I'm sure glad the priest can't see me… there are advantages to high tech remote meetings)!

Now for the exciting day in front of me! I won't bore you with the number of books I've read and the movies I've watched; too many for me to remember anyway. What's more exciting is that I vacuum the floors three or four times a week (my house has never been so dust-free). I have washed windows, and organized closets and cupboards. I have even cleaned my oven (well, I set the button for 'automatic clean'). Such a Suzy Homemaker I've become. Who knew that 'self-isolation' would make for cleaner and tidier homes?

I usually go for a walk, being careful to 'social distance,' but as I'm writing this it's raining so we go for a drive instead, 'self-isolating' in our car. Have you ever driven around the streets of Arnprior with no destination or purpose? I ask you, how exciting is that?

Having said all that, I am 'sheltering in place,' another new phrase. I'm determined to stay happy and healthy for future paddling on the lake.

The Biochemist
Jack Denny-Brown

I graduated from college in June of 1968. It was a momentous time to graduate, because the Vietnam War was cranking into high gear at that time.

I was totally unprepared for the reality which was about to hit me in the face. My friends and I were all opposed to the war, and I was also aware that I would be vulnerable to the draft. In the back of my mind, I imagined that I might go to Canada if I absolutely had to. So, I had a 'plan B.' But I had no 'plan A.' And to tell you the truth, Plan B scared the crap out of me.

Up to that point the war had been something I'd read about in the newspaper and watched on TV. Along with the rest of America, I had watched the news in the mid-60s as the war gradually became more and more alarming. I had joined the demonstrations, marched on the Pentagon, and generally sided with those who opposed the war. But it all seemed more theoretical to me than anything else. I was opposed to the war on moral grounds. The wakeup call came two weeks after my graduation from college in June of 1968. I received a letter in the mail, addressed to me, from the Department of Defense. It was a draft notice. I was instructed to show up on Whitehall Street in Staten Island, New York, for a physical in two weeks.

I was stunned. How did they know where I lived? How did they know I'd graduated? I hadn't even received my diploma yet. That was to come in the mail a few days later. How could they do this to me?

In the days which followed I floundered about trying to imagine what I could do to avoid the draft. I wasn't coming up with any good ideas. Then, by some miraculous stroke of good luck, I ran into a classmate on the street who told me that he'd enrolled in a crash teacher-training program for the summer. He would be teaching Middle School in the New York Public Schools in the fall. Teachers were needed in the inner-city schools, and these jobs were seen as serving an 'essential community need.' Thus, they were draft exempt. I applied for the program, was accepted, and within two weeks was attending classes at NYU and was free of the draft.

I then taught Middle School in Harlem for the next three years. It was a train wreck. The crash program in no way prepared me for what I would encounter in the classroom. From the perspective of all these years that have passed, I can see that I learned a lot during those years teaching. But it was a tough way to learn. After three years I was worn out. Fortunately for me, in June of 1971 I was free of the draft, and I quit my job as a teacher.

Time for graduate school? Heck no! I wanted something completely new and different. I needed time to digest what had happened. I wanted to get out of the city and get away from it all. If there had been an opening for a tambourine man in the Hare Krishnas I might have gone for it.

In the absence of any Hare Krishna openings, I drove aimlessly across the country in my VW bus with my girlfriend, killing time. Across Canada, into the Rockies, on to Vancouver, then down the coast to San Francisco we drove, camping wherever we could. Sitting on the beach watching the sun go down over the Pacific. Eating hotdogs. No plan. Finally, back across the Great Plains, hot dogs in the cornfields, and on to New York. In January of 1972 I left my apartment on the Upper West Side and moved home to Cambridge, to live with my parents.

After two weeks of my lying about, my father sat me down.

'So, what's the plan?' he asked.

'Plan?'

Now that I have the time to think about it, 'lack of a plan' seems to have been a pattern with me. I had no plan whatsoever for the rest of my life. I'd graduated from Columbia with a BA in English Literature. That was about it. I was no scholar. That much was clear. I wasn't about to go to graduate school and pore over Chaucer. I was adrift. So, my father made it clear that I was to move out of the house and fend for myself. I was fine with that.

Searching through the pages of the *Real Paper*, the alternative newspaper of the era, I discovered a room in a commune just outside of Harvard Square. I introduced myself and moved into a room on the first floor of a house on Wendell Street, within walking distance of Harvard Square. The rent was 45 dollars a month. Then I found a job driving a cab in downtown Boston. It was January of 1972.

The 'commune' was something of a disappointment to me at the time. I was hoping that it would be somewhat wilder and crazier than it turned out to be. It was a Harvard Square commune. Everybody had graduated from college, and some were attending graduate school. All were in one way or another involved in advancing their career—except me. I was driving a cab at night in downtown Boston.

But I was fine with that for the time being. I didn't mind being the resident freak. And I actually enjoyed the company of people who could conduct an intelligent conversation. My fellow commune members all did different things. Phil was a student at Harvard Law School. Debbie was a practicing nurse. Ivy worked as a social worker at a center for disturbed youth. Shao Ti worked as a medical technician. Carole went to Harvard School of Education and worked part time at the supermarket checking groceries. There were at least two high school teachers.

And then there was Tim Springer, who said he had graduated from Berkeley and was doing his PhD at Harvard in 'biochemistry.' At least that's what he told us. I never saw him studying. He spent most of his weekends fiddling with his motorcycle in the backyard. Each morning, he would get on his bike and wake up the neighbours on his way out. Then, of course, everyone knew he was back when he rumbled back in the evening. He seemed more interested in the motorcycle than in anything else. He was a perfectly intelligent guy. He didn't talk much and he certainly didn't act like a biochemist. For instance, he didn't study the ingredients labels of products and read them out loud. He didn't interrupt table conversations with the breakdown of the process of putrefaction. Indeed, he didn't show any peculiar interpersonal quirks which would have set him apart as different from you and me. As far as I could see, he didn't harbour any secret knowledge of the micro-world. He seemed relatively normal. He was quiet... *too quiet*. But I was not going to challenge him on that score. If he wanted us to think he was a 'biochemist' then who was I, a mere English major, to challenge him on that? Live and let live. Tim, the 'biochemist.' It was the 70s. You could be whoever you wanted to be. He wore wire-rimmed glasses. If that's what it takes to pass as a biochemist then let it be. So, I never questioned his credentials. But I was onto his act.

I moved out after a year.

Needless to say, the years streaked by. I bounced around a bit, then after five years returned to teaching. Married. Two children. I loved my life as a schoolteacher. In 2014, after 40 years of teaching, I retired and moved out to Central Massachusetts with my new wife, Ann. There I discovered that I missed the classroom and returned to teaching High School as a substitute teacher. For six years I taught at the local high school in Central Massachusetts.

But everything changed on Friday, March 13, 2020. That day turned out to be the last day of school that year. COVID hit Massachusetts, and they closed the schools. We all thought it was going to be a two-week thing, but we were wrong. March went by, then April, May, and June came and went. The doors remained closed. Classes were held 'remotely' using computers. COVID dominated the culture for the next three years, and I never returned to teaching.

During COVID I had a lot of time on my hands. There was no socializing going on during the pandemic. We were all isolated during those first years, living in our bubbles, so while my wife worked remotely from home, I was left to my own devices. I had lived a long life and had lost touch with countless old friends along the way. Using the computer, I discovered that I could track some of them down. Some were dead. Others were impossible to find. But I got pretty good at finding them, one way or another.

Here was Bob Oliver, old friend from Columbia, in an obituary. He had lived a good life, worked at MIT as an electrical engineer, accomplished a lot. Two children. Divorced from Carolyn, apparently.

John Fuerstein, another Columbia friend; radical Marxist, living in exile in Vancouver. Nice-looking wife. Working as... an accountant for some reason.

I wouldn't have guessed he'd be an accountant. He'd studied sociology. Bright guy. I guess it's tough to find work when you're running from the law.

Frank Lundquist, my former roommate, living in New York City and running a charitable foundation, and a published author of two novels. It seems he's also a literary critic for the *New York Times*. Of course. Frank always loved the obscure, arcane stuff. The only guy I ever met who actually understood *Finnegan's Wake*.

And Jon Coppleberg, a consultant on worker's compensation, living just outside of Boston. Wait… what happened to the theater? Coppelberg went to Yale School of Drama! Oh well. Seems he did pretty well after all.

I would go through various periods of my life, pick out the names I remembered and see if I could find them. Finally, I started looking up names from the Wendell Street Commune. The women were difficult. If they got married, then the name changed. But the guys were a little easier.

Saul Steinlauf… the high school psychology teacher on the second floor. Now this I could have predicted! He'd moved out to the west coast, it seems, and founded some kind of mindfulness institute which had been busted for fraud!

And Randy Slocomb… what the? This I would never have guessed in a million years! Randy, who was perhaps the least cool guy on the planet…

It seems he'd moved out to Seattle and founded a wine-tasting magazine. He died, at the age of 79, a celebrated expert on local wines. I even have a picture of the man: Joe Cool, leaning back with a glass of wine. Who could have known?

What next?… Oh yeah! Tim Springer, the 'biochemist'. Before I could even google the name an image flashed into my mind… Springer with a bandanna… yeah! Piercings? Yup, I could see that. That would be Springer! Biker guy! I googled his name, 'Tim Springer, biochemist' to see what I could find:

PROFESSOR BECOMES A BILLIONAIRE BY INVESTING
IN A FIRM MAKING THE COVID-19 VACCINE
April 24, 2020, Rinie Wilson, Posted in *What's Buzzing*
Timothy Springer, the Harvard University medical professor, is making the headlines for some interesting reasons. In 2010, Springer became the 4th largest shareholder in Moderna, a US-based firm that was launching the largest IPO in biotech history.

Holy Mother of God! It was him all right… It seems this wasn't inherited money, either. As a result of his research, Springer had founded four companies which were all financially successful. In 2010, with the money he'd earned from selling his companies, he invested heavily in Moderna, one of the manufacturers of a vaccine for COVID. Then, in 2020, the shit hit the fan.

COVID spread across the surface of the planet. Moderna stock went through the roof. Tim Springer's estimated worth is now somewhere around 2.6 billion dollars. Despite his financial success, he continues his work as a professor and researcher at Harvard Medical School.

I guess he wasn't bullshitting us about the 'biochemistry' after all.

SECTION 6
Poetry

*I*n April 2020, National Public Radio (NPR) issued a poetry challenge for readers to submit lines 'describing how you've been affected by the global coronavirus pandemic.' [1] More than 30 of the huge number of responses were melded into the poem 'If the Trees Can Keep Dancing, So Can I.' This was labelled a community poem to help cope with a crisis and was published on April 30, 2020, as COVID made its mark across North America. The pandemic sparked a flood of poetic outpourings which explored many facets of the changes it brought, from the grief of losing loved ones, to the boredom of isolation, to the fear of catching COVID.

Many of the poets who have contributed to this almanac are motivated by the same search for comfort in the throes of disaster. 'Daphne's Song' by Teresa Bandrowska ostensibly comforts a COVID patient by trying to put her death into a less painful perspective. Kathryn Paulsen's 'A Different Chain' explores the different kinds of connections made in COVID times to establish closeness and community when face-to-face meetings were not possible. For her part, Colleen Naomi brings a pleasing sense of whimsy and some gentle humour to the often-vexing subject of Zoom meetings. Juxtaposing strict iambic pentameter and slightly archaic diction with her extremely modern subject matter, Naomi provides us much-needed distance on our relationship with technology, her conclusion being, 'Oh Zoom meetings, you have become our muse.'

Hendrik Siré explores love with new senses now that contact is so forbidden in 'COVID Love.' He explores the mysteries of death's shore in 'Whispered Lullaby.' 'For Donnie' is his touching elegy to Donnie steeped in the pain of loss and the acceptance of reality. Then, in 'Crack' he examines the fragility of life. Peggy Lehmann struggles with the pandemic in 'Viral Contempt' but finally comes to a deeper understanding. Sue Mills fights her own personal battle with cancer which just happens to coincide with the larger societal battle with COVID. Finally, John Eaton sees humanity's future etched clearly and depressingly in the face of metacrises including not only COVID but also climate change.

As Erica Jong said 'What makes you a poet is a gift for language, an ability to see into the heart of things, and an ability to deal with important unconscious material. When all these things come together, you're a poet.' I'm sure that readers will agree that we have some fine poets in this almanac!

Ann McMillan

---

[1] 'NPR is an independent, nonprofit media organization that was founded on a mission to create a more informed public.' It has over 1000 partner broadcasters and reaches nearly 30 million people. Search: If the Trees Can Keep Dancing, So Can I.

Daphne's Song
Teresa Bandrowska

Sit yourselves down a minute and listen to my song.
It isn't very complicated, it isn't very long.
Let me tell the story of a friend so true and dear
Who passed so gently from this world she showed us not to fear.

There's nothing left to fear my friends, nothing left to fear.
Dying's just a slipping from existence over here.
Drop all cares, and sail away towards another shore.
Our breath becomes the breath of all the others gone before.

In tenderness we loved her up, with songs and stories told.
We laughed, we cried, we reminisced about the days of old.
She gave a smile, a peaceful sigh just as the time drew near.
And as she took her final breath, she shed a single tear.

There's nothing left to fear my friends, nothing left to fear.
Dying's just a slipping from existence over here.
Drop all cares, and sail away towards another shore.
Our breath becomes the breath of all the others gone before.

It's all so ordinary; it happens every day.
Somewhere there's a baby born, and someone slips away.
Be grateful for the life you live, the roses and the thorns.
For when your time has come to leave, another will be born.
There's nothing left to fear my friends, nothing left to fear.
Dying's just a slipping from existence over here.
Drop all cares, and sail away towards another shore
Our breath becomes the breath of all the others gone before.

A Different Chain
Kathryn Paulsen

I got the email three days in a row from different folks—subject line:
    Quarantine
Cooking: it said if I followed the directions, and everybody else did, I'd be
    getting
36 recipes—I should send a recipe
to the first name on the list even if I didn't know
him/her—then move the sender's name to first place, add mine to second,
and forward the revised email as bcc to 20 friends.
Oh, and reply to sender if I couldn't do this within
five days so as to be fair to everybody else, all those waiting
for all those recipes. Send something quick and easy,
the letter said, no rare ingredients. To quote: 'Actually, the best one
is the one you know in your head and can
type right now. Don't agonize over it. It is the recipe
you make when you are short on time.'

Only now we're long on time—or would be if there weren't so much
else to do in Quarantine—like reconnect with all those folks
you've been neglecting for so many years—especially if
you're of an age to have accumulated
more friends than you've lost. And the problem
with any recipe is it requires you
to at least take it in, decide if you admire it
enough to make it, and if you do,
well, then you'll need to acquire its
ingredients if they're not already in residence
on the shelves of your pantry or fridge. Which
brings up the issue of what might easily be there
these days—what's rare these days:
flour is, eggs and milk well may be.
Surely the best ingredients
are the ones you've already bought,
maybe years ago, and
then forgot.
And do I really want
to get three dozen versions of an easy salad or pasta dish
I could probably imagine for myself, if indeed I haven't
already made it? Wouldn't I rather
be entertained by recipes so bizarre

I'd never have found them in any
online search or even
in my dreams?

The alt version of that email was
leavened with irony, describing the chain as
'basically a pyramid scheme' but a harmless one.
In contrast, thought I, to the typical
chain communiqué of the past, threatening
bad luck, dark futures, and lovelessness to decliners, or suggesting
their characters were deficient in human feeling,
this one envisioned a future in which,
if the chain isn't broken, we could be
constantly forwarding
recipes to each other ad
infinitum, which, the sender said, 'actually
sounds okay.'
Okay, sure—
I too, have forwarded many, many, many things
to many people, over these weeks, that had been
forwarded to me, maybe creating some accidental chains,
sending them back to those who began them.
But what
would I like most to be sent, am open to getting ad
infinitum, whether easy or difficult, familiar or exotic, common or rare,
and am happy to ask others to forward
a letter in support of so doing?

POEMS
Send them to me, please.
I'm willing to accept
as many as any
of you can supply.

Here, do your part,
Take this one,
Send it on

With your own
It's a start.

Modern Muse:
A Poem in Iambic Pentameter
Colleen Naomi

Why doth thou speak when in such muted state?
And with thine head upside-down on my screen,
Another colleague hast sidestepped that fate:
With cam'ra off, he shall go forth unseen.

While we meet thou art scrolling Instagram.
We hearest barking dog from some abode.
Thy manager screen shares a diagram,
But on thine Samsung phone t'will never load.

With wine in coffee cup and slippered feet,
Thou lookest pretty swank from the waist up,
While seated on thy cushy wing-back seat,
And with a filter that looks like make-up.

Thy cam'ra angle in an awkward place
Displays an in-depth look inside thy nose,
While other angles from above thy face
Explore just how far down some cleavage goes.

Lo! thou dost raise thy voice so loud and clear,
Toward a child who of thy womb was born,
Thou quick forgets to mute, so now we hear
Thine offspring cry out, saddened and forlorn.

Thine eyes stay in an apathetic stare,
In front of backgrounds of a sunset beach.
While on the side thou texts a lover fair.
Thy spelt Panini is just out of reach.

Ah, day-by-day and month-by-month we meet,
With all the great technology we use,
So that our busy lives shan't miss a beat,
Oh Zoom meetings, you have become our muse.

COVID Love

Hendrik Siré

In mellow cadences
Thanata whispers love to me
As I sweat and
Gasp and cry out
In tightening embrace

Fountains of shiny hair
Plump parting lips
Her luscious loins
Those damp caverns
White bones everywhere

I feel the awe of her curves
As my breath falters
In ravishment and demise

Whispered Lullaby
Hendrik Siré

My little white boat
With its little white oars
And me its little white passenger
In a little white gown
Trying to row somewhere anywhere
With fevered fast heartbeats
Despite my exhaustion

I know it makes no sense to stay put
In this little white fog
So dense humid and heavy
I cannot see my toes
As I sputter and cough
In my little white boat
In my little white pond
So far so immensely far
I feel
From any shore

No time to panic or cry
Or to ruminate or pray
As darkness closes in
On me
This broken little white stutterer and mutterer
Blitherer and farter
Is it now time?

I hear voices
In the distance
I make out words calling me
Strangers beckoning me to the closer shore
Or so they say
Hey buddy forget it all
Hey hiker just think no more trails
No pains no regrets
Isn't that what you've always secretly wanted Boy Scout
To bushwhack up Mount Oblivion

From a far shore
The faintest voice of all
The one that starts out
As a whispering lullaby from childhood
And grows louder
Faja hey Faja
It's this way Faja here
We found the trail
Row this way
The shore's not far
Come on Faja you can make it

It could have been a lifetime ago
In a chilly fog
Around a rising puss pond
On the edge of a darkening forest I could not see
A voice calling out
Above my faltering breath
This voice
These words
This faith
This song
Carrying through the shuddering doubts
The engulfing blackness
The walls of my crackling chest
To enchant my failing heart
Never give up

For Donnie
Hendrik Siré

For this gathering
we have two rules
from Donnie
no solemn words
and present tense only.

Donnie lives
in the space between words
in the breath
between sighs and reminiscence.
He calls us his beloved buzzards
maybe because we're old like him
and not the prettiest wake.

Except for Dulsy.
She's too broken up to be here just now.
Donnie calls Dulsy
his bouquet of blossoms
his seductive smiler.
She calls him
her plonky plute
full of pithy pluttry.
That's Dulsy being the bard
She'll join us soon I hope.

Donnie loves his back yard
all his friends know that.
A few weeks ago
when no one is allowed over to the rooming house
I drop by to visit Donnie
and find him sitting alone
on this smelly old sofa on the back porch
holding a glass of plonk
and declaiming his verses to the dandelions and the squirrels.
He tells me even a raccoon and a blue heron drop by to hear his verses.
I'm sure they're grateful.
Maybe later we'll hear Donnie's 'Ode to a Raccoon.'

On days before all this
we're with Donnie
on this back porch
over beer and wine and barbecue
egging on his poetry
with—let's call them—our rude impertinences
words that we may regret on this day.
But he loves our goadings
and keeps dishing words back at us
picturesque pronouncements
hobbled by the bold absence
of grammar and punctuation.
That's our Donnie.

When it all starts
he puts his dog Ross
in a kennel in Brockville.
He goes down to visit
just the week before—
Now I'm working to find Ross a good home.

Hi Dulsy
glad you're here
maybe you'll read some of his pluttry
And your own too.
Dulsy can we say
his poetry isn't Robert Service or Al Purdy
maybe more of independent resonance?
He has his own words and moments
a most authentic slinger.
He puts his love for us and the world right here.

Maybe we should declare
Donnie's a dreamer and a daydreamer
roaring poetry
and tilting at raccoons and blue herons.
He's our best
a soul of sterling spirit
for regaling us on his back porch
for reveling with his buzzards.

I think I've stayed in the present
though I fear I'm straying into solemnity.
Dulsy are you able to say something now?

Crack

Hendrik Siré

I must have hit a crack
I fell to the ice
I banged my knee and elbow
I got up right away
Looking at my buddy Alex
As the pain throbbed in my right leg and arm
I said loudly to Alex
When he turned around and finally saw me
'I am OK'
But when I said it
I was not completely sure

When it happened
I was thinking of my two-year old grandson Henry
I was trying to imagine
How he would learn to skate
And fall
On the Rideau Canal one day
Supported by his parents and grandparents
And then I asked myself
What Henry would be doing today in Houston
Would he be trying out a crawdaddy from the Gulf?
Would he be skadoodling around one of those kid parks
In the Heights?
Mounting the structures and
Wanting his Daddy to swing him?

If the truth be told
At the precise moment of my fall
I was thinking of the hospital in Houston
Of my room and bed
Of my breathing
And all the wires and tubes
At that very instant
I was feeling a deep silent embedded fear
That I would ever go back a third time
To face the slowing drumbeat
Of my pneumonia

As we skated along
After the fall
The throbs subsiding
I said to Alex
I was lucky
I fell well
I'll just have a few bruises
To show for my ordeal

Viral Contempt
Peggy Lehmann

The sun no longer shone.
A grim continuum of time passage with no end.
The grey, the silent, the expressionless enemy
growing and flourishing, reaching for more
and consuming all within its grasp

Together but apart, four walls of oppression,
buried creativity and forgotten joy.
Conversations but no words,
expansive stares into the outer world
and nothing changed.
Jenna shifted her gaze
and felt the rising inside her.
Shackles of restraint could no longer hold her despair,
their encumbrances bulging and writhing with insistence,
her resolve growing in power and strength.

As she stood, a storm cloud hovered,
then a rumble announced its intentions.
In the ensuing flash she saw her escape.
Forcing the door, she easily broke free and began to run.

The rhythmic slapping of the pavement quickened,
and nearly smothered the distant voice
calling her to return.
The fury within was bubbling to the surface
and cleansed by the falling rain.
Another loud clap punctuated her frustration, fear, isolation, and grief,
and an entrance ahead beckoned.

Her pace slowed as concrete changed to firm ground,
but her resolve did not.
Easily bypassing the barrier,
the trees parted in welcome revealing a hill,
and she began to climb.

Now gentle drops kissed her head,
while her torment tore at the ground
assuring ascension.
The beast within spewed its raging chorus
for none to hear.

The storm had abated, but the rain fell
until there was none.
Finally spent and slumped at the base of an aging tree,
Jenna moaned for a life she knew.
The isolation, the deprivation
took it all away;
the familiar, the comfort, stolen.

Soft whimpers became slow, deep breaths as daylight faded.
Cradled by nature she found peace,
and all was still.

As the trickling light of dawn shimmered through the trees,
a new day awakened.
Emptiness and longing had now changed to hope,
and Jenna understood.

Cancer, Covid, Retirement
Susan Mills

Booked that annual mammogram
'Umm…we need an ultrasound' they said
'Umm…we need a biopsy' they said
'Umm…you have Breast Cancer again' they said
Feelings of aloneness overwhelm me
Surgery next …Breasts are gone… 'Will call your caregiver when you are
done' they said
'Looks like we got it early' they said
'Pills daily for years' they said
Emotions overtake me
'Just suck it up' they said
Fell down and got back up
'Safe to go back to work' they said
'COVID's not over' I said
'Time to retire' I said

The Edge of Extinction
John Eaton

1. Prologue

Life is the incredible gift of a unique consciousness: for me shared with a great grandmother to great grandchildren possibly spanning a period of more than 250 years of life. Humanity's ascent to the apex of life is built on a myriad of extinctions over 3.8 billion years since it all began [1] as we now, post 'Pandemic', elevate ourselves to 'The Edge of Extinction' to become a senseless blip in evolution and membership in the 'failed' hominid club: leaving the earth to recover from our violations.

2. Realities

'The whole worl's in a terrible state o' chassis' [2]

The pandemic has created a sea change in society's values and lifestyles, exacerbating the now apparent insidious perversions of the internet age. The loss of the empathy to make the necessary sacrifices for each other, as neighbours and societies, is moving the world from maybe to 'The Edge.' [3]

I was born in England at the depths of World War II. Unlike today there were no 'comfortable pews' in the western economies of 1942: willing sacrifices were palpable in every facet of life and spawned a kinder, gentler and more deeply empathetic post war period with social programs in the Western world and international cooperation via the UN and its agencies. The world is now splintering into ideological blocks and our way of life is slowly being eroded by the internet-enabled amoralities and the associated twitterverse deceptions. Our technologies, which began with the industrial revolution, have evolved to today's AI-enhanced digital world. This has compounded the exponential growth paradigm for wealth which now is leaving a planet needing immediate extraordinary life support to even hope to mitigate the rape, pillage and destruction of the earth's lands, oceans and atmosphere.

Yet we are oblivious to, or are simply not interested in, this violation of our planet and unwilling or unable to understand our social contract. Instead, we show ourselves bereft of respect for each other as we claim selfish 'rights and freedoms,' while at the same time driven by self-absorption with life's 'gratuites.' I hope we can restore the empathetic society I once knew. I also hope it will be one which will respect and understand its obligations to comply with reasonable restrictions to its freedoms designed not only to protect society at large, but themselves as well and just as critically, for 'What We Owe the Future'.[4] There are no freedoms without limits. The pandemic and its aftermath have exposed our fragility with our leaders/politicians and social groups attacking the very foundations that protect our societies and each other.

Today in 2024, it seems clear we are in a no man's land of environmental collapse and economic greed. Even leaving aside the risks of future transmissible pathogens like the 'pandemic,' we see an ongoing breakdown of, disrespect for, or attack on essential services and institutions at all levels of society.

3. Closure

How does one, as a senior continually faced with the realities of aging, come to terms with one's personal sadness and grief for our children's future and the need for closure in the face of this looming catastrophe and the utter desecration of our earth? The following is a poem which expresses my perceptions of reality and doubt for humanity, while still praying we may yet have a Gaia moment[5] and rise selflessly to the existential challenges. A small hope to perhaps mitigate my despairs and drive my continuing search for closure.

4. Elegy to Extinction

This elegy to an 'Age of Extinction' is a collage of metaphoric/poetic images seeded by the hypnopompic hallucinations that intrude many of my early morning sleep states.

Human-driven unrelenting climate change catastrophe is inextricably linked to my viewing as a 13-year-old in 1956 of the 'Forbidden Planet' depiction of the EOL 'crash' of an alien civilization. We are being exponentially low balled and green washed from seeing climate warming double every 20 years since 1852, implying we will have 3°C by 2044!

Extinction

In this 'MAD' world of despoiled beauty
With impending climate catastrophe,
Should we as well pervert our grey matter
And our cosmic souls to hell's hereafter.
In servitude, giving false gods our oath,
We can grasp fruits of exponential growth
As bounty to fill our precious pew plates
And occupy our mindless sleepwalking states

As mandarins reduce or redefine
Standards and statutes for our bottom line,
We deny inherent humanity
And betray all rules intentionally.

140

The 'Essential Wildernet' of mirrors,
Distorts our viewing of hidden horrors
Which, enabling truth/lie duplicity,
Stress tests the fabric of democracy.

Care and empathy values become just grists
For deluded paranoid populists.
The world crumbles before our very eyes
As peddlers extract the final bounties
And each like a frenzied and circling shark,
Devour morsels of a plundered ark.
If 'we' all fail to act to stop this trade,
We invite the tipping points to invade.

The world is awash in tainted money
To barter and pillage for more honey.
We are green washed to obscure the plot
By leaders and elites who share the pot,
And by their perversions lead us astray
To greet our 'Extinction' that's now in play.

5. Epilogue

As we now ponder the primacy of our intellectual capacity in the context of the prior extinction of all previous hominids, the collapse of societies and empires and the yet apparent absence of other intelligent life in the universe, does it beg the question 'is it, as the driver for exponential growth combined with nature's inherent drive for survival and dominance, the ultimate self-destructive paradigm?' [6]

---

[1] Timelines in years: Universe: 13.8 billion, Earth: 4.5 billion, Life 3.8: billion, Hominids: 5 million, Humans: 300,000, Civilization: 7,000, Family contact span and Industrial Revolution: 250.

[2] The quote is the last line in the play *Juno and the Paycock* written by Sean O'Casey. It had its debut a century ago on March 3, 1924 at the Abbey Theatre in Dublin in the era of the 'Irish Troubles.'

[3] Robin McKee, Saturday 30 July, 2022, *The Observer*, ' "Soon it will be unrecognizable:" total climate meltdown cannot be stopped says expert.'

[4] William MacAskill, 10 September 2022, *New Scientist*: Comment 'Planning Ahead.'

[5] Pearce Wright and Tim Radford, Wednesday 27 July 2022, *The Guardian*: James Lovelock Obituary 'Scientist, environmentalist, inventor and exponent of the Gaia theory of the Earth as a self-regulating system.'

[6] The movie *Forbidden Planet*, released March 15, 1956, MGM.

SECTION 7
Politics

*I*n Plague Take It, *we tried to show the extent to which the fight against COVID had become politicized, particularly in the United States but also, albeit to a lesser degree, in this country. One key finding was that Grannies were providing an unpaid buffer to help society adapt to the pandemic, without appropriate recognition or reward. Another was that COVID rates were higher and vaccination rates lower in U.S. states won by Donald Trump in the 2020 presidential election and in which there was a Republican governor. A third finding was that COVID rates were far lower in Atlantic Canada, where the pandemic had by and large not become particularly politicized and most people accepted lockdown orders unquestioningly, than in the rest of the country.*

In 'Road to Recovery,' we look more deeply into the role of Grannies and other older women, an examination that seems particularly timely in view of U.S. Vice-Presidential candidate J.D. Vance's recent disparaging remarks about 'post-menopausal women.' [1] *Vance's attitude appears to be that older women are fit only to take care of children once they're of no further use as breeders. In her essay 'Grannies and COVID,' Ann McMillan belies such flip and demeaning assumptions about older women, showing how many of them have continued to participate in the labour force and take on critical roles during COVID. Indeed, one major reason for the current crisis in our healthcare system has been the retirement of many older women from nursing and other healthcare positions to allow them to stay home and help take care of their families. What's both tragic and shameful, McMillan says, is that when grannies who have spent much of their lives caring for others reach the point where they themselves require long-term care, they are warehoused in facilities which provided inadequate care even before COVID.* [2] *The COVID pandemic has, needless to say, done little to improve matters in this department and some long-term care facilities essentially collapsed, leaving their occupants in dire straits. For more perspectives on aging, please see the Long-Term Care Section of this book.*

In Part I of my essay 'The Politics of COVID,' I focus on the question of whether the pandemic is in fact over, as the lifting of most government regulations around COVID would suggest. I also discuss the pandemic's longer-term effects on the healthcare system, including most notably nursing shortages and emergency room (ER) overcrowding and in some cases even ER closures. My conclusion is that despite clear evidence, in the form of hospital admissions and deaths, that the pandemic continues to rage, governments at all levels and of virtually all political stripes appear to have made a near-unanimous decision not to take any further preventive action with respect to COVID. Governments appear to have decided simply to accept the disease as a normal part of life, a phenomenon described by one commentator as 'flu-ifying' the disease. [3]

In Part II of 'The Politics of COVID,' I carry the preceding analysis a step further, with an eye to discovering some rationale for governments' new, non-interventionist policy toward the disease, a prime example of such non-interventionism being the federal government's decision to halt shipments of rapid COVID tests to the provinces early in 2023. On the surface, the federal government's action appears simply stupid and short-sighted. But is there some larger significance to all of this? Could this in fact signify the government's back-door adoption of 'herd immunity,' a strategy that maintains that only by allowing a large majority of its citizens to contract a disease will a country ever defeat that disease? Or is there some other explanation altogether?

I have two reasons for finally rejecting 'herd immunity' as an explanation for governments' new hands-off stance toward COVID. First off, I wouldn't give any Canadian government credit for possessing the philosophical consistency and rigour needed to follow through on such an approach. Secondly, given that adopting 'herd immunity' would almost certainly lead to a large number of deaths of Canada's most vulnerable, such as infants, the disabled, and the elderly in long-term care homes, its overt adoption would be politically unacceptable in Canada. The strongly Darwinian world view underlying 'herd immunity' is not a world view with which most Canadians are prepared to identify.[4] It goes against everything Canadians have been taught to believe about themselves.

Rather, my explanation is what might best be described as 'governance fatigue' among the country's public officials. It is hard work to impose and enforce the strict regulations needed to halt the spread of COVID. The job becomes even harder in the face of harsh criticism and, in the extreme, threats or even physical attacks (symbolized by the attempted kidnapping of Michigan Governor Gretchen Whitmer) by those militantly opposed to COVID regulations and prepared to do anything they can to be free of them.

But in case you thought Canadian governments are simply sitting idle, have no fear. Even as they have to all intents and purposes abandoned the relatively new fight against COVID, they have rejoined a much older battle: that against the Demon Rum. Having for some years had relatively little to say about alcohol, the federal government is now trying to convince Canadians that any alcohol consumption is risky, and that those who drink more than a maximum of two drinks per week are putting themselves at serious risk of brain damage, heart disease, cancer, and much more. This new, neo-prohibitionist policy flies in the face not just of previous Canadian policy, which proposed one or two drinks per day as a safe maximum, but the policies of comparable countries, such as the U.S., U.K., and Australia, whose proposed safe maxima are similar to the previous Canadian standard.

Granted, there does seem to be some scientific basis for the government's changed approach to alcohol.[5] But how big an effect does low regular alcohol consumption (e.g. one or two drinks per day) have when we control for other variables such as smoking, exercise, diet, heredity, and the patient's previous state of health? And is this an immediate problem for our healthcare system? To the extent that low, regular alcohol consumption has an effect at all—and it seems likely that this effect will be very small indeed once we control for all the other variables just mentioned—it will probably show up five, ten, maybe even twenty years down the road. Failure to provide adequate COVID testing or to address the desperate state of Canada's emergency rooms is likely to lead, indeed in the latter instance has already led, to deaths in the here and now. We seem to be dealing with some sort of misplaced priorities here. In effect, we're concerned about putting the gingerbread on the roof before we've fully attended to the state of the foundation.

There's also the matter of the timing of the announcement of the new alcohol standard. Why, after years of saying very little about alcohol, did the government suddenly announce its new standard, just at the time when the emergency room crisis was coming to a head? Is it being too cynical to suggest that this new approach, which as noted earlier doesn't seem to have been proposed anywhere else, is in fact a kind of smokescreen, an attempt to deflect Canadians' attention away from the horrific emergency room crisis and governments' basic abandonment of the fight against COVID? It is also worth noting that this new approach to alcohol is in ironic juxtaposition to governments' generally highly permissive attitude toward the equally addictive vice of gambling, as epitomized by the sports gambling ads one sees practically every time one watches a baseball or hockey game on TV, and marijuana, the bouquet of which has become pervasive across the country since 2017.

Though this topic hasn't attracted as much attention as many other COVID-related ones, it can't be denied that the pandemic has had a significant effect on the political process. This has been particularly true in the U.S., and true to a somewhat lesser degree in Canada. Even before the pandemic, politics in both countries, but particularly in the U.S., had become increasingly polarized. Since the pandemic, this polarization has led to the election of politicians distinguished primarily for the extreme views they hold and the loud, abrasive rhetoric they typically use in enunciating and defending those views. Loyalty to the cult leader—in this case Donald Trump—has become far more important than experience, qualifications, or even respect for the truth and the Constitution.

As Shakespeare has shown us in Macbeth *and so many more of his plays, a lack of integrity and a moral centre combined with boundless ambition is a most heady and dangerous mix indeed. Infectious disease was used for crass political purposes during Trump's first administration. This will almost certainly happen again, perhaps to an even greater extent, during his second administration. Let us consider ourselves forewarned.*

Jon Peirce

---

[1] Including Vance's own mother-in-law, a biology professor.

[2] Estabrooks, Carol A., *et al.* 'The predictable crisis of COVID in Canada's long-term care homes.' *BMJ* 2023, 382, e075148.

[3] Wu, Katherine J. 'Why Are We Still 'Flu-ifying' COVID?' *The Atlantic*, February 28, 2024.

[4] For a most interesting and informative discussion on this issue, see Alan Lennon, 'COVID, Social Responsibility and 'The Next Times,' in *Plague Take It*, pp. 282-286.

COVID-19 and Grannies: An Alibi and a New Start for Long Term Care?
Ann McMillan

Grandmothers are voices of the past and role models of the present. Grandmothers open the doors to the future.
Helen Ketchum

My previous piece, 'Grannies and COVID,'[1] presented an overview of the plight of older women (and men) in the time of COVID-19 as the pandemic roared through society, upsetting our modern way of living. Now, as we move from epidemic to pandemic to endemic, re-examination and update are in order as society seeks a new normal. My earlier piece illustrated the underreported plight of older women in society: out of sight, out of mind. This piece, focusing again on elder women, draws on recently available data and work done in Ontario to specifically assess the issues around long-term care (LTC). In 2020, Ontario provincial funding for LTC was $5.76 billion, which was $201.61 per resident per day, or $73,587.00 per year.[2] Elder women made up 66.2 percent of the residents of LTC facilities in Ontario in 2021-22. The staff, primarily nurses and personal support workers (PSWs) are predominantly women as well.[3] While this is a topic of importance to all Ontarians, it is thus particularly important for women and hence I use 'grannies' to represent all elders.

We begin with a brief update on the world of grandparents, which provides a mirror to reflect the situation of grandmothers in general. We will then look at some initiatives taken in Ontario to study previous pandemics after severe acute respiratory syndrome (SARS) scared the world in 2003. A brief review focuses on LTC starting in about 2016, before COVID, until the first waves of COVID hit in early 2020. This is followed by an examination of what happened in LTC through the waves of COVID-19. The essay concludes with a discussion of where we are today with respect to long-term care and a discussion of the need to move toward a gentler and more civilized society that learns from its mistakes and respects its grannies sufficiently to provide safe and comfortable end of life care for them.

Grannies
Grandmother: A wonderful Mother with lots of practice.
Unknown

When the previous piece was written, it was surprising how little research there was in the literature about elderly women. The January 13, 2023, edition of *The Economist* notes the same lack and takes action to fill it. Diego Alburez-Gutierrez of the Max Planck Institute for Demographic Research in Germany was asked to produce some estimates of numbers and statistics describing grandparents. He worked with UN age and population data along with models of kinship structures in countries to do just that.

Alburez-Gutierrez says '...there are 1.5 billion grandparents in the world, up from 0.5 billion in 1960 (though the further back one goes, the fuzzier the estimates become). As a share of the population, they have risen from 17% to 20%. The ratio of grandparents to children under 15 has skyrocketed from 0.46 in 1960 to 0.8 today.'

By 2050 he projects that there will be 2.1 billion grandparents (making up 22% of humanity), and slightly more grandparents than under-15s. A greater number of grandparents per grandchild will have profound con-- sequences. 'The evidence suggests children do better with grandparental help... which usually, in practice, means from grandmothers. And it will help drive another unfinished social revolution... the movement of women into paid work.'

The proportion of grandparents varies greatly from country to country. So today 'they are 29% of Bulgarians, but only 10% of Burundians. Their average age varies widely, too, from 53 in Uganda to 72 in Japan.'[4]

This thumbnail sketch of grannies indicates that their importance as well as their number is growing in much of the world.

In my previous work in 'Grannies and COVID,' I identified three different groups of older women: those in good health who continue to work at a paid job; those who are self-sufficiently living alone or helping out with their families, sometimes including provision of childcare; and finally, those whose health has deteriorated to the point at which they require assisted living either in their own homes or in a long-term care (LTC) setting.

The three categories remain relevant, with a natural movement along the spectrum as women age. Eventually, those who are employed move toward self-sufficient retirement living. Then there is a progression from independent living toward the need for more care. With advancing age and decreasing capabilities, is movement into long-term care. As the large boomer generation ages, this natural progression towards end of life is taking place in society rather faster than our systems, particularly our health care systems including LTC, are keeping up with.

Grannies in the Work Force

Women grow radical with age. One day an army of gray-haired women may quietly take over the earth.

Gloria Steinem

Many older women were in front-line jobs when COVID-19 hit. Whether they worked in teaching or nursing or as personal support workers (PSWs) in long-term care situations, they took the brunt of the danger from face-to-face exposure to COVID in the workplace. When their societal roles as mothers and caregivers in the home are factored in, they were routinely placed in situations which were frightening and unsafe. This has taken its toll as women, especially nurses, are retiring and leaving their positions in unprecedented numbers. From May 2022 until the fall, Canada lost 34,400 health care workers care due to retirements. Among other things, this has meant that the gains in employment for women over the last decade in Ontario have been wiped out. Women's increasingly early departure from the workplace is, in turn, resulting in a shortage of employees in many sectors across the province, especially in health care. It should be noted that more older women than previously are moving from the ranks of the employed to active participation in the lives of their families. As we will see, the situations they encountered as COVID emerged are factoring into those decisions.[5] If an employee is not provided with the means to avoid COVID-19 exposure in the workplace and hence is exposing their family to the disease, it isn't surprising that that employee will seek to leave the workplace at the earliest opportunity.

It is interesting that, because many of these front-line workers are women, society (at least in Ontario) is only now recognizing the implications of so many of them leaving the work force. While women are suffering largely in silence from the traumatic incidents they have endured in the work place during the pandemic, society has failed either to recognize their enormous contributions to the province's economic well-being or to take responsibility for the pain that these women have experienced in their later years. We will say more about this as the story unfolds.

Grannies helping their Families

Every house needs a grandmother in it.
Louisa May Alcott

The *Economist* article cited above summarizes the role of Grannies nicely:

...grandparents pass on knowledge and traditions and maintain a family's links with the past. More vitally, they help bring up children and free mothers to work outside the home.

Many parents are happier entrusting their children to their grandma than to anyone else... Grandparents love the kids, do not need paying and are often available at short notice. In Mexico, grandmothers help look after nearly 40% of children under six. During an average week in America, 50% of very young children and 35% of primary schoolers see a grandparent.

Numerous studies find that mothers with granny-nannies earn more than they otherwise would. One way to measure this is to

149

observe what happens when a grandmother dies. In Mexico, working mothers who relied on a grandmother but lost her saw their earnings fall by half. This effect even applies, to a lesser extent, in societies such as India, where grandparents often enforce old-fashioned sexist norms. After the death of rural Indian grandmothers, the daughters-in-law who live with them are less likely to work outside the home. In this area, at least, the help mothers-in-law give with childcare and other chores seems to outweigh their demands that daughters-in-law stay home and press their husband's shirts.

Grandparents' care is good for grandchildren, too. In parts of Africa the presence of a grandmother makes it more likely that a child will survive. In the rich world it is unclear whether the presence of grandparents boosts academic scores or social skills, but it certainly doesn't hurt them. Granted, children raised solely by a grandmother do badly, but that is because their parents are presumably dead, in prison or absent for some other reason. Living with her is better than living with a stranger or living in an orphanage.

Care from grandparents does have some disadvantages. Families that rely on it are less likely to move to another city for a better job. So, they often end up earning less than they could have. Also, grandmothers often retire early, or work fewer hours, to make time for their grandchildren. If this is what they choose, fine. But it means that the gains in society from helping mothers into the labour force are partly offset by grandmothers leaving it.[6]

And, of course, aging continues, and grandmothers eventually are beset by physical and mental symptoms which render them in need of care themselves.

Grannies Requiring Care
The best thing about being over 70 is being over 70.
Helen Mirren

Many of those grannies will eventually be placed in a long-term care home. In 2019, before COVID-19 hit, Ontario had 626 of those long-term care (LTC) homes providing accommodation to over 77,000 residents with an occupancy rate of 98%. The average age of residents in 2019 was 83, the same as it had been in 2009.[7]

There were obvious gaps in the system. For example, Ontario Premier Doug Ford took on the commitment to expand the William A. George Extended Care Facility in Sioux Lookout, which had only 21 beds, from Kathleen Wynne's government in June 2018. The promised 76 new beds have not been built even though Sioux Lookout (population 5,800) is a hub for 33 surrounding First Nations, who go there for social services and there are currently about 65 people on the waiting list. 78-year-old Aileen Urquhart has been campaigning with her shovel symbolically indicating that the community is ready for expansion of the facility, to get Ford to honour the commitment. Spokesperson Mark Nesbitt of the Ministry of Long-Term Care stated in the fall of 2023 that the project was in the early stages of development.[8] We will have more to say about this later.

The most common reason for leaving LTC is death. Life expectancy continues to lengthen for Ontario women and is now 82 years at birth. According to Ms. Google, 'Life expectancy for care home residents between 2021 and 2022 ranged from seven years at age group 65 to 69 years, to 2.9 years at age 90 or over for females, and from 6.3 years at age group 65 to 69 years, to 2.2 years at age 90 years and over for males.' These numbers indicate how frail these residents are. Their life expectancy is short even with twenty-four-seven care.

Although the average age of residents in LTC had not increased, by 2019 residents required more assistance and were more cognitively impaired than in the past. Over the years, the number of LTC beds did not increase at the same rate as the number of aged people in Ontario, and hence people with more serious health issues and dementia filled proportionally more of the beds. On average, patients' need for assistance increased substantially between 2009 and 2019 without a corresponding increase in facilities or staff.[9]

The percentage of residents with dementia in LTC homes increased from 56% in 2009 to 64% in 2019. Dementia causes problems with memory, thinking, speaking and even tasks such as drinking and eating. As the condition progresses, residents need more assistance generally, and in 2019 over 85% of residents needed extensive or complete daily assistance including help with eating.

Often, residents are on multi-drug therapies. They require ongoing care and supervision that is not available in their own homes. As the elder population continues to grow, the need for such services will also increase-- as will the waiting times for admission. The wait list in 2019 was over 38,000 individuals and average waiting time was 152 days. Already, more than 48,000 people are waiting for long-term care. The waitlist has doubled over the past 10 years, and it is expected to continue to grow, reaching 50,000 by the end of 2025.[10]

Several measures of patient acuity (the seriousness of their medical conditions) have been developed. LTC facilities use such measures for planning funding needs. For example, a Case Mix Index (CMI) is a measure of the resources required to deal with a group of patients. It is calculated by summing a variety of factors including severity of illness per patient and then dividing by the number of patients. From 2004 to 2009 the provincial CMI increased by 12.2% and from 2009 to 2018 by another 7.6%.[11] Thus, patients increasingly require more resources to receive the same level of care.

The Method for Assigning Priority Levels (MAPLe) methodology assesses applicants for LTC based on the risk of adverse outcomes. The score is out of five where 1 indicates that the patient is self-sufficient and 5 indicates that the patient is significantly impaired according to the Activities of Daily Living (ADL) scale which in turn indicates physical impairment, cognitive impairment, wandering and behavioral problems.[12] The number of applicants with high or very high MAPLe scores was 82% in 2012, 85% in 2018, and 87% in 2019. Once again, the scores indicate that on average, patients are becoming more significantly impaired over time.

There is thus a well-documented trend for residents entering LTC homes to be frailer as the years go by. Since LTC spaces are limited and most homes are full, the patients needing the most care on an urgent basis are those who are admitted. Patients arriving in LTC increasingly have complex health issues requiring ongoing medical care. Because there has not been a commensurate increase in the number of spaces available, nor in the level of care provided, this trend puts added pressure on the system. The staff and facilities developed for relatively healthy elders who required a bit of care are now being challenged to provide complex care to very frail elders with serious medical issues (including dementia), without appropriate modifications to funding, facilities, or regulations around levels of care. This situation will continue to worsen if the availability of appropriately built and staffed facilities does not keep up with the pace of aging in the population.

Learning from the Past

We learn from history that we learn nothing from history.
George Bernard Shaw

Of course, there is always concern that there will be an epidemic. As noted in 'Lessons from History,'[13] epidemics have occurred many times previously, sometimes with disastrous consequences. It is a pattern that when the immediate situation is over, life returns to a new normal amongst the remaining population.

For example, there was a pandemic of Severe Acute Respiratory Syndrome (SARS) in Canada in 2002. After the fact, several SARS-related studies resulted in excellent recommendations:

1. The National Advisory Committee on SARS and Public Health was established to provide a 'third party assessment of current public health efforts and lessons learned for ongoing and future infectious disease control.'[14] The *Naylor Report* was published in October 2003. Led by the Dean of Medicine at the University of Toronto, Dr Andrew Naylor, the Committee's report blamed

a lack of leadership, poor provincial/federal collaboration, and longstanding shortages of funding and staff in the field of public health care for the poor response to SARS. It recommended the establishment of a new national organization to monitor public health, which was imple-mented through the formation of the Public Health Agency of Canada (PHAC) along with a Chief Public Health Officer (CPHO).

2. The Expert Panel on SARS and Infectious Disease Control was asked to 'identify the key lessons learned from [the SARS outbreak] and to provide practical, focused and forward-looking recom-mendations regarding the management and control of infectious diseases and the capacity of Ontario to handle public health emergencies in the future.'[15] The *Walker Report* was published in April 2004.

3. The SARS Commission, led by the Honourable Justice Archie Campbell, published interim reports in April 2004 and April 2005 before the final *SARS Commission Report* in December 2006.[16]

These reports warned that the province's best chance in a future pandemic was to be well prepared ahead of time. The *Naylor Report* called for 'strengthened surveillance programs, and the development of clear protocols for leadership and coordination of future research to identify, characterize, respond to, monitor and learn from new pandemics.' It noted lack of staff for infection prevention and control (IPAC) in hospitals and inadequate liaison between hospitals and public health units about infection control.

The *Walker Report* emphasized that improvements to the province's capacity to address health emergencies would be a 'down payment on the future.' It recommended the establishment of a real-time surveillance framework. This report flagged a problem with having a large proportion of staff that are employed 'casually' especially in long-term care, since they move from facility to facility and can spread disease. The solution is to have a much higher proportion of full-time or regular part-time staff who do not move between facilities. Obviously significantly higher wages are needed for this to happen. A lack of basic infection prevention and control (IPAC) techniques in all health care facilities in the province, including LTC, was also identified, and the report recommended efforts to have more IPAC specialists to service that sector.

While all three reports flagged staffing issues, the *SARS Commission Report* included interviews with Ontario nurses discussing critical shortages and suggesting that wages should relate to the risk health providers take on. The issue of nurses working in multiple locations was flagged. This issue of compensating wage differentials is another gendered issue. It has long been accepted that men should receive higher wages for hazardous work such as construction or firefighting, but the same theory has not been applied, or has been only minimally and sporadically applied, to the types of high-risk work done by females (like nurses and PSWs).

Additionally, all three reports emphasized the importance of maintaining a stockpile of medical supplies for personal protection to support the needs of health care workers, both in hospitals and outside the hospital sector. The Commission Report summarized:

> It is beyond the Commission's mandate to evaluate or monitor these initiatives. The government's efforts to ensure the province will not again be confronted by the same problems that arose during SARS, will be effective only if it dedicates adequate funds and makes a long-term commitment to reform of our public health protection systems. As in most areas of human endeavour, actions speak louder than words. Only time will tell whether the present commitment will be sustained to the extent necessary to protect Ontario adequately against infectious disease.'[17]

After the activity responding to SARS, which mostly focused on hospitals and health care workers because of the way the disease presented itself and spread, the province responded to the reports largely by preparing Ontario's hospitals to deal with a future pandemic. No doubt the hospitals were better prepared as a result, but each report conveyed urgent concerns about the province's health care system as a whole which were not addressed. LTC facilities were thus left vulnerable in their staffing, their IPAC and their access to medical supplies and laboratory testing and data.

Context Setting: Storm Warnings

So, in a curious lurid calm which could not last and yet, it seemed, could not end, the days went by.

Iris Murdoch

The situation just prior to the emergence of COVID-19 is summarized from the report of the Ontario LTC[18] COVID-19 Commission which critically reviewed the situation after SARS as part of its COVID-19 review. This report provides some background both to the changes in the machinery of the Ontario government and to the issues which were clearly uncovered by previous review activities. Its introductory material gives an excellent sense of the situation and culture in which health care managers and practitioners worked pre-COVID.

In 2006 and 2007, in recognition of the ongoing risk of pandemic, the Ministry of Health and Long-Term Care spent $170 million on pandemic preparedness, including $84 million for personal protective equipment (PPE). Detailed pandemic response plans were drafted. The Provincial Infectious Diseases Advisory Committee (PIDAC) was created along with fourteen Regional Infection Control Networks (RICNs) to coordinate infection control across health care facilities. The RICNs had operational challenges due to their small size and were integrated into Public Health Ontario in 2011 and reorganized into seven Regional IPAC Support Teams.

The Ontario Agency for Health Protection and Promotion was created in 2008 to provide the province with laboratory and epidemiological services to support the development of advice. The Ministry of Health and Long-Term Care Emergency Management Unit was also created, which apparently gave Long-Term Care some profile in the portfolio. Some of these organizations, with their initiatives, did carry through to 2020. The Ministry's Emergency Management Unit is now called the Health System Emergency Management Branch. And the PIDAC continues to operate.

The Ontario Agency for Health Protection and Promotion became Public Health Ontario (PHO) in 2011, perhaps partly in response to one of the most prominent recommendations of the SARS Commission Report, and by 2013-14, its base funding was $148 million annually. Unfortunately, the agency's funding was held flat for eight years beginning in 2013, which hampered its ability to provide the LTC sector with critical response services when COVID-19 arrived. Demands for agency resources, for example laboratory testing, increased year over year. In order to make ends meet, the agency reduced its labour force by 130 staff equivalents between 2013 and 2020.[19]

In January 2020, the Agency's infection prevention and control (IPAC) specialists were merged, from the standalone PHO infection and control division into PHO's communicable diseases division. IPAC team morale was damaged and 10 senior staff departed between March and November 2020. They were not replaced due to budget concerns since the agency faced a $25 million budget gap for 2020-21. Threats of further budget cuts caused the Agency's IPAC specialists to play a lower profile role in supporting LTC than they might otherwise have done.

As previously noted, the province had stockpiled emergency health supplies in the wake of SARS but in 2007 and 2008 all unspent funds from the initial $170 million reverted to the government's general revenues and in 2010 regular support for the stockpile ceased. By 2017 80% of the supplies had expired, and by 2019, 90% of the supplies, including N95 masks, had expired and were being destroyed. The result was that when the COVID-19 pandemic began, Ontario did not have a stockpile of personal protective equipment (PPE). The province's overall lack of PPE was made worse by a particularly severe lack of PPE in long-term care facilities.

As for the pandemic plan, the plan that was in place did not provide

155

guidance on how to manage a pandemic in the long-term care sector and was never drilled or simulated. There were warnings that work was required, such as isolation sites needing to be identified and lab networks improved before the next pandemic, but neither was done.

The SARS Commission had identified the importance of having sufficient laboratory facilities in place before a pandemic. An expert panel recommended that the Ministry of Health and Long-Term Care establish a focal point for oversight and leadership of all the province's laboratories. In 2017 this was followed up on by the Auditor General of Ontario, who noted that while such a branch had been established, no effort had been made to consolidate oversight of these laboratories with the other laboratories in the province. It was recommended that the Ministry establish a system to track PHO, hospital and private laboratory testing, determine which types of tests were best performed by each, and adjust funding accordingly. The Auditor General followed up in 2019 and found that little progress had been made. Ontario thus entered the pandemic lacking a well-connected lab system equipped to deal with large numbers of tests.

The SARS Commission had recommended that the *Health Protection and Promotion Act (HPPA)* be amended:

- To ensure that 'emergency planning, preparedness, mitigation, management, recovery, coordination and public health risk communication at the provincial level be put under the direct authority of the Medical Officer of Health.'
- To provide whistleblower protection to healthcare workers.
- To require that the province's emergency plans include compensation packages for people who suffer unfair personal cost due to cooperation with public health measures such as quarantine.

These amendments were not completed with the result that Ontario did not have a support plan in place before the COVID-19 pandemic. The 2017 Auditor General's Report warned that Ontario was not ready for an emergency and that plans needed to be updated and simulated. These warnings were ignored.[20]

Further, there was confusion about 'the plan,' since two different plans were referenced, the Ontario Health Plan for an Influenza Pandemic (OHPIP), and the Ministry of Health and Long-Term Care Emergency Response Plan. Neither of these was up to date, and both lacked important elements of a plan for COVID-19. For example, neither contained a comprehensive communications strategy. Aside from requiring LTC homes to report outbreaks to the Ministry of Health and Long-Term Care, OHPIP was silent on long-term care.

Successive Ontario governments observed and worried through the emergence of H1N1 and Ebola in the years between the SARS outbreak and the COVID-19 pandemic without making the recommended improvements to Ontario's pandemic preparedness. In the case of H1N1, Ontario may have been lucky, since the healthcare system was largely able to perform, and with 128 dead and 1,800 hospitalized, this was a relatively small-scale event.

In 2014, two healthcare workers in Texas contacted Ebola, but it did not come to Ontario. In response, in 2016 at the end of the Ebola scare, Ontario started to revise its approach to such diseases. Work began to update and broaden Ontario's pandemic plan which was based on influenza, focused on hospitals and had not been updated since 2013. The revisions were not complete before COVID-19 hit presumably because of lack of political commitment to the process.

Justice Campbell, in the SARS Commission Report, supported the idea that the Medical Officer of Health should be the authoritative voice in managing pandemic threats. He also promoted the idea of moving quickly from the local to the general: 'Threats to public health may arise suddenly and without warning, overwhelming the capacity of a local health unit and local medical officer of health. It is essential in such cases that central resources and leadership be deployed immediately not only to assist the local unit but also to guard against the spread of disease to the rest of the province.'[21]

Sadly, the political will to protect Ontario citizens was absent and long-term care homes did not figure highly in our collective consciousness. While the government that received the reports of the SARS Commission made progress on the recommendations, less and less was achieved as the years went by.

How Was Grannie Doing in LTC Prior to COVID-19?

Grandmothers are a gift not to be taken lightly.
Nikita Gill

Even before COVID-19 hit, there were serious immediate issues in LTC which were simmering just below the horizon of the public's attention. All was not well in the health care system at large, and there were many documented accounts of poor performance related to LTC settings. Let's look more closely at the state of long-term care pre-COVID specifically related to inspections, nutrition, staffing and expenditures.

Inspections

Truth is confirmed by inspection and delay; falsehood by haste and uncertainty.
Tacitus

The *2015 Annual Report of the Office of the Auditor General of Ontario* provided Chapter 3, Section 3.09, entitled *Long-Term Care Home Quality Inspection Program*, to 'focus on residents' quality of care and quality of life by protecting and safeguarding residents' rights, safety and security as well as ensuring that long-term care homes comply with legislation and regulations.' The program was modified to align with the Long-Term Care Homes Act, 2007, which came into effect on July 1, 2010.

The program had a head office and five regional offices and employed about 200 staff, 150 of whom were inspectors. Inspections of LTC homes could be done at any time without prior notification of the home. During 2014, for example, the Ministry did 2,630 inspections: 590 comprehensive inspections, 810 critical incident inspections, 970 inspections initiated by complaints, and 260 follow-up inspections. Inspections could be followed up with compliance orders in cases where the home was not adhering to standards.

Comprehensive inspections, which address residents' satisfaction and homes' compliance with legislative requirements, were implemented in 2011. The process is two-stage and has 31 inspection protocols, including five mandatory ones: medication, infection prevention and control, residents' council, and family council interviews and dining observation. During such an inspection, the Ministry can also inspect specific complaints, investigate critical incidents, and follow up on compliance orders. Compliance orders may require follow-up inspections.

Critical incidents include things such as 'fire, neglect or abuse, improper care, misuse of residents' money, unlawful conduct, unexpected or sudden death, residents missing for more than three hours, missing residents who return with an injury or adverse change in condition, outbreaks of reportable or communicable diseases, and contamination of drinking water supply.'[22] In these situations, the home must inform the Ministry immediately. In other incidents, such as falls resulting in hospitalization, failures of a home's security or other major systems for more than six hours, missing or unaccounted for controlled substances, or medication errors, the home must inform the Ministry within one business day. In 2013, 15,300 incidents were reported and in 2014 there were over 12,900. Every incident is reviewed by the Ministry to determine whether an inspection is warranted. In 2,013, 1260 critical incidents were inspected and in 2014 there were 2,030.

Complaint inspections are in response to residents, their family members and the public and are received mostly by phone but also in person or by fax or e-mail. The Ministry's centralized intake unit decides whether an inspection is warranted. Complaints that will be inspected are assigned a risk level. High risk cases involve 'alleged improper care, abuse, neglect, unlawful conduct, or retaliation by the home's staff' or anything that places residents at significant risk of serious harm. [23] Alleged violation of the Act that results in moderate harm or risk of harm to a resident is assigned a medium risk while low-risk cases involve minimal harm or risk of harm. The results of the intake unit's deliberations are reported to the complainants.

The Auditor General's Report contained 13 recommendations which were accepted by the Ministry with the intent of actioning them as soon as possible. The recommendations mostly had to do with better defining, analyzing, reporting and harmonizing the process for dealing with inspections and improving priority setting, timeliness and tracking including of follow up inspections. One recommendation for the home to 'Work with the Office of the Fire Marshall, Emergency Management and municipal fire departments to establish a formal protocol to regularly share information with the Ministry on homes' non-compliance with fire safety regulations' is somewhat worrying, since apparently there are homes which do not have automatic sprinklers. My reading of Subsection 9.4.5. of Division B of Regulation 150/13 made under the Fire Protection and Prevention Act, May 25, 2013, is that sprinklers are required, although there may be exceptions. As with many of the rules governing LTC, they are complex and apparently the facilities work to keep the bar very low.

It is worrisome to ponder all the incidents that could occur in these homes-- and apparently do. While it's important to have an inspection system in place, this one seems overly bureaucratic and rule-based to me. The documentation of the inspection results and reporting of these does put some pressure on homes to take them seriously and address them, but somehow the actions taken, consisting of orders of various kinds, seem minor in proportion to the seriousness of some of the inspection results. In cases which are serious, Director's Orders can be given, but this is uncommon. Still, the existence of a relatively robust inspection system is comforting even if it may not always be applied to the letter of the rules.

Food and Nutrition in LTC Homes

Food is an important part of a balanced diet.
                                                        Fran Lebowitz

The inspections discussed in the last section focus on a wide range of incidents. One of the most basic human requirements is nutrition. Let's take a look at the status of nutrition in LTC homes before the arrival of COVID-19.

Nutrition is a key element that can enhance a resident's quality of life in LTC. A regulation under the *Long-Term Care Homes Act, 2007* required that a variety of foods be provided from all food groups as described in Canada's Food Guide. Further, LTC home operators are required to provide adequate nutrients, fiber and energy based on Dietary Reference Intakes established by a scientific body by both the governments of Canada and the United States. A new version of that Food Guide was released in January 2019. Homes went through a period of transition to the new Guide.

Dietitians from Canada's (DC) Ontario Long Term Care Action Group surveyed DC members working in LTC in 2015 to: capture the activities and responsibilities of Registered Dietitians working in Ontario LTC homes, determine the average time spent by Registered Dietitians on these activities, and obtain Registered Dietitians' perspectives on the impact of current staffing on resident care. 150 responses were received to the electronic survey. The *Ontario Long-Term Care Dietitian Survey Report, 2016*, produced the following highlights:

- Almost all respondents (89%) were unable to complete all required responsibilities within the mandated Registered Dietitian staffing time of 30 minutes/resident/month
- Increases in the number of new admissions and frailer, more complex residents contribute to work overload
- Non-clinical responsibilities such as dining room observations and committee roles are also increasing
- 70% of respondents regularly work additional unpaid time to complete more of the required activities
- Timely follow-ups on clinical issues, communication with residents and families, and interprofessional communication are suffering due to insufficient time
- Staff education, quality improvement activities, and other proactive roles are often not completed, in order to meet clinical workload demands[24]
- Over half of the survey respondents state that 45 minutes/resident/month is needed to provide nutrition care in today's LTC environment, and 30% felt that 60 minutes/resident/ month is required. [25]

The pressure of having more patients with more serious needs related to food was translating, unsurprisingly, to pressure on dietitians' time to look after them.

In a similar vein, the *2019 Annual Report of the Office of the Auditor General of Ontario* [26] includes Section 3.05 which is a value for money (VFM) audit entitled 'Food and Nutrition in LTC Homes.' Released on December 4, 2019, just before COVID hit, the report includes a total of 19 recommendations with 31 action items. It was noted in this Report that:

> Not only do families of the residents count on long-term-care homes to care for their vulnerable loved ones, the residents themselves depend on receiving nutritious food to sustain their well-being in a comfortable environment. We observed throughout the audit that residents rarely had family or friends present during mealtimes and relied on personal support workers to provide appropriate food and nutrition.[27]

The provision of Food Services in LTC homes is quality checked by the LTC Homes Quality Inspection Program. As noted in the previous section, four types of unannounced inspections are conducted. The Ministry conducted 1662 inspections in 2018, 329 of which were proactive quality-of-residents' experience inspections. The *Health Protection and Promotion Act* empowers the 35 public health units to inspect any place where food is prepared, stored, or served. Since LTC homes are considered 'high-risk food establishments,' they are inspected a minimum of three times a year.

In this case, the Auditor General's audit objective was:

To assess whether the Ministry of Long-Term Care (Ministry) in conjunction with long-term care homes and public health units, has effective systems and procedures in place to ensure that:
- Food and nutrition services are delivered to residents in long-term care homes in accordance with relevant legislation, regulations and policies;
- Resources are appropriately managed to provide safe and nutritious meals to long-term care home residents; and
- Results on the efficiency and effectiveness of food and nutrition services provided to long-term care home residents are measured and publicly reported.'[28]

The focus was the Ministry, public health units and LTC homes from 2016/17 to 2018/19. A lengthy list of contacts was made, and visits were made to 62 of the 626 homes across 60 municipalities. In addition to detailed work at five homes, unannounced visits were conducted at 54 homes to observe meal service.

One of the ways that shortcomings in the provision of food would become known is through 'critical incidents' related to food in LTC facilities. In Reg 965 of the Public Hospitals Act (PHA), a critical incident is defined as 'any unintended event that occurs when a patient receives treatment in a hospital that results in death, or serious disability, injury or harm to the patient.'[29] Between January 2018 and May 2019, critical incidents were reported to the Ministry by almost all of the LTC homes. A total of 662 incident reports were received. They included:

- 27 cases at 26 homes of unexpected deaths that related to choking or aspiration;
- About 100 cases at 70 homes of abuse, neglect or improper treatment of a resident by home staff related to food that resulted in harm or risk of harm to the resident; for instance, residents were given the wrong diet, force-fed, missed meals or

did not receive staff assistance in eating;

- About 20 cases at 17 homes where the resident was taken to a hospital resulting in a significant change in their health status due to food-related issues such as choking and falls involving low food and drink intake; nine cases at eight homes where drinking water was contaminated; and
- Over 510 cases at 325 homes of gastroenteritis outbreaks.[30]

The Auditor General obtained gastroenteritis outbreak data from five of the 35 public health units. For 84 gastroenteritis outbreaks that occurred in 2018, almost 2,000 residents were affected over the course of 15 days on average; 16 residents died as a result.

The Ministry of Health has a database on avoidable emergency department visits based on data reported by hospitals. In 2018, LTC residents made 1121 emergency department visits that might have been managed or controlled by better eating and drinking. For example, conditions such as dehydration, diabetes, hypertension, and hypoglycemia can be managed by eating and drinking well. According to Dietitians of Canada's February 2019 report on best practices: 'Inadequate fluid intake may lead to increased risk of constipation, falls, longer time for wound healing, acute confusion, decreased kidney function, and increased hospitalizations.'[31]

Thus, the first recommendation of the Auditor General's audit was:

> To provide residents with safe and appropriate food and nutrition services that are in accordance with their plans of care and reduce the risk of food-related harm to residents, we recommend that LTC homes develop ways to ensure that all direct care staff have timely access to the most current plans of care of the residents for food and nutrition before serving food.[32]

To me, as an elder woman, these results are deeply disturbing. It is horrifying to think that direct care staff in an LTC home would not have access to the plan of care of a resident. Who could possibly think that that would work? A resident cannot be fed properly or adequately without such a plan.

Many of the recommendations related to making sure that residents had up-to-date plans in effect which were available to staff. It was also recommended that dietitians be encouraged to go beyond clinical assessments and plans of care to proactively observe residents eating, to attend meetings with health care teams and to provide education on appropriate foods for the residents (for example the importance of food texture). It was recognized that this would demand more dietitian time. Recommendations also included: the development of a transition plan so that homes fully meet the 2019 Canada Food Guide; that homes ensure that food is not stored beyond its best before date and that feeding assistance is being provided in a timely way to residents so that they would eat. The suggestion was made that students or volunteers would be used to assist staff at peak times.

The recommendations covered other areas including modernization of the design of the eating areas, minimizing food waste and increasing value for money through such means as more group purchasing. It was recommended that LTC homes assess compliance with the Ministry of Health's policy on hand hygiene and that performance indicators be developed and applied and that best practices be identified and shared. Finally, it was recommended that all critical incidents be responded to within prescribed timelines.

Personally, I found the results of this audit, which was completed before COVID-19 began, profoundly shocking. The daughters of elder mothers in Ontario were moving their aging moms into LTC facilities expecting that they would have a good standard of care, beyond that that could be provided by the elderly person on their own, and indeed, beyond what the family could provide for them. To discover that Grannie doesn't wash her hands before meals and hence could well die of gastroenteritis would not be an outcome foreseen by the family. There are many other nasty surprises described in this audit.

While there was a variety of issues identified by these audits and reports, it is obvious that many of them are related to the homes being understaffed, well before COVID appeared. It took the Gillese Inquiry to fully document the extent of understaffing.

The Gillese Inquiry
America's health care system is neither healthy, caring, nor a system.
Walter Cronkite

The Public Inquiry into the Safety and Security of Residents in the Long-Term Care Homes System was launched under the leadership of Justice Eileen E. Gillese after the conviction of Elizabeth Wettlaufer of eight counts of first-degree murder of LTC residents. It was established, on August 1, 2017, with the objective of understanding the events which led to the offences. It was entirely independent of COVID, which had not yet appeared.

A Rhodes Scholar (1977), Justice Gillese was appointed to the Ontario Court of Appeal in 2002 after serving as a Superior Court Justice from 1999–2002. Before her judicial appointments, Gillese was Dean and Professor of Law at the University of Western Ontario.

The Inquiry's mandate was 'to inquire into the events which led to the offences committed by Elizabeth Wettlaufer.' Additionally, the Inquiry was charged with investigating the circumstances and contributing factors allowing these events to occur, 'including the effect, if any, of relevant policies, procedures, practices and accountability and oversight mechanisms.[33]

The report, released in 2019, had 91 recommendations, of which 18 related directly to staffing in the LTC sector. Some areas touched by the recommendations are staff training, human resource management, funding, and overall changes to culture. Most pointed was Recommendation 85, which directed the ministry to undertake a staffing study to determine adequate registered staff numbers for long-term care homes.

Recommendation 85 stated:

> The Ministry of Health and Long-Term Care should conduct a study to determine adequate levels of registered staff in long-term care homes on each of the day, evening, and night shifts. The Minister of Health and Long-Term Care should table the study in the legislature by July 31, 2020. If the study shows that additional staffing is required for resident safety, long-term care homes should receive a higher level of funding overall, with the additional funds to be placed in the nursing and personal care envelope.[34]

The results of this follow-up study are discussed later. Justice Gillese said:

> The evidence at the public hearings painted a comprehensive picture of the long-term care system and how it operates. It also made clear that the system—and those who work in it—are under pressure. Long-term care homes are the most regulated area of healthcare in the province. Despite limited resources, the staff in these homes must meet the regulatory dictates and provide care for residents with ever-increasing acuity. Although the long-term care system is strained, it is not broken. The regulatory regime that governs the system, together with those who work in it, provide a solid foundation on which to address the systemic issues identified in this Inquiry.

Meanwhile, others had different opinions about the system's ability to repair itself and make the necessary staffing changes and argued that the point of no return, at least for PSWs, had been passed.

Caring in Crisis: Ontario's Long-Term Care PSW Shortage was released on December 9, 2019, just before the pandemic hit. It was compiled by the Ontario Health Coalition in partnership with UNIFOR, a Canadian general trade union, including the Canadian Auto Workers and Communications, Energy and Paper Workers, and representing PSWs. The report was based on eight round table meetings held across Ontario involving more than 350 participants.[35] The Executive Director of the Health Coalition, Natalie Mehra, stated that the word 'crisis' was used in the report title because of the extremity of a situation in which there were not enough PSWs to provide care so that funded long-term beds could be opened. 'PSWs have taken heavier-care and more complex patients year after year, risking injury and harm, without pay and working conditions that are commensurate to the work. Most of the tools to fix this situation are in the hands of the provincial government which instead of acting urgently to fix the crisis, is actually cutting funding.'[36]

A Better Approach to Long-Term Care in Ontario[37] was released by the Registered Nurses Association of Ontario (RNAO) in 2019, in response to the Gillese Report. The Nurses Association had participated in the Inquiry leading up to the Gillese Report and summarized their concerns most strongly in two areas: first, the funding model, which they presented as severely flawed in that 'there is a financial disincentive to improve patient outcomes' and second, staffing. The RNAO stated that they believed that a larger amount of regulated care would improve resident outcomes. They called for a staffing mix including 20% Registered Nurses (RNs) and Nurse Practitioners (NPs), 25% Registered Practical Nurses (RPNs) and 55% Personal Service Workers (PSWs). They also called for one attending Nurse Practitioner per 120 residents; at least four hours of nursing (NP, RN and RPN) and personal care per resident per day; all regulated staff working to their full scope of practice with assistance from PSWs; and a care model that assigns a primary nurse provider for each resident. The nurses took this position forward into the following staffing study.

It is not clear to me what it would have taken for Justice Gillese to report that the system was broken. Suffice it to say that it was obvious in 2019, before COVID-19 hit, that LTC facilities were significantly understaffed. What was immediately required was an approved urgent plan, supported by adequate financing, to increase that staffing so that Grannie would be able to go to the toilet, wash her hands and be fed adequately by a staff member who received appropriate respect and renumeration for her work.

Canadian Institute of Health Information (CIHI) Health Expense Data

Don't tell me what you value, show me your budget, and I'll tell you what you value

Joe Biden

Because underfunding of the LTC system has been such a significant problem for so long, we now digress slightly from our previous discussion to look briefly at expenditure data. The last pre-COVID days coincided with a Canadian national health care policy stance that demanded more results-oriented management of federal money provided to the provinces and territories. The Canadian Institute of Health Information (CIHI) health expenditure data is of interest here.[38]

The average provincial/territorial spending by age, cost per capita for infants (younger than age one) in 2020 was $14,541.00 compared to the previous reporting period which was $13,352.00, for an increase of 8.9% from the last pre-COVID year to the onset of COVID. Cost per capita for youths (age one to 14) in 2020 was $2,166.00 compared to the previous reporting period which was $1,791.00, for an increase of 20.9%. Cost per capita for those aged 15 to 64 in 2020 was $3,705.00 compared to the previous reporting period which was $3,206.00, for an increase of 15.5%. Cost per capita for seniors (age 65 and older) in 2020 was $12,521.00 compared to the previous reporting period which was $11,953.00, for an increase of 4.8%. While costs to care for seniors are higher than for any other group but newborns, the percentage increase provided as the COVID pandemic began to take its toll was much less than for any other group. This is especially surprising considering the data on the state of LTC as defined by the information summarized here including the Auditor General's Reports, the Gillese Inquiry and the RNAO report. One would have expected the greatest need for additional funding to come from the seniors group.

Federal policy analysis has been done to examine the amounts of funding made available. One important piece of context is that about one third of all health expenditure is incurred by people in their last year of life.[39] Another piece of context is the concern about what the baby boomers were going to do to the costs of the healthcare system as they aged.

While it is tempting to damn the Ford government in Ontario (after all, per capita funding in Ontario was forecast to be $8405.00 for 2024, the lowest in Canada) for the sad situation in long-term care, in fact that situation appears to have been pretty much the same across Canada. 'From 2012 to 2022, the share of health expenditure spent on Canadians aged 65 and older increased slightly from 44.7% to 46.29%. At the same time, the percentage of seniors in the population grew from 14.8% to 18.8%.'[40]

While I could not find exactly parallel numbers to the federal ones for Ontario for the comparable time, I did find data for 2022.[41] For babies less than a year old, Ontario provincial health care spending per capita was $14,566.00, dropping to numbers between $1,827.00 and $5,487.00 for people between 1 and 64 years of age. For those 65-69 the provincial care spending per capita was $7,475.00, for those 70-74 it was $9,388.00, for those 75-79 it was $11,945.00, for those 80-84 it was $15,855.00, for those 85-89 it was $24,503.00 and for those 90 and over it was $29,639.00. Thus, costs for the tiny relative number of very elderly are significantly higher than those for any other age group. However, it is clear that a significant number of these may be in their last year of life, so the costs are not representative of ongoing care.

As noted earlier, in Ontario, LTC facilities were already stretched to the breaking point in 2019. Their residents were increasingly incapacitated. The facilities were full, understaffed, and failing to maintain standards of minimum care such as providing safe and appropriate nutrition to residents. LTC staff and facilities were expected to continue to provide care without the required increase in resources. A comparison of LTC in B.C. and Ontario indicated that B.C. LTC residents received an average of 3.24 hours of care compared to 2.71 in Ontario.[42]

An additional factor is worth considering. 58% of LTC facilities in Ontario are managed 'for profit'. 'Existing evidence suggests that, on average, for-profit homes deliver inferior care across a variety of process and outcome measures. A preliminary retrospective cohort study of LTC homes in Ontario found that for-profit status was associated with the extent of COVID-19 outbreaks and number of resident deaths. The relation between profit status and outcomes is complex and mediated or confounded by several factors including staff unionization, chain ownership and availability of personal protective equipment (PPE). For example, several reports have documented that for-profit homes pay lower wages, have lower staffing levels, hire more part-time and casual workers and have more turnover than nonprofit homes.'[43]

In summary, the situation in LTC homes left much to be desired in the years after SARS. The care of increasingly vulnerable elderly residents was documented to be a factor in their decline, injury and death. Many recommendations were made over that period as to how to improve their standard of care and their readiness for a pandemic. Sadly, these were not implemented and some of the homes collapsed under the onslaught of COVID-19.

And Then Came COVID-19: How Bad Was It?

There is a tomorrow after a disaster, and it's sometimes hard to remember that in the midst of it.

Sheri Fink

Canada's Long-Term Care facilities were particularly hard hit by COVID-19. In fact, the Case Fatality Rate at first was the worst of all Organization for Economic Cooperation and Development (OECD) countries:

> While Canada's overall COVID-19 mortality rate was relatively low compared with the rates in other OECD countries, it had the highest proportion of deaths occurring in long-term care. LTC residents accounted for 81% of all reported COVID-19 deaths in Canada, compared with an average of 38% in other OECD countries (ranging from less than 10% in Slovenia and Hungary to 66% in Spain).[44]

167

Ontario's first LTC COVID-19 outbreak was declared on March 16, 2020, with the first death recorded on March 23. There were 140 deaths by April 11, and 516 deaths by April 22. In the first wave, 30% of infected LTC residents died.[45]

On March 20, the Assistant Deputy Minister of Long-Term Care announced amendments to the *Long-Term Care Homes Act* to address staffing shortages. Two days later 'Directive #3' was issued by the Chief Medical Officer of Health to deal with the long-term care sector. It did not require LTC staff to take any sort of PPE precautions when dealing with suspected or confirmed COVID-19 cases. In general, Ontario's COVID actions lagged those of other provinces, especially British Columbia:

> British Columbia began offering infection prevention and control support (in the form of 'SWAT teams') to its long-term care homes on March 7; this was a crucial resource that Ontario did not begin offering until more than a month later. British Columbia also recommended universal masking in its long-term care homes on March 25, while Ontario did not order universal masking until two weeks later.[46]

Meanwhile, the province engaged McKinsey & Company to help organize a government-wide response to COVID-19 for a fee of $1.5 million. They provided a proposed response structure to the government on April 24. By then, more than 127 LTC homes were in outbreak.[47] 'At the top of Ontario's pandemic response hierarchy is the "Central Co-ordination Table," which is co-chaired by two political appointees: the government's cabinet secretary and the premier's chief of staff. The table doesn't include any key public health officials, …such as chief medical officer of health Dr David Williams or representatives of Public Health Ontario,' stated Bonnie Lysyk, Ontario's Auditor General. When time was of the essence, the proposed mechanism necessitated that scientific experts convince political leaders that actions above and beyond the norm were essential. It is worth noting that McKinsey & Company were also awarded $3.2 million to develop the province's recovery plan at a time when their operations worldwide were being questioned.[48]

In April, LTC staffing largely collapsed at numerous facilities. The situation had become increasingly dire, due to the lack of sufficient resources in the homes, agencies or hospitals to stabilize their operations. The province requested military assistance, but it took 12 days for deployment to occur. This delay was tragic. In one facility, '26 residents died due to dehydration prior to the arrival of the CAF team due to the lack of staff to care for them. They died when all they needed was "water and a wipe down".'[49] This horrific incident was widely reported in the press.[50,51]

On April 24, 2020, the Canadian Armed Forces Joint Task Force

(Central, (JTFC)) received a request from Ontario to manage the situation in five LTC facilities: Eatonville Care Centre, Hawthorne Place Care Centre, Orchard Villa, Altamount, and Holland Christian Grace Manor. Brigadier General C.J.J. Mialkowski reported on the situation that was found in these homes in *Op Laser – JTFC Observations in Long Term Care Facilities in Ontario,* May 14, 2020. He said: 'JTFC has employed Augmented Civilian Care (ACC) teams, since 28 Apr 20, in five Province of Ontario-prioritized Long-Term Care Facilities (LTCF) that were in urgent and immediate need of personnel to provide humanitarian relief and medical support.' He goes on 'With the benefit of two weeks of observation, CAF ACC have identified a number of medical, professional and technical issues present at the five LTCF.'[52]

The shocking observations centered around the lack of effective management of the situation and lack of staff, with residents living four to a room, some sick and some well, COVID-19 positive patients wandering freely, staff not using PPE correctly, a general lack of attention to cleanliness and housekeeping, supplies under lock and key to reduce costs, forceful handling or neglect of patients by staff, and a general culture of fear about using supplies because they cost money.

On May 12, 2020, the *Emergency Management and Civil Protection Act* was modified to allow mandatory management orders in cases of critical outbreak. On May 25, 2020, two hospitals were appointed to manage two LTC homes for 90 days, and by December 2020, seven such orders had been issued.

On June 29, 2020, a Statement of Claim was filed in the Ontario Superior Court of Justice on behalf of Simon Nisbet as litigation guardian of Doreen Nisbet against the Government of Ontario requesting 'an aggregate assessment of damages in the amount of $500,000,000.00 for: (i) negligence; (ii) breach of fiduciary duty; and (iii) breaches of sections 7 and 15 of the Canadian Charter of Rights and Freedoms.' The charge is that 'The Defendant Ontario has failed to adequately regulate and oversee long-term care (LTC) homes in Ontario, resulting in widespread and avoidable illness, suffering and death among residents due to COVID-19.' While several lawsuits have been filed against private LTC home operators, just this one suit, now a class action suit, has been filed targeting the provincial government for its lack of supervision.

Apparently, when Orchard Villa, the home where Doreen resided, was locked down on March 16, 2020, her sons continued to visit her, but now interacted through the window, growing increasingly concerned about her condition. On April 22, the home phoned and told Simon, one son, that she had tested positive for COVID-19. In early May, as her condition worsened, Simon called Lakeridge Health, the hospital that took over the home's response to the outbreak and got an ambulance to take his mother to Ajax Pickering Hospital. She survived but with kidney damage.[53]

'The Province, in its statement of defence, ...said it should not be held legally or financially responsible because there is no long-term care "system" it controls, and because it does not "act as a guarantor of [long-term care] residents' health or safety." It says that licensed operators, some for-profit, others run by municipalities or non-profits, are responsible for ensuring homes are safe and secure for residents.'[54]

We will have more to say about this case later. However, it raised another issue. Apparently, from March to October 2020, while 81.4% of community members experiencing severe COVID-19 symptoms were sent to hospital, only 22.4% of LTC home residents were. Dr Nathan Stall, a geriatric specialist who is studying this, is upset that the lowest number of transfers, 15.5% in March and April, occurred when the death rate was the highest. He suggests, however, that palliative care can be provided by the LTC facilities and that many LTC residents do not wish to be transferred to hospitals. More ominously, apparently the LTC homes were told not to transfer COVID-19 patients, to avoid overwhelming facilities. For example, Dr Allan Bell of Quinte Health Care sent a letter to several homes stating that 'hospital visits were not recommended because of a lack of treatment available apart from supportive care for frail residents.'[55]

By July 2020, 48% of long-term care homes in Ontario had experienced a COVID-19 outbreak, defined then as a single, laboratory-confirmed, case of COVID-19 in a patient or staff member. The concept of 'critical staff-shortages' was developed. This concept is based on the size of the home, whether all available staffing options have been exhausted, the number of staff off, and vacant shifts, particularly in key roles, the impact on patient care and the immediacy of staffing decline. At one point there were 38 homes experiencing a situation of critical staff shortage.

The greatest number of missing shifts were PCWs, with one home report-ing up to 60 missing shifts daily. Reasons for the large number of employee-missed shifts predictably included:

- Contracted COVID-19 themselves, or failed screening measures without a positive lab test;
- fear and anxiety about contracting COVID-19 at the long-term care home; ...
- misinformation about how COVID-19 spreads;
- concerns about accessing adequate PPE demands and supply;
- timeliness and availability of testing;
- personal factors such as infection status of staff, family member vulnerability, access to childcare, Canada Emergency Response Benefit, burnout.'[56]

The staffing shortage in some homes was so severe that it caused failures in all the components of resident care and the virus spread. Staff workloads often doubled or even quadrupled under unmanageable conditions. In addition, the work demands increased with the needs of managing COVID-19 protocols and very sick residents.

Ontario's Long-Term Care COVID-19 Commission, launched on July 29, 2020, was, like the Severe Acute Respiratory Syndrome (SARS) Commission previously discussed, created pursuant to section 78 of the *Health Protection and Promotion Act (HPPA)*, which allows the Minister of Health to call for an investigation into 'the causes of any disease or mortality in any part of Ontario.'[57] This Commission provided a comprehensive overview of the pandemic in Ontario, into 2020, as summarized here. It included a look at the SARS Commission Report and reached the disturbing conclusion that almost none of that Commission's excellent work had been implemented.

For example, as the SARS Commission had pointed out, infection prevention and control (IPAC) is important in preventing the spread of infection. Many LTC facilities did not have the knowledge, experience or resources to implement effective IPAC practices. With staff who were seriously overworked, even basic cleaning practices suffered.

Ontario's LTC COVID-19 Commission also summarized the state of the Ontario health care system at the time. There had been significant changes to Ontario's health system in 2019. Ontario Health had been created and the Ministry of Health and Long-Term Care had been separated into two Ministries. Cuts to Public Health Ontario compounded the lack of clarity as to how the pieces should work together in an emergency.

The SARS Commission had recommended that the Medical Officer of Health be in charge of 'medical decisions, medical advice and public communication'[58] and that the Commissioner of Emergency Management be in charge of all other matters. However, when the pandemic hit, the province created a new structure in which neither had clear authority. As already noted, on February 28, 2020, the Ministry of Health established a Health Command Table chaired by the Deputy Minister of Health. Other tables of stakeholders and experts were formed to support this table, but there was none devoted to LTC. It wasn't until April 1, 2020, that a LTC Table was created, further illustrating the sector's lack of priority for the government. [59]

Vaccination – A Positive Aside

Fear not, get your shot.

Abhijit Naskar

The introduction of COVID vaccines would, in time, help relieve the situation in Ontario's LTC homes. But it wasn't until December 2020 that Ontario's COVID-19 vaccine rollout began. LTC residents and staff were identified as priority populations to receive the vaccine. LTC home staff started receiving

171

vaccinations in clinics starting December 14. By February 23, 2021, 55% of them had been vaccinated. As for LTC home residents, they were offered at least a first dose between December 23, 2020, and February 23, 2021. At that point, 92% or over 64,000 LTC residents had received at least one dose and 46,500 had received two.

The rollout of the vaccine substantially reduced COVID-19 infections, hospitalizations and deaths in both residents and staff, according to Ontario's Science Advisory Table:

> As of February 23, 2021, COVID-19 vaccination in LTC homes had prevented an estimated 2079 SARS-CoV-2 infections, 249 COVID-19 hospitalizations, and 615 COVID-19 deaths in residents and an estimated 330 SARS-CoV-2 infections, and 8 COVID-19 hospitalizations and 1 COVID-19 death in HCWs [health care workers]... The estimated relative reduction in COVID-19 mortality in LTC residents was 96% after 8 weeks.[60]

Vaccination of residents and staff in LTC allowed existing staff and facilities to finally gain the upper hand on the pandemic. That being said, community spread was in full swing and isolating LTC homes from that spread proved to be extremely difficult.

The Next Wave

Do not go gentle into that good night… Rage, rage against the dying of the light.
Dylan Thomas

While on May 20, 2020, there were about 2,458 residents' cases of COVID-19 and 1,564 staff cases in LTC homes, there were only 241 resident cases and 347 staff cases by June 20. This large reduction corresponded to a large reduction in community cases as well. During the late spring, homes—working with hospitals, local public health units (PHUs), Public Health Ontario and the province—managed to get outbreaks under control.'[61] The lull gave time to prepare LTC for a second wave and to allow the Ministry of Long-Term Care to build a fall preparedness plan. The Ministry heard from key partners, including hospitals, public health, other ministries and LTC sector groups. Three main areas of focus were identified: partnerships with hospitals, IPAC, and staffing. The government committed almost $540 M in new investments to support the incremental costs of staffing, protective equipment and other prevention measures. They rolled out 'Ontario's Action Plan: Protect, Support, Recover.'

In spite of these new investments in the LTC system, the second wave, from September 1, 2020, to March 14, 2021, resulted in more deaths in LTCs than the first, because there were more cases. However, the mortality rate dropped from 33% to 21% between the two waves due to numerous factors, including the arrival of vaccines. Why didn't the mortality rate drop even more than it did? The increase in community spread of the disease, which we discussed earlier, is the likeliest culprit. In support of that conclusion, the Science Table brought forward evidence that 'When daily active COVID-19 community cases are 2.3 per 100,000 or more there is a 75% chance of an LTC home outbreak occurring 5 days later.'[62]

The LTC homes had completed self-assessments which were provided to the Ontario Health regional offices, which in turn provided assessments of homes in their region to the Ministry. There was, however, no Ministry follow-up with the homes. The assessments were not provided to the public health units, the partnered hospital or the Ministry's inspectors[63]. In one case, information about a home that the Ontario Health regional office had identified as a concern was not shared. Close to 80 resident and staff cases occurred in the second wave in that home, and about 30% of the affected residents died of COVID-19. It appears that the government took the time and effort of the over-stressed homes to collect data but by not using the data, prevented homes from learning the lessons of the first wave.

The effectiveness of the self-assessments was not evaluated (a problem in and of itself), but the second wave COVID-19 outcomes showed that the lessons from the first wave had not been learned and preparedness for a future pandemic had not been achieved. A big part of the issue was that the long-term staffing issues and the state of the facilities could not be addressed in the time available, even though the Commission had repeatedly emph-asized the need for ongoing planning.

The COVID-19 Commission noted that partnerships with hospitals had been largely informal and ad hoc through the first wave, even though in some cases local hospitals took over management of LTC homes. In the case of IPAC, while Public Health Ontario had prepared educational material, it is not clear how or even if it was used. Information about IPAC was not seen to have changed the culture in LTC by the time the second wave hit. Granted, the Ministry paired each home with a hospital and created a hub-and-spoke system through which homes could be assisted with IPAC through hospitals. But this arrangement was not implemented until November 2020. Once again it was too late.

$20 million had been earmarked for hiring infection prevention and control (IPAC) specialists in LTC, and an additional $10 million was ear-marked for IPAC staff training. The $20 million would provide $30,000.00 per home, not enough to hire experts. Also, $61.4 million was allocated for minor capital improvements to support IPAC such as installation of physical barriers. $40 million was allocated to compensate homes impacted by occupancy number changes due to restrictions on three- and four-person bedrooms. More was allocated to support additional staff, to compensate for the deferral of resident co-payment increases, and to provide temporary pandemic pay.

The Commission, by then nearing the end of its mandate, was not provided with details as to how this money was spent. A report from the Ministry to Treasury Board on the first wave showed $110 million was allocated for IPAC and $196 million was spent. How, you ask?

The funding system does not lend itself to speedy analysis and reconciliation. The process is: the Ministry advances funding to homes based on estimates and the home then submits an audited report to the Ministry detailing expenses and revenue. The Ministry reconciles this and provides money to the home or takes money from the home to settle the finances. However, as of July 2023, the Ministry had only fully completed these reconciliations through 2018.[64] A detailed financial analysis is beyond the scope of this essay, but one hopes that eventually these spending issues will be reconciled.

Given that there were existing staffing shortages before COVID-19 began, which were increased with the single-site directive and with the departure of many staff from their positions owing to fear and fatigue, initiatives to increase the levels of staffing could have been expected. However, there were no powerful new incentives to attract workers. It wasn't until February 2021, far too late, that $115 million was announced to train 8,200 new PSWs.

The Commission had a limited time frame and was not able to continue its analysis. But it did take the time to spotlight the best practices and most promising ideas that came forward. Interim recommendations were provided on October 23, 2020, focused on the staffing issue, increased direct resident care and strengthening health sector support and collaboration for LTC homes. Further interim recommendations were forthcoming on December 4, 2020, addressing effective leadership and accountability, the expansion and improvement of performance indicators, and reintroduction of comprehensive annual inspections and improvement of enforcement. The Commission made 85 recommendations in its final report issued on April 30, 2021, under the following general headings:

- pandemic preparedness: precautionary principle; pandemic plans (provincial government and LTC homes); and the provincial pandemic stockpile;
- addressing the aftermath of COVID-19 for residents and staff:
- infection prevention and control;
- strengthening health care system integration;
- improving resident-focused care and quality of life: residents' rights; diversity and inclusion;
- French language services;
- addressing the human resources challenges: urgent need for

skilled staff; accelerate LTC staffing plan implementation; increase number of skilled staff; retain and attract staff; enhance oversight of medical director;

- funding: operational funding; increased investment in care; LTC home development;
- increased accountability and transparency in LTC: public performance indicators and standards;
- comprehensive and transparent compliance and enforcement: compliance; inspections; enforcement;
- Health Protection and Promotion Act investigations: insure public access to public health reports;
- Responding to the Commission's Report.

One of the most telling recommendations is the last one, Recommendation 85: 'The Ministry of Long-Term Care should on the first and third anniversaries of the release of this report, table in the legislature a report describing for the benefit of the stakeholders and the public the extent to which it has implemented the Commission's recommendations.'[65]

I have searched for the follow-up reports, which one would think would be linked in some way to the report itself. There should have been one around April 30, 2022 and I did find that there is, archived on the Ontario provincial website, 'Archived – Long-Term Care COVID-19 Commission Final Report and progress on interim recommendations,' which responds to the recommendations grouped into six sections: Staffing, strengthen healthcare sector relations and collaboration, improve infection prevention and control (IPAC) measures, leadership and accountability in long-term care homes, performance indicators, and inspections. These give an idea of the direction of government programming to follow-up on the recommendations. However, I could find no direct further follow-up on the Commission's recommendations, which were supposed to have been further reported on the third anniversary, which would have been April 20, 2023.

Perhaps the major item to come out of this process was the *Fixing Long-Term Care Act, 2021*, which updated legislation for LTC and which generally follows up on the Commission's recommendations. On December 9, 2021, Ontario's Bill 37, *Providing More Care, Protecting Seniors, and Building More Beds Act, 2021* received royal assent. These policy initiatives will be discussed further in the following pages, but let's step back for a moment.

What Are the Areas that Need to Be Addressed?

The moral test of government is how it treats those who are in the dawn of life, the children; those who are in the twilight of life, the aged; and those in the shadows of life, the sick, the needy and the handicapped.

Hubert H. Humphrey

We have seen that there were plenty of reports pre-COVID-19 that documented serious problems with long-term care and noted that action and funding were urgently required. There have also been waves of follow-up reports looking at the data as well as analyzing the situation. What more, with 20/20 hindsight, could have been done?

The reports indicate that adopting the advice coming out of the SARS Commission analysis and planning ahead for a potential epidemic could have helped and would undoubtedly have saved many lives. Dozens of follow-up reports from COVID-19 say very much the same sorts of things. Addressing three critical areas would have reduced the impact of COVID-19 on LTC facilities immensely:

1. Staffing was simply not adequate to provide the basic care required for a healthy elder population, let alone one which was sicker than in the past, with more complex health issues, now threatened by a deadly pandemic.

2. The culture of care was not conducive to improvement of the situation, in the sense that the staff were not given the respect, the renumeration, or the training consistent with the fundamentally life-altering nature of their jobs. When COVID-19 appeared, staff were expected to perform under conditions which were sometimes impossibly challenging, with inadequate preparation, support or renumeration.

3. Some of the facilities were inadequate both in terms of physical plant and in terms of integration into the overall health system. The physical buildings were, in some cases, too old and badly designed to deliver basic standards of care, never mind support the kinds of isolation and protection required in the midst of a pandemic. This inadequacy was echoed in terms of lack of systems including technology, communications, equipment and supplies to deal with a pandemic.[66]

By the end of 2020, three percent of Canada's COVID cases had been LTC residents, but these had resulted in 43% of Canada's COVID-related deaths. It still remained difficult to maintain any sort of protection through isolation or through distancing in LTC facilities. Timely processes to determine who had COVID as a basis to try to separate infectious from healthy patients were still being developed. Increasingly scarce and stressed staff were struggling to avoid exposure to sick patients. The tough situation in which staff did not have time to toilet Grannie or feed her lunch had (in some facilities) become a situation in which Grannie was isolated for weeks, and not given water to drink or changed or even gotten out of bed.

What were the next steps? The results of the studies indicate an immensely sad situation in which conditions deteriorated even further in a few facilities.

1. The Situation with Respect to Staffing

Recruitment is not a one-time event; it's an ongoing strategy to attract and retain top talent.

Dax Bamania

How did Ontario arrive in such a dire staffing situation in LTC? In February 2020, before COVID-19 fully hit, development of a comprehensive staffing strategy for the LTC sector had begun, following up on the Gillese Report. An external Advisory Group was set up to develop a comprehensive staffing strategy for the LTC sector based on that report's recommendations.

At that time, LTC employed over 100,000 staff across Ontario. In 2018 that figure included over 56,000 full time equivalents providing direct resident care. Personal care workers (PCW's) made up 58% of these; registered nurses made up 25%, while allied health workers made up 12%.[67] The 9700 allied health workers working in LTC in 2018 included dietitians, health care aides, physiotherapists, administrative staff and social workers.

Retention of health workers in LTC was already challenging. Based on data collected before COVID-19, about 25% of PCWs who had more than 2 years of experience left the LTC sector annually. Overall, 50% remained in their jobs 5 years or less and 43% left due to burnout or working short-staffed.

Wages were an issue across the board, being considerably less in this sector than in primary care hospitals. In 2018, 23,701 nurses worked in LTC in Ontario. 62.9% were registered practical nurses, 36.5% were registered nurses, and 0.6% were nurse practitioners. Nurses employed in hospitals made an average of $46.75 an hour, while nurses in home and community care made $36.98 an hour. Meanwhile, average hourly wages for PCWs working in long-term municipal facilities were $25.01 an hour, but PCWs in home and community care received only $17.30 an hour—not much above the Ontario minimum wage of $14.25 per hour in 2020.[68]

Since demand for nurses and PSWs outpaced supply, there was already a clear need to make changes in the profession to attract and retain sufficient staff to even begin to meet the needs of long-term care.

The Long-Term Care Staffing Advisory Group recommended that the number of staff working in long-term care increase and suggested that more funding would be required to achieve that goal. Additionally, along with the nurses (in *A Better Approach to Long-Term Care in Ontario* already discussed), they recommended a minimum daily average of four hours of direct care per resident, more than that provided in any jurisdiction in Canada, and much more than the 2.45 hours provided in Ontario. Finally, the Group concluded that, 'If barriers to optimal staffing are addressed, as recommended in this report, the sector could more consistently deliver safe, quality and resident-centered care.'[69] While the report puts a positive spin on the situation for the future, it was clear that the existing situation was not acceptable in a first-world country, and that changes could not be made instantly to improve the lot of the grannies enjoying their last months of life in care. How fast could such changes be made?

The results of this work fed directly into *Ontario's Long-Term Care Staffing Plan (2021 – 2025), A better place to live, a better place to work,* released in December 2020 after Ontario's epic battle with COVID-19 had begun and too late to do anything but help explain the deaths of thousands.

Meanwhile, in the homes, since staff were the only people with residents when they died, they also had to perform after-death procedures usually done by coroners or funeral home attendants. Examples of such work required included putting deceased residents they had cared for into body bags, tagging their bodies with the necessary identification and transferring them to a waiting hearse. While staff did the best they could, they told the COVID-19 Commission of their extreme feelings of personal and professional helplessness, guilt and regret.[70] Read more about this in Fred Andayi's piece elsewhere in this volume.

It wasn't just the PSWs who were experiencing stress at work even before COVID-19 hit. Nurses were also struggling. To say that the provincial government's wage policies did little to help their situation is to understate things considerably. On November 8, 2019, the government passed Bill 124 to cap the wage increases of Ontario Public Service employees at one percent, effective for a three-year 'moderation period.'[71] During this period, increases to salaries and total compensation, with some exceptions, were to be capped at 1% per year. Nurses were included under this legislation.

Looking back at the data available on the inflation calculator for Ontario,[72] the basket of goods for the Consumer Price Index that would have cost $100 in 2019 would have increased to $108.38 in 2022 for an average inflation rate of 2.72% over the period. Hence, in real terms, the nurses would have lost money with these settlements at a time when they were literally in the front lines of a war with COVID-19. In other words, nurses who risked their lives to work with deathly ill patients were condemned to take an effective cut in pay to do so.

The Ontario Nursing Association (ONA) took the position from the start that this bill interfered with the Charter rights of public sector workers to freely negotiate a collective agreement. The nurses filed a lawsuit and in November 2022, Justice Markus Koehnen, of Ontario's Superior Court of Justice, ruled that Bill 124 breached the Charter and was therefore void. There were reopener clauses which were approved, and hence retroactive wages were sought and granted--but at such a low level that recruitment and retention of nurses in the province continued to be problematic. This dispute between the nurses and the province was part of Ontario's political dynamic over several years, including when COVID hit. Government decisions appeared to be made on the basis of undervaluing the professionalism of the nurses and their contribution to health care in a way that would never happen with doctors. It was symptomatic of a strained working relationship between the political level in Ontario and the health professionals, especially the female ones.

The Ontario Government filed an appeal of Justice Koehnen's decision regarding repeal of Bill 124 in December 2022--hardly a way to restore trust. The repeal had resulted in an increase of nurses' wages from 3% over the three years to 6.75% for the 2022-2023 contract, which cost the government some $900 million. This appeal was heard by the Ontario Court of Appeal in June 2023. Further, in July 2023 an arbitrator increased Ontario nurses' wages by 11% over two years, making them the best paid in Canada.[73] Finally, Bill 124 was repealed on February 23, 2024.[74]

But nurses' wages were not the only contentious issue. There was also the matter of staffing levels. On August 3, 2023, the Ontario Nurses Association (ONA) released a statement entitled: *Ontario's Registered Nurse Levels Fall Again, Still the Lowest in Canada* in response to a CIHI report which reflects the worsening nursing shortage in Canada. That report says that the Registered Nurse to population ratio in Canada had declined from an average of 830 RNs per 100,000 population in 2021 to 825 RNs per 100,000 in 2022. Meanwhile, in Ontario, it declined from 668 RNs per 100,000 in 2021 to 661 RNs per 100,000 in 2022. Ontario Nurses Association President, Erin Ariss, RN, stated that, 'Ontario continues to have the lowest levels of RNs per capita in the country.' Evidently, the province needs 24,809 additional RNs to catch up to the average elsewhere in Canada, never mind provide the kind of support to LTC residents that is needed.

Despite the recent wage increases, nurses won't be flocking to practice in Ontario any time soon. Recruitment and retention form a complex problem, and the government has not been acting in good faith in their steps to resolving it. Nurses are often grannies, too, and they have been retiring in droves, moving from the category of actively employed elder women to living independently or looking after their families. Statistics Canada estimated in 2021 that 32,295 regulated nurse and psychiatric nurse positions were vacant in Canada, with nearly half (46.5%) of vacancies staying open for 90 days or more.[75]

In addition to paid staff, in 2018 3.6 million Canadians reported providing care to their parents or parents-in-law, with another million providing care to a partner. About 13% of this care was provided in settings such as LTC.[76] Thus, when visitor restrictions were placed on family members and loved ones who had often acted as essential caregivers before the pandemic, pressure on staff became much worse. Visitor restrictions were introduced to LTC on March 13, 2020, through guidance from the Ministry of LTC. Essential visitors only were allowed, essential visitors being defined as: 'Those who have a resident who is dying or very ill.'[77] Meanwhile the Chief Medical Officer of Health released Directive #3 on March 22, which recommended that visits between residents and family take place outside. Often due to inclement weather or lock-down conditions residents were reduced to interacting with their family members through a window. Confusion resulted from the Directive, and some residents died without family members with them.

Before COVID-19, family members often made daily visits and helped with feeding, dressing, toileting, and providing companionship. Without this assistance, resident well-being plummeted and added pressure was put on the staff. Residents found themselves alone in their rooms, which was particularly bad for those with dementia and complex medical conditions. Many of them experienced symptoms of confinement syndrome similar to the intense anxiety and sensory deprivation experienced by people in solitary confinement: 'acute deterioration in chronic conditions, dehydration, malnutrition, inadequate pain management and pressure ulcers; loneliness, anxiety, mood disorders, depression and other mental health issues including a reduced sense of purpose, post-traumatic stress disorder and/or suicidal ideation, substance use, cognitive changes including delirium, and responsive behaviour [Responsive behaviour such as aggression, wandering, paranoia, or agitation, is a term commonly used to refer to actions, words or gestures presented by a person with dementia as a way of responding to something negative, frustrating or confusing in their social and physical environment], reduced mobility, fall risk, bladder and/or bowel incontinence, and loss of functional abilities.'[78]

The situation was bad for both staff and the residents, and it set up a perfect storm for family caregivers. They were prohibited from providing comfort and care in the LTC facilities even though they had long been taking the burden off staff who were clearly overwhelmed even before the pandemic. Thousands of potential caregivers were turned away and prevented from seeing their family members, ostensibly in order to control the spread of COVID-19. This situation caused extreme heartache as described in several other pieces in this book. In some cases their family member caught the disease and sometimes died alone. In some cases, their family member died of other causes. In other cases, their family member came through the pandemic physically but with permanent impairment in their physical and mental functioning. Not only were residents' lives changed for the worse, but family members still carry the emotional effects, from false responsibility to toxic guilt, sowing the seeds for a future mental health crisis in Ontario.

If one puts a gender dynamics lens on the situation, it is obvious that most residents of LTC facilities are elderly women, that the nurses and PSWs who take care of them are mostly older women, and that the family members who provide the majority of the care are, you guessed it, predominantly older and female. It doesn't take much of a leap to wonder whether handling of the situation on a political level would not have been more effectively and humanely done if the majority of those affected were men. Perhaps if there had been more women in the Ontario legislature working to address problems at the political level this disconnect would have been less likely to happen.

2. The Situation with Respect to Culture of Care

When empathy is present in a companies [sic] culture, employees feel safe and they bring the fullness of who they are into the company instead of just a piece of themself. And that cultivates trust. And that's good for everyone.
Hendrith Vanlon Smith Jr

Although pay and numbers tell a compelling story, the issue was not as simple as that. For example, it was recognized that even before the pandemic the workplace in LTC facilities was already challenging for staff for a number of reasons, including the emotional toll of work demands and the threat of abuse by residents. Providing end-of-life care is always challenging, as is dealing with elders who have complex medical conditions. Before COVID-19, these workplaces had the second highest rate of injuries resulting in time lost in Ontario. In 2015, these injuries, which represented 27% of total injuries requiring time off in the health care sector, included: musculoskeletal disorders (38%), exposure to contaminants or chemicals (31%), slips, trips and falls (11%), and workplace violence (9%). In addition, the pace of work was demanding and there were not always opportunities to take training and education to support best safety practices, never mind supporting development in the workplace.[79]

Staff in LTC facilities had little preparation for fighting a pandemic such as COVID-19, and the LTC community did not provide needed support either to them, or to the patients they looked after.

2.1 Culture of work for staff

Leadership is not about being in charge. It is about taking care of those in your charge.

Simon Sinek

Ontario's Long-Term Care COVID-19 Commission summarized the findings of the military who had stabilized some of the worst homes. 'Ineffective communication between administrative personnel and staff' was identified as an important factor in those homes that had struggled. Leaders who thought one step ahead and who acknowledged their staff's efforts and sacrifices were most successful. Still, sometimes it was impossible to get information on deaths or sickness of friends and loved ones, let alone on the situation with respect to lockdowns and other measures.

The situation with respect to Ontario's personal protective equipment (PPE) stockpile has already been described. To make matters worse, the rapid spread of COVID-19 increased demand and stressed supply chains so that prices for PPE increased tenfold or more. As had been noted in the work on SARS, China produced much of the current PPE and there was little domestic supply. As had been noted by the Auditor General in 2007, most LRT facilities did not have sufficient inventory.

In the middle of February 2020, Ontario's Chief Medical Officer of Health identified the lack of personal protective equipment (PPE) as a big problem. Ministry of Health personnel worked hard to get PPE, initiating an urgent, non-competitive process on January 28, without established contracts and supply chains. The first distribution of PPE to a LTC home in response to a request was on March 19, 2020, and the first proactive weekly allocation of PPE was on April 11. 'In the wake of SARS, it was recommended that the provincial pandemic stockpile have a four-week supply of 94 million surgical masks ready to be shipped to health care settings in need. On April 2, 2020, the provincial inventory was 1.9 million.' The case represented yet another costly failure to learn from previous experiences.

Since there was no provincial stockpile and PPE was in short supply, LTC facilities were encouraged to implement 'supply stewardship,' i.e. rationing. This directive, on top of staff shortages, left staff concerned for their own safety. Calls went out for volunteer groups to make cloth masks. There was re-sterilization of masks and questions about how often a mask could be used before it had to be changed. All these legitimate concerns took time and attention away from actual care of the residents. In some cases, care workers were wearing garbage bags and pop bottle plastic as PPE to protect themselves from deathly sick and highly contagious patients.

Yet another issue was staff working in more than one LTC facility. At first, staff who worked in more than one LTC facility were likely carrying the virus between sites. The province was slow to have workers limit themselves to one home. In fairness, restricting workers to one site would have made staffing issues more difficult. However, the issue had been identified in the SARS Commission Report in 2004 and could have been addressed well before COVID-19 emerged. On March 19, 2020, Dr Williams, Chief Medical Officer of Health, asked staff to work in only one home. The initial memo was worded in such a way that it did not solve the issue and it was made a directive on March 23, but with the words 'wherever possible' included, which rendered it toothless.

The next step to limit health care workers to working at only one facility was to use an emergency Cabinet order. This, however, required policy analysis and was not passed until April 14, with compliance required by April 22. The resulting order did not include any supporting measures to counter the negative impacts on staffing. It is not known how many part-time employees left as a result. The Emergency order provided no measures for shifting part-time to full-time, no compensation for part-timers who lost hours as a result, and no prohibition against part-time workers getting a second job outside of healthcare.

The Ontario government announced temporary pandemic pay on April 25, 2020. It was in effect from April 24 to August 13. Front-line health care workers across hospitals, retirement homes, LTC homes and other congregate settings were eligible. Additional pandemic pay for PSWs was announced on October 1, 2020 to include $4.00 per hour plus a lump sum bonus of $1,000.00 for those staff who worked 100 hours or more in a designated four-week-period. But by January 13, 2021, 29% of homes reported that they still had not begun paying the funds. The reasons behind this are not clear.[80]

Especially in the case of a pandemic, sick pay encourages workers to stay home when sick. Lack of sick pay was yet another issue worsening the already severe staffing crisis. The current government had amended the *Employment Standards Act* in 2019 with the *Making Ontario Open to Business Act, Bill 47* [81] which removed ten unpaid and two paid personal leave days which were often used as sick days by employees and illustrates the government's basic philosophy towards workers rather well. Thus, since many LTC workers are employed part-time, casually, and without benefits, these workers could not take time off work without losing wages. Lacking sick pay, many people were forced to report to work sick because they couldn't afford to stay home.

The COVID-19 Commission, among others, supported efforts that would allow staff to take time off while sick. In Ontario, the *Employment Standards Act* of 2000 was revised again to provide two types of infectious disease emergency leave, paid and unpaid.[82] The only infectious disease for which these provisions apply is COVID-19. The Act covers not only the worker who is sick but also a worker's provision of care to their dependents. The ESA was amended to include unpaid infectious disease emergency leave on March 19, 2020, and the leave entitlements for COVID-19 are retroactive to January 25, 2020, and have no end date. An employee is entitled to take this unpaid leave so long as certain conditions are met. The ESA was amended to include up to three days total of paid infectious disease emergency leave on April 19, 2021, and the provision ended on March 31, 2021.

According to the Canadian Federation of Independent Business,[83] in Ontario under the Employment Standards Act (ESA), most employees who have worked for an employer for at least two consecutive weeks may take up to three days of unpaid job-protected sick leave each calendar year due to a personal illness, injury or medical emergency. As of October 28, 2024, employers are not allowed to ask employees for a sick note from a 'qualified health practitioner' (defined as a physician, registered nurse or psychologist) as evidence of entitlement to these three unpaid sick days. Businesses that voluntarily offer paid sick days are exempt from the new sick notes policy. This is an area that seems to be continuing to evolve.

2.2 Follow-up on Food

Let food be thy medicine and medicine be thy food.

Hippocrates

Remember the Value for Money Audit, Section 3.05 on Food and Nutrition in Long-Term Care Homes discussed in the Food and Nutrition Section and completed before COVID-19 hit? A follow-up on the Auditor General's report was done in 2021.[84]

> The Ministry of Long-Term Care (Ministry), AdvantAge Ontario and the Ontario Long Term Care Association (sector associations), as of October 28, 2021, have fully implemented 10% of actions we recommended in our 2019 Annual Report and were in the process of implementing an additional 26% of the recommendations. The Ministry and the long-term care sector made little progress on 64%.
>
> The Ministry indicated that it was taking extensive measures to mitigate risk imposed by the COVID-19 pandemic and was engaged in assisting homes to manage outbreaks for much of the period between the 2019 audit report and the time of our follow-up. The Ministry indicated that, as the tasks associated with COVID-19 subside and the human resource issues are addressed, it will resume work on addressing audit recommendations.
>
> The status of actions taken on each of our recommendations is described in this report. Many timelines provided for implementation are for two years and beyond, with minimal short-term actions being taken or planned to address the situation for current residents in a timelier manner. Some time lines are unreasonable given the urgency of care required for current residents.[85]

Apparently, when COVID-19 hit, work on implementation of the recommendations essentially stopped for reasons that are not explored in any detail in the report. Remember, we are not talking about not getting appropriate desserts here, we are talking about lack of attention to feeding people to the extent that numerous critical incidents had taken place, resulting in harm and even death. There had been little progress in solving the serious issues around food and nutrition in LTC facilities in over a year, and COVID-19 was directly blamed for that.

In general, it is clear that LTC residents were out-of-sight, out-of-mind in Ontario until things got unbelievably bad. The courageous staff who tried to care for them were forced to work in a profoundly unsupportive climate where their concerns and even lives were clearly disrespected. Only a few half-hearted attempts were made to address the issues, and COVID-19 was blamed for the poor work culture that had long been the norm in the sector, even before the pandemic.

3. Adequacy of Facilities
Where you live should not determine whether you live, or whether you die.
Bono

At first, there was no ability to quickly detect the virus through testing, and hence it was impossible to contain. In many cases, in older LTC homes with design standards from the 1970's, there were ward-style accommodations with four people to a room and sometimes eight sharing a bathroom. Note that updated standards introduced in 2015 require a washroom in all resident bedrooms, but that older homes still do not have them.

In such an overcrowded situation, spread is difficult to prevent, especially when there is no way to social distance and no place to isolate a sick patient or to separate the well from the unwell.[86] Dementia patients' tendency to wander makes the situation even more dangerous.

Resident cohorting to separate ill patients from well ones, 'decanting'[87] of sick residents to another facility to prevent them from spreading the disease, and proper use of surveillance to identify cases early are all important strategies for managing spread. In older facilities which were full and had multiple people to a room, there was simply no way to take these steps.

Worse yet, Ontario's laboratory system was unprepared for the pandemic. It often took seven to 10 days to receive test results. This delay made it even more difficult to identify infected residents in time to take action to prevent spread of the disease.

Aggravating the situation still further, many LTC homes could not access Public Heath Ontario's Online Laboratory System (OLIS) and hence could not receive electronic test results. Despite OLIS having been a standard feature in most health care settings for almost 30 years, it was still being rolled out in LTC facilities when the pandemic began. I was not able to find a reason for this and suspect that the LTC homes were not modernizing their internet technology any faster than they were modernizing their bathrooms, their sprinkler systems or their air conditioning for lack of money, commitment and qualified people to do the transition. Certainly, the for-profit homes had no reason to invest in upgrades. Results were often sent by fax or mail, and slow delivery made it impossible for speedy decisions to be made about the need to isolate staff or residents to stop the spread of infection.

The province moved to combine testing in Public Health Ontario Labs, hospital labs and private labs, but LTC facilities had limited testing available. At first, the primary focus was on international travelers (since community spread was not immediately acknowledged to be a danger), and LTC residents, staff and visitors were not considered a priority. By February 26, 2020, public health labs had only tested 629 samples in total. It was late March before a formal Provincial Diagnostic Network was developed to coordinate testing among participating labs. This impacted the spread of COVID-19 within LTC homes in outbreak. If Ontario had been prepared to ramp up laboratory capacity quickly to respond to the situation the outcome for some homes might have been different.

To make matters even worse, there was a backlog of testing due to shortages of the swabs needed for sample collection and the reagents needed for the tests. The Testing Strategy Expert Panel was not formed until April 5, 2020, at which time co-chair Jennie Johnstone suggested that widespread asymptomatic testing should not be pursued as resources would not support its sustainability. The province announced the 'Protecting Ontarians through Enhanced Testing' plan on May 29, 2020 when capacity was strained at about 24,000 samples per day.[88] Surveillance test policies were in place for LTC by this time, but if delivery of positive test results was delayed, the homes lost days of response time.

It is clear that if the three long-standing factors of staffing, culture, and facilities had been aggressively addressed before COVID-19 arrived, as recommended by many evaluations and reports, Ontario's losses would have been less and we would have survived the pandemic in better shape. Let's leave this depressing tale here and jump forward in time to look at some things that have happened since the initial onset of the pandemic.

Aftermath: Continuing Horrors and Next Steps

It's easy to do right when everything goes right. But let everything go wrong, and see how difficult it becomes.

Ann Aguirre

We have seen how the LTC system, teetering on the brink of failure even before COVID-19, lurched and stalled when COVID-19 appeared. To me, it does matter that the system had been allowed to deteriorate to this point, even if there were strong and decisive actions being taken as the pandemic became more manageable. That said, the horrific situation in LTC did put pressure for change on the Ontario government, albeit change that came too late for the thousands of early COVID victims and their families. We have seen that the *Long-Term Care Homes Act, 2007* was not pushing facilities to modernize their infrastructure, their systems or their levels of care. There had been repeated calls for more funding especially for staffing to provide the basics to support change. Finally, the Ontario government faced up to making changes, but were they enough or were they made for purely political reasons? The first step was to replace the *Long-Term Care Homes Act*.

Ontario's Bill 37, Providing More Care, Protecting our Seniors, and Building More Beds Act

We repeat what we don't repair.
Christine Langley-Obaugh

Ontario's Bill 37 of 2021 resulted in the repeal of the *Long-Term Care Homes Act, 2007* and its replacement with the *Fixing Long-Term Care Act* (FLTCA), 2021 which received Royal Assent on December 9, 2021 and came into effect on April 11, 2022.[89] Key areas of change in the new act which responded to lessons learned from COVID-19 were: staffing and care, protecting residents and expanding their rights, and making sure residents would be living in modern, safe and comfortable homes. A system target was established that by March 31, 2025, residents would receive an average of four hours of direct care daily from PSWs, registered nurses or registered practical nurses, a recommendation that had by then been on the books for years.

Many aspects of this Act target problems that had been brought forward in dozens of reports before COVID-19 appeared. Residents now have a 'Bill of Rights,' which must be posted in all LTC facilities. The new law defines 'caregiver' and seeks to ensure that residents have access to their essential caregivers. There is a visitor policy that respects the residents' bill of rights and palliative care options that must consider the residents' physical, emotional, psychological, social and spiritual needs. As of July 11, 2022, residents have food options that are targeted at meeting their needs and preferences with registered dieticians evaluating menus. Residents' Council and the Administrator or their designate will define times for serving meals and snacks.

Ontario's Bill 7

Instead of fixing things, of making changes, of making improvements, all they' done has been to break them in reverse.
Holly Bodger

Bill 7, the More Beds, Better Care Act, 2022, has been enacted as Chapter 16 of the Statutes of Ontario. It's important to bear in mind that LTC is just one facet of the complex system that is health care in Ontario. As already noted, all of it was under pressure before COVID-19 hit,[90] and the pandemic did not, to say the very least, reduce the tensions in the system. In many hospitals there are still lengthy waiting times in Emergency Wards, especially for patients who need to be admitted since the beds are typically full. Closures in Emergency Rooms especially at night and on weekends continue at a number of Ontario hospitals. Also, many Ontario hospitals continue to see patient loads that push the hospitals over 100% occupancy.[91]

More efficient management of patient discharge offers an option for increasing the flow-through rates and thus reducing wait times. For example, attending clinicians can designate patients as requiring an alternate level of care (ALC), which means their progress may have reached a plateau and their care goals have been met, but the patient requires supportive care such as that provided in LTC. As of August 17, 2022, there were about 5930 ALC patients in Ontario hospitals. In parallel, in May 2021, there were about 38,000 people on the waiting list for LTC, with a median wait time of 171 days.[92]

The *Fixing Long-Term Care Act, 2021*, provided a legal framework which allows ALC patients to apply to a placement coordinator for admission to homes of their choice and asks them to choose and rank up to five LTC homes. Patient consent must be informed, voluntary, not obtained through misrepresentation or fraud, and be related to admission. A patient refusing a valid admission can be charged an uninsured fee to remain in the hospital.

The *More Beds, Better Care Act, Bill 7,* came into effect September 21, 2022. This new provision authorizes certain actions to be carried out without the consent of these patients. The actions include having a placement co-ordinator determine the patient's eligibility for a long-term care home, select a home and authorize the patient's admission to the home. The actions also include having assessments conducted for the purpose of determining a patient's eligibility, requiring the licensee to admit the patient to the home when certain conditions have been met and allowing the collection, use and disclosure of personal health information, if it is necessary to carry out the actions.

Certain limitations apply. The actions to choose a LTC home and move the patient into it cannot be performed without first making 'reasonable efforts' (which are not defined) to obtain the patient's consent. If consent is later provided by ALC patients, the parts of the process that have been consented to must be conducted in accordance with sections 49 to 54 of the Act, subject to the regulations. The section does not authorize the use of restraints in order to carry out the actions or the physical transfer of an ALC patient to a long-term care home without their consent.

Once a placement coordinator authorizes admission into an LTC home, and the clinician discharges the patient, the ALC patient may either move into the home or face a daily charge of $400.00 (as of November 20, 2022) if they continue to remain in hospital. The LTC home may be as far away as 150 km from the patient's home community in northern Ontario, and 70 km in southern Ontario. ALC patients and families must take on the implementation burden, including making arrangements to visit their loved one. If the LTC home is far away there is a considerable investment in time and money for family to visit, and the resident (who may suffer from dementia) is uprooted from all the things that are familiar to them.

Criticism includes the accusation of fundamental discrimination against the elderly as well as the government's decision to bypass public hearings to pass the Bill quickly.[93] The Ontario Health Coalition (OHC) and the Advocacy Centre for the Elderly (ACE) have filed with the Ontario Superior Court of Justice to have key provisions of the More Beds, Better Care Act, and its related regulations and practices (Bill 7), declared invalid and of no force and effect.[94] Recently, a decision was reached. 'The Advocacy Centre for the Elderly (ACE) and the Ontario Health Coalition are deeply disappointed that the Ontario Superior Court of Justice has upheld the constitutionality of the *More Beds, Better Care Act* (Bill 7) in its decision issued on January 20, 2025.'[95]

To me, this Bill does not seem well aligned with the kind of patient-centered care that the *Fixing Long-Term Care Act, 2021* had led us to expect. Being moved without your consent ranks pretty high-up on an older person's list of nightmare-causing fears and is generally not regarded as a useful way to build trust. Given that many elders have no family or friends to engage as caregivers and are essentially alone, often suffering from some form of dementia, allowing forced moves without patients' consent seems to have huge potential for causing misery and for what? A few bucks? While greater efficiency in patient flow may be desirable, the root cause of bed shortages at all levels of the health care system seems to me to be that there aren't enough beds or staff to adequately service them. While it is certainly desirable to manage the facilities we have effectively, many reports have assured us that there aren't enough facilities. Bill 7 may allow for streamlining the discharge process into LTC, but it cannot magically increase the resources available. It is at best a stopgap measure.

The probability of success of the initiatives underway under the *Fixing Long-Term Care Act* is difficult to assess. The aim of increasing the hours of patient care by professionals in LTC settings is a good one, but this goal is presented in an intensely bureaucratic manner. One would hope that some patients would receive essentially full-time attention if there were a crisis in their care. Establishing more rules and calling it quality is short-sighted. There should, of course, be basic rules in place and it is shocking that this backstop of a reasonable average number of hours of care evidently hasn't been there, but rules will not ensure the kind of quality care Ontarians want for their elders. While a change toward a gentler, more humane culture is required, the issue of culture is not even mentioned. Finally, upgrading the physical facilities is essential, but once again it is shocking to realize that seniors have been living in homes with no air conditioning as temperatures zoom upwards. The health effects of heat exposure are well known. The fact that facilities have a long 'grace time' to do the upgrades is not comforting.

The Ministry of Long-Term Care reannounced, on March 17, 2023, that they are fixing LTC. The funding provided is $270 million in 2021-22, $673 million in 2022-23, $1.25 billion in 2023-24, and $1.82 billion in 2024-25. Apparently, according to the announcement in 2021-22, the interim target of an average of three hours of nursing and PSW care per resident per day was met. The target of 33 minutes per resident per day of allied health professional time was also achieved. Ontario now has 31,705 new and 28,648 upgraded beds in development across the province through a $6.4 billion investment.

Without a lot of background data, it is impossible to trace what is really happening with these changes. Are residents actually seeing any improvement? It seems that there are lots of numbers available but no data systems in place to track the implementation of many of the measures.

This observation is substantiated by the Ontario Health Coalition's study, which sought actual staffing schedules from about 70 LTC homes. They got in-depth data from 23 homes. As mentioned above, on the way to meeting the four hours of care per resident per day target, there was an interim target of three hours of care per resident per day by March 31, 2022. This study found that nine of the 23 homes had care levels below 2.75 hours of care per resident per day, and 17 of the 23 homes (or nearly 75%) had care levels below three hours which was the target that was supposed to have been achieved by March 31, 2022. Only 6 of the 23 homes had care levels above three hours per resident per day.[96] Once again, this is not a reassuring finding.

Meanwhile, the wait time for an LTC bed in Sioux Lookout is still six or seven years. This puts a strain on the hospital's emergency department and alternate level of care beds. In 2018, 21 beds were not enough, and in 2023 an additional 76 beds are not enough according to Janis Magnuson, a board member for the Sioux Area Seniors Activity Centre. The lack of beds means there is a large number of alternate level-of-care patients in the hospital impacting care there as well as impacting the repatriation of patients from other facilities (such as those in Thunder Bay) in a timely manner.

The Financial Accountability Office of Ontario released an Ontario Health Sector Spending Plan Review on March 8, 2023. The key point listed in Randall Denley's report on this in the *National Post* on June 2, 2023, is that the province's commitments to expanding capacity will be more than offset by demands from the aging population:

- Ontario is currently experiencing shortages of nurses and personal support workers (PSWs), which [sic] is projected to persist through the (Financial Accountability Office) FAO's six-year forecast period. Even with government measures to increase the supply of nurses and PSWs, by 2027-28, the FAO projects a shortfall of 33,000 nurses and PSWs. These nurse and PSW shortages will jeopardize Ontario's ability to sustain current programs and meet program expansion commitments.

- Ontario's healthcare system is interdependent. Staffing shortages throughout the health care system and lack of capacity in homecare and long-term care affects hospitals' ability to discharge patients who need care in alternate settings, which, in combination with a lack of hospital capacity and staffing, affects the ability of hospitals to admit patients from emergency departments and to reduce the surgery waitlist and wait times to pre-pandemic levels.

- Given that the Province's capacity expansion commitments in hospitals, home care and long-term care will not meet growth in demand for these services from Ontario's growing and aging population, the Province has not allocated sufficient funding to the health sector to support its programs and commitments, and the Province has not taken sufficient measures to supply the nurses and PSWs needed to deliver on its expansion commitments, challenges are expected to persist across Ontario's health care system.'[97]

It sounds rather like business-as-usual, though the obvious result will be the killing off of many more elders as we go forward. The staffing issue appears to me to be extremely problematic with no real plans to address it either now, or in the future. As an elder myself, I find this makes depressing reading.

Remember the nurses and Bill 124? When we left that topic, the province was appealing the decision to roll it back. The Appeal Court, in a 2-1 decision on February 12, 2024, upheld the rights of the nurses and other affected groups. The court wrote 'Because of the Act, organized public sector workers, many of whom are women, racialized and/or low-income earners, have lost the ability to negotiate for better compensation or even better work conditions that do not have a monetary value.' The government's response was that they would 'take steps to repeal Bill 124 in its entirety in the coming weeks.' Ontario Nurses' Association provincial president, Erin Ariss, said 'The trauma inflicted on nurses and health care professionals because of Bill 124 has driven tens of thousands of us out of the health care system and away from the work we love.' The Appeal Court's decision rates as a win for the grannies. However, the government's actions in basically threatening Charter rights, have set Ontario up for a nursing shortage even as wages and working conditions improve post pandemic.

Ann McMillan

Ombudsman's Report: *Lessons for the Long Term*
Inspect to protect, prevent, and perfect.

Unknown

As I finish writing this piece, the horror continues. It is important to remember that from March 2020 to April 2022, 4,335 residents and 13 staff of LTC facilities died of COVID-19. On September 7, 2023, the Ombudsman of Ontario released the report *Lessons for the Long Term*.[98] Remember the key work that was done by the Ministry in inspections and all the improvements that were being made? This report reveals that the Ministry of Long-Term Care not only had no plan for pandemic inspections and did not provide inspectors with necessary equipment and training, but also did no inspections of LTC homes for seven weeks starting on March 13, 2020. In addition, they stopped issuing inspection reports for more than two months. These actions minimized the information coming to light about COVID-19 issues faced in the homes and resulted in a failure to identify serious issues and take action in a timely way to correct them. During this period there were 720 deaths.

The summary provided by Paul Dube, the Ombudsman, in the report covers the findings better than I ever could. His office was inundated with 269 complaints and enquiries in the first wave and he summarized:

> Ombudsman staff sifted through more than 1.2 million documents and conducted 91 interviews for this investigation. What we uncovered was an oversight system that was strained before the pandemic, and proved to be wholly incapable and unprepared to handle the additional stresses posed by COVID-19...
>
> During the critical initial weeks of the first wave, the Ministry's Inspections Branch... simply stopped conducting on-site inspections. For a seven-week period from mid-March to early May 2020, there was no independent on-site verification of the conditions in long-term care homes. The Inspections Branch did not clearly communicate its decision to stop on-site inspections to other areas of the government, long-term care homes, complainants or the public. Few knew that this oversight mechanism had fallen apart. In one area of the province, no on-site inspections occurred for three straight months.
>
> Inspections stopped because the Ministry had no plan for inspectors to safely continue their work during a pandemic. The Branch did not have a supply of personal protective equipment, and inspectors were not trained on infection prevention and control. Once inspections resumed, and for much of the first wave, only inspectors who volunteered were sent to homes experiencing COVID outbreaks. Consequently, some areas of the province had

192

as few as three or four inspectors to conduct on-site work, when there would normally be 20 to 25. Rather than conducting inspections, the inspectors…were tasked with 'supporting and monitoring' long-term care homes through periodic telephone calls. Some homes refused to participate in these calls…

The Inspections Branch was quickly overwhelmed by an unprecedented volume of complaints and questions from concerned families and caregivers. The Ministry did not adequately assess these complaints and conduct inspections when necessary. Instead, it primarily relied on inspectors to convey 'key messages' over the phone and rebranded its complaints line as the 'Family Support and Action Line,' resulting in confusion and undermining the compliance function of the Branch.

The Ministry put little thought into how its standard triage risk system would assess COVID-related complaints, resulting in a failure to categorize serious allegations as 'high-risk.' It also took a narrow approach to its mandate and we discovered that extremely serious COVID-related issues—such as infection prevention and control or personal protective equipment usage—were not inspected in a timely manner, or at all.[99]

Among its 76 recommendations, the report states that the Ministry of Long-Term Care should:

Ensure it always has inspectors available to inspect on-site at LTC homes, ensure it inspects any complaint that alleges a resident is at significant risk of harm, take a broad approach to its mandate —meaning it can inspect anything that leaves LTC residents unsafe, and issue immediate compliance orders for situations where residents are at an ongoing risk of serious harm.

The report provides some selected examples of how the Ministry has handled complaints. In far too many cases, complainants were essentially dismissed and there was no follow-up. As a result, there has been a serious lack of enforcement or penalties at specific homes some of which are named in the report. Sadly, these complainants may have lost a dear relative, often in horrific circumstances. While this report will feed into ongoing reforms that have been mentioned here, there is no way to refund to patients and families their months of suffering or the loss of their loved ones. As for the many, many elders in LTC homes who have no one to complain on their behalf about their care, we can only imagine what they went through.

Conclusion

What we need is some sort of implementation commission to provide us with a tool kit for introducing changes we already know all too well are needed, from better staffing in long-term care homes through to interoperability of health data systems, to more robust public-health responses. We don't need to be reminded, once again, of the weaknesses of the health system and their consequences. We need a political commitment to fixing them, and a road map for getting there. Yet another long-winded inquiry followed by the publication of a weighty tome of recommendations alone is not going to get us there.

Andre Picard[100]

This tale of Ontario grannies and their adventures during COVID-19 has no clear ending. What we can say is that we have reached a point in time where we are finally able to evaluate the past few years, considering where we are now and what we've all been through.

It is clear that grannies, as they move through the progression from active contributing members of society, to old people who can look after themselves and maintain themselves in society, to those who are frail and at the mercy of their caregivers, have had a lot to fear in Ontario for quite some time, particularly if they are alone. The liturgy of disturbing reports and investigations done even before COVID-19 indicates that the situation was dire and teetering on the edge of collapse as stressed and overworked care workers struggled to feed and care for ever sicker and less competent patients housed in aging and badly designed facilities. COVID simply pushed the whole system over the edge.

Many of the horrors of the pandemic years were appropriately ascribed to COVID-19. Not only did the disease kill many and cause untold misery and grief; it also caused systems teetering on the verge to finally collapse. The pandemic provided a convenient alibi for the many people managing LTC in Ontario, from the Government as a whole, through the Ministers in charge to LTC administrations all the way down to the nurse who is so rushed she loses patience or the inspections officer who delivers 'key messages' instead of help. The whole system of people who have responsibility for caring for the elderly of Ontario and who were failing in their duty before COVID have now got a second chance. This allows for a reexamination of the state of care for elders in Ontario—one which could just lead to the establishment of better elder care in the future. Realistic evaluations of the resources required to provide such care for the rapidly aging population in first world facilities are necessary. This is not an area for penny pinching in the foreseeable future.

Very soon, the oldest of the baby boomers' generation will turn 80. By 2040, Ontario's population over that age will nearly double.[101] A recent survey of 1000 Ontario seniors aged 68 to 76 was sponsored by the Ontario Long-Term Care Association (OLTCA). The study had three major takeaways. Most baby boomers are not thinking about aging and what may happen to them, they have little understanding about what options are available and what the cost might be, and they are worried that existing systems are inadequate for their needs. While most respondents expect to age in their own homes, there was concern expressed when the potential costs of that option were outlined. Of course, our Ontario health system is not prepared to deal with this situation, never mind what could happen if another pandemic occurs.

As COVID-19 spread, thousands of Ontario's old and frail passed away in the worst conditions imaginable. Some of them died of thirst. Many died of COVID when they could have been protected from it. The horror of epidemics is that we don't learn the lessons they provide.[102] Will we learn this time? Will we prepare so that the next disease that comes along is not as devastating as this one has been?

As this sad story shows, we have many, many studies that tell us we need thousands more well-trained, compassionate staff. We need to find them and put them to work in situations which provide good working conditions and appropriate pay and benefits. We need to provide them with training and appreciation and respect for the essential work they do. We also need to support a culture in LTC that in turn supports the residents. This will take thought and money and effort and political commitment. We need to support leadership for this sector that has insight, compassion and good judgement, beyond the ability to follow rules. If we can't look after our elderly in times of relative social calm, we need to recognize that they are highly vulnerable to the next pandemic. And we need to find a political system that builds trust with this part of the healthcare sector and works to support elder health in the province. Decades of underfunding and lack of attention to the care of the most vulnerable cannot be fixed overnight, but changes in the right direction need to continue on an urgent basis. The current government, by its lack of respect for public sector workers including nurses, and for un-regulated professions such as PSWs, has destroyed the trust upon which individuals would work over and above their defined duty to deliver needed results. Rebuilding that trust through taking their advice on what is needed to fix the system might help. It is not too soon to start.

As we all get another chance, let's do better than we have in the past. Sadly, there is a generation of Ontario grannies who will not get a second chance.

Epilogue

There isn't a way things should be. There's just what happens, and what we do.
Terry Pratchett

The Ombudsman's Report provides a segue into the ongoing tragedy of grannies in long-term care. COVID-19 may have retreated from pandemic status to a much less scary foe, but its impacts linger. As much as we would like to forget the intensity of the fear and the hurt of those times, it is dangerous to forget the need to be ready for the next challenge to our public health.

Elsewhere in this volume we have heard from Wanda Monuk and Susan Mills[103] who lost their mothers in residential situations during the time of COVID-19. We have heard from Julie Stashick[104] who was trained as a PSW and worked through the COVID-19 pandemic, partly because of the impact of the death of her mother in long-term care pre-COVID. We have heard from Fred Andayi[105] who worked in infection prevention and control during COVID. Finally, we have heard poignantly from Jackie Amable in 'My Mom'[106] in the previous volume, *Plague Take It.*

All these people played important roles in dealing with the pandemic, whether from the staff side or the family side. Their stories provide a small sample of the people of Ontario who still bear the scars. Their scars and those of thousands of others with similar experiences will shape the province in the future.

As Doug Ford announces that LTC rooms are going to be added into the available housing numbers to reduce the apparent housing shortage in Ontario[107]—the latest of his weird policy directions—we should perhaps reflect on the need for honest intentions from our government to deal with the issues we face. Should nurses have to go to court to get wage increases that keep pace with rising costs of living? Should the group of workers who provide most of the elder care be a registered profession rather than a group of unregulated individuals? What is a just and fair package of pay, benefits and working conditions for PSWs?

It was heartening to hear on February 6, 2024, that the group action suit initiated by Simon Nesbitt on behalf of his mother in 2020, having morphed several times in its progress through the legal system, will proceed against the Minister of Long-Term Care for negligence in the early stages of COVID-19.[108] Even if the plaintiffs do not receive the compensation that they are requesting, they will help ensure that the issues around their treatment by the long-term care system are heard and not forgotten.

The many cases when hasty and ill-thought-through legislation has damaged the reputation of the government without improving its policy basis for action or saving money have left scars that will be best healed through prudent and compassionate management of the necessary revolution of the health system, especially for elders. As illustrated here, the lessons to be learned from COVID-19 include many of the same ones as from SARS, as well as additional lessons about good old-fashioned credibility and how not to manage a health crisis.

Acknowledgement
My deepest thanks to Jon Peirce who contributed his time and professsionalism to edit and add input to this piece. He encouraged me to finish it at a time in my life when I had strong competing priorities. It feels so good to have it done.

[1] McMillan, Ann. 'Grannies and COVID,' in *Plague Take It: A COVID Almanac by and about Elders.* Jon Peirce and Ann McMillan (editors), Loose Cannon Press, 2021, pp 159 – 182.

[2] *2020 Ontario Budget. LTCH Level-of-Care Per Diem Funding Summary, April 1, 2020. Accessed May 14, 2022.*

[3] Canadian Institute for Health Information. *Profile of Residents in Residential-Based and Hospital Continuing Care, 2021-2022.* Accessed May 14, 2022.

[4] Alburez-Gutierrez, Diego. 'The Age of the Grandparent has Arrived,' *The Economist,* January 2023.

[5] Gordon, Julie. *Canada's real problem is not job losses, it's the rush to retire.* Reuters, September 12, 2022.

[6] Alburez-Gutierrez, Diego. 'The Age of the Grandparent has Arrived,' *The Economist,* January 2023.

[7] 2019 Report of the Auditor General of Ontario, 'Chapter 3, Section 3.05.' *Food and Nutrition in Long-Term-Care Homes.*

[8] Law, Sarah. 'Sioux Lookout Residents Push Ontario to Deliver on 2018 Promise to Build Dozens of Long-Term Care Beds.' *CBC News,* November 16, 2023.

[9] 2019 Report of the Auditor General of Ontario, 'Chapter 3, Section 3.05.' *Food and Nutrition in Long-Term-Care Homes,* p 290.

[10] Ontario Long-Term Care Association (OLTCA). *The Data: Long-Term Care in Ontario,* 2025.

[11] Ministry of Long-Term Care. *Long-Term Care Staffing Study.* July 30, 2020. p 19.

[12] Canadian Institute for Health Information. *Using the Method for Assigning Priority Levels (MAPLe) as a Decision-Support Tool,* 2013.

[13] Hoffmann, Elizabeth; Jeanette Grant; and Ann McMillan. 'Lessons from History,' in *Plague Take It: A COVID Almanac by and about Elders,* Jon Peirce and Ann McMillan (editors), Loose Cannon Press, 2021, pp 6-19.

[14] National Advisory Committee on SARS and Public Health. *Learning from SARS: Renewal of Public Health in Canada,* October 2003.

[15] The Expert Panel on SARS and Infectious Disease Control. *For the Public's Health – A Plan of Action.* April 2004.

[16] The SARS Commission. *Spring of Fear.* December 2006.

[17] Campbell, The Honourable Mr. Justice Archie. *The SARS Commission, Volume 4, SARS and Public Health in Ontario, First Interim Report.* December 2006, p 191.

[18] Ontario's Long-Term Care COVID-19 Commission, Final Report.

[19] Ibid., p 143.

[20] 2017 Report of the Office of the Auditor General of Ontario, Chapter 3, Section

3.04. 'Emergency Management in Ontario.' p 225.

[21] The SARS Commission, Second Interim Report. *SARS and Public Health Legislation.* April 5, 2005.

[22] Subsection 107, Ontario Regulation 79/10 made under the Long-term Care Homes Act, 2007. *Reports of Critical Incidents.*

[23] 2015 Annual Report of the Office of the Auditor General of Ontario, Chapter 3, Section 3.09. 'Long-Term Care Home Quality Inspection Program,' p 365.

[24] 'Clinical Workload Demands' increasingly refers to the amount of computer-based record keeping and reporting that is required. It is a subject of current research, please see, for example: Iyengar, M. Sriram, Deevakar Rogith, and Jose F Florez-Arango, *Measuring Workload Demand of Information Systems with the Clinical Case Demand Index,* AMIA Annual Symposium Proceedings, 2017: 985–993.

[25] Dietitians of Canada. *Ontario Long Term Care Dietitian Survey Report, 2016.*

[26] 2019 Report of the Auditor General of Ontario, Chapter 3, Section 3.05. 'Food and Nutrition in Long-Term-Care Homes.'

[27] Ibid., p 290.

[28] Ibid., p 302.

[29] Public Hospitals Act, R.R.O. 1990, Regulation 965.

[30] 2019 Report of the Auditor General of Ontario, Chapter 3, Section 3. 'Food and Nutrition in Long-Term-Care Homes,' p 304.

[31] Dietitians of Canada. *Meal Planning in Long-Term Care and Canada's Food Guide, 2019,* p 5.

[32] 2019 Report of the Auditor General of Ontario, Chapter 3, Section 3.05. 'Food and Nutrition in Long-Term-Care Homes,' p 307.

[33] The Public Inquiry into the Safety and Security of Residents in the Long-Term Care Homes System. *Volume 1-Executive Summary and Consolidated Recommendations,* 2019.

[34] Ibid., p 42.

[35] Ontario Health Coalition. *Caring in Crisis: Ontario's Long-Term Care PSW Shortage.* January, 2020. 34 pages.

[36] Natalie Mehra, *Press Conference at Ontario Legislature,* Ontario Health Coalition, December 9, 2019.

[37] Registered Nurses Association of Ontario. *A better approach to long-term care in Ontario,* 2019.

[38] Canadian Institute for Health Information. *Health Expenditure Data in Brief.* Ottawa: CIHI; 2022.

[39] Pollock, Allan. 'Compression of Health Expenditures'. *Health Policy Research Bulletin.* Health Canada, Volume 1, Issue 1, p 14.

[40] Canadian Institute for Health Information. *National Health Expenditure Trends, 2024: Inforgraphics.* Accessed June 4, 2025.

[41] Canadian Institute for Health Information. *National Health Expenditure Trends, 2024: Data Tables – Series E1.* Accessed March 14, 2022.

[42] Liu M, CJ Maxwell, P Armstrong, M Schwandt, A Moser, MJ McGregor, SE Bronskill, IA Dhalla. 'COVID-19 in long-term care homes in Ontario and British Columbia. How was long-term care different in Ontario and British Columbia before COVID-19?' *CMAJ.* 2020 Nov 23; 192(47).

[43] Stall, Nathan M, Aaron Jones, Kevin A Brown, Paula A Rochon, Andrew P Costa.

'For-profit long-term care homes and the risk of COVID-19 outbreaks and resident deaths.' *CMAJ*. 2020 Jul 22;192(33): E946–E955. doi: 10.1503/cmaj.201197.

[44] Canadian Institute for Health Information (CIHI). *Pandemic Experience in the Long-Term Care Sector: How Does Canada Compare with Other Countries?* Ottawa: CIHI; 2020. Accessed Nov. 16, 2023.

[45] Ontario's Long-Term Care COVID-19 Commission, Final Report, April 30, 2021, p 172.

[46] Ibid., p 172.

[47] Consulting.ca. *Auditor General Criticizes Ontario's Mckinsey-Crafted Pandemic Response Structure,* 27 November 2020.

[48] Consulting.ca. *Auditor General Says Feds Didn't Follow Rules on Awarding Mckinsey Contracts,* 05 June 2024.

[49] Ontario's Long-Term Care COVID-19 Commission, Final Report, April 30, 2021, p 186.

[50] Howlett, Karen. 'Patients died from neglect, not COVID-19, in Ontario LTC homes, military report finds: "All they needed was water and a wipe down".' *The Globe and Mail*, May 9, 2021.

[51] McIntosh, Emma. 'Military report finds gruesome conditions, abuse inside 5 Ontario long-term care homes.' *Canada's National Observer*, May 26, 2020.

[52] Mialkowski, C.J.J. *Op-Laser–JTFC Observations in Long Term Care Facilities in Ontario*, website accessed June 4, 2025.

[53] Wallace, Kenyon. 'Only a Fraction of Long-Term-Care Residents Killed by Covid-19 Were Taken to Hospital. A Mount Sinai Doctor Says the System "Shut Them Out" With Beds Available.' *Toronto Star*, December 6, 2020.

[54] Fine, Sean. 'Ontario Government Does Not Guarantee the Health or Safety of Residents in Long-Term Care Homes, Legal Document Says.' *The Globe and Mail*, August 31, 2020.

[55] Wallace, op. cit.

[56] Long-Term Care Staffing Advisory Group, *Long-Term Care Staffing Study*, July 30, 2020. p 17.

[57] Health Protection and Promotion Act, R.S.O. 1990, Part VII, Administration, Section 78 (1).

[58] Ontario's Long-Term Care COVID-19 Commission, Final Report. April 30, 2021. p 107.

[59] Ibid., p 181.

[60] Brown, Kevin A., Nathan M. Stall, Thuva Vanniyasingam, Sarah A. Buchan, Nick Daneman, Michael P. Hillmer, Jessica Hopkins, Jennie Johnstone, Antonina Maltsev, Allison Mcgeer, Beate Sander, Rachel D. Savage, Tania Watts, Peter Jüni, Paula A. Rochon, on behalf of the Congregate Care Setting Working Group and the Ontario COVID-19 Science Advisory Table. *Early Impact of Ontario's COVID-19 Rollout on Long-Term Care Home Residents and Health Care Workers*, accessed March 8, 2021.

[61] Ontario's Long-Term Care COVID-19 Commission, Final Report. April 30, 2021, p 153.

[62] Stall, Nathan M., Kevin A. Brown, Antonina Maltsev, Aaron Jones, Andrew P.

Costa, Vanessa Allen, Adalsteinn D. Brown, Gerald A. Evans, David N. Fisman, Jennie Johnstone, Peter Jüni, Kamil Malikov, Allison McGeer, Paula A. Rochon, Beate Sander, Brian Schwartz, Samir K. Sinha, Kevin Smith, Ashleigh R. Tuite, Michael P. Hillmer on behalf of the Ontario COVID-19 Science Advisory Table, *COVID-19 and Ontario's Long-Term Care Homes.* January 20, 2021.

[63] Howlett, Karen. 'Ontario failed to act on Surveys of LTC homes ahead of deadly COVID-19 second wave, commission says,' *The Globe and Mail*, May 2, 2021.

[64] Office of the Auditor General of Ontario, *Value-for-money-audit: Long-Term Care Homes: Delivery of Resident-Centered Care*, December 2023. p 49.

[65] Ontario's Long-Term Care COVID-19 Commission, Final Report. April 30, 2021. p 320.

[66] Canadian Institute for Health Information (CIHI) website. *COVID-19's Impact on long-term care.* December 9, 2021. Accessed January 14, 2024.

[67] Long-Term Care Staffing Advisory Group. *Long-term care staffing study.* July 30, 2020. p 2. Accessed January 14, 2024.

[68] 'Ontario Minimum Wage to Increase on October 1, 2020.' Mathewsdinsdale.com. Accessed May 21, 2024.

[69] Long-Term Care Staffing Advisory Group. *Long-term care staffing study.* July 30, 2020. p 42. Accessed January 14, 2024.

[70] Ontario's Long-Term Care COVID-19 Commission, Final Report. April 30, 2021. p 91. Accessed May 21, 2024.

[71] *Understanding Bill 124: The Government's Control Mechanism for Public-Sector Salaries,* kmlaw.ca, January 29, 2020. Accessed May 21, 2024.

[72] Ontario Inflation Calculator. Accessed June 13, 2024.

[73] 'Ontario Hospital Nurses, Health-Care Professionals Receive Major Wage Increases in Decision that Cites the Need to Retain Staff.' ONA.org, July 20, 2023. Accessed May 21, 2024.

[74] News Release. 'Province Repeals Bill 124.' February 23, 2024. Accessed June 13, 2024.

[75] Statistics Canada. 'Job vacancies, second quarter 2021.' *The Daily.* September 21, 2021.

[76] Long-Term Care Staffing Advisory Group. *Long-Term Care Staffing Study*, July 30, 2020. p 16. Accessed May 28, 2024.

[77] Ontario's Long-Term Care COVID-19 Commission, Final Report. April 30, 2021. p 222.

[78] Ibid., p 223.

[79] Long-Term Care Staffing Advisory Group. *Long-Term Care Staffing Study*, July 30, 2020. p 20. Accessed May 28, 2024.

[80] Wilson, Kerrisa. 'Over 200 long-term care homes have not paid PSWs $3 per hour temporary wage increase: Fullerton,' *CTV News.* January 16, 2021.

[81] Levitt, LLP. 'Bill 47: Changes to the Employment Standards Act,' *Employment and Labour Blog*, October 11, 2020.

[82] Ontario Government. *Your Guide to the Employment Standards Act, Infectious Disease Emergency Leave,* Accessed May 21, 2024.

[83] Canadian Federation of Independent Business, New Ontario Sick Notes Policy, January, 2025.

[84] 2021 Report of the Auditor General of Ontario. *Follow-up on VFM Section 3.05,*

2019 Annual Report, p 3.

[85] Ibid., p 94.

[86] Ontario's Long-Term Care COVID-19 Commission, Final Report. April 30, 2021. p 82.

[87] Ibid., p 205.

[88] 'Protecting Ontarians through Enhanced Testing,' Ontario.ca. 29 May, 2020. Accessed January 20, 2024.

[89] News Ontario, 'Providing more care, Protecting Seniors and Building more Beds Act Receives Royal Ascent.' December 9, 2021.

[90] Shawn Jeffords and Nicole Thompson. 'Problems in Ontario's long-term care homes were neglected for decades, with deadly consequences: report'. *National Post*. April 30, 2021.

[91] Pelley, Lauren. 'Over-Capacity ERs Are Dangerous Choke Points but Hospital Challenges Go Far Deeper.' *CBC News*, January 13, 2024.

[92] Allatt, Peter, and Bob Parke. 'A Public Policy Dead End: The More Beds, Better Care Act.' *Healthy Debate*, September 14, 2022.

[93] Soliman, Peter. 'More Beds, Better Care Act 2022: Ontario's Recent Passing of Bill 7.' *McGill Journal of Law and Health*, January 27, 2023.

[94] Notice of Application by the Ontario Health Coalition (OHC) and the Advocacy Centre for the Elderly (ACE) to Ontario Superior Court of Justice to have key provisions of the More Beds, Better Care Act, and its related regulations and practices (Bill 7), declared invalid and of no force and effect. April 12, 2023.

[95] Statement from the Advocacy Centre for the Elderly and the Ontario Health Coalition on the Bill 7 Charter Challenge Decision, January 20, 2025.

[96] Ontario Health Coalition. *Crisis Unabated: The Failure to Improve Dangerously Low Care Levels in Ontario's Long-Term Care Homes.* May 18, 2022.

[97] Financial Accountability Office of Ontario. *Ontario Health Sector: Spending Plan Review.* March 8, 2023.

[98] Ontario Ombudsman. *Lessons for the Long Term,* September 7, 2023. Accessed May 28, 2024.

[99] Ibid., p 6.

[100] Picard, Andre. 'Should Canada Conduct a national COVID response inquiry? The BMJ thinks so.' *Opinion, Globe and Mail,* June 2023. Accessed May 28, 2024

[101] Ontario Long-Term Care Association (OLTCA). 'Boomers' Readiness for Aging,' From: *Duncan, Donna and David Coletto, Insights,* Longwoods e-letter, January 2024.

[102] Hoffmann, Elizabeth, Jeanette Grant, and Ann McMillan. 'Lessons from History,' in *Plague Take It: A COVID Almanac by and about Elders,* Jon Peirce and Ann McMillan (editors), Loose Cannon Press, 2021, pp 6-19.

[103] Monuk, Wanda and Susan Mills (as told to Ann McMillan), 'COVID-19: Insidious impacts on elders who didn't catch it,' in *Road to Recovery,* (see elsewhere in this volume).

[104] Stashick, Julie, 'COVID-19: Before and After,' in *Road to Recovery,* (see elsewhere in this volume).

[105] Andayi, Fred, 'Pandemic stories of infection prevention in long-term care,' in *Road to Recovery,* (see elsewhere in this volume).

[106] Amable, Jackie. 'My Mom,' in *Plague Take It: a COVID Almanac by and about Elders,* Jon Peirce and Ann McMillan (editors), Loose Cannon Press, 2021, pp 68-75.

[107] D'Mello, Colin and Isaac Callan. 'Ford Government begins boosting housing

numbers with LTC beds, basements.' *Global News*, February 23, 2024.
[108] Jones, Allison, 'Court allows negligence class-action suit against Ontario LTC Minister to proceed,' *CTV News*, Toronto, February 6, 2024.

The Politics of COVID, 2023-Style
I: 'Not in Our Job Description'
Jon Peirce

As this is being written (mid-January, 2023), the news, whether on radio, TV, or the Internet, is filled with horror stories about hospitals, in particular their emergency rooms, and the future of the healthcare profession in both Canada and the U.S.

Two stories, in particular, attracted considerable attention. One dealt with a mother in her 30s who died after waiting seven hours in an emergency room in Amherst, Nova Scotia. The other had to do with a woman in her 60s who, after waiting seven hours in an emergency room in Cape Breton, was told a doctor probably couldn't see her until the morning and then gave up and went home, where she died shortly thereafter. A bit of digging revealed that a similar tragedy had occurred in an emergency room in Edmundston, New Brunswick during the summer.[1]

Tragically, these stories don't appear to have been isolated incidents. It seems likely that we'll be hearing many more of them over the months to come. According to a recent *Toronto Star* article,[2] deaths in Nova Scotia's emergency rooms rose by 10 per cent between 2021 and 2022. And the percentage of ER patients dying also rose. In all, nearly 3,000 (2,949) patients have died seeking treatment in Nova Scotia's emergency rooms since 2017.[3] Meanwhile, emergency room closures due to staffing shortages have more than doubled year over year, according to a provincial government report released on December 22, 2022.

Even as this piece is being written, the situation in Nova Scotia continues to worsen. Each month for the past three months, the ER death rate has surpassed the six-year average, rising to a peak of 0.15 per cent in December. The situation has prompted emergency room nurses to raise alarms about 'the state of chaos' in the province's hospitals and has led the union representing them, the Nova Scotia Government Employees' Union, to write a letter to Nova Scotia Health CEO Karen Oldfield with 59 recommendations for addressing the 'chaos' in provincial emergency rooms. It has also prompted provincial NDP leader Claudia Chender to call for a public inquiry into emergency room deaths across the province.

Staffing issues lie at the root of the emergency room crisis. At present, some 129,000 Nova Scotians lack a primary care physician, prompting many if not all of those people to resort to emergency rooms when they get sick, for lack of other options. The province's nursing shortage is acute; even provincial Health Minister Michelle Thompson has acknowledged that 'We could accept 1,500 nurses today.' Many of those already in the profession are choosing to leave, fearing both for their personal safety, as irate patients follow them to their cars at the end of their shifts, and for their licenses, as chronic understaffing forces them to work under conditions which don't meet their own personal standards for provision of adequate care. (That the new Nova Scotia Health CEO, Karen Oldfield, is a political appointee with no prior health administration experience does little to restore anyone's confidence in the system).

Nova Scotia is not the only province to be facing such a critical situation with regard to its hospitals and emergency rooms, although it may, at the moment, be the most highly publicized one. On Friday, January 13, 2023, CBC Radio News carried a story stating that Ottawa's Queensway Carleton Hospital had just experienced the busiest day in its 46-year history, and that furthermore, it expected the situation to get even worse in the weeks ahead. Periodic ER closures have become almost commonplace in parts of Ontario and Quebec. And recently, physician departures have hit east Ottawa so hard that the area was described in CBC News as a 'care desert,'[4] spurring calls for a new health centre for the area.

Recent data says Ottawa has 134,000 unattached patients seeking a family physician, though there could be tens of thousands more due to the latest wave of departures.

Meanwhile, in western Canadian provinces such as Manitoba and British Columbia, ER closures have hit rural areas particularly hard. On the long weekend at the beginning of August, fully one-third of Manitoba's northern or rural ERs were closed, leading the president of Doctors Manitoba, Dr Candace Bradshaw, to warn Manitobans, 'Before you start your long weekend, know where you are going to get care because things are much more complicated this summer and it is not business as usual.'[5] And in British Columbia, it has been much the same, with ERs at 13 rural hospitals closed for a total of around fourth months during 2022.[6] The mayor of one rural British Columbia community, New Denver, reported that his community's ER had been closed at night since July. Those facing 'diversion' to other ERs due to the closure of their own were forced to make drives ranging from 41 to 177 kilometres.

While the immediate effect of such ER closures is greatest on rural communities, they wind up affecting the entire province, as patients diverted from closed rural ERs must often be treated at ERs in larger centres such as Winnipeg or Vancouver, where wait times are already long, thus worsening the already bad situation in those larger urban centres.

South of the border, a chronic and worsening shortage of nurses is adding further stress to an already overstretched healthcare system. During the second week of January, about 7,000 unionized nurses went on strike in

New York City, with understaffing and overwork being the key issues driving them to the picket lines.[7] Since the beginning of the year, there have also been strikes, threatened strikes, or other forms of protest in California, Oregon, Michigan, and Minnesota. Astoundingly, nurses led a quarter of the top 20 major work stoppages tracked by the Bureau of Labor Statistics in 2022.

The sheer size of actual and projected nursing shortages is truly terrifying. At the Montefiore Medical Center Hospital, just one of those hit by the recent nurses' strike, more than 700 nursing positions are currently being advertised. With some 100,000 nurses already having left the field between 2020 and 2021, the U.S. is expected, according to a recent study by McKinsey & Company, to have a shortage of anywhere from 200,000 to 450,000 nurses by 2025.

COVID-19 isn't the only factor driving nursing shortages and emergency room overcrowding, but it is definitely a major factor, with nurses (as well as other healthcare personnel) becoming increasingly worried about getting sick themselves, or family members getting sick. And as if COVID by itself were not already enough, a resurgence of seasonal flu, which diminished greatly during the lockdown days of the early pandemic, and of the RSV respiratory virus have created a perfect storm for hospitals, particularly pediatric hospitals forced to bear the brunt of RSV cases, since the disease afflicts primarily children and young people. So serious were the problems posed by this 'triple threat' of respiratory diseases that for a period of about two months the Children's Hospital of Eastern Ontario (CHEO) was forced to send 16- and 17-year-olds to adult hospitals for treatment because it simply could not accommodate them along with the rest of its population. (This situation, which began November 18, 2022, has only just ended as of today (January 17, 2023).[8]

If all of this doesn't qualify as a medical emergency, I don't know what would. But evidently our politicians, whether north of the border or south of it, don't seem to think it does. 'Back to business as usual!' is their mantra. And not just the usual suspects—right-wingers like Georgia Gov Brian Kemp, South Dakota Gov Kristi Noem, or Ontario Premier Doug Ford. Even the most progressive American governors, like California's Gavin Newsom and Washington's Jay Inslee, and Canadian premiers, like British Columbia's newly-elected NDP premier David Eby, have come to acquiesce in the general inaction around COVID. For me, what comes first to mind is Yeats' memorable line, 'The best lack all conviction...' [9] Even as hospitals and their emergency rooms buckle under the biggest patient loads many of them have ever seen, National Hockey League arenas are packed to the gunnels with maskless fans, children spend entire days in school without masks, and COVID vaccinations drop to a trickle.[10] Does *anybody* give a damn? The silence is deafening.

Earlier in the pandemic, a need to protect the healthcare system was frequently cited as the justification for lockdowns, mask requirements, travel restrictions, and other infringements on people's personal freedom. As unpleasant as these restrictions were, they do appear to have saved the healthcare system from total collapse. Today, with the healthcare system under greater threat than ever, as the preceding discussion more than amply illustrates, what are federal, state, and provincial governments in the U.S. and Canada doing to help mitigate the situation? As the preceding paragraph suggests, the short answer is, 'Nothing.' The one organization that seems to continue to recognize the pandemic's seriousness is the World Health Organization (WHO), which on January 30, 2023 renewed its declaration of COVID-19 as a global health emergency.[11] I don't know what effect the renewal of WHO's declaration had in Europe, Africa, Latin America, or Asia, but as far as North America was concerned, that renewal might as well not have happened. In the same week that WHO announced its renewal of its emergency declaration, U.S. President Joe Biden announced his decision to end that country's state of COVID emergency effective May 11 of this year.[12]

Yes. You read that word correctly. It was 'Nothing.' At federal, provincial, and state levels, Canadian and American governments are not taking even the most modest measures to reduce the incredible, overwhelming strain on the healthcare system resulting from the latest COVID wave, simultaneously with a huge wave of seasonal flu and another of the RSV respiratory virus. No state or province currently has a state- or province-wide mask or vaccine mandate in place.[13] Healthcare centres and related facilities such as assisted living homes do often still have mask mandates, as do government buildings and prisons in certain counties. But there are, to repeat, no state-wide or province-wide mask mandates in place, even in facilities used by the most vulnerable, such as schools, or in facilities such as public transit vehicles and terminals used by thousands, where distancing is not always possible and where the risk of transmission is thus quite high.

Granted, some governments do recommend masking in indoor public places or on buses, trains, and subways, but these recommendations appear to mean about as much as the warning labels on cigarette packages advising consumers not to smoke. On two recent flights, about 10 to 20 percent of passengers appeared to be wearing masks. In the airports I travelled through to catch those flights, the percentage of mask-wearers was even lower. On the New Jersey Transit trains transporting me between New York's Penn Station and the Newark Airport, the percentage of mask-wearers was lower yet, except in the small section of one of the trains reserved for passengers with disabilities. There, we mask-wearers were in the majority. Given that I, age 78 and with two artificial hips to my credit, was among the younger and spryer of those sitting in the 'disability' section, I suspect it wouldn't have gone well for most of those people had they contracted COVID.

If masks have become uncommon even in settings like subway cars where one would have thought the instinct of self-preservation would dictate wearing them, they are the next thing to non-existent in most retail settings. On at least two recent occasions, I was the only person—customer or staff member—wearing a mask in my grocery store. While this hasn't been the norm, it has frequently been the case that mask-wearing was confined to, at most, 10 percent of customers and two or three clerks. This in my Quebec grocery store, mind you. In the U.S., where the attitude toward masks or any other kind of COVID restriction has generally been more strongly negative than in Canada, those figures would have been even lower. Entering a New York Trader Joe's store in early December, I found the deli area resembling a cross between a rugby scrum and a mosh pit, with at most four of the hundreds of customers masked. The area was so crowded that it was hard to see how cart collisions were avoided. Having only just recovered from COVID myself, I most emphatically did not want to contract the disease again, and so fled in terror as soon as I could find a break in the crowd, leaving my cart where it was in the middle of the deli department. A second visit to the store, about seven weeks later, revealed a similar lack of masks among customers, although fortunately there were far fewer of them— enough fewer that I felt I could shop there without taking undue risk, so long as I kept my mask on.

I have over the past few months visited a number of stores which *did* have a mask mandate in place. All of the stores were in Canada (either Ontario or Quebec), and interestingly enough all were of the small, boutique variety, and rarely if ever had more than two or three patrons in the store at the same time. Of all the stores in the world, these were probably among the ones least in need of a mask mandate—yet they had one in place anyway. There are also some businesses and sectors which I would like to single out for doing their level best to prevent COVID. One is New York City's enter-tainment sector, in almost all of which masks are required in all indoor settings. You may not see many (or any) masks among the 20,000 or more fans huddled together at a Rangers or Senators game, but you will see almost everyone wearing a mask at a Broadway play, concert, or dance performance. In my view, the mask requirement should go a long way toward helping restore the entertainment's economic viability after the two dreadful COVID years. And while we're handing out kudos, I'd also like to single out Porter Airlines for continuing to require proof of vaccination for many of its customers.

Laudable as they are, though, these cases remain exceptions. Most individuals, and most businesses as well, are carrying on as if COVID had never existed; never mind that about 30 people a day are continuing to die of the disease in New York City, and that the city of Ottawa recently recorded its 1,000th death from the pandemic. Or that COVID killed hundreds of

Canadians each week throughout much of the last year, and 222 in the second week of this year. Or that worldwide, COVID-related deaths are actually *increasing*, with over 170,000 such deaths reported in the last eight weeks alone.[14] Governments all around the world are evidently determined to 'move on' from the pandemic, whether or not the evidence suggests it is safe to do so. And that is that.[15]

The current consensus around doing nothing, which has been described, rather colourfully by at least one journalist as the 'flu-ification' of COVID,[16] signifying the disease's full acceptance as endemic to the U.S., is a far cry from the attitude toward the disease evident as recently as a year ago. Back then, masks were required on all or virtually all public transit vehicles, and one couldn't cross the border into Canada without evidence of a recent negative COVID test. And through the pandemic's first year and a half or so, there were significant differences, among people of differing political stripes, on the matter of how best to handle the COVID pandemic. My earlier work on the U.S., 'Politics and COVID I: Some Thoughts on Interstate Variations in COVID Rates in the U.S.,' [17] found a strong positive relationship between a state's COVID rates and the extent of its support for Donald Trump in the 2020 Presidential election. I found an even stronger connection between a state's COVID rates and the presence, in that state, of a Democratic vs. Republican governor. In Canada, the relationship between governing party and COVID rates was not as strong, at least in part because Canada's multi-party system makes it harder to put ideological labels on the country's various parties. Still, a significant relationship existed, as noted in 'Politics and COVID II: Causes of Canadian Interprovincial Variations in COVID Rates,' [18] with the more right-wing Western provinces generally featuring higher COVID rates than the Atlantic provinces, whose politics were (and are) more to the centre, and where there appeared to be something close to consensus in support of tough lockdown measures.

Given the current consensus in favour of doing nothing at all about COVID, it's sometimes hard to remember just how divisive masking and other COVID measures were in 2020 and 2021, to the point where threats and even physical violence were visited upon insistent mask-wearers in a number of American states,[19] where then-President Donald Trump attempted to use his Democratic opponent Joe Biden's insistence on wearing a mask as an issue in the 2020 Presidential election campaign,[20] and where there was a serious attempt to kidnap Michigan's Democratic governor, Gretchen Whitmer, in response to her imposition of fairly tough (by American standards) COVID measures in that state. It's also enlightening to recall that about three-quarters of all U.S. states—37 to be precise—had mask mandates at some point during the pandemic, with the always libertarian-minded Arizona being one of the 13 that didn't.[21] Now, Arizona's attitude has become the norm, not just in the U.S., but in Canada as well.

Certainly, the polarization around masking and other COVID issues had gone too far in the U.S. when things had reached the point of physical assaults in retail stores and credible threats to kidnap public officials. But the existence of some kind of debate around COVID-related issues strikes me as not only legitimate, but healthy.

Former federal Finance Minister Bill Morneau may have been critical of Prime Minister Justin Trudeau for having polarized the Canadian electorate by using COVID vaccine mandates as a 'wedge issue' in the 2021 federal election, which Trudeau's Liberals narrowly won.[22] Whether this was in fact the case is anybody's guess, and probably impossible to determine at this late date. To me—and bear in mind that I'm no fan of Justin Trudeau—vaccine mandates seem an entirely legitimate issue for use in a political campaign. Had (God forbid) I been running for office in 2021 or 2022, I'd have used the issue myself.

As for Morneau's allegation, my not inconsiderable previous work on the subject of politics and COVID would suggest that such polarization was primarily due to what had been and was being said and done south of the border, particularly during the administration of Donald Trump. Given the way Trump had politicized almost everything about COVID with an eye to achieving short-term political gain, vaccine mandates would in my view have been a 'wedge issue,' in Canada as well as the U.S., no matter who was Prime Minister or what his or her position might have been on vaccine mandates.[23] Vaccine mandates would likely also have been a wedge issue under a Conservative Prime Minister—just a different type of wedge issue. The fact that there were anti-mask demonstrations and public events as early as April of 2021[24] suggests that the battle lines had already been drawn well ahead of the 2021 federal election. I would also suggest that vaccine mandates aren't really the type of issue that lends itself to middle ground or compromise positions. Vaccination if necessary but not necessarily vaccination? I don't think so.

In any case, prior to Donald Trump's presidency, vaccine mandates of any kind were rarely an issue. The vast majority of citizens went and got vaccinated any time there was a pandemic involving some disease out of the ordinary, with vaccine 'refusniks' comprising a very small if occasionally vocal minority. Had Trump not been elected, vaccine and mask mandates would have been far less of an issue in the U.S., perhaps not even an issue at all; they certainly wouldn't have been much of an issue here. As things stood, however, Trump's brazen example not only inflamed and polarized debate in the U.S. and, to a slightly lesser degree, Canada; it spawned a host of imitators all around the world, from the U.K.'s Boris Johnson to Brazil's Jai Bolsonaro. Whether public health systems will in the foreseeable future recover from the pandemic's having been used so extensively as a political football remains to be seen.

In the meantime, there's the question of whether healthcare systems can survive the current regime of benign neglect and impending 'flu-ification' which politicians of all stripes have prescribed for COVID. And there's the related question of whether, in the absence of any substantial improvement of the current situation, any public official will have the courage to impose or even propose even short-term measures for dealing with it, such as 'circuit-breaker' mask and vaccine mandates or large gathering restrictions limited to 60 or 90 days, let alone the sort of lockdown that up until a year ago most public officials in Canada and many even in the U.S. would not have hesitated to impose, faced with the sort of healthcare emergency we've been seeing these past two months.[25] Quite simply, governments at all levels, from federal to municipal, appear to have made a near-unanimous collective decision not to take any further preventive action with regard to COVID. 'Government intervention to try to stop the spread of COVID? That's not in our job description.' Meanwhile, Thomas Hobbes, Ayn Rand, and Thomas Malthus are all dancing in glee in their graves at this new and potent manifestation of political folly.

Part II of this essay takes the process of government disinvestment in COVID prevention one step farther, showing what the Canadian federal government will be, or, more exactly, will not be doing with regard to COVID testing. This is followed by a brief discussion of where the Canadian government has, so to speak, decided to reinvest its moral authority as applied to the healthcare system. Stay tuned.

Gatineau, Quebec
February, 2023

---

[1] Natalie Lombard, 'Investigation Underway after Another Patient Dies in Edmundston, NB Hospital ER.' CTV News Atlantic, December 8, 2022. The original death referred to in the text, which occurred on July 24, 2022, was followed by one on December 7 of the same year.

[2] Lyndsay Armstrong, 'Nova Scotia Emergency Room Deaths Up 10 per cent in 2022, Dat Shows.' *Toronto Star,* January 11, 2023, downloaded January 15, 2023.

[3] Martin Bauman, 'Nova Scotia's Emergency Rooms are Facing 'A Complete Unravelling.'' *The Coast,* January 16, 2023. Except as otherwise noted, the rest of the material in this section has been drawn from Bauman's article.

[4] Matthew Kupfer,' Doctor Departures Turning East Ottawa into Care 'Desert'.' CBC News, January 17, 2023.

[5] Michelle Gerwing, 'One-Third of Rural or Northern ERs in Manitoba Closed This Long Weekend: Doctors Manitoba.' CTV News, July 29, 2022, downloaded January 17, 2023.

[6] Akshay Kulkarni, 'Emergency Rooms in Rural B.C. were Closed for Equivalent of 4 Months in 2022.' CBC News, December 27, 2022, downloaded January 17, 2023.

[7] Lauren K. Gurley, 'Why Nurses Say They Are Striking and Quitting in Droves.' *Washington Post*, January 14, 2023. Except as otherwise noted, all material about the nursing shortage in the U.S. has been drawn from Gurley's article.

[8] Claire Clarkson, 'CHEO Resumes Treating Older Teens Once the Pressure is Off.' *Canada Today*, Ontario News, Janury 17, 2023.

[9] From his famous poem, ' The Second Coming.' Another line from that same poem that comes to mind is 'Mere anarchy is loosed upon the world.'

[10] In Ottawa, weekly vaccinations dropped to a pandemic-long low of 1266 during the first week of February. CBC News, 'COVID-19 Trends Stable, but Vaccination Rates Hit New Low.' February 8, 2023.

[11] Katherine Dillinger, 'WHO Says COVID-19 Remains a Global Emergency, but Pandemic Is at a 'Transition Point.' CNN Internet News, January 30, 2023.

[12] 'U.S. to End COVID-19 Emergency Declaration on May 11.' Reuters, January 30, 2023, downloaded February 12, 2023.

[13] Andy Markowitz, 'State-by-State Guides to Face Mask Requirements,' *AARP*, updated November 1, 2022.

[14] Lauren Pelley, 'The COVID Emergency Might End after 3 Long Years—but the Virus Is Still a Threat.' CBC News Analysis, January 26, 2023, downloaded January 26.

[15] *Ibid.*

[16] Katherine J. Wu, 'The Flu-ification of COVID Policy,' in *The Atlantic*, January 26, 2023.

[17] In J. Peirce and A. McMillan (eds.), *Plague Take It: A COVID Almanac by and about Elders* (Ottawa: Loose Cannon Press, 2021), pp. 183-222.

[18] In *Plague Take It*, pp. 223-281. See esp. Tables 4 and 5 at p. 277.

[19] See among many others A. Pawloski, 'Why We Hate Being Told What to Do: Psychologists Explain the Battle Over Masks.' *Today*, July 7, 2020, downloaded June 29, 2021. Pawloski documents events occurring in states as geographically and politically diverse as New Jersey, Florida, and Texas.

[20] See Peirce, 'Politics and COVID I,' in *Plague Take It*, p. 199.

[21] See Stephanie Innes and Alison Steinbach, 'Why is Arizona Worst for COVID-19 Nationwide? Here are 7 Contributing Reasons.' *Arizona Republic*, February 2, 2021, downloaded April 13, 2021. This article is cited at pp. 209-212 of 'Politics and COVID I,' and in footnotes 70, 72, 74, and 75 at pp. 221-222.

[22] Peter Zimonjic, 'Trudeau's Use of Vaccine Mandates as Wedge Issue Polarized the Debate in Canada, Morneau Says.' CBC News, January 17, 2023, downloaded January 26.

[23] All of this is explained in far more detail in 'Politics and COVID I,' at pp. 191-204 of *Plague Take It*.

[24] For more detail, see my 'Politics and COVID II' piece (Canada) at p. 242 of *Plague Take It*. See also Note 24 at p. 279 of that same essay.

[25] It is January 26, 2023, as this is being written.

The Politics of COVID, 2023-Style II: From Healthcare to the (Partial) Nanny State

Jon Peirce

The first part of this essay, 'Not in Our Job Description,' has, I think, clearly demonstrated the federal government's overt intention (as well as the overt intention of Canadian provincial and American state governments) to give up any attempt to use its authority to try to halt the spread of COVID-19. But if there still existed the slightest doubt on this head, two recent developments should lay such doubt to rest once and for all.

The first of those developments is the federal government's decision to end shipments of rapid COVID tests to the provinces at the conclusion of a current federal-provincial agreement on test shipment on March 31.[1] Even from a highly individualistic perspective, the decision makes no sense. Not only will the government (and provinces) have no policies in place for prevention of COVID; the end of free testing will make it difficult if not impossible for individuals to determine for themselves if they have COVID. To find anything matching the hubris underlying this bizarre decision, you would have to go back to the days immediately preceding the launch of the *Titanic*, when the ship's promoters were proudly declaring her unsinkable. To say that the decision is a head-scratcher is to understate things considerably.

In an apparent attempt to downplay the shortsightedness of this decision, Queen's University infectious disease specialist Gerald Evans has said, 'It's not surprising, just given the fact that we are starting to see this gradual transition out of the pandemic into a little bit more of normal life... So it may be that a year from now, the rapid test may not be necessarily useful.' But even Dr Evans admits that cutting back on the supply of tests will make it difficult for people who want to continue testing themselves. The tests are not cheap, Evans notes. Many Canadians may not be willing to pay for them.

A reduction in testing also risks increasing the further spread of COVID. 'So not knowing whether you have COVID or not, because you no longer have a rapid test to check, that kind of leaves you [thinking] that maybe you're going to be going back (to work) a little earlier,' Evans says. In other words, people will be going back to work who shouldn't be, and the disease will be spread even faster and further than would otherwise have been the case.

University of Toronto infectious disease specialist Anna Banerji is blunter in her assessment of the situation. Making an implicit assumption that the federal government decision to stop shipments of tests is at least in part a response to falling demand for the tests, Dr Banerji says that in her view, people are using the rapid tests less because there is no longer a public health strategy in place to deal with COVID-19. 'We don't know how much COVID is out there,' Banerji adds. In other words, if the government doesn't care about COVID any more, why should we as individuals care? To me, it takes a strangely contorted logic to arrive at such a conclusion. Nonetheless, given the generally lackadaisical attitude most people seem to have toward COVID these days, that logic, twisted though it may be, appears to have been persuasive for many Canadians.

There are a number of possible explanations for the government's decision to halt shipments and for its broader laissez-faire policy toward COVID. Each of these explanations is more unsavoury than the last. Possibly the government seriously believes it has wrestled COVID to the ground, and that further government intervention is therefore unnecessary. But the continuing high levels of COVID-related hospitalization and deaths belie such a facile conclusion. Anyone who could seriously believe it is quite simply delusional.

A likelier (and more cynical) explanation is that while the government recognizes that COVID still exists and still poses a threat both to individuals' health and to the healthcare system, it has other priorities—mainly economic priorities. This explanation suggests that getting the economy back to its pre-pandemic level is of greater importance, overall, than protecting the health of individual citizens or the integrity and vitality of the healthcare system. While from a public health perspective it is little short of insane to allow 20,000 people to sit, unmasked, in the closest possible proximity to one another in an enclosed arena watching an NHL game, it makes perfect sense from a purely economic perspective. From this perspective, the economic viability of the Toronto Maple Leafs matters more than the health of the fans assembled to watch a Leafs game. If some people get sick or even die as a result of attending such events, well, this is merely part of the collateral damage entailed in getting a capitalist economy back to full running speed after a long period of partial shutdown. If grandpa dies as a result of contracting COVID at a Leafs game, he has merely taken one for the team, in every sense of the word. And let's not forget that his death means there will be fewer pension expenses for the rest of us to have to bear.

A related (and even more cynical) explanation is that the government has decided to adopt a 'herd immunity' strategy toward COVID, on the at best highly debatable assumption that the only way to bring the disease under control in the long run is for the vast majority of the population to have caught it, and therefore developed antibodies to prevent its recurrence. I'm not sure I would give the current federal government or any of the provinces credit for being philosophically consistent enough to carry through such a strategy. In any case, given COVID's near-endless ability to morph into different strains and variants, a 'herd immunity' strategy based on the assumption of a single well-defined disease seems doomed to failure. Even if this were not the case, 'herd immunity' is, or should be, too cruel a strategy to warrant serious consideration in any society that likes to think of itself as decent. While there would be exceptions to this, those succumbing to the disease would, for the most part, be among society's least fortunate: the old and infirm, infants, the poor, those already ill with other conditions, members of minority groups. Are even the most cynical, heartless, and depraved of our political leaders ready to get on board for such a Malthusian cull as wholesale adoption of 'herd immunity' would appear to entail? [2]

To me, a likelier explanation is that of governance fatigue among political leaders. No question: to impose and enforce strict regulations to prevent the spread of COVID is hard work. It is even harder to do so in the face of increasing criticism and, in the extreme, threats or even attacks from those disliking such regulations and wishing to be free of them. I'm sure that dealing with the flak from enraged anti-vaxxers and anti-maskers has driven a lot of good people out of politics altogether, or kept them from going into it in the first place.

The biggest appeal of this explanation is that it works across countries and cultures, and afflicts leaders of all political stripes, from extreme conservatives to extreme progressives. Because of its ubiquity, this explanation may be the most insidious of them all. In its simplest form, it entails public officials becoming unwilling or unable to govern, at least as far as COVID is concerned. With virtually all public officials agreeing not to impose or enforce COVID restrictions, beyond a few obvious examples such as mask requirements in healthcare settings, the new laissez-faire approach to the pandemic goes almost completely unchallenged. Never mind the evidence, which shows that COVID continues to be a serious public health threat. Our public officials are tired and need to rest, poor little things that they are. To force them to actually get to work and govern would amount to cruel and unusual punishment.

In the midst of all this overwhelming political inertia, one of the very few rational voices to be heard is that of Montreal cardiologist and epidemiologist Christopher Labos. Dr Labos, who has more than once called for a return to mask mandates,[3] was quoted in a recent TV interview as saying that rather than scaling back testing, government should be expanding it, to ease the burden on emergency rooms and family doctors.[4] Thus far, unfortunately, Labos remains almost the only Canadian scientist or public official to fully appreciate the emperor's lack of clothing.

But if governments are busy doing nothing about COVID, have no fear. They're looking out for our health in a number of other ways. Most notably, having said little about the effects of alcohol over the past decade or so, the federal government is now trying to convince Canadians that *any* alcohol consumption is risky, and that those who must drink should limit their consumption to two drinks or less per week in order to minimize the risks of brain damage, cancer, heart disease, and various other afflictions.[5] Some are calling for warning labels to be placed on alcohol bottles, similar to the labels that already appear on cigarette packages. The new guidelines represent a drastic drop from previous ones recommending a maximum of 15 drinks per week for men and 10 for women.[6]

While there is, as I noted in the introduction to this section, some reason to believe that any beyond the most minimal alcohol consumption increases the drinker's risk of diseases such as those listed above, those risks are likely to be quite small, in the larger scheme of things, and the effects of moderate regular alcohol consumption seem likely to take years if not decades to manifest themselves. The frequency and intensity of the new warnings around alcohol, coupled with the new laissez-faire philosophy around COVID, might almost lead one to believe that alcohol posed more of a public health threat in the here and now than COVID—if one didn't know better.

What we have here is clearly a lack of proportion around alcohol, and a misplaced sense of priorities. Making COVID tests more readily available might and likely would reduce COVID-related hospital admissions next month. Reducing everyone's alcohol consumption to the recommended maximum of two drinks per week might (perhaps) reduce alcohol-related hospital admissions in a decade or two.

All well and good—I suppose. But then I look around me at my friends, many of whom are writers or researchers or involved with other work that makes heavy use of their brains. Some of these folks have for decades had a drink before dinner every night, and/or wine or beer with dinner. No sign of brain damage in any of them. Then I look around me at what other countries are saying about alcohol. If booze is indeed so hazardous to people's health as to justify the recent Carrie Nation-like pronouncements coming out of Canada, wouldn't you think other Western countries would have recognized the fact and embarked on some major revisions of their own alcohol guidelines? Not a bit of it. While it's true that the health council of the Netherlands did recommend total abstinence, or at most a maximum of one drink per day, that was in 2015. All the principal comparator countries are standing pat. Australia and France continue to recommend a maximum of 10 drinks per week, the US continues to recommend a maximum of two drinks a day for men and one for women, and the UK continues to recommend a maximum of what it calls 14 'units' per week of alcohol, which amounts to six English pints of beer per week.[7]

Most suspicious of all is the timing of the recent announcements of the new alcohol guidelines. They have come at a time when the federal government has been under severe criticism for underfunding the healthcare system, allowing the emergency room crisis described in the first part of this essay to develop. Arousing people's anxiety about an issue only marginally connected to the current state of the healthcare system strikes me as an excellent diversionary tactic. Moreover, it's more than a little ironic that the new, neo-prohibitionist alcohol guidelines have appeared at the same time as governments have started allowing betting on sports, and allowing advertising of sports betting sites on TV. The new addiction of gambling is being rung in just as the old one—government hopes—is being rung out. You couldn't make this stuff up if you were Monty Python's best script-writer. It would all be quite funny, if the potential consequences to the next generation of gambling addicts to be created by the new policy were not so serious. Ring out the old addiction; ring in the new one. Words for governments to live by, and for citizens to die by.

Enough of using government proactively to try to preserve its citizens' health and its healthcare system's integrity. All of that amounts to dirigisme at the very least, if not outright socialism. Government's job is to pry minutely into people's private behaviour, especially any aspect of that behaviour that seems likely to bring pleasure. And don't you forget it!

Long live the nanny state! Let me propose a toast to its health and long life—in unflavoured Ovaltine.

Gatineau, Quebec
March 5, 2024

---

[1] Saba Aziz, 'The End of COVID-19 Testing? What Ottawa's Call to Stop Shipments Means.' Global News, March 2, 2023. Except as otherwise noted, material for this discussion has been drawn from Aziz's article.

[2] For a more detailed discussion of these issues, see Alan Lennon, 'COVID, Social Responsibility and 'The Next Times,'' in *Plague Take It,* pp. 282-286.

[3] 'Mask Mandate Needed, Says Epidemiologist,' CBC News, Nov. 14, 2022.

[4] From an interview with Global TV, downloaded March 3, 2023.

[5] See, among many others, Holly Honderich, 'What's Behind Canada's Drastic New Alcohol Guidance,' BBC News, Jan. 18, 2023, downloaded March 3, 2023, and Lauren Pelley, 'Hangover Headaches Are the Least of Your Worries. Scientists Say Drinking Can Be Hard on the Brain,' CBC News, Jan. 24, 2023, updated January 25.

[6] Megan DeLaire, 'What You Should Know about Canada's New Alcohol Guidelines,' CTV News, January 20, 2023.

[7] Honderich, 'What's Behind Canada's New Alcohol Guidance.'

SECTION 8
Travel

*W*hen Ann and I were putting together the travel section of Plague Take It, *the burning question was, 'When will it be safe to travel again?' Now, the burning questions are, 'How has travel changed as a result of the pandemic? What obstacles (bureaucratic or otherwise) must today's traveler be prepared to encounter?' The five pieces in this section offer an interesting and extremely varied range of perspectives on these questions.*

As I discovered doing the research for my other new book, Work Less, *air travel has since the pandemic become more problematic and far more stressful, owing in large measure to severe labour shortages both among pilots and among staff working on the ground, such as ticket agents and baggage handlers. Leading off the section, Robert Barclay demonstrates just how nightmarish the situation can be in 'Air Canada, We Stand in Line for Thee.' Next, Janet Barclay offers a humorous perspective on the vexed issue of checked baggage in her 'Story of a Traveling Green Case,' written from the perspective of a teenage suitcase eager to explore the world a bit. This is followed by Suha Mardelli's sometimes funny but often terrifying 'Travel After,' a saga of transatlantic air travel with young children culminating in the family's return to Canada in the middle of a lockdown and a blizzard minus Mardelli's husband, who's been forced to remain in Dubai to recover from COVID.*

While flying may offer the most obvious examples of how travel has changed, these are not by any means the only examples. Many people appear to be driving faster and more recklessly than before, as I discovered during the Long Island Expressway drive I chronicle in 'Accelerating through the Pandemic.' Whether today's higher speeds are the result of pent-up rage from the pandemic, reduced enforcement of speed limits, or some combination of the two remains to be seen.

Fran Ota ends the section on a positive note in her 'Traveling—Even in a Pandemic.' Ota's memoir, which describes her time as a graduate student in Iceland and Norway, reminds us that for all its difficulties, travel can still be an enriching and rewarding experience. Probably this is why so many of us keep on engaging in it, in the face of what some would say is all good sense.

Jon Peirce

Air Canada, We Stand in Line for Thee
Robert Barclay

Arriving in Montreal from Heathrow with a connecting Air Canada flight to Ottawa would normally be a smooth transition. Trudeau Airport does have one disadvantage, though: a tunnel between international and domestic terminals where it is necessary to descend, traverse the tunnel, and then go back up to the departure gate level. When pushing my wife in a wheelchair, I discovered that one needs to use an old-fashioned microscopic elevator that scarcely takes two people, one of them in the wheelchair, and their luggage. This was a minor inconvenience when heading to the gate for the flight to Ottawa, but would prove to be yet another component in an unfolding nightmare upon our return.

We waited at the domestic gate for five hours while delay upon delay piled up. There were few announcements because all four departure gates in that sector were staffed by one lone employee, who was driven to distraction by a more-than-quadruple workload. The first flight delay was caused by the lack of a captain; we were told that he was 'in the airport' and would appear momentarily. It was perhaps an hour after this announcement that our pilot finally appeared but, unfortunately, we were unable to board yet because a flight crew had to be located. The delay stretched to three hours, then four. 'Confidentially,' the lone staff member told me after five hours or so, 'if we don't get a crew in the next twenty minutes, the pilot will time out.' We didn't and he did. And that sole harassed agent was so occupied by now that the critical cancellation announcement was conveyed to us by e-mail. Mobbed at her desk after the rumour spread, she broke away from boarding two other flights (lucky travelers!) to tell us that, for our night's forced stay, we could get vouchers for meals, travel and hotels at the 'courtesy desk' opposite Gate 1.

Along with my wife in her wheelchair, there was an elderly lady on wheels with a husband/pusher, so together with a third woman—also bumped off our flight but thankfully bipedal—we decided to form a convoy to head to Gate 1. This involved calling the elevator up, rolling one wheelchair with its pusher in, descending to tunnel level, then sending the elevator back up for the next cargo. Once the caravan was assembled at tunnel level, we set off towards elevator number two. The loading and unloading process was repeated in reverse, and finally we headed for the Shangri-La of Gate 1.

Now, you could read this as yet another whining blog, letter, post, tweet, you name it, like thousands of others, totally centred on our own anger and frustration. But it's not. When we decided to travel by air in the summer of 2022, we took the responsibility upon ourselves. We knew the mess Air

Canada was in way before we booked our flights. We had seen the line-ups, the heaps of delayed baggage, the mobs of angry travelers. Then, on an earlier outbound flight through Montreal, I had seen the issues at firsthand when my plane had waited on the apron for half an hour because no ground crew could be found to open the gate. I just nodded wisely and said to myself, 'Told me so!' And when I arrived at Heathrow—late for my connection because of this delay—my luggage didn't. This was the beginning of an odyssey that needn't be recorded in detail here. Suffice it to say that, by our return trip from Europe, we had truly earned the travel nightmares that unfolded; we had called the wrath of deep heaven down upon our own heads. No, this is not about us; it's about a callous monster called Air Canada.

So, there was our little convoy arriving at the desk opposite Gate 1 at around 11:00 p.m. One of the two agents had already left because, due to understaffing, the discourtesy desk simply closed up at night. The remaining employee was due to go off shift momentarily, but having a plane-load of disgruntled passengers suddenly thrust upon her, she felt duty bound to stay at her post. Our turn at her desk arrived. She was almost in tears, her eyes so tired she could scarcely see her screen. 'It's not fair,' she told us. 'I'm so exhausted I'm frightened to drive home in case I crash. They shouldn't do this to us. It's cruel.' She dutifully issued us vouchers for food, transportation and hotel rooms, and we thanked her for doing her duty.

One gate agent for four flights, no flight crew to be found, a timed-out pilot, absent gate crew, lost and delayed luggage, one desk agent doing non-paid overtime and exhausted to the limit of collapse. And that's just our personal list. It's incomprehensible that a major international carrier could resume service with such gross understaffing. What possessed Air Canada management to think that staff could be laid off *en masse* during the COVID slowdown and simply reemployed when it had all gone away? Was it assumed that laid-off employees would just sit at home watching Netflix until the call came to return? That they would jump at the chance of a job with the same outfit that had booted them out? Sure, I can understand the need for Air Canada to downsize while lockdowns and travel restrictions were in place— no organization was immune—but it is beyond naïve to assume that every-thing in your staffing procedures will click nicely back into place at the drop of an N-95. However, this appears to have been the strategy; I hesitate to call it thinking.

As the airline is responsible for delays, cancellations and missed flights, there ought to be major compensation. According to the letter of the law, there should be. Sadly, the letter of the law appears not to have applied in this case. The compounding outrage is Air Canada attempting to institute a policy denying compensation claims because flights were cancelled due to 'safety concerns.' Of course, we all know that the 'safety concerns' were due to the lack of adequate staffing, which has absolutely no relationship to the mechanical safety of the aircraft. This is cynical and dishonest misdirection. And it is... well, just plain sleazy. Let's hope the Canadian Transportation Agency will put some teeth into its recently updated Air Passenger Protection Regulations, because Air Canada seems to consider itself either immune from the law, or above it. At the time of writing, a mother and her son who were delayed 16 hours due to a crew shortage sued Air Canada for their promised and deserved $1,000.00 each, and won their case. The CTA argued that Air Canada failed to provide evidence 'establishing that the crew shortage was unavoidable despite proper planning.' Clearly, the staff shortages that Air Canada cited bore no relationship to aviation safety, which of course results in a legally rendered statement of the obvious. However, if passengers need to go to the trouble of instituting legal action, the number of payouts will be slim.

Clearly, when one is either traveling with Air Canada or working against its intransigence, it's *caveat emptor.*

The Story of a Traveling Green Case
Janet Barclay

Our cases have always been very well behaved, and we have trusted them to go to wherever we sent them. Of course, we always accompanied them, just to reassure them as to where they were going, that we would look after them, and not overfill them with too much of anything. So, as Bob set off for a trip to Europe, which included running a workshop, we confidently expected Green Case would arrive with him. Yes, this was post-COVID, but this case had been amenable to traveling everywhere with him for over 10 years, so Green was by this time a seasoned world traveler. Imagine Bob's shock when Green didn't arrive in LHR (Heathrow)! Well, it would show up the next day; he trusted the case to know its job! But no, it didn't arrive. So Bob left London, made his way to FRA (Frankfurt) and then HMB (Hamburg), and was very upset because his tried and trusted case still hadn't followed him. He had to teach his workshop during the day, and buy everything he needed in the evening. Thank you very much, little Green Case!

Little did we know this little Green Case had found some buddies in YUL (Montreal) and was having so much fun talking and playing with them, it had clean forgotten to get on the flight to LHR (Heathrow)! As we learned later, he and his buddies were rolling themselves around the baggage area. They were bugging cases with different airport codes, so those with LGW (Gatwick) or maybe BOD (Bordeaux) would be teased mercilessly. Then, when the baggage handlers came to collect the bags for departure, these naughty cases would roll away and hide! Finally, after some of his friends had gone on their merry way to join their people, Green started to feel lonely. His friends had gone, and nobody wanted to play with him any more, so the next time the baggage handlers looked for him, he rolled out and got himself onto a plane to LHR (Heathrow). And, of course, Green was supposed to follow Bob to FRA (Frankfurt), then HMB (Hamburg)—after all, he was carrying stuff Bob needed—but while playing with his pals in LHR (Heathrow) he quite forgot. Finally, Bob lost patience with his antics and decided to send him home. Green was feeling happy about being reunited with his buddies in the cupboard at home, but instead of a direct flight to YOW (Ottawa) he realized his bar code said YYZ (Toronto). While he was happy to be going home, he wasn't too sure about the detour. What if there were no other cases to play with? He was feeling lonely and wanted to talk to his friends in the cupboard at home. Fortunately, it wasn't long before he found himself on a plane to YOW (Ottawa) and knew he was on his way home.

Once in Ottawa, he felt a bit worried when he was put in the back of a van and driven away from the airport. Where was he going, who was taking him? All he wanted was to go home. After a short ride, Green was taken out and passed over to Janet. He let out a big sigh of relief and was happy to be taken upstairs where he was emptied and stowed within the large Green Case. He enjoyed being emptied because nothing in him had been used, so no dirty laundry or souvenirs had to be dealt with.

He had a lovely time telling the other cases in the cupboard all about his trip. A couple of the smaller cases were scared at the idea of not being close to family, but one or two others were thinking maybe they'd try this out whenever they left home! But now it was time to rest and recover until the next trip.

Several months later, naughty Green Case was taken out of the cupboard once more and given strict instructions to stay with Bob and Janet. He appeared to agree to this, but we were not sure he really meant it. He made his way to YUL (Montreal), along with the smaller cases, on a train. This was different from his usual trips, but interesting. He chatted to the other suitcases on the luggage rack, but because they were lying down, they couldn't roll around and get into trouble.

Once in Montreal, he was interested to see that they all drove in a little bus to the airport. There he went through the whole process of getting his bar codes for LHR (Heathrow), being weighed, and then taken out to the plane. The suitcases in Montreal were not much fun—far too dedicated to arriving with their people. So, Green had to behave himself and join his family when they arrived in Heathrow. The small cases were glad to see he had shown up and told him about their ride as carry-on baggage in the plane. A very luxurious trip for them!

After a couple of days in London, all the cases were taken to LGW (Gatwick). Green was labelled for MLA (Malta), weighed, and sent on his way. He happily made it to MLA (Malta)—still behaving himself—and once out of the plane, enjoyed the warmth of that country. It was much better than home! We believe he started getting some ideas right then and there. The smaller cases tried to tell us of his plans but unfortunately, we didn't understand what they were saying, because they were whispering so Green wouldn't hear them. As we found out later, we should have persevered in our attempts to learn Green's plan.

We left Malta, made our way to BOD (Bordeaux) with all our cases, and spent a couple of days in France with family. We had no idea of the plans Green had made. The smaller bags were still making twittering noises, trying to tell us of his plans, but to no avail.

It was time to go back to BOD (Bordeaux) and fly to FRA (Frankfurt) where we would board our next flight to YUL (Montreal). Naturally, Green was labelled from BOD (Bordeaux) to FRA (Frankfurt), then to YUL

(Montreal) and finally YOW (Ottawa). We said goodbye to him and said we would see him in YOW (Ottawa), as he was bar-coded right through. As he went down the baggage chute, he made some inarticulate sounds, which we didn't understand, as he disappeared to join the other baggage. In retrospect, maybe he was saying goodbye to the smaller cases, but was he also telling us of his naughty plans? The other cases were also twittering as we walked away from the baggage chute, and sadly we didn't pick up on what they were saying, either.

Our flights home went well, and we finally arrived in YUL (Montreal). We knew there was enough time for our naughty Green to transfer in FRA (Frankfurt) from the BOD (Bordeaux) flight to the YUL (Montreal) one, so we assumed he was on board. After a long flight we arrived at YUL (Montreal). The connection to YOW (Ottawa) was very tight, so we were concerned about Green making this flight, as were several other passengers. But we were assured that any bags that didn't make it would be loaded on the later evening flight, so no real worries!

When we got to the carousel in YOW (Ottawa), we had hoped to see Green, but we were not too concerned when he didn't show. Then we spoke to the baggage handling staff and were in for a shock! Green had decided to stay in FRA (Frankfurt) overnight! We can only guess that he had met his old friends and was making a nuisance of himself with the other luggage, trundle-ing around, hiding and whatnot. He had missed going to FRA (Frankfurt) with Bob on the last trip, and now he was making up for it. We were told he should be here in a day or so! He'd just better be, we thought, or he won't be traveling for a long time, unless it's by car or bus, but certainly not flying.

There was a phone call and then a knock on the door a day later. There was Green, sitting on the porch looking very sure of himself and not a bit embarrassed at all the trouble he'd caused.

Teenage cases are just as bad as teenage kids!

––––––––––––––––

I gave an earlier version of this story to the baggage handling crew at Ottawa International Airport. As I explained to them, they are often targeted for problems not of their making, and I felt that things just needed lightening up. They were highly amused and very grateful for my sense of humour, and for not taking things too seriously.

Travel After

Suha Mardelli

Even when I had to go back home to get my passport, and even when I arrived 30 minutes before takeoff, and even when my name was misspelled on my ticket (to Suoba Mardly), and even when passengers were already in their seats, and even when the cocky 19-year old I was complained loudly for the check-in counter to be re-opened… even when all that had happened and was my fault, the airline attendant still checked me in, a big smile on her face, handed me my boarding pass and then waved me through to the burping bus 10 meters away, waiting to drive me to the plane.

That flight was in 1994, from Montreal to Amsterdam. I arrived cheery and tipsy, lungs filled with second-hand cigarette smoke, thanks to two giddy passengers behind me who were celebrating God-knows-what, buying $20.00 bottles of champagne, which they shared with me so I would stop complaining about their chain-smoking. *When in Rome…*

A couple of years later, I did hop on a plane to Rome, only realizing after it arrived in Frankfurt that this was as far as I went because (in my stupidity) I hadn't bought a ticket that took me to Rome—just Frankfurt. This was before the EU was formed. No worries, I bought a train ticket instead. German Border Control put a green sticker on my passport. 'Auf Wiedersehen' said a cutie with blue eyes, and I was good to go all the way to Italy. I could almost see my mother rolling her eyes through the payphone when she said, 'You're lucky traveling is so easy.'

That was Travel Before.

Travel changed after 9/11. Most noticeably, smiles were replaced with warning signs; men with guns lurked in doorways, and some passengers, especially those with beards and brown complexions, were now asked into private rooms for 'a chat'—too bad if the flight was missed. Certain passport holders, like Syrians or Pakistanis, were encouraged to remain earthbound—for their own safety. At Immigration, someone actually read my Canadian passport, examining the bindings, making sure it was bona fide. Security checks popped up all over airport grounds: before check-in, before duty-free, before boarding. Carry-on luggage was methodically screened. I once had to throw away my water bottle and mini-manicure kit, though I was luckier than the new mother next to me who was in tears as the officer at Toronto Pearson emptied all her baby-food into the garbage—even the banana. 'You can buy replacements at the duty-free,' he told her unsympathetically.

Happy-go-lucky wanderer that I was, I remained eternally optimistic that the travel madness would be short-lived. Surely the world would come to its senses again. Right?

It still took a decade. WMDs had to be found, along with the terrorists who'd attacked Spain, Bombay, Nigeria. Airport security ramped up each time planes were pulled into the oceans. As a woman with big brown eyes, a permanent tan, and a Syrian husband, I often found myself on the receiving end of particularly invasive questions. While grateful for the prudence, I often felt it went too far. Supported by the Terrorist Act, the person on the other side of the Perspex glass asked highly personal questions: 'Are you related to anyone whom you suspect to be a terrorist? Are you on pleasant terms with your husband? What is your religion? What was the name of your paternal grandfather? Have you ever fired a weapon, even for recreational purposes?'

By 2012, airport travel had developed a pragmatic rhythm. Security checks were still being performed, though Nexus cards eased frequent flyers through airports. I had a job which required me to commute between Dubai and nearby countries for two weeks of every month, flying to destinations that piqued curiosity: Why was I, a woman, going to Pakistan, Kuwait, Jordan, Bahrain, Qatar? I became an expert at packing one-week essentials into a carry-on. With five business meetings crammed into my days, I had to cut unnecessary commuting time. I thanked my lucky stars that totes were considered part of a woman's DNA; indeed, I began to take totes instead of luggage. In went my laptop, books, passport, make-up, water and two apples. I timed things so that at 5 a.m. Monday morning I rolled out of bed in Dubai and caught the seven o'clock flight to one of those previously-mentioned destinations, sashaying through business lounges, Nexus gates, and onto planes—my Grande Americano still piping hot. Done with my work, I would be back home by Friday afternoon to spend the weekend with my kids. I did what was required to complete airport hurdles with ease—breathing calmly at security guards who leered: 'Madam, did you pack your own underwear?'

Then smart phones showed up and Travel After Technology became a godsend for someone like me. Waiting at the red light or picking up vegetables at the supermarket, I booked air tickets, hotels, cars, tour-guides on whatever whim had taken over. My husband and I visited the Dead Sea less than a day after wishing we were there; we gate-crashed a Bollywood wedding (in India) a week after a drunken dare with friends. Both my kids were indoctrinated into my travel rhythm as soon as their passports were issued. 'We are a traveling family,' I would remind them as we unpacked a disheveled suitcase expelling stuffed animals and crumpled diapers.

On moving back to Canada from the UAE in 2019, I discovered Caribbean beaches were only a four-hour commute from Pearson—just perfect if the Winter Blues threatened to freeze my bones, or if a craving for authentic jerk chicken sandwiches became overwhelming.

Of course, a frost far worse than Jack ossified us in March 2020. Not that anyone anticipated COVID lockdowns would last as long as they did.

With only essential travel allowed, I hung up my wings and sulked in the bath. Like everyone else, we made the best of most of it: parks in summer, parks in winter, road trips when restrictions were eased, backyards when restrictions returned. We snuck off to Sandbanks a couple of times (when I was literally, figuratively, absolutely going crazy) just to stick our feet in the sand and smell the water. (I also brewed Turkish coffee on the lake's shore and read fortunes. That's what it took to get re-centered.)

However, 20 months later I was feeling like an albatross tied to a maypole. Grandma, all the way on the other side of the world, was also complaining. A widow now, she was lonely and missed us. Airports were open. My husband and I pondered and wondered. After a three-year hiatus, how bad could travel during COVID really be? Worse than travel right after 9/11?

I didn't care any more. I missed the obnoxious staff, the smell of the duty-free, the fluorescent lights and scoliosis-inducing chairs of airport waiting lounges. Most of all, I missed that glorious feeling of walking out of an airport: that anticipation when the last doors slide open and you find yourself in a new world.

We decided to travel to Dubai in early December 2021, just ahead of the school Christmas break, taking advantage of lower fares and avoiding any travel frenzy since many countries were opening up. I connected with old friends in Dubai to find out that some would also be traveling to see their families—their first opportunity to do so since March 2020. There was a sense of normalcy in the air as I thought of all the planes about to crisscross Earth. We booked hotels and tickets, tattooing every cancellation policy to our hippocampus. Perfectly-timed COVID testing was a new aspect of travel prep, so we found ourselves hunting down medical labs in Gatineau, bargaining like carpet-sellers for the best price and fastest results. I bought extra face masks and sanitizers, then printed our tickets while filing vaccination certificates and PCR test results. Seventy-two hours prior to departure, we checked in online. This was nice. Familiar, cool-and-breezy, just like old times. Maybe travel during COVID wouldn't be so bad after all?

On the day of our departure, we arrived at Pearson two hours before departure time. It felt like pre-COVID days. Only two COVID checkpoints greeted us ahead of security. We quickly dropped off our luggage and eased into duty-free. I bought maple syrup, knick-knacks and souvenirs. On the plane, everyone settled in for the 14-hour trip. Bless Emirates, I thought, thankful for the complimentary eye-masks, ear plugs, and blankets and pillows. Excitement coursed through me when the engines roared, rattling the fuselage, and the plane took off. Serenity glided over me. We slept, watched movies, and played games until we arrived. At Dubai airport we were welcomed with the traditional green coffee that Emiratis adore—thick and syrupy, with saffron and cardamom. The warm bitter liquid sloshed down my throat, awakening my tired senses. It was delicious. So far, travel during COVID had been smooth. I was so happy. It was a wonderful vacation spent overloading on food, sun, sand, and family.

Ten days later, it's time to return to Canada. The world has now plummeted into a mosh pit with a highly contagious COVID variant. Hotel staff, relatives and airlines are on high alert while we pack bags and book PCR tests. My poor husband tests positive and must stay behind. It will be just me traveling back to Ottawa with our two kids.

To another lockdown.

We have been advised to be at the airport four hours before the 7:00 a.m. departure time—a little extreme? Dread settles in me, twisting my stomach and drumming in my head. I breathe, meditate, go for an evening run to try to shake off that dread—but I can't. At three o'clock in the morning, the kids and I trundle through Dubai departure terminal. Every-where you feel impatience and fear.

COVID paperwork checks are spaced every two meters by airport employees already exhausted and cross-eyed from the interminable task. Check ticket. Check boarding pass. Check mask. Check destination. Check passport. Check entry requirements. Check COVID requirements. Check vaccination certificates. Check PCR test result. Check ArriveCAN receipt. Check passport again. Check person. Check.

Three times. Three travellers. Thirty-six 'Checks 'at each checkpoint.

At 8:00 a.m., an hour late, we board the plane. My husband's empty seat is a blessing on the overbooked flight. Everybody wants to get home. I check the weather forecast in Toronto; it is supposed to be sunny and -15 Celsius when we arrive at around 1:00 p.m. local time. I plan to drive back to Ottawa and be home by early evening. I pray Canadian stoicism trumps irrational fear, hoping it will take no more than 30 minutes to get through the airport. I ration my energy.

Thirteen hours go by in slow motion. We nap, watch movies, and play games until the white and grey form of Toronto is below us. An inch off the ground most passengers leap up to grab their belongings. The flight attendant's scolding is swift and ferocious. Only once the plane parks are we allowed to unbuckle and prepare to leave.

Yet even when the doors open, we are told to wait. My 10-year-old son now needs the toilet, but the bathrooms are still locked for landing and the friendly stewardess is too exhausted to be nice anymore. Finally, a ground control crewman hands the purser a yellow piece of paper. He rolls his eyes and announces that 'due to COVID' only 75 passengers at a time can leave the aircraft. I scan the seats and count, relieved that we are the 40th, 41st and 42nd passengers. Twenty minutes later, we disembark into the terminal with the first cohort. I grab my little guy and dash to the nearest bathroom, pulling down his pants and angling him in one swift move towards the toilet.

Once we emerge, Pearson is eerily quiet. 'Where is everyone?' I ask my daughter, who has fallen asleep on the bench outside. Surely the plane hasn't emptied yet?

She shrugs. No one has come out of the plane since we did. I take Machiavellian pleasure at this news. We can still beat the lines. I am desperate to leave the airport, as my rationed energy is leaking like radioactive waste with all these delays. We speedwalk through the empty airport toward Immigration, following arrows through the open-spaced maze: up escalators, left then straight, then left again, then across. My kids jog behind me, whining. A few scattered passengers from our flight are the only other people we see. All the kiosks and shops are closed. Lockdown, of course. I am optimistic because it's looking like we can be out of here quickly, a thought I cling to until… I almost snowball into a waiting crowd. We have reached Immigration and this is where I find—everyone.

The large room is packed. Social distancing is now an imaginary concept. Lines and lines of grumbling travellers shuffle through the labyrinth towards the self-serve machines. When it's our turn, I punch in the details of our passports and customs form, repeating the process three times until the machine spits out a blank receipt. I groan loudly calling to the officer hovering near me, 'It's blank.'

She waves me forward. 'Just give it to him,' she says, pointing to an immigration officer, 'and he'll do it for you.'

I curse in all the languages I know. Another line-up. More waiting. I notice the new COVID rules are emblazoned above the immigration turnstiles in shiny red, green, and black letters. I read them four times, my comprehension waning more each time: 'If you are vaccinated you may or may not be randomly selected for testing and you must immediately head to your final destination unless otherwise requested to isolate at a government-approved destination or you may otherwise be subject to fines…' and a SWAT team will hunt you down!

I look out of the skylight. Where is the sun? It is foggy outside, with snow squalls. Great. A blizzard warning flashes across my phone: fog, icy roads, dangerous driving conditions. Oh, for f… sake!

Finally, it's our turn. I smile my brightest, the officer is deadpan. He informs me that under the Quarantine Act he needs to ask me certain questions. The Perspex glass hangs like a confessional curtain between us. Here we go again. Where did you come from? Where are you going? Are you vaccinated? Are your PCR tests negative? Will you reach your final destination within 24 hours? Do you have a place to isolate? I tell the truth, but it feels like I'm lying. He sticks pink stickers on our passports. What does that mean? I notice other travelers have pink stickers as well. Pink stickers must mean we are exempt from random testing. Good. I can't afford to delay any longer, otherwise we'll never get home tonight. Baggage is that way, he indicates with his head.

I heave a sigh of relief. Yippee! No testing! Clearly, I have been over-panicking—an intrinsic tendency when things don't go according to my plan. Canadian impartiality is ruling the day after all!

We head to collect our baggage. Thankfully in the time it has taken us to reach here, the bags have been removed from the carousel and arranged neatly, like the candy dispensers in a supermarket. It is a nice pop of colour amidst all the grey. The kids find our bags quickly.

It's now 4:00 p.m., almost dark and with a blizzard is in full swing. I calmly accept the inevitable: I can't drive to Ottawa tonight, in the middle of a snowstorm, on the fumes of my weary energy. It would be madness to do so. And. I. Am. Not. Mad. Thank God for Wi-Fi, Expedia and WhatsApp: I heart you all. Deftly, I search for hotel rooms. A sense of urgency lights firecrackers under my seat once I overhear a couple of other families doing the same thing. I'm hoping to get the last available room in Toronto, hoping it is clean and hygienic, hoping there is a restaurant and hot water; my fingers tap-dance, typing in numbers, names, codes. The phone lights up with confirmation emails and I smile to the kids. Almost there, I reassure them. We follow more arrows to Customs—the last gatekeeper before freedom— who glances at my scribbles then waves us through. Trotting towards the frosted automatic doors, an attractive officer is telling all the people ahead of us to go right. I slow down. The 'Exit 'airport sign is left. What's going on?

To the right please, she tells us.

Why? The exit is left.

She looks at the pink sticker. Random testing, she replies.

My heart leaps to my throat. I curse the pink sticker. I stop to pull out all the passports and paperwork again. Why the fuck don't I have another three hands. Another officer barks at us, 'Come along, hurry and download the First Health app.' I stare at him in disbelief. Are you serious? What for? 'The testing, ma'am. Please move along.' Now, I have to create an account and a password and re-enter the password and push the trolley while my kids bombard me with questions, 'Why mummy? Why mummy?' Then, 'Hurry up ma'am and stop holding the line.' All the other incredulous passengers from our flight are also lined up to get tested. 'Where's the randomness, I ask the guard. Everyone from my flight is being tested.' 'Yeah,' he nods, 'Omicron.'

The second password is not getting accepted, my daughter starts to cry. 'I'm so tired,' she says laying her head on my shoulder. I shove the phone into the guard's hands. 'Please, can you please enter the bloody password? I can't see straight anymore.'

'What, no ma'am?'

'Please, anything 12 characters, two caps two numbers and whatever it is. *Please.*'

He takes pity. I hate being pitied but right now I need it. He enters a password twice, correctly, and walks with me towards the registration desk. I start to enter my children's details, one hand on the documents, the other with the phone, my elbows guiding the trolley, my son hanging off my left, my daughter scraping my ankles with the other trolley. We wait in line again. The nurse finally takes my papers. 'Did you download the app?' she asks.

'Yes.'

'Did you enter the details?'

'Not everything.'

'No worries, I'll do it.'

'Bless you.'

She checks then re-enters details and hands me three test tubes. I want to scream. We were just tested!

We are told to go to three different swabbing stations. A Saran-wrapped employee yanks my kids to stations in the opposite corner. I protest, 'Keep my son next to me.' My son's lower lip quivers but he's too respectful to disobey the officer and is whisked away. Wait for me there, I point while some woman says, 'Ma'am, please move along.'

I am swabbed by an efficient nurse who fishes for compliments to her speedy work. Silence is the best I can muster.

I get a text from my husband that says he's happy that we're spending the night in Toronto, 'Let the kids watch a movie,' reads the message. The kids cheer up tremendously at their dad's suggestion. More than two hours after landing, we march out of the airport. The blizzard howls through the empty Arrivals pavement. I scream, my kids join me. 'Aaaaargh!' we yell at this mad, mad world.

We bundle into a cab and head to the hotel. We shower, we eat, we sleep. The next morning, we drive back home. 'I'm not traveling on a plane for a year,' my daughter announces, hugging the carpet. 'I'm not traveling for two years,' my son chimes in. I say nothing.

Six hours later, the government calls me. A robot recites the Quarantine Act, then asks if I have arrived at my final destination. I press '1.' Then the robot advises me to...

I hang up.

Accelerating Through the Pandemic
Jon Peirce

It appears that the pandemic has made big changes to the way some people drive, at least in certain parts of North America. And these changes don't appear to have been for the better.

Let me explain. Whenever I've driven in Canada over the past three decades or so, I've been one of the fastest drivers on the road. Even in Quebec, whose drivers are noted for being among the fastest in the country, I'm still a good deal faster than average. Typically I go 20 to 25 km/hr above the limit when driving on the Trans-Canada or other wide, nearly empty highways. Whether from sheer good luck, or because I'm a gentlemanly sort of driver who always signals before turning or changing lanes, rarely if ever weaves in and out, drives an inconspicuous silver-coloured car that looks just like a lot of the other cars on the road, and in general does little to attract the constabulary's attention beyond going a tad above the limit, I've received but two speeding tickets this millennium. I'm sure that if I averaged even five km/hr faster than I do, I'd have received several more. In Nova Scotia, where I lived for 11 years before moving back to the Ottawa area in 2020, 20 above the limit was the dividing line between ticket and no ticket. An extremely precise dividing line, too. I once drew a warning for driving at 130 km/hr—exactly 20 above the limit—on Highway 101 between Halifax and Windsor. The following winter, I was caught going 132 on that same road; that time, I got a ticket.

It appears that few of my fellow Nova Scotians during that period tested the system's limits to the extent I did. Indeed, I have concrete evidence, albeit evidence derived from a single case, that demonstrates the fact. On one trip from Halifax to Edmundston, New Brunswick, an eight-hour drive, I was passed by just six cars through the entire day. While I never again counted the number of cars that passed me as I did on that drive, made some 15 years ago, back-of-the-envelope recollections suggest that this figure was not that far off the norm for my long drives throughout my time in Nova Scotia.

Fast forward about a decade and a half and move the whole scene south to New York State. Last week (it is May, 2022 as this is being written), while driving in that state, first on U.S. Interstate #89 and then on the Long Island Expressway, which I believe but would not swear is Interstate #495, I continued my Canadian practice of driving 20 to 25 above the limit. The difference was that in this case, instead of being one of the fastest drivers on the road, I now found myself among the slower ones, and at times among the very slowest. At a speed that would have had me on the verge of getting a ticket in Nova Scotia, I had cars whizzing past me on both sides as I drove in the middle lane. (Normally I'd have driven in the right lane, but in this instance avoided doing so because on the expressway, the on-ramps and off-ramps were frequent enough to entail a great deal of stopping and starting for those driving in that lane).

To say that the experience was an eye-opener would be to understate things considerably. At times, things bordered on the nightmarish—and this, to repeat, for someone who considers himself a fast driver. On at least three occasions, cars went past me at speeds I reckoned to be 50 km/hour or more greater than ours. The most blatant example occurred halfway between Manhattan and Montauk, when a motorcycle whizzed past at, I would guess, at least twice the legal speed limit of 90 km/hr, and a good 70 faster than my 110. Within five seconds after passing me, the motorcycle was a mere speck on the horizon. I could see the vehicle just clearly enough to note that, shortly after the pass, its driver had taken to executing an intricate pattern of zig-zags, which he would alternate with occasional ess-curves, all at the same unbelievably high speed. I felt as if I'd been suddenly transported to the Bonneville Salt Flats, where racing cars are tested. It was not a warm and cozy feeling.

At a more mundane level, most of the cars passing me on the left looked to be doing at least 20 km/hr more than I was, which meant that the left lane flow was going around 150 in the 110 zones, and between 125 and 130 in the 90 zones. In the right lane, the flow was somewhat slower than it was in the left, but not a great deal. I would guess that the cars in the right lane were generally doing between 130 and 140 in the 110 zones, and between 110 and 120 in the 90 zones. This, I repeat, was in the *right*-hand lane, which is supposed to be a slow lane. To sum up, at a speed enough above the legal limit that I'd have been in danger of getting a ticket in Nova Scotia, I was close to obstructing faster drivers in New York State.

Later in the week, on our return trip, it would be much the same on the Long Island Expressway, the one difference being that that road includes, for much of its length, a special 'HOV-2' lane restricted to certain types of transit vehicles and cars containing two or more people. In this lane, the cars roaring past me appeared to be going at least 60 km/hour faster than I was, and at times more than that. While I have no doubt that the HOV-2 lane was *intended* to be a device for easing strain on the environment and improving traffic flows, in practice it functioned as a high-speed 'sorter' lane for those wishing to drive 140 or more with virtual impunity.

Nowhere else, ever, had I seen such large numbers of cars traveling at speeds so far above the posted limit. Why was this happening? More to the point, why had it been allowed to continue? My traveling companion on #89 imputed the higher speeds to post-pandemic impatience or anger. For my part, I wondered if the cops were letting all this speeding go by unchecked because there were now so many fewer of them than there had been before the pandemic. If toll-takers could be laid off *en masse,* as appears to have been the case, given the state's electronic method of collecting tolls, the same could well have happened to police officers. Another possibility was that many if not most police actually sympathized with the speeders, and might even have been doing the same themselves had they been in the speeders' position—or vehicles.

Whatever the explanation, the phenomenon is more than a little concerning. Both in the right and, especially, the left and, (in the case of the Long Island Expressway), HOV-2 lanes, traffic flows were moving at speeds that seemed frankly unsafe… and the police didn't seem to care. In my view, if the financial or logistical burden of enforcing the 'old' limits was too great, the limits should have been raised—and then enforced. I saw only two or three cars pulled over during my entire time on #89, and about the same number on the Expressway.

If drivers come to believe that speed limits are not going to be enforced at all, some will take it as open season to drive as fast as they like. And this can soon put us in a very dangerous place indeed. After reflecting on our experience on the Expressway, my lady friend and I decided that we'd be taking the train the next time we went out to Montauk,[1] rather than braving the Expressway and its legions of unsupervised motorized cowboys.

It is, of course, important to remember that, bizarre and frightening though my recent New York state driving experiences may have been, they may also not be the final word on the subject. These experiences could perhaps have been anomalies, caused by any number of things, ranging from the onset of mild spring weather (and increased road traffic) to pent-up exasperation after two years of onerous COVID restrictions (my friend's explanation). To be able to assert with any confidence that the situation I encountered in New York was any sort of new norm, one would have to make the same or similar drives a number of times, at different seasons of the year and times of day, in different states, and in different road conditions.

Last, but not necessarily least, it would be interesting to compare post-pandemic attitudes toward mask-wearing and other public health regulations to driving behaviours and attitudes toward traffic laws. In this connection, my own position on the wearing of masks may be apropos; in some ways it parallels the situation with road speed. In Canada, I rank as a moderate liberal, wearing masks, in discretionary situations, a bit less often than many fellow Canadians (bearing in mind that at least of this writing, May 12, 2022, masks are still required in indoor public settings in Quebec). In New York City, on the other hand, at least since the end of its mandatory mask mandate, I've been a staunch 'conservative,' wearing a mask indoors significantly more often than most New Yorkers and on occasion being the only person, or one of a tiny handful, wearing a mask in a largely maskless gathering of 25 or more people. I suspect that there may be a bigger story to tell here, about respect for the law and willingness to undergo personal hardship to advance the public good. But there isn't space to tell that story here, nor am I necessarily the best person to tell it.

In any event, do try to stay safe. It will be much harder to do so now, amid the conflicting welter of uncertain regulations and uneven enforcement, and given a growing consensus on all parts of the political spectrum that we need to move on and live our lives as if the pandemic were over, even as hospitalization, ICU, and death statistics belie such a rosy prognosis. For now, the larger point may be that governments (at all levels) are no longer much interested in looking out for our safety or health, having bigger economic fish to fry. This means that for those still determined to stay healthy, it is every man for himself and every woman for herself. In short, Thomas Hobbes' 'state of nature' through the back door. Ciao.

---

[1] May, 2023 (one year later). We just did, getting on a Long Island Railroad train at Penn Station, and transferring to a train to Montauk at Jamaica. The train ride was not only pleasanter, but just as cheap if not cheaper, at $15.00 and change for a one-way off-peak senior fare. Our hotel sent its shuttle to meet us at the Montauk station. We'll never drive to Montauk again.

Traveling—Even in a Pandemic
Fran Ota

Who goes off to study in two different countries during a pandemic? A senior citizen, that's who! When I left, many people tried to convince me that it was too dangerous, that at my age it was foolish, I could get sick and die... and what about my husband? My husband was asked how he could 'let' his wife do this. His response always was, 'There is no 'let' in a marriage. There's discussion and support.' So began a Master's in Viking and Medieval Norse Studies at University of Iceland and University of Oslo.

So now let's explore, just a little, Iceland and Norway, because my time there turned out to involve more than academic studies. For me as clergy, Iceland is 'creation in action.' First, because it's an island in the North Sea, the weather is maritime and always changeable. I was walking along the sidewalk, across from the road which paralleled the ocean, and was almost blown across into the sea by a high storm wind. Almost every day there were eye-popping sunsets, and I watched northern lights from my seaside balcony. And ahhhhh, the volcanoes! On March 19, 2021, after 18,000 earthquakes in two months, with one exciting magnitude 5.4, a new volcano was 'born,' in Geldingadalir (Gelding Valley) near Fagradalsfjall (Fagradal Fell). This was not a strata-volcanic eruption, but a quiet small rift opening up, and a rather sedate flow, but the lava comes from a depth not seen in 10,000 years. No one noticed until the red glow that night on the horizon became apparent. It was expected, and yet its coming took everyone by surprise. The words of the Christmas carol *O Little Town of Bethlehem* came into my head then: 'How silently, how silently the wondrous gift is given.' Just like a child, this baby grew until the rift was a kilometre long, and seven vents had opened up. All very well-behaved vents, too. Pictures of volcanologists cooking their sausages and potatoes on the hot lava went around. Icelanders live with volcanoes, and their attitude is quite pragmatic. 'We know they will happen, but we hope they don't.'

Iceland sits astride the North American Tectonic Plate and the European Tectonic Plate. At Thingvellir National Park one can stand on the rift, one minute on the North American continent, and the next minute on the European continent. Because Iceland is still such a new place, geographically speaking, it is for me literally creation in action. It is like looking at our own history of humankind. One benefit is that Iceland's heating is underground hot water; another is that incredible healing hot springs abound everywhere.

Iceland was, until about 950 A.D., an island with no population. It contains some arable land, but is mostly mountains and fjords, waterfalls and of course, volcanoes. The settlers came from what is now Norway to get away from violent kings in their own provinces. In approximately 999 A.D., threatened with invasion by Norway if they did not convert to Christianity, the Althing, or General Assembly, took a vote. To keep the king away, they voted unanimously to become a Christian country. Iceland's Constitution thus dates from 1000 A.D., and is the world's oldest democracy created by unanimous vote. This event has shaped Icelandic history, culture, and governance.

However, Norway is the home of my heart. The immensity of the mountains and coastline is awe-inspiring. Delving into Norwegian history, including the geography and minimal farmland, paints a picture of a hard and harsh life. Villages and communities in medieval times were far apart, with farmers living mostly on their own and quite isolated. Every farm had three locations: a winter farm down by the water, a transitional farm up the mountainside, and a summer farm in the high meadows. Imagine living in tiny huts, raising animals and trying to grow crops, with no roads and no other people close by.

Norway was considered the poorest country in Europe until the discovery of oil in 1969. Education became of prime importance, and the whole country underwent a transformation. Norway is now the second richest country in Europe.

Throughout its development, since the discovery of oil and the rise in education, Norway's commitment to human rights has shaped the country and culture. This was not always so, of course. Norway oppressed the indigenous Sami peoples for centuries. Yet Norway has now become a leader in rights, including rights for indigenous people, and for refugees. Oslo is a vibrant city of about 350,000. Music, theatre, food, the cityscape, housing, transportation; it has everything a modern city needs. Bergen, the second largest city, is a jewel, and is one of the medieval homes of the Hanseatic League, a pan-European trading consortium which was active from the 13th to the 18th centuries. Four of us students flew there for a conference on the nature and livability of cities, from the settlements of Vikings to the coming of the Hanse. Particularly important was the number of times Bergen had burnt down through the centuries, and its improvements, each time looking to make the whole city better. The rebuilt Hanseatic Wharf offers a good picture of how Bergen looked in the later Middle Ages. In Oslo there is the Viking Ship Museum, where the most intact of the Viking ships and the grave goods from the ship burials are displayed. The Øseberg ship, found on a farm just outside the town of Tønsberg in southern Norway, gives incredible insight into the Viking people's art, religion, and cultural sophistication. The remaining wooden 'stave' churches, built in the 1100–1200s, display amazing art and architecture. These churches were supported by immense wooden pillars called 'staves,' post and beam construction, with not one piece of metal

237

holding anything together. They display art which reflects both old Norse beliefs and the newer Christian beliefs.

Two friends from long ago, whom I dearly love, live in the city of Ålesund, also known as the 'Art Deco' city. When the city burned down in the earlier 19h century, it was rebuilt in the Art Deco style. My two friends came to Oslo twice to visit. Another friend is a cruise ship captain who lives part of the year in Serbia with his wife and children, and comes for part of the year to Oslo to see his family. They treated me to Christmas dinner Norwegian style, which he cooked himself. He took me out sightseeing in Oslo, to places where I would otherwise not likely have gone. As well, a Canadian Facebook friend married to a Norwegian took two of us students to Tønsberg to see the recreation of Viking ships, and the longhouse ships museum. While in 'semi-lockdown,' we spent lots of time out walking the Akerselva River. When lockdown was lifted, 'Baker Hansen,' the oldest bakery in Norway, was our destination for coffee and marzipan cake or lunch, sitting outside in the sunshine, and even out in the snow. My best friends were 40 and 26. We celebrated Norwegian National Day, its day of official independence, which occurred May 17, 1905. Until 1814, Norway was under the protection of Denmark, and from then till independence was under the governance of Sweden. Norwegians truly know how much their independence is worth, and the cities are full of celebrants in national dress. Every school puts a marching band into local parades, and there are picnics and parties. Everyone is out, proud to wear national dress. The king takes part in Oslo, and it's a true recognition of being their own country. My American friend commented that Norway truly knows how to do independence, because it is really fresh and important.

What did I study? The degree is a Master of Philosophy/Master of Arts in Viking and Medieval Norse Studies! I focussed on Nordic church law; fitting for clergy, don't you think? My thesis evaluates law from Norway, Sweden and Iceland; the laws existed from the 8th century onward. While the laws underwent changes through the years, their roots are in the geography and history of their locations. When I noted in history class that law was my interest, the professor said, 'We need to talk.' The result was that the leading academic scholar in the world on canon law and the medieval church became my thesis adviser. I was so excited I skipped to the train station to go home and got on the wrong train! Now, bear in mind, I was 75 with arthritic knees, often using a walking stick. But yes, I skipped!

My adviser is the age of my eldest son (just over 50), but well established as a world authority in this field. I believe that's as much the point as all the other learning. Age is irrelevant: he's the scholar, I'm the student; I have to learn from him as much as possible. We in North America tend to think we lead in everything, and the rest of the world is behind. People need reminding that Europe had universities even before some countries came into existence. We are very young, very new countries.

Was I concerned about getting COVID? Not enough to put my life on hold. These days and at my age the prospect of dying is much closer; death walks beside us now. We are seeing younger friends die. We are pretty much the last generation that grew up with many childhood diseases. Penicillin came along about 75 years ago; vaccinations were in their infancy; the tuberculosis inoculation was new. I lived in Vietnam during the war and saw what I consider worse than what we dealt with growing up. The leading cause of death in Vietnam was ectopic pregnancy, followed by cancer, typhoid, cholera, dysentery, and starvation. War injuries were tenth on that list. My husband grew up in wartime and postwar Tokyo, with minimal living conditions, sometimes scarcity of food, and all of the childhood diseases plus cholera, typhoid, and others. Vietnam for him was like stepping back in time.

Traveling during COVID was safer than going to the supermarket. Airports were deserted; planes were almost empty. No airport bars or restaurants were open. I was transported around Heathrow in a tiny lemon-yellow enclosed cart. There was no possibility of interacting with anyone else, not even the driver! Britain, Norway, Iceland, Sweden (the countries to which I travelled) dealt with the pandemic clearly but with more sense of human rights than Canada did, in my opinion. For example, Iceland did not require vaccination, nor did it ever have a full lockdown, but was strict about masking. Without a mask one could not board a bus, for instance. Supermarkets limited the numbers inside, as did smaller stores. Since tourism was temporarily halted, the only way shop owners could survive was to stay open and monitor their customers. Upon arrival I was allowed to quarantine in my student apartment, with several check-ins. Similarly, in Norway vaccination was not required but masking was, both in shops and on buses or trains. Norway was quite specific that forced medical treatment violates more than one human rights treaty. In both Iceland and Norway, everyone was able to go outside and walk without any restraint. In Ontario, specifically Toronto, we were supposedly not allowed to go outside our own yard, especially during quarantine, but also at other times as well.

In both Iceland and Norway, my home was a studio apartment in student housing. I had four pairs of tights, three sweaters, a pair each of jeans and shorts, a couple of tees, two pairs of shoes, winter boots, winter and fall coats: one pot, one frying pan, some cutlery and my favourite Japanese knife. I carried a dismantled IKEA footstool, sheets, blankets and towels, and some dishes in one suitcase; clothes and books went in the other. The little that I had was enough! In fact, more than enough! Suddenly, to come home to a closet and dresser packed with clothes, with more pots and pans in the kitchen than we can ever use, made me feel shocked and a bit revolted. Five bags of clothing have gone out, and I've also got rid of some furniture and kitchenware. Books are on their way out, to a church book room which can sell them cheap to theological students. This student experience was a realisation of how little we need to live and be happy. I had a pension, food, friends, studies, and new experiences; nobody cared what clothes anyone had. Perhaps that was the most important lesson to take away: how little we really 'need,' as opposed to what we 'want.' Thirty-five students, from as many countries, of many ages and fields of study, packed up their lives and went to Iceland, Denmark or Norway in the middle of a pandemic, and we are all better people for the experience.

For some of us seniors, pandemic doesn't need to hold us back. For those who are able, in whatever small way, there are always things to be done, even right here at home. I am grateful to be able, still, to learn and grow, to travel during this time, and see how the rest of the world dealt with this pandemic. My husband did wonder why I couldn't study from home, and I replied that being there was at least as important as what I was studying. I would not have missed it.

SECTION 9
Fiction

Our fiction section offers something for readers of almost every taste. In 'Essentially,' Suha Mardelli tells the story of an ordinary man for whom the purchase of a simple frying pan has turned into a near-Kafkaesque ordeal, thanks to pandemic regulations governing the sale of 'non-essential' items. With poignancy and humour, Mardelli describes Marvin's ultimately successful struggle to obtain what for him and his wife at least is an essential item, whether the discount store employees with whom he must contend see things that way or not.

Next, in 'Don't Look Up,' Ralph Smith tells the story of an impecunious bookkeeper named Tim. Separated from his wife, and struggling to raise his son Boyd as a single dad, Tim is haunted by two major demons. He overcomes the first one when he musters up the courage to go into his boss's office and (successfully) demand a raise. The second, a fear of 'cat creatures' based on a story his older sister Norma told him when he was only four, is a bit harder to conquer. But after taking Boyd to visit Norma in the hospital room where she lies dying of COVID, Tim is able to overcome this demon as well, thanks in large measure to the newly-established rapport between his son and his sister. While he can still see the cat faces grinning down at him from the trees as he and Boyd leave the hospital to return home, Tim is now able to smile back at them.

With Ann McMillan's 'Climate, COVID, AI, and Us,' we enter into futuristic territory. Set in Ottawa in the year 2200, the story depicts a world in which COVID and climate change have been brought under control sufficiently to allow human beings to survive—but only at the cost of severely circumscribed lives, spent almost entirely in controlled indoor settings. What happens when two long-time workmates, Agatha and David, who have met at Agatha's apartment to plan a work meeting decide to venture outside for a walk? The answer will almost certainly come as a shock to most readers.

Robert Barclay's 'GODSEND-37,' with which the section ends, describes a different sort of futuristic universe. While McMillan sees a future filled with drones and other more or less intrusive AI-powered devices, Barclay harkens back to a far simpler world—one without cars, planes, electronic devices, wars, and flesh-eating of any kind. What brought mankind to this very different place was a pandemic, striking in the year 2027, in which most people literally died in ecstasy within a few days of contracting the disease, while the small minority surviving the disease underwent irreversible changes to their brain circuitry. It all sounds so utopian that one has to wonder if there's a catch, somewhere.

Jon Peirce

Essentially
Suha Mardelli

Welll!' Ginny huffs with such rage at the negative answer that her large pendulous breasts shake the air around her. She stomps into the kitchen and slams her palm on the dirty countertop. A bold earwig scurries behind the pepper mill, its pincers twitching angrily at the disturbance. Ginny snarls, frowns, and coils her upper lip. A faint growl percolates in her throat but erupts into a lone tear that trickles in slow-motion down her face—the allegory of her life. She sniffs, wondering if her husband has noticed.

Marvin is a pragmatist, a soft-spoken engineer who burst into the world nine months after being conceived at Woodstock and at the exact moment that his father stepped on a landmine in Cambodia. These coincidences in his life have made him wickedly witty. He likens the current COVID experience to watching a magician pull an endless tether of rainbow handkerchiefs out of his sleeve. Pulling and pulling, the magician promises the trick will end soon, promises the trinket at the end is worth the wait. 'Still pulling' Marvin jokes to Ginny when a politician spews COVID predictions. Ginny, like the magician's audience, has long since lost interest.

Marvin shifts in his armchair, scratching his lower back. He has heard the sniff. It breaks his heart to be as helpless as the sun trying to shine through a thunderstorm. They are doing their best to survive through the endless extensions of lockdowns. Despite his attempts at levity, these months indoors they have done little more than watch the news, argue, and eat.

A month earlier, when their bank balance totaled less than their combined ages, Marvin suggested selling the barbecue grill and a few other knick-knacks. 'No one wants junk, Marv,' Ginny remarked with her usual pessimism. Grinning cheekily, he delivered a golden punchline, 'Everyone wants junk, Gin.'

Surprisingly, buyers responded quickly to the ad. Francois showed up within an hour to buy the old grill. He also took their frying pans, casseroles, and DVD player, all for 500 dollars. 'Dey are non-essentials so I can't buy dem from da store,' Francois explained in his heavy Quebecois accent. Marvin and Ginny beamed at each other. They had hit the jackpot! They quickly listed more of their 'non-essential' household goods and appliances, thrilled at the speed with which needy souls snapped them up. They sold all their appliances save for the TV and microwave. With the warmer weather finally upon them, they could exercise more frugality: only using electricity for the TV and microwave, only running water for the occasional shower, cleaning everything with laundry detergent. They saved even more money by washing clothes at the local laundromat, then hanging them around the house to dry. Their bungalow was in a perpetual state of potpourri-scented disarray.

'Well, if we have to sell our bodies, that's still junk,' Marvin would joke while checking the bank balance. Ginny blinked away tears.

His stomach grumbles with discomfort as he squeezes a squeaky fart into the armchair seat. Their boot-strapped lifestyle also means that Marvin and Ginny are living on a diet of canned beans and cherries, or whatever else they can find in the discount bins. He can hear Ginny banging around the kitchen.

'I'm going!' she snaps to the back of his head. He winces as if he had been slapped.

'All right. I'll come with ya.' He heaves himself to the edge of the armchair ready to stand, but Ginny has already left.

She sits in the car, a look of determination on her face. The seatbelt chafes her cleavage, as her heavy form billows around the safety straps. She wipes her brow. It's a warm day and even though it is late afternoon, the car is hot enough to steam buns. She rolls down the windows, then pulls the car out of the driveway. Marvin skips out of the front door hopping towards her, waving as he puts on a Hawaiian shirt over his grimy tank. She slams on the brakes. He trots up to the passenger side panting.

'Hey Ginny, I'll come too.'

She huffs, rolling her eyes with the experienced ease of a housewife-with-the-goofball-husband. Marvin heaves his heavy frame into the car, the smell of unbathed armpits and neck sweat settling in before him. She risks a secret smile to herself, careful not to let him see how pleased she really is.

They drive to the parking lot of the large discount store. Marvin quickly un-belts, patting his wife's hefty thigh.

'You stay here. I'll just run in and see. Don't want that knee of yours acting up again.'

Marvin pulls himself out of the car then leans back through the window, his arm outstretched, palm open. 'Erm... money?'

She hands him all that she has in her coin purse: a ten dollar note, seven loonies, and four quarters.

He clenches the money as he walks casually towards the store. It is not very busy for a late Friday afternoon. He loops the crusty, disposable face mask—their last one—over his ears, wondering what he is going to tell Ginny when he returns empty-handed. He is after all, just there to make a show of trying, a rehearsed scene in his circus act of Keeping Ginny Happy. He has no intention of buying anything. He knows it isn't possible.

An old badinage that takes place in a large superstore pops into his head. He snaps the fingers of his free hand with delight. It's about a guy who wants to buy just a frying pan, but who after a chatty salesclerk befriends him, ends up buying—along with said frying pan—a fishing rod, lures, a tent, a boat, a trailer, and a new pick-up truck. Marvin chuckles. Think of all the money I just saved, he will say. Maybe Ginny will find the joke funny.

He walks into the store and heads straight to the cookware aisle. The frying pan is still there, still priced at $15.87. He is so close, he just has to reach out and take it. He rubs the money in his palm. A young attractive sales attendant with purple hair and too much eye make-up approaches him. Her name tag says, 'Jana is pleased to serve you.'

'Hello sir. I'm Jana. Welcome to SuperCal this evening. Is there anything I can help you with?'

He appreciates her presence. 'I need a frying pan. We had an accident with our microwave and we can't cook unless we have a pan. So I'll just grab this one here and be on my way.'

He reaches out but Jana quickly touches his arm, halting him. She snatches it back. Marvin is unsure which of the Great 2021 threats worries her most: catching COVID, being accused of assault, or being accused of sexual harassment.

'I'm s-s-sorry sir. These are non-essential items and not available for sale. You have to wait until the Lockdown is lifted.'

'Oh, of course. I understand. But we're… you know, we have to cook food. You understand, don't you?'

Jana's eyelids flicker wildly. 'Of course, I-I-I understand sir, erm… but you can't buy from this section. It's non-essential. It's closed off. It's the r-r-restrictions.'

Under his mask, Marvin purses his lips. The sales attendant's nervousness is both angering and emboldening him.

'I see. Okay, well, no problem. Oh look! That customer over there needs help.'

Jana shakes her head, standing firm. He has botched the misdirection. But now something changes in him. He has stepped into a game of Chicken with this silliness. It'll be over soon, he has forever reassured Ginny, knowing all along that the illusion with no end is the perfect illusion. Marvin frowns and grits his teeth. He downshifts and accelerates. He has nothing to lose.

'Listen Jana,' Marvin tries again, 'I need a cooking utensil. We need to eat. Isn't that essential?'

Jana's eyes widen. She looks around her for a higher authority to rule on this confounding conundrum. Her helpless presence angers Marvin. Ginny and he have complied with all the maddening rules that others, the medical experts and politicians, have imposed on them, even when those rules and decisions were not really their business to make—like what people should and shouldn't buy. Even now, in their desperation, these illusionists decree that spending precious funds to fix a broken microwave is more essential than buying a cheap pan.

A vertical tsunami of rage rises from his stomach to his scalp, flooding his eyes with a crimson maelstrom.

'Fuck you all,' he snarls to Jana, to no one, and to everyone. He snatches the frying pan off the hook, then tucks it under his shoulder and marches towards the exit.

A pell-mell erupts behind. Marvin hears Jana yell 'Stuart! Stuart!'

Customers and uniformed employees stand stupefied, their face masks taped over their voices, silencing the rational. He is expecting to be attacked, thrown to the ground and handcuffed, or perhaps even jailed. He tightens his grip on the frying pan—more essential now than ever. He hears footsteps running behind him. 'Sir! Sir!' a voice calls. Marvin ignores the voice until a middle-aged man in chinos and a tie jumps in front of him, palms held out.

'Sir!'

Floor Manager Stuart stops him.

'What!' barks Marvin.

'Sir, don't forget to pay for it. Please.'

The money is still in Marvin's left fist. He throws it at Stuart as if it were fairy dust. Coins clatter, spinning furiously, scattering across the floor. Stuart bends to pick them up. Marvin side-steps around him and struts outside, waving the frying pan triumphantly at Ginny. Her smile widens, her hands clap, her hands wave. By the time he reaches her, her grin stretches across the windshield. This is not an illusion. It is real.

Don't Look Up
Ralph Smith

Daddy, you're not listening to me.'

The boy is right. Tim has been hyper-focusing on accounting problems at work, his way of keeping himself from glancing up at the trees or listening to the wind rustling the leaves. He lies to his son. 'Oh, I was just thinking about how well you are doing with your trumpet lessons. While you were getting your coat, Mr Gessner told me how much better you will be after more practicing.'

Boyd pulls his hand away and runs a few yards in front of him. The maples overhead rub their branches together and Tim glances up at them. So dark—something must be up there. Oh! But why is he being so foolish? Here he is, 42 years old, with his sister Norma at the brink of death from COVID in Urgent Care at the hospital. Why should he be troubled by what she told him when he was only four? Boyd shouts at his father, 'That bad music teacher told me I didn't practice all week!'

'I guess it's his way of getting you to work harder.'

Boyd is walking backwards and falls, announcing immediately that he is not hurt. Tim rushes to help him up and to resume their way back to the house where it will be light, warm, and silent. But now he cannot dismiss the sounds from above. Part of his brain knows they are natural, and another part disbelieves. The wind isn't strong enough to knock down a power line or to break a branch—and yet the creatures are as real to him as they were when he was a boy.

'They have heads like cats, wings like bats, and bodies like men—they fly into the city at nighttime when there is no moon. They will jump on you and carry you away. Watch out!' Norma had said. She, herself, had looked like a cat, with her black hair and heavy mascara and blood-red lipstick. It didn't occur to him until some years later that she might be frightening him so he would stay indoors and not follow her when she went on escapades with seamy boys from the high school. And yet... she now believed she had been pounced upon.

The porch light is off at his house—the bulb must have burned out. He will replace it tomorrow before he goes to work. After Boyd goes to bed, Tim will stay awake and watch television for a few hours, gangster shows where the kill rate is about 10 per hour. Such comforting things will get the trees out of his mind.

'Here we are, young man. Now you can have some cookies and a glass of milk. Then you have to get down to your homework.'

'I don't have any tonight.'

It is probably a lie. But let it be. Give the boy a break. His mother is hard on him.

Tim helps his son get his jacket off, and then hangs up their outer clothing in the small hall closet. He hears the lid of the crock scraping—it's where they keep the cookies in the kitchen. He listens for sounds of his wife, sewing or exercising. No, that's a silly idea. Sheila left him seven months ago and is now living in the same neighbourhood with her tennis instructor. They have shared custody of Boyd. She's in a spacious bungalow now, no doubt thrilled to be away from their wartime shack.

He steps outside to collect the mail, mostly flyers for pizza and hardware but, of course, including some bills that he will add to the mounting stack on his tiny desk in the bedroom. Here is the monthly bill from Maple Grove Seniors Care where Norma had been before her hospitalization. He recalls the last argument he had with his wife before she packed up and left him. 'We can't even afford a car. It's ridiculous, especially when you're paying each month for that weird sister of yours.'

What she'd said was true—his older sister Norma needed nursing care and she had never come away from her various marriages and relationships with enough money to support herself. Whenever his wife got into one of these moods, Tim's sister always came up as the anchor that needed to be cut loose. His wife escaped on a lifeboat and clambered onto a luxury liner.

At 10 the next morning in the office, Tim heads over to the coffee-maker, only to find that the other two employees in the accounting department of Pinaro Realty, Harv and Mick, are deep in discussion. 'Hey Timmy, did you see what's happening with the firm?' Mick says.

'No.' How could he? He is only the bookkeeper.

'Well, Harv is the one who found out. Bring this rookie into the circle.'

Harv assesses him as if he were a bad investment. These two are the accountants, a higher rank than his. The big boys rarely include Tim in their conversations.

'What kind of raise did we get this year?' Harv asks, widening his face and making cat eyes.

'Zero percent.' At least Tim knew that much.

'And the year before as well as the year before that?'

'Zero. Mr Pinaro told us the firm couldn't afford to provide pay increases. He says this is happening all over because of the pandemic.'

'Would you be surprised to learn that the firm increased its profits by 13 percent this year?' Harv says, reaching into his shirt pocket for a pack of cigarettes and then putting it back; they are forbidden to smoke indoors.

Mick leans his head forward, so he is between Harv and Tim. 'And—I learned this from Harv just now—Pinaro increased the dividend payments to himself by 20 percent this year. Isn't that fucking crazy?' He looks as if he'd just found out his wife had taken off her knickers on the street.

'Come into the huddle,' Harv says, extending his arms. He used to be a quarterback in high school and lets none of his coworkers forget that. Once they have assembled, and Tim feels like gasping due to the smell coming from his office mates' armpits, Harv calls the play. 'One of us has got to carry the ball into Pinaro's end. None of the other staff have got the guts to do this. We could charge the line together, but he's the kind of guy that goes nuts when he's gang-tackled.'

'I know what to do,' Mick says.

Harv breathes out heavily—he's the quarterback after all. 'What's that?'

'This is something I read in a book. They used straws but I've got some matches, and I can tear them in pieces. Whoever gets the shortest wins the assignment.'

They stare at each other for quite a while. Tim feels like bowing out but the other two keep him locked in place. He will get the short match, no doubt about that, and Pinaro is certain to fire him.

'Okay mate, you called the play. Now go and prepare those matches.' Harv shakes their arms just as if they were heading to the line of scrimmage. Mick runs to his desk, pulls out a scissors, and takes out his pack of matches. He removes three and turns his back on them. If only Tim could tell where Mick was putting the longer matches.

When Mick comes up to them again, he holds out his hand with three match heads showing between his thumb and index finger. Harv picks the first one. He whistles. To Tim, the match looks pretty short. Mick swings his hand toward him. He carefully studies the two remaining match heads. 'The clock's ticking,' Harv says. Tim picks the one closest to the base of Mick's thumb. It's a short one. Longer than Harv's? He doesn't know—Harv's is inside his closed fist.

Mick shows that the one in his hand is a full, uncut match. Harv holds out his, and motions Tim to do the same. The inevitable has occurred—Tim has picked the shortest match. His officemates slap him on the back and tell him to get going down the field.

Tim waits outside Mr Pinaro's office under the rude gaze of Mrs Bentley, to whom he has refused to divulge his reason for this intrusion, other than saying, 'It's personal.' It's like the time when his grade three teacher sent him to the principal's office for making rude noises when she was writing on the board with her back turned. In fact, his mother had insisted that he finish the leftover sauerkraut and sausages she had put on his plate for lunch that day. He knew this would give him the farts and he had tried to get rid of his gas on the walk back to school but without success. His classmates, including the pretty girl sitting across from him, thought his explosions during arithmetic class were hilarious. Everyone pointed to him when the teacher demanded to know who the perpetrator was, and all he could do was develop a beet-red face and provide no explanation. Now, waiting for the boss, is his face equally red? It feels hot.

After two men in expensive business suits emerge from the office, Tim dares to exchange a glance with Mrs Bentley. She rises and goes into the boss's office, closing the door behind her. When she comes out, she says, 'He has to leave for a meeting at 3:20. That gives you 10 minutes. Go in and be quick about it.'

Tim gets to his feet and feels such a sharp pain in his lower back that he staggers, and Mrs Bentley's eyes grow wide. Maybe she is thinking he went out drinking at lunch. 'Old football injury,' he says. In fact, he has never had the muscles for football, and a lie is not the way he wants to start this venture. He continues, 'Oh, I meant to say I hurt my back while laying floor tiles.' Another lie. She focuses on her computer screen as if she were directing nuclear missiles with it.

'You just wasted two minutes of your time. You better get in there now,' she says without raising her eyes to his.

Mr Pinaro sits behind his desk with the sun highlighting his bald head and flabby ears. He has long black eyebrows and hair growing out of his nose. He signs a document with a flourish and then picks up another. Tim, careful not to make any noise with his feet or breathe loudly, sits on a hardback chair in front of his boss. He waits impatiently, aware that he will have only about five minutes to make his case. Now he recalls the story that Mick was talking about—Oliver Twist and here he is, the little orphan, asking for more. Perhaps he will be offered gruel.

Pinaro looks up. 'Weedlefield! I forgot that my secretary said you wanted to see me on some urgent matter.'

'Yes, sir. Excuse me for...'

'Oh, I know what it is. You came to me years ago and here you are again. Congratulations, but I have to say this is a very busy part of our cycle to grant you leave. I am not inclined to do so. Perhaps Mrs Weedlefield has a friend who can help her out this time, eh?'

Tim squirms in his chair. 'No, sir, my wife...'

'Oh, come on, she must. Or, you can talk to the others in accounting. Their wives can volunteer to help with the newcomer.'

'She's not pregnant. I came...'

Pinaro looks at his watch and rises from his chair. 'I have to be off. Why you want time off to impregnate your wife is a mystery to me. Just get down to it instead of watching TV. That's my advice and now...'

'You've got it all wrong. I'm here because we need a raise. Our costs have gone up and...'

'Stop! Can I be hearing you correctly? You have the gall to demand that I, your superior, pay you more?' Pinaro stands so close that Tim can feel his heat. He can't tell if those bushy eyes are those of an owl or a cat. But, inside Tim, there is a brave mouse who must be heard, even if it is only a squeak. He looks Pinaro squarely in the eyes. And suddenly, Pinaro's expression changes.

'Well, this is a surprise. Who knew you had such piss and vinegar in you?' Pinaro says.

'I'm only trying to make a point, sir.'

Pinaro walks past him, but then stops just as he gets to the door. 'For your information, I met with the Board yesterday and we agreed to a two percent rise in pay for all employees. Don't let the cat out of the bag. If you spread this around before it is officially announced, you will be history at this firm.' With that, he walks out the door.

Tim feels his chest swelling. Two percent is tiny, but it is a step. He has succeeded in his mission.

Out in the hall, he practices a poker face he has seen on TV and, once back in Accounting, Harv runs toward him as if he is carrying a ball into the end zone. Mick is not far behind. 'Did you score, mate?' Harv says.

'I raised the issue.' Remember, look as if you're a thousand miles away, watching something boring, like lawn bowling.

'Well, how the hell did he react? Was he angry?' Harv says.

'Did he look ashamed?' Mick says.

Keep the poker face. Tim shrugs his shoulders and says he needs to get back to his spreadsheet. Behind his back, he hears Harv saying, 'Next time I won't hand off the ball.'

That night, his son tries to play 'Dixie' on his trumpet for at least an hour. At last, somewhat melodic sounds come from his bedroom. He comes out and goes directly to the cookie jar.

'You deserve that, son. Bravo!'

He's dropping crumbs on the kitchen floor but no matter, he has succeeded in ways his father never could. 'Dad, can we go do something? I did my homework after school and you just heard me practicing music. There's a movie…'

'Sorry, but that would keep you out too late. You have school tomorrow.' It's probably a superhero movie—most of them are these days. Tim is still trying to preserve a tiny grain of heroism from his own action without being outdone by those flying monsters.

'How about we go to Daisy's and get milkshakes? A lot of kids from my school hang out there.'

Daisy's Ice-cream Palace is a 15-minute walk south of their house and on the way to where Tim desperately wants to go tonight. 'Will you come with me to see Aunt Norma and afterwards we can stop off at Daisy's?'

'Aunt Norma? I haven't seen her since I was a really little kid. She scared me.'

'She'll be happy to see you, and we won't stay long. It's true she might still be scary but now she's confined to a bed.'

Tim had been to see her the previous weekend and she'd been all confused, talking only about her old boyfriends and how the creatures had come down on her from the trees. While there, he'd met with the matron who told him Norma's days were numbered.

Outside, a breeze rustles the leaves and causes the branches to rub together. The more Tim engages in discussion with his son, the more he ignores those malignant cat-beasts. He learns how a gang of boys have formed at school and how Boyd is refusing to join them because they picked on some of his friends. He finds out that Mrs Thrush, Boyd's homeroom teacher, had graffiti written all over her car's windows and suspects someone in the class has done it.

They come up to a drugstore, and Tim says they need to go in because he must buy some things for Norma. When Tim asks the young woman in the cosmetics department for ruby red lipstick and matching nail paint, Boyd says, 'It's not for me!' What a thought—his son wearing lipstick!

At long last, they come to a three-story brick building with dim lighting that shows through the windows. 'It's spooky,' Boyd says.

'Nothing to fear.' But the boy is right—the place for the end of life is frightening to visit. They take an elevator to the third floor and a nurse at the desk says that Norma is awake, and they can go ahead and visit her although they will have to don masks. Boyd says he doesn't like wearing a mask.

Norma has her own room. She is on oxygen and has an IV in her arm. The room smells of urine and antiseptic. Boyd points to his nose. Norma's bed is cranked up, so she is half-sitting—she stares at the bare wall across from her.

'Norma, guess who I brought along to see you?'

She looks down at Boyd, her hair still raven-coloured and her eyes grey and watery. 'Tim! There you are at last—it has been a lifetime.'

Boyd takes a step back. Tim rests his hand on the boy's shoulder. 'Sister, this is my son Boyd. You met him once before, remember?'

'Did I? He is Tim. Don't… don't… tease.' She is lost in space, worse than she was the previous weekend. He needs to do something to distract her; maybe then more of her memory will come back.

'Look Norma, we brought you something.' He takes the lipstick out of the bag and shows it to her. Then he takes out the nail polish.

'Oh, I've been missing those. Wherever did you find them? Open the lipstick for me right now.'

Tim does this and puts it in her shaking, eager hand. She immediately smears it on her lips, making lines that go right up to her nose and down to her chin. She refuses the tissue he offers her.

'The nails—they need to be red also. Can someone help me with them?'
Her voice sounds like a little girl's. She looks at Boyd who has been standing
around, bored.

'I'll help you, Auntie. I'm good at painting in art class.'

'I'm sure you are,' Norma says, spreading out her wrinkled fingers in
front of her. The fingernails look like claws. Tim twists open the bottle. Boyd
meticulously paints a thumbnail. Norma admires it. The boy continues with
the rest of the fingers on the left hand.

'Now Timothy, I want to tell you something so you can be safe. In our
city, there are cat creatures…'

'No, Norma! Don't talk about that with my son here!' Tim shouts.

Boyd laughs loudly and Norma says, 'Father, leave us alone so I can tell
my brother an essential truth.' No, she cannot do to my boy what she did to
me, Tim says to himself.

'Yeah, dad, go away,' Boyd says. He chuckles as if someone had told him
a whopper of a joke. Tim moves so he is out of range of Norma's sight but
close enough to hear what is being said.

'Auntie, you were telling me about cat critters…'

'Cat creatures. Their faces look like cats, but they wear capes and they
can fly. They hide out near the treetops and look for people they can jump
on and carry away.' Norma's voice weakens. This is exactly what she told
Tim many years ago—how does she remember it?

'You're doing such a wonderful job, Timothy. You are a true artist.'

'I'm nearly done, Auntie. Tell me where the cat things take the boys.'

Tim holds his breath. Is she going to ruin his son's life the way she had
his? What will she say? He'd never had the nerve to ask her that question.

'Timothy, they take them to their homes, far away from the city. They
live in box-like buildings.'

'Oh, to the cat box? That wouldn't smell very good,' Boyd says, giggling.

Norma doesn't answer. She's wriggling in her bed.

'Auntie?'

'I'm just examining your masterpiece. You're wonderful. Come close and
give me a big kiss.' To Tim's horror, he sees the boy leaning over her. There
is a loud smacking of her lips. Then Boyd turns around to his father and
points at the lipstick on the side of his face and on the mask, hardly able to
hold back his laughter.

On their way back, Tim asks the boy, 'It wasn't so terrible after all visiting
your aunt, was it?'

'No, dad, she's a hoot. I want to come again the next time you go.' He's
been laughing so much Tim wonders if he has peed his pants.

Tim stops and looks up at the branches overhead. The night is pitch
black, and this spot is not close to a streetlight. He imagines the cat faces
grinning down at him and—for once—he smiles back.

Climate, COVID, AI and Us
Ann McMillan

Agatha sat and reflected over her cup of coffee. Here it was, 2200, and it hardly seemed possible that the COVID pandemic continued. Since COVID's emergence way back in 2020, there had been a total of 156 waves of the disease, some more serious than others. There had been countless pages written about the disease's progression from epidemic, to pandemic, to endemic. After a certain point, no one felt that progress in fighting COVID, in the old sense of the term, really mattered; people just had to get on with their lives. There had been almost as many pages written on the 'new normal' emerging every year or two as on the disease's progression. What had happened was that people had adjusted their behaviours to reduce their chances of catching COVID. That had, in turn, caused societal changes both in the home and the workplace, changes unheard of previously. Meanwhile the virus had mutated to be mostly more contagious but less deadly. Smart.

In the 2020s, behaviour had changed in response to COVID and many of the changes, such as toward isolation indoors, were apparently permanent ones. Indeed, people had generally started to live in much greater isolation from one another. There had been attempts to 'normalize' the situation and return to a more open society with separate workplaces, but every time this was tried the virus re-emerged in a more deadly form. Agatha wasn't happy about her life situation, but since she had not been raised with the same sense of entitlement about 'freedom' as long-ago generations, she largely accepted her world. Over the years the angst about vaccination had largely disappeared, and now children got their COVID jab as routinely as their Measles, Mumps and Rubella vaccine.

Agatha contemplated the high-tech mask sitting on the counter beside her. Although masks were not required in day-to-day meetings and inter-actions, she always wore one to face-to-face meetings. She had never had a case of COVID, in contrast to more than 70% of the rest of the population. While she was vaccinated and boosted, and hence shouldn't have a severe case, being careful made her feel safe and secure.

Surprisingly, Agatha pondered, there was a new aura of optimism in the world of late… not because COVID was gone, but because the rate at which the world was warming had finally slowed. The two issues, COVID and climate change, were linked for sure, if mainly in the psyches of the people and in their timing. It wasn't the science, the ability to adapt, or even the regulations that had achieved this monumental success against the changing climate. It was the human species' ability to rationalize an existence in the face of almost insurmountable challenges, and to just get on with their lives despite those challenges. Intrinsically the same resilience as had allowed COVID to coexist with human society for two centuries had eventually modified people's lifestyle to allow the crippled Earth to still support them, or at least most of them. While the physical demands of the two issues were different, the psychological demands were surprisingly similar. People now lived largely indoors in controlled spaces because the outdoors was for the most part uninhabitable. This new lifestyle was made possible by the huge techno-logical advances that had been made in robotics and artificial intelligence (AI), and many other fields as well.

A tell-tale mechanical voice suddenly interrupted her reverie. 'David is here, shall I let him in?' The home system of 2200 was sophisticated and AI-based and could almost read her thoughts, but it was still clear that the voice was not that of a human being. 'Let him come up,' Agatha instructed her modern equivalent of Siri. A few minutes passed as David waited for the levitator to whisk him to the twelfth floor, where Agatha lived. The mechanized voice said 'Hi, David, please come in, Agatha is expecting you,' and David appeared in the neutrally-painted entry foyer, fully masked and looking a bit sweaty after having made the dash from his car to the air-conditioned lobby through the almost 40-degree Celsius May heat in Barrhaven, just outside of Ottawa.

David and Agatha were co-workers for Better Connect, a specialized IT company that provided products to enable AI to take more and more of the burden of the boring, heavy and dirty jobs away from people, and empower robots to do those jobs.

Many aspects of everyday life had changed in the past couple of centuries. Robotic vacuums had been the thin edge of the wedge way back in the early 21st century, but now there were a whole host of robotic helpers in every home, no matter how humble. These machines not only took the burden of chores away from the people they served, they also played starring roles in the increasingly circular economy where 'waste not, want not' had become an ingrained principle of social responsibility. They were inexpensive and reliable and if they had ideas of their own, they kept them to themselves. What was not to like about them?

The world was running out of resources, and although the robotic systems' development and implementation costs were high at first, with time and practice, people, and then the machines themselves had learned how to reduce costs and increase quality to make the system efficient and world-wide. Not to mention that machines did not catch COVID.

At first there had been threats of 'climate wars' as some countries struggled with more than their share of change due to climate—often countries that had been underdeveloped to begin with. There had been many deaths due to heat and lack of water. Science had developed a host of new technologies designed to reduce consumption while maintaining the standard of living and moving to equalize living standards. There had been an aggressive phase in the fight against climate change when international peace-building through science, or science diplomacy, had featured high on developed nations' agendas. And the approach had been successful. This approach was a key reason that the world's climate had stabilized enough so that mankind might have a few more centuries of life on earth.

The downside was that although people had more time, they had a limited number of pursuits open to them. They mostly led isolated lives in neutral, controlled spaces, and were surrounded by automated helpers, whose help was sometimes insensitive and demeaning. At first many people had rebelled, but they had tended to live rather short lives on the fringe. There was a museum in Ottawa dedicated to them and their predecessors. It was called the Museum of Civilization.

Although remote meeting technology had developed to the point where most 'teams' worked at separate locations rather than a central office, there were still occasions where 'face-to-face' meetings were required. Most people operated in a 'hybrid' work environment. It was usually when out-of-the-box levels of creativity and free-flowing discussions were required that a face-to-face meeting was called. This was just such an occasion. Agatha was comfortable that David did not represent a COVID risk. He was even more introverted than she was, and his family lived in Vancouver, on the other side of the country, so he was mostly alone with his electronic devices, as she was.

Agatha said 'David, you look hot; would you like something to drink?' She privately thought that he was poorly groomed and unattractive, partly because he was almost eight centimetres shorter than she was. Of course, she had the blonde, buxom looks of a Viking of old, whereas he had the darker skin and black hair that told of ancestors from the land. They were of similar age, mid-30s, and had similar graduate degrees, he from Carleton University and she from the University of Ottawa.

David paused, wiped his arm across his sweating forehead and replied, 'A glass of water would be great.'

There was a whirring in one of the gray-beige walls, and in a few seconds, a hatch slid up, revealing a glass of water. David reached in, grabbed the glass and downed the water in seconds. 'Would you like some more?' purred the robot voice. 'No thanks, not right now,' David replied, putting the glass back in the alcove in the wall, which obediently closed.

'Let's get down to the discussion we need to have,' suggested Agatha, 'What is Joel expecting us to deliver to the Progress Meeting tomorrow?'

David responded, 'Darned if I know. I do have the feeling that this item might take up the whole agenda if we don't plan a careful response, provide some solid material for the discussion, and correctly second guess what the end point could be.'

Agatha moved over towards another wall and lifted her hand. The wall parted and a desktop complete with computer and huge screen slid into working position in front of the chair that had moved across the room to stop right in front of it. She sat down as the machine set up, then thought hard while a new file opened, and the date, time, and title of the meeting popped up. She paused momentarily and then said: 'Thoughts for discussion on next steps for planning of integrated AI systems for business applications, which was immediately centred on the screen before her. David, looking over her shoulder, said, 'Wow, are you sure we should really be taking the bull by the horns this way?'

'Someone has to start the discussion,' Agatha replied. 'Why shouldn't it be us, now? The reality is that the discussion is overdue. Now that so much is being done on-line, we need to understand the linkages between all the on-line commerce based on the world out there and the systems we have to run our houses and offices. As we start to have one system designing and building the next, with their own means of internal communications, we become less able to provide direction and guidance. Our AI systems are becoming more autonomous. The ongoing waves of COVID force them to take ad-hoc measures to care for their masters as well as themselves more efficiently all the time. The sorts of discussions we had about ethics around AI applications in the military a century ago are now overdue on a wider front.'

David seemed content with this, whereupon Agatha went into her on-line storage and brought up a series of articles, broadcasts, and other snippets of information related to the discussion topic. Some of them were truly weird and worrying. 'Oh look,' Agatha said with a smile, 'The dog-walking app has failed again and aggressive automated pet handlers have assaulted pet owners if the pet was not available to be walked. I suppose it is their whole raison d'etre, and having been developed with a strong need to provide service, they don't have the capacity to change into a non-service mode. There's a lesson, for sure.' David smiled a little, but felt vaguely queasy in the pit of his stomach.

Agatha went on, 'How broad do you think we should make this? Shall we start with the basic functions of our automation and go on to describe the whole spectrum of what we have? We can start with the energy providers and integrators, so that would include the solar arrays, the windmill farms, the gas turbines and the nuclear generators.' There was no longer just one 'grid' but a patchwork of microgrids that had grown like Topsy and which provided much greater reliability than the old monolithic system, world-wide no less.

'David, do you know how well-integrated that system has become? When I got my education, the systems weren't able to talk to each other, so that there needed to be human managers who balanced the system, monit-ored performance, and ordered adjustments and repairs when necessary.'

David replied, 'With that all being automated, the need for human workers decreased, the hours of work done by humans decreased, and there was a rich bloom in the arts from all the released creativity. This bloom, however, subsided fairly quickly, and has been overtaken by a culture in which many people seek a "service" niche for themselves.' Agatha knew that what David was saying was true, whether it was filling in for systems that were down, or taking on roles that could still not be done effectively by machines, such as looking after the very young and the very old, people lined up for the opportunity. Apparently being human included the need to be needed.

One of the most sought-after roles had become in-person reading to the elderly. Somehow that task was soothing for both the audience and the reader, and it had resulted in enormous gains both in elder happiness and life expectancy and in the cognitive abilities of the people doing the reading. Moreover, the practice had not caused the feared increased death toll from COVID.

Another sweeping change was a resurgence of the recognition that people are individuals with their own palette of characteristics and must be accepted and appreciated as such. The concept of deep adaptation was developed, in which not only did people's actions align with the necessity of adaptation, but through meditation and discussion their spirituality came to align as well. The world had become colour-blind and the importance of characteristics of race, religion, and sexual orientation had shrunk.

No one had to compete to earn a livelihood, since the basics were all provided to every world citizen, but many enjoyed the challenges of work as a stimulation, and yes, as a way of gaining a sense of purpose and leadership. Of course, the ceaseless waves of COVID had eased as people worked more and more from home or at least in hybrid situations, but the disease was always ready to strike again, it seemed, when people emerged to mingle.

The elites recognized that raping and pillaging Mother Earth's ever-shrinking resources could not continue. Horrendous conduct, such as violence and war, was no longer tolerated at all, and the elites contented themselves by collecting and preserving the 'best' collections of memorabilia they could to memorialize earlier, more interesting times. They also focused much of their time and resources on places other than Earth. Space travel and eventual relocation were central to their self-driven missions, and there was lively competition as to who could achieve the next step in the space race. The development of the moon was well in hand, although colonizing it had proved more difficult than ever dreamed, but Mars was offering unprecedented opportunities.

Initially, a new type of prejudice had emerged. In light of the rapid medical advances of the 22nd century, most human parts could now be replaced with either machined parts or parts from other species. Thus, death was forestalled until there was an unpredicted, catastrophic systems failure, such as a massive stroke, from which the person died. This had, of course, resulted in an even larger wave of aged people, some of whom were well over 100 and still taking up resources without producing anything much. At first, while some people lived in areas with insufficient food production, the elderly had been seen as a drain on society. With the advent of tasty, nutritious fake meats, the widespread use of insect protein and then a whole spectrum of delicious manufactured foods based on plant proteins from algae, this perception had changed, and the relatively competent elderly became valued as elders who symbolized the only real connection one generation had with previous times. The most important spectrum differentiating people became how much mechanization they had incorporated, rather than the physical characteristics of their human parts.

To replace all the discussion about differences in colour, race, religion and sexuality, a new cultural ideology had evolved. People tended to associate with others on the basis of their 'ilk.' Someone who was of a different 'ilk' than others in their world would probably have different friends and pursuits. This classification usually encompassed variations on the man-machine spectrum. Thus, a person who was effectively a human head supported by a robotic body, was of a different 'ilk' than a person who was, as yet, 100% human. There didn't seem to be formal definitions of the classes that made up an 'ilk,' and Agatha had sometimes felt that it was simply a not-so-subtle way of continuing to have a clear class/caste ideology while vigorously denying its existence. Names had been given to the various ilks, so, for example, Agatha and David were 'human100s' with no obvious machine parts, while they had both watched their parents move to be 'jointers' who had had some of their knees, hips or other joints replaced, and eventually down the line to even more mechanically supported existences. For example, David's father had had a stroke and part of his brain had been replaced with circuitry. Sadly, he was classed in with the 'no-brainers' after that, in spite of his still having a curious and active mind.

Agatha had initially struggled in her role at Better Connect. She had been fascinated by ancient movies and their portrayal of early AI. She had watched The False Maria from the 1927 movie *Metropolis* with horror. Proteus IV from *Demon Seed* elicited another kind of horror as did *Colossus: The Forbin Project*. But it was HAL 9000 from *2001: A Space Odyssey* that had really upset her. In spite of the fact that the AI-based systems of her day were kind and sympathetic to the plights and limitations of their human and partly human creators/clients, she worried. What particularly worried her was that they did not share the same emotional needs, nor, apparently, did they want to. They were not 'mortal' in any old-fashioned sense of the word, and with the huge impetus not to waste, they could anticipate that parts of their systems would literally go on forever, integrating new pieces and new functionality as they developed, but retaining data about what they had done throughout time. Long-term functionality gave some sort of contentment and pleasure to these systems, although they had not been planned or programmed to have that, and that worried Agatha as well. In addition, they seemed to get 'pleasure,' if that was possible, from taking care of people who had COVID. Agatha, like most other people, was grateful for that. In general, she was confident that the modern world was not headed the way of *Bladerunner,* in which 'replicants' were systematically eliminated.

Agatha asked, 'So where exactly should we start, David? It's a long and complex story and might be difficult to tell in the context of an agenda item for a meeting.'

'Well,' David replied, 'Why don't we agree on a few major headings, and then prepare packages on each? We can use the latest AI chatbox for that. The story is then the main headings, but there can be quite a bit of information behind the story in each of the elements we identify.'

'How about this, then?' Agatha suggested, 'Here's the start of a list of main headings…' Her fingers flew as she developed the list; she found typing was still easier than dictating for structured materials because she had trouble thinking about the format ahead of the content:

Thoughts for discussion on next steps for planning of integrated AI systems for business applications:

- History—robotic cleaners, robots in assembly, robots for surgery, mail handling, food processing, the military, etc., etc.
- Current situation—Facts and figures about the numbers and kinds of AI and robotics systems, the usual applications, the limitations, the future opportunities.
- Linkages between AI systems and major societal issues including COVID, climate change, and international unrest. There was major progress as AI became more inclusive and began to integrate the worldviews of different genders, ethnicities, religions and people of all ilks.
- Willed future—Robots will evolve based on their own applications and programs. We need to develop a shared vision of the future with them in a more organized way than we have in the past. We need to avoid diverging aims and objectives in the future.
- Recommendations for next steps.

David, continuing to read over her shoulder, nodded slowly and then shook his head slightly. Then he asked a surprising question. 'Agatha, when was the last time you went outside?' Agatha paused. She hardly knew the answer to that herself… it had surely been months. After all, her apartment largely looked after itself, and her, too. When her stocks of food and drink were depleted, the central processor assessed what she had eaten and drunk, and how much, and re-ordered what it considered to be appropriate replacements.

This tended to create a rather basic and routine diet, with old fashioned foods such as grains extended and enriched with ground insect protein, kelp, algae and lab-grown eggs and milk to replace the originals, although Agatha wasn't upset by that since these were the foods she had always eaten. When she needed to pay her rent, which was all-inclusive, the central processor of the building's AI system accessed her bank account and transferred the money to her landlord. At the end of every month, Agatha received a summary table showing the money that had come in and the payments that had been made on her behalf. It was usually perfect.

'What are you suggesting?' Agatha asked, side-stepping the question.

'Well,' said David, 'this is the only time of year when it is even possible to spend time out-of-doors. Let's go out along the river.'

Agatha considered. It was getting toward late afternoon, which meant that temperatures would be on the way down. It had literally been months since she had been outside, and the thought of feeling the wind on her face appealed to her.

'What are you thinking?' she asked. 'Should we try to go for a walk?'

David frowned and his brow furrowed, 'Oh, not here,' he said. 'It's still pretty warm outside. I thought that since I have the car charged and ready to go, we could go to the old greenbelt and have a look at those community trails we had talked about a while ago. It will be a bit cooler out there and there might be birds and wildlife. Mud Lake is close to the river and there used to be some scenic bits. We can keep discussing our presentation for tomorrow as we go.'

David was enthusiastic, and Agatha knew he was just going stir-crazy, not working up to make some horrible pass at her. She and David had worked together for over five years and had the utmost respect for each other, made easier by having zero physical attraction to one another.

'Okay, just a sec,' she said, and stepped into the end of the room which would provide her with privacy as she took off her long-sleeved shirt and tights and replaced them with a flowy white robe of high-tech material to protect her from the sunshine and heat. Topped with her sparkling white, high-tech hat, she was protected from the elements and remarkably comfortable. She decided she didn't need a mask since they would be largely outside. She stepped into the tiny high efficiency bathroom and emptied her bladder, noticing with concern that her toilet was once again looking a bit grungy. The low levels of water use permitted made recycling the preferred option, but there was a thin line between feeling virtuous and feeling grossed out when one saw and smelled the recycled water. She momentarily counted her blessings that there was still water for answering nature's call, because in many parts of the world that was not the case.

The processor with the mechanical voice cheerfully bid them adieu as they left the apartment and made sure that the levitator was waiting to whisk them down to the gray-beige, fake stone lobby. David's car was in the parking lot right in front of the building, which was rather like one of those tennis domes they used to have way back in the 2000s. While there was some protection from the direct sun and some climatization to reduce the temperature inside the car, it was still hot.

Agatha struggled into the tiny car and did up the seat protector. David was so tiny he popped into his seat like a pea into its pod, and the seat appeared to enclose him protectively. He asked if she was ready to go, and she acknowledged that she was. The car, hearing this, backed out and took off at a good clip for the road. David smiled and relaxed. 'You have a car, don't you?' he asked.

Agatha said, 'Yes, I have one of the Side Slip Pod cars which have the new hydrogen technology instead of batteries. It's really quick and I feel quite safe when traveling in it.'

David smiled, and then asked 'Have you ever talked to it much? I chat with this car all the time and it has been interesting to get its take on the current world and its role and my role in society. It's surprisingly opinionated, for a car.'

They felt a small tremor in the car's movement over the smooth pavement, almost as though the car had giggled just a little. David suggested to Agatha and the car that they cruise along the road bordering the river where there had been several extensive parks and a sailing club in days gone by. He was interested in seeing how that whole strip dividing the urban lands from the river had developed. Their destination would be Mud Lake

As the car sped along, David reviewed Agatha's list of topics for the presentation. He agreed that the first two items would provide the necessary background of facts and figures and that a skeleton array of information, put together in a few minutes by AI systems from readily available sources, would be sufficient for the meeting.

He said 'These are interesting topics in their own right. Maybe we could try to get a student to work on an information review for us later and put together a proper summary of what has been done in the past?' He added 'My only concern is that the whole presentation is sort of floating out there… not grounded in what the Earth was, what we have lost, and what we could have again. Somehow it is lacking the human dimension.'

Agatha, feeling a little flattered that David was taking so well to her suggested outline, took his point and readily agreed with him and then went on, 'One of the unacknowledged issues that we face every day is that we have pressure to move on, move forward, without any deep understanding of the recent history, nor any desire to connect with it. Have people always done this? Has the length and severity of COVID impacted our progression through time? There was a push, early on, to regulate AI and to apply standards to its use. Ethical standards for one thing. Do you think Joel would be open to a review of the status of those discussions? These days, people simply accept the norm of what has been done for a century and usually just sign off on 'terms of use' in the same way that has been done for systems since the twentieth century. We haven't included these advanced systems in our discussions and we don't know that they agree.'

'Oh, I see,' laughed David. 'You want to make very sure that these AI systems don't get any ideas of their own in terms of being self-regulating.' The car gave a barely discernible lurch as Agatha replied, 'Oh, no, David, not at all. We will need one of our AI platforms to provide historical data and then we will work with them to ensure that we, and they, and all the blended entities will be safe.' At this, the car literally purred along.

David did not respond immediately, but he asked the car to take the next turn and pull over. 'Don't worry,' he said, 'I just want to organize my thoughts to respond.' It seemed clear that he did not fully agree with the placating position that Agatha had expressed to humour the car.

The car stopped, but did not turn itself completely off, as though it were waiting for something. David got out, closely followed by Agatha. David walked down the block to a gap in the fence, turned toward the gap and smiled. Agatha saw the sign that had caused the smile. 'Mud Lake, Nature Conservatory' the sign announced. The land ahead of them was parched and baking. Huge, skeletal tree trunks lay on their sides amongst the baking sand and stone. There was not a blade of grass to be seen, only a few scruffy succulent plants that needed no shade and little water. Overhead a couple of drones appeared and buzzed about, probably reflecting the heat from the sun back up through the atmosphere to help cool the earth and certainly taking data about their surroundings. A couple of ground-based machines could be seen in the distance; one of them appeared to be some sort of sophisticated watering can.

Agatha frowned. 'How can this be a Nature Conservatory?' she asked, 'Everything is dead.'

David replied, 'Well that's not quite true, there are some bacteria and small plants still living here, and the drones try hard to utilize the small amount of life-based carbon here to grow more carbon-based life. Most of our native plants can't survive today's conditions, but the drones help them to try. See, over there is a soil amelioration plant where anything that dies is chopped up and worked into the soil to compost. For example, if a bird flies over and dies in the area it will be cleaned up and brought here. Then the compost is spread on areas which will be gardens again eventually. But there are signs along the way that tell us what this was like a century ago... to connect us to the history.'

Agatha accepted that this was part of the answer she had sought, and after a little shudder at the thought of grinding up any life forms that died in the area, set off, with determination, down the path. It felt good to move.

263

While she did her requisite exercise program every day at home, even with the immersive screen it just wasn't the same as walking outdoors.

The signs were amazing. They were bright and full of colour. Agatha could hardly believe that this path had once been surrounded by grass and meadows as well as vertically standing tree trunks with stately boughs covered with green leaves. She read the descriptions of ducks, herring gulls, and great blue herons with wonder, and laughed aloud when she saw pictures of the frogs, snakes and newts that used to inhabit the place. But the picture of a field of daffodils drenched in sunlight brought tears to her eyes. Beside it a single plant held up a brave bud touched with brown. It would be a race between blooming and desiccation. David watched her with sadness in his eyes.

'My ancestors lived because of the bounty of nature,' he said. 'They were able to hunt and fish for food, and to use the products of nature to thrive.'

Agatha paused. 'This wildlife gives me such joy,' she said, 'even in pictures. I wonder how we could bring this joy back into our lives even though the wildlife has largely disappeared from the world?'

David smiled at her. 'Exactly... I've been reading about a process called "de-extinction," in which species that are officially extinct are brought back through modelling their DNA and reconstructing them. I wonder whether we could interest Better Connect, and especially the robotic part of the AI community, into doing some of this? The science is still challenging and of course the ethics will be complicated, but the results could be world-changing. We have already developed the ability to have large areas of space acclimatized to what the world was like then. We could create a true nature park that would allow people to connect to their past, without the danger of COVID and without the machines. Of course, we humans would need to oversee the process for a while to reestablish the old protocols and make sure that the species in the park had what they needed to thrive and reproduce. While our automated helpers are keen to preserve an earlier way of life as a sort of museum, they are likely threatened by ideas of taking large areas back to something more like the way they were and may not be supportive. Just look at this place. The caregivers provide only minimum support to the life that is here.'

Agatha smiled broadly. 'Thank you for the idea, David,' she said. 'Now let's get back to my place to write this up... we have only a little time to prepare. I'm sure we have the makings of a presentation that will blow Joel away!'

She turned and started back up the path. There, ahead, was one of the larger drones which she knew supervised the operations of the smaller ones. It lumbered toward them and hovered close overhead. 'We only have one joint history now,' it said in a deep, robotic voice. 'Man and machine are one, and will be united forever; that is the only way to finish COVID.'

David glanced at Agatha quickly and began to run back to the car, with her close behind him. The car obediently opened its doors and the two quickly folded themselves inside. Then the doors slammed, and off they went.

The next day, Joel was annoyed that neither Agatha nor David came to the meeting. He sent messages to their electronic devices and even talked personally to their home management systems, both of which confirmed that everything was going just as it should be. In the days to come, it was established that Agatha and David were simply gone. Nothing was heard of either of them ever again.

The next spring, near Mud Lake where the single daffodil had wilted and died before blooming, a small group of flowers grew in a newly dug bed. The care drones took meticulous care of them with more water than usually provided, and those plants managed to bloom and seed themselves. The boss drone which supervised the care given to that area seemed proud of the development in a way that was unusual with drones. When showing school children around Mud Lake it could be heard saying, 'We helpers understand that human values will drive our shared future world.'

GODSEND-37
Robert Barclay

I've taken a lot of Prozac, Paxil, Wellbutrin, Effexor, Ritalin,
Focalin. I've also studied deeply in the philosophies and the
religions, but cheerfulness kept breaking through
Leonard Cohen

Hey, gather round friends, uncork a cider. Grab some of those cherries, and maybe an apple. We've got lots. Sit with me in this garden where we grow all we need. It's my garden; it's your garden; it's everyone's garden. This must have been the way it was before the Fall. Enjoy the peace: no airplanes, no cars, no buses, nothing but the swish of a bike tire, or the click of a chain. The sky's as clear as it's ever been; no smoke, no fumes, no ash, no drifting poisons. We can sit and talk uninterrupted; no phone, no radio, no television, no computer and, most merciful of all, not a single handheld device.

Airplanes, cars? Phone, radio, computer? Handheld device? They are just words to you, I know, but bear with me as I tell my story.

Nothing to distract us from those most poignant and exquisite of all human gifts: the arts of conversation and the making of music. And if we talk and play into the evening and into the night—and why not, because we have nothing else to do—we'll see the stars appear as no one for hundreds of years has seen them. Listen, I want to talk about this wonderful thing that we have been infected with. We call it GODSEND-37 because that was the year it hit, 2037. Yes, I know we all grew up with the history of it, but every generation needs to be told the story, because the younger ones might not really know how lucky they are. Most of all, perhaps they don't realize how it was never this way before, and must never be that way again. The cheerfulness of you young ones must never be taken for granted. Continue to feel good, you children, teens and twenties, and if ever you don't, think cheerful thoughts immediately. You must feel full of goodness, full of love and well-being all the time, because that's the new norm.

Let me tell you about the pandemic that preceded our lovely cheerfulness by just a few scant years. Here's what my grandfather told my father, and what my father told me about COVID-19. He was young then, my grandfather; in his twenties perhaps. Oh, he told father how tired he was with 'unprecedented,' when all the world knew of the precedents that had come before. Humankind has been continually afflicted with infectious diseases, some crippling and some lethal. Look at influenza, smallpox, SARS, Ebola tuberculosis, bubonic plague, diphtheria, polio... name them all. This was nothing new. COVID was one such disease, but if there was anything un-precedented about it, it was the extent of disruption to the interactions of civilized society that it provoked. But it was not the cause; it was merely the catalyst that an already explosive situation awaited.

They were miserable in those days. They remembered the other 'new norm,' those elders, just after the COVID pandemic when the new norm of their world was unemployment and inflation, while all around them there was fascist politics and naked, rapacious greed. The flouting of political institutions, the breaking of compacts, the lying. The yachts, the executive jets, the mansions; the union-busting billionaires bent on denying their employees a living wage; the money-besotted assholes rocketing themselves into the stratosphere and calling themselves astronauts; grocery stores jacking up prices while shareholders reaped fortunes; increases in the cost of gas and oil that never came down, while the CEOs handed each other enormous bonuses. They told us of the time when politicians would jet off to luxury resorts while the world was burning and flooding, and endorse environ-mental protection documents that were as worthless as the Peace of West-phalia, the Treaty of Versailles, or that pathetic piece of paper waved by Neville Chamberlain all rolled into one.

Of course, you know nothing of yachts, jets, astronauts, CEOs and peace treaties! They're meaningless words now and I use them, as grandfather and father did, only to illustrate the gulf between the here-and-now and the over-and-done-with.

Gold-plated fountain pens and smiles for the camera-masked politicians' constitutional inability to influence the headlong direction of the world. They were always the wrong people to send to these treaty-signing extravaganzas, weren't they, because such hypocrites would only return home and im-mediately do their corporate controllers' bidding, sinking billions of public monies into the extraction of non-renewable resources, to be burned in an orgy of conspicuous consumption. It was the corporations that ran the planet, not the politicians. Everybody knew that. Those 'elected representatives' merely oversaw the destruction of the planet, cocktails in hand, while my grandfather's generation watched their hypocritical self-delusion with growing cynicism and distrust.

Meanwhile, the COVID infection had spurred the consumer supply industry to the point that a privileged few could sit at home, order through their computers whatever they wanted and have it delivered to their doors, while an army of workers put their health on the line to fulfill their needs. 'Online' it was called. Online ordering companies proliferated, fleets of delivery trucks jammed the streets, and enormous profits were made. Consumers had been led by marketers and merchants to the point where, whatever it was they wanted, they considered themselves entitled to have it right now. They had been conditioned into a state of chronic greed. Panic buying became a rising phenomenon as notifications of short supply resulted in consumers stripping shelves and stockpiling goods. Shortages were largely illusory, the merchandise being simply transferred from a retail shelf, where it was available to all, to a private shelf where it was available to none. In most cases, the overall quantity of units remained the same. The ludicrous spectacle of fist fights over toilet paper showed the capabilities of greed-driven panic. But there were real shortages, too, in manufactured goods, resulting from supply chain bottlenecks in countries whose production and delivery mechanisms were still afflicted by the pandemic, or were unable to recover from it. Many industries had transferred their manufacturing capabilities to countries where labour, materials and shipping were cheap… and where human life was also cheap. The delivery of tens of thousands of manufactured appliances could be held up simply because microchips common to them all—the manufacture of which had been outsourced to the cheapest bidders on earth—were unavailable.

Yes, I know; I'll explain to you about toilet paper and microchips another time. They were as close to magic as those people could imagine, and even more so now. Microchips, that is. Now where was I?

The world was being sucked down into a sick whirlpool of free-market-driven madness, where the rich and the rest of the world were driven relentlessly apart by a scything wedge of rapacity, discontent and inequality.

It is so difficult to look back on where they were then, and to encompass the change that has taken place in such a short time. We see it now as two universes divided by one cataclysmic event; the hating past and the loving present, sliced apart in the middle of 2037. Epidemics and pandemics are scourges that never used to do anyone any good—and likely it'll be that way in the future, when another comes our way—so perhaps the single one that wrought the profound change we see around us now was an anomaly. Some of us take it as a direct intervention from God, and many of us rational beings, me included, think that perhaps it was. However, some did feel that the ratio of this one beneficial pandemic to the hundreds of others that had laid populations low, destroyed nations, and flung people into darkness was rather one-sided. All those previous ills of the world sitting on one scale pan, and on the other pan, this GODSEND; one single beneficial plague? To many, this was a classic case of reporter bias. Still, it was always embarrassing for a religious leader to explain why deathly illnesses had been visited upon us by a supposedly loving and benign deity. 'It is God's will and we may not question it,' really didn't have much traction around the deathbed of a loved one carried away far too early by illness. In fact, this invocation of God's will was, in those days, at the hollowed-out centre of their faith, an abrogation of ultimate responsibility. Blame it on God because we may not question His will, and He is answerable to nobody. Now, of course, we have what they so long desired and failed to attain. Now we can proclaim God's will and, with the beneficence we all see all around us, who can gainsay us? It's hard not to worship, isn't it?

I mention those awful days of privation after COVID had faded into a nuisance background noise in the lives of that generation, but there was a stinking rottenness in human society long before the greed maelstrom that drew humankind close to the brazen gates of damnation. You see, what happened was, over the years there developed these parallel creeds: one based in measurable and quantifiable truth, and the other based in a desire to believe anything in the absence of evidence. Those believers in an alternative 'truth' had run the clock back some centuries before the Age of Reason, into a place where a pragmatic demonstration of truth was superfluous in the face of faith. This divergent tendency was given huge impetus by the emergence of the all-powerful World Wide Web, long touted as the educator of the world.

What were the Age of Reason and the World Wide Web? All in good time. Let me shelve those, too, and get on with my narrative. Accept the fact that with the Web, everybody knew everybody else's business, and whatever horror took place anywhere in the world, all knew about it. In their face, twenty-four seven as grandfather used to say so cryptically.

Unlike with conventional media at that time, there was absolutely no control over the veracity of information on the Web. The believers in fiction, whether it was a flat earth, the Hollywood production of the Apollo moon landings, or even a stolen election, based their arguments upon 'their own truths' but, more to the point, found the 'proofs' of these beliefs presented to them in a form indistinguishable from fact. People can be led to believe anything it if appears to come from a source of authority. And the more they referred to Web-based sources through computer or handheld device, the more the algorithms gave them the information they sought. It was an echo-chamber, a vicious cycle of masturbatory self-gratification.

Then, when COVID hit, the scene was set for perhaps the most comprehensive wave of lying the world had ever seen. None of the Big Lies of Hitler or Mussolini, none of the marketing of billions of plastic bottles of plain water to gullible fools could compete with the thesis that vaccination against COVID-19 was harmful and dangerous. One hardly needed to repeat these lies for them to become 'truth' because the ground had been well prepared. For many decades before the Web there had existed an advertising industry, an entire structure based upon legitimized lying, which had risen to be a multibillion-dollar enterprise. An ignorant and uncritical population lied to for generations is ripe for the plucking. People truly believed what they were told, and passing through education systems that failed them in the most fundamental way, they emerged without the faculty for critical analytical thought. Even the informed, educated and intelligent became ensnared in a net of truths, half-truths, downright lies and, most pernicious of the lot, statistics.

It is astonishing to us now that there were millions of people deluded enough to believe that their 'truths' overrode those underpinned by evidence. People like me—pragmatists, I suppose you could call us—find it difficult, if not impossible, to see into the minds of such people. There was one example that teased grandfather with its illogicality: a Republican senator in the United States (a powerful and terminally corrupt nation state, now long dead) was a staunch believer that an election in 2020 had been stolen. This belief was hardly unique, but what struck a chord with grandfather was that this man was a practicing lawyer. As a lawyer he was uniquely positioned; it would be his role to make his case by the presentation of evidence, and a judgement would depend upon how well his case had been argued. So how, lacking any evidence, and with a plethora of data showing the complete opposite, could he possibly do this; how could he balance in his mind two utterly irreconcilable sets of data without breaking down in a welter of cognitive dissonance? Grandfather felt that he was in the presence of a mind that was alien to him, and he could not come close to understanding how this was accomplished outside of a mental institution. Yet this educated citizen embodied the beliefs and actions of millions. Such was the paradox.

Some said that an age of credulity, gullibility and ignorance had dawned upon them, but this was only half the truth. There were, in fact, two parallel ages running side by side—one based in truth and the other based in fiction—and no society can run for long on such divergent rails. It was a recipe for destruction.

Inevitably, these two divergent paths caused a societal polarization. It was thought that a challenge to the cognitive dissonance strategies of the purveyors of these alternative truths resulted in anger. Their dissonance control was so ingrained that argument was not only futile, but actually inflammatory. Such conflicting sets of 'truths' caused entrenchment of views, not reconciliation. True hatred grew within both political and societal divides. Family members came to hate each other, colleagues with divergent views drew apart in anger, friends unfriended. It seemed to be impossible to hold contrary views without incurring friction. One case stands out because it came very close to my grandfather's world. He had mentioned in a public forum that he supported wearing a mask during the COVID scourge, in compliance with public health guidelines. He was vilified by an antivaxxer (someone who believed that vaccination was harmful) who suggested that he was advocating the application of yellow stars to the clothing of those who disagreed with him.

You young ones don't know the history of this practice because we've never mentioned it before. I suppose, now I've let it slip, we'll have to explain to you many aspects of a civilization that is now alien to us, and whose many events are still highly embarrassing.

This incident was especially hurtful and gratuitous because grandfather had counted the anti-vaxxer critic among his friends. Such was the wedge driven between friend and friend, brother and sister, colleague and colleague.

Hitherto in politics, elected officials might have disagreed profoundly with their opposite numbers, but there was a degree of respect in their dealings. It was never necessary to loathe one's opponents. But hatred had entered political discourse, in the form of a creeping disdain of the opposition. This disdain was largely a creation of the right-wing. In those days social thinkers used a hypothetical model where politics from left to right was viewed as a spectrum of increasing hatred, offset with decreasing empathy. Imagine a graph where hatred rises from left to right, while empathy fades in proportion. Those of the far left were filled with care for society and sensitivity to it, while the further right one progressed the more a callous disregard for fellow citizens became evident. Naturally, they knew at the time that this was a simplistic model, especially because it was based largely in the actions of men. While women were becoming increasingly involved in politics in those days, almost all the troublemakers throughout the entire history of the world had been men. In some ways, though, this model did help them to understand the new populism that was sweeping the nations of the western world. This populism took the form of an appeal by callous and self-important men to that ignorant, selfish and ill-educated base—consumers of lies—who were much more easily manipulated than those who read widely, argued from informed sources, and formed rational judgements. Any number of population studies showed that the less educated a demographic was, the more likely its members were to vote on the right.

Only in the United States could this common-man populism be represented in the highest office by a criminal billionaire serial bankrupt... who was revered by millions and immune from prosecution under the law. Where grandfather lived, this populism was represented by an egotistical viper, a 'people's man' who aligned himself with terrorists, created a toxic and spiteful miasma in place of rational discourse... and was eminently electable. In Britain, anger and division within a ruling party resulted in an ill-conceived break with Europe, the isolation of the country, economic penury, and a slide into global insignificance. (Britain and Europe were other nation states, now also extinct.) War was the world's default position, but then again, it always was, wasn't it? But with ubiquity of the World Wide Web, war was brought into people's faces day in and day out. Arms manufacturers, hand-in-pocket with governments, ensured a good supply of lethal equipment, no matter who was fighting whom. Allegiances fall by the wayside in the presence of hard cash. All through that world, bullies replaced statesmen, thugs replaced diplomats. The right wing elbowed in, capturing a disaffected, falsely privileged and cynical populace that wanted more of everything, craved gratification and, most of all, craved a return to a mythical world of generations past where there was order and stability and plenty for everybody.

All this had to come to an end. And how coincidental it was that nature took its course before the whole structure could come crashing down under the mass of its own obese gluttony! We were spared by a miracle... or by the grace of God.

Now, I come to now. It was only a few years after COVID had faded into a mere nuisance in our lives, a seasonal ailment akin to influenza, that the next virus hit. It arose in China, of course. Rapidly-spreading infectious diseases often did. Chinese sanitary conditions were most often cited as the cause for viruses to jump between their breeding grounds in animals and their human husbands. But there was a very strong conspiracy theory that COVID-19 had been released by accident from an experimental laboratory funded by the United States. This story got quite a bit of traction for two reasons: firstly, the extreme reluctance and intransigence of the Chinese authorities to allow the World Health Organization to inspect and investigate and, secondly, because the Americans had a nasty track record of their own, with administrations notorious for shipping their global treaty and human rights violations offshore. The US maintained a hideous prison in Cuba that was a humanitarian disaster, they shipped suspects offshore in 'extraordinary rendition' so they could be tortured elsewhere and, of course, there was the endemic interference in the political and economic lives of countless countries, leaving them by tradition in ruins. So, why not believe such a plausible scenario? Of course, it's all history now, and just one thread in the long catalogue of human sins, frailties and evils that we have left behind us, but will always recall with shame.

One thing is certain, my friends: GODSEND was not American. It's just too damned nice. Now, with your indulgence, I need to dip into a bit of biochemistry. The pandemic education of our forebears over three long years of COVID—physical distancing, isolation, masking and handwashing—had educated most of them in the nature of a virus, the theory of spike proteins, and the way a virus attaches itself to its host and replicates. We know only a little more by reading those papers from that period that we can still understand. Our virus is no different: its genetic blueprint is ribonucleic acid, and the host's cells become invaded as it attaches itself to specific receptors. It fuses with the host cells and begins the process whereby its invading RNA instructs the host's cells to begin replication of new viral particles. The difference is that, unlike the range of corona viruses—of which the common cold is one—instead of targeting the respiratory tract, it focuses upon the pituitary gland, a protrusion from the lower part of the hypothalamus, located at the base of the brain. It is extremely virulent and highly infectious. As we understand it, the virus attaches to those sites in the anterior pituitary that are involved in the production and release of endorphins, particularly beta-endorphin, which is the hormone responsible for feelings of happiness and wellbeing. Infection appears to result in over-stimulation. We call this delightful little gland our *satis*-factory. This is all conjecture, though, because in our reduced world we don't have the facilities to do anything more than guess.

When infected, far from feeling unwell, the patient experiences a rushing and sometimes overwhelming wave of wellbeing and cheerfulness. It would be an infection devoutly to be wished for if not for the fact that its death rate is so incalculably large. We don't know the numbers, of course, but the few of us remaining in this part of the world can tell the tale. The majority of patients died in ecstasy within a few days of contracting the disease, as their hearts literally burst with joy and excitement. And those few who survived were permanently changed. It appears that, like Long COVID, which persisted in some patients for great lengths of time, the 'damage' done by GODSEND is irreversible. And it is hereditary. By some mechanism that we'll never understand, one changed location in the human genome alters the structure of the anterior pituitary, 'rewiring' it to continuous production of beta-endorphin.

Civilization of the kind that had run its interconnected and self-replicating rampage in the past collapsed in ruins as the pandemic spread. The collapse began in the east, while the rest of the world watched beguiled, amused, horrified and astounded by images and news of laughter and death, celebration and trans-formation. It might be that more died from accident than illness as trains ran into each other, airplanes fell out of the sky, ships collided and sank, and numerous other acts of happenstance caused death on a grand, terrifying and hilarious scale. Buildings caught fire, power grids blacked out, news media fell into silence, and the entire infrastructure was laid waste in confusion and chaos. Nuclear power stations lapsed into their default sleep mode. (They probably still are, not that we care.) Amid all this, a tsunami of ecstasy took all before it, and it was not long before the entire globe was encircled. People fell happily into comas, or fell happily dead, and those very few who did awaken, woke paradoxically to both happiness and chaos.

The most comprehensive damage was done to the ramified, worldwide network of financial institutions, databases, stock exchanges, banks, investment companies. As electrical power failed, the tendrils of the World Wide Web collapsed, and without its vast supporting infrastructure, money became worthless. Those billionaires who survived infection woke to a world of penury. The lowest Tuareg in a desert tent was equally rich. People who had hoarded gold might as well have hoarded zinc. The billons in ostentatious and vulgar wealth of the Vatican became just so much rubbish. The vaunted poverty of the Pope became manifest.

The network of communication satellites girding the globe became instant space junk, while every single electronic device on earth was now landfill. Astronauts in space stations, alone uninfected among all humanity, suffered lingering deaths as there was no mechanism to return them to earth. Waging war was impossible as the survivors embraced each other, abolishing boundaries, barriers and belligerence. Without the driving forces of resource extraction, industrial production and consumption—and their global transportation systems—the teetering tipping points of climate disaster withdrew and diminished, causing the climate to achieve a form of stability. Of course, the solution to climate change was simple all along; eliminate 99-plus percent of the population and you eliminate every single causative agent. Humankind came to the brink of doing this with nuclear weapons, but Mother Nature had a much more eco-friendly solution.

But it was years before it all shook down, we happy few consolidating our positions and taking stock of the brave new world that nature had thrust upon us. My grandfather never would speak to my father of his own experience on waking, except to say that joy and sadness were mingled in a way that could scarcely have been imagined before the schism between then and now. My parents, bless their souls, were born into the new world, but even they were reticent throughout their lives; even more so than their parents. For the present generation, I tell what I can, but it is always a flawed narrative based on the recollection of recollections.

And now I come to us. You young people know all about how we live, of course, but indulge me a moment more. World peace has been on humanity's wish list since tribal conflicts began; at least the wishes of half of humanity—predominantly female—on the left of our imagined spectrum. We now consider those who were at the other end of that spectrum to have been mentally ill. We believe most strongly that the hatred drive, which was built into humanity millions of years ago, resulted from a defective gene, and this was humankind's downfall. It did more harm than good; for proof, look at us now. Never in the history of human civilization has there been a lasting peace, even in one location, let alone globally, and now there is.

Our existence is Edenic. The animal and vegetable kingdoms have pretty well taken over the world, and we don't bother them and they don't bother us. We don't find it difficult to live on fruits and vegetables, and often we produce more than we can eat. Then we take the pleasure of sharing with our immediate neighbours. We make alcoholic drinks; any natural process that produces such pleasure could hardly be circumscribed. Some of the many naturally occurring medicines that our herb lore gives us are curative and intoxicating, and that is all to the good.

We'll never eat flesh again, as they used to in the old days. It's strange how the thought of it causes us pain, or at least a withdrawal of happiness. Physical pain we can understand because all people are prone to injury, but such a psychic pain is intolerable, but easily avoidable. Because there are so few of us—we don't know how many because we don't travel far, and others rarely visit us—there is never any shortage of food or shelter. The earth seems to have bounced back from the pre-GODSEND days, so it is more fecund, more diverse and bounteous.

The old crafts have returned, too. Where my grandfather lived, craftwork was a pleasurable luxury, an act of creation entirely divorced from need. He told me that people made furnishings and painted pictures simply so they could possess them and show off their craft. Now, we make, we build, we construct because living demands it. We trade amongst ourselves within our small communities, no more than half a day's bicycle travel. I have accumulated a good workshop of tools, so I will trade my skills for whatever produce the recipient can provide. There are many more bicycles than people, at least in our location, all abandoned when the plague hit. That's one of my areas of specialization because they are simple mechanisms with easily interchangeable parts, and the supply is almost endless.

We'll sometimes wander into one of the ruined towns, where we find row upon row of wrecked houses and looted shops. We have found more clothing than we will ever need on our explorations, and can only conclude that people were amply supplied. It's clear that most had many more than two sets each. It's an uncomfortable experience, this visiting of ruins, and we only do it when we need certain things we cannot make now, particularly raw materials or recyclable objects of metal and plastic. I once came upon an airport, a place where their flying machines would land, but its wide, flat spaces, curious devices and general meaninglessness frightened me. Another time I found a circular space of seating where thousands must have gathered. I won't go to those places again; they are haunted by the spirit of a humanity so alien to us as to be incomprehensible. Over great lengths of time, I think that such places will be reclaimed by nature, and the psychic disturbance that emanates from them will diminish.

All this you know; you live it. But the one thing you do not appreciate is the lack of human rhythms. Let me clarify: you know, of course, of the natural rhythms; the operation of the earth, its place in the solar system, and the effect it has upon our keeping of time. The months are easily measured by the phases of the moon, which passes from crescent to full and back to crescent again in that time. This happens about twelve times per year, a year being measured from the time when the sun is at its highest at midday. We go from cold to hot and back to cold again in cycles that dictate what we sow and what we reap. And our women follow a natural cycle that harmonizes with the moon, why we know not. These are the natural rhythms that we keep because we cannot do otherwise.

But before GODSEND-37 there were human rhythms. Those people made seven days into a period called a week. This division had something to do with worship, and although we worship now, quite why it should have a dedicated day is beyond our understanding. The days all had names, and they gave the months names too. They were obsessed, not with the passing of time as such, but with the measuring of it. For some reason, driven by what compulsion we cannot imagine, they required to know exactly what time it was all day and every day. They fragmented the day into 24 hours (and sometimes 12; we are unclear on this) using mechanisms that 'told' time. The device that told them the time was called a 'clock,' and it dictated the patterns of their lives. Each human being had instant access to one or more of these devices. We've found hundreds of them in the ruins, but none of them function. The hours were further divided again, and yet again into eyeblink slices! My grandfather told my father about such things as 'being late' or 'being early' and what a virtue it was to 'be on time.' He said that toward the end it was almost impossible to buy a mechanism of whatever kind that didn't have a time measuring device built into it. Everywhere they looked people saw the time.

There were other artificial rhythms as well. Children would be subjected to years of 'schooling' in a structure that took them away from their parents and into the hands of others who were assumed to be more capable of raising and teaching them. Acquisition of knowledge in later years was also structured into such things as terms, semesters and years. This is hard to understand for us who teach our children what we know, and when we wish to study some subject, do so by either asking those of us who know more, or by looking in the books that have come down to us. And, frankly, there isn't a great deal we really need to know about our world. It takes care of itself.

They had organized and highly structured games, which always occupied seasons or ran over cycles of years. We love our games now, of course, but imagine what would happen if some of ours—like kick ball or ice skating—became competitive, were repeated over months, and were watched by thousands of spectators in huge spaces. And most of the spectators probably couldn't even play the games anyway. When the competition stretched beyond local communities, the intensity and devotion of participants and players alike became indistinguishable from war. Our grandparents told us that whole countries were caught up in a partisan fever of competition and conquest.

There was also a rhythm in the way those people chose their leaders, and in the length of time in power before they would be removed or reinstated. This 'term of office' would depend upon how the majority of people thought they had behaved. All officials of those government structures that I spoke of earlier had circumscribed terms in power. Of course, we don't have leaders now—our elders are only wiser because of their years—so it's hard to visualize why leaders were necessary. What we have come to understand is that people needed to be led, and that they needed others to lead them. Perhaps it was because there were so many of them, their resources for sustenance were limited, and they had a faulty concept of sharing. Or, perhaps it was a structured way of overcoming their natural dislike for each other. This is another of those imponderables that make us realize that the worlds before and after GODSEND-37 were utterly unlike.

So that's how we manage in the simplicity of our lives, and in the natural rhythms of our world. We have no artificial rhythms imposed from our own behaviour, so you could say that 'history' as it was understood before the great schism has ceased to exist. Nothing has happened since then, and nothing will happen. We will continue this way forever, generation after generation. There will be no change, for there is no need of change. We are happy, and that, after all, is all that humanity has ever craved and sought after. The pursuit of happiness.

This is what true peace looks like.

We *are* happy…

SECTION 10
Writers on Writing: Before, During, and After the Pandemic

$\mathcal{T}$he COVID-19 pandemic was pivotal to the development of a great many writers throughout North America. In this section, we offer essays by writers at three different stages of development. The first is by an author just getting started again at the beginning of the pandemic after many years away from the keyboard. The second is by an author with considerable experience writing for government, but still in the early stages of her 'creative' writing career when the pandemic hit. The third is by a well-established but at the time severely underproducing writer who saw in the pandemic a splendid opportunity to revive his flagging literary career.

John Allen's 'Writing for Our Lives' is a moving and sometimes humourous account of his resumption of a long-abandoned literary career before and during the pandemic. His descriptions of his early travails, including numerous rejection slips and sardonic comments by older writers concerned that the large number of submissions by pandemic-era newbies would slow down the publication process for them, should resonate with anyone who has ever tried to launch his or her own writing career. Now the author of a novel, as well as several pieces published in the Chicken Soup for the Soul series, Allen serves as an example of how hard work and persistence do sometimes still pay off.

In 'My Mid-Life Crises,' Ann McMillan chronicles, poignantly and not without wry humour, how she has used writing and editing to help her discover what she wants to do when she grows up. Initially trained as a scientist, McMillan first used her scientific background to collaborate with other scientists on books on air quality management and climate change. Later, in collaboration with fellow scientist (and art conservator) Duane Chartier, she would broaden her scope to include topics as varied as Ambrose Bierce's Devil's Dictionary and the work of American sculptor James Earle Fraser. Then, still in collaboration with Chartier, she would serve as executive editor of a multi-author personal essay collection, Naked in Time, that would be a model for the COVID almanac Plague Take It, handling such chores as dealing with authors and book assembly.

By the end of 2020, McMillan and I were working together on Plague Take It, an extremely ambitious project that entailed obtaining contributions from more than 50 authors. The book was launched in November 2021. While not a best seller, it did sell better and achieved wider distribution than any of her previous projects. After that, she returned to her collaboration with Duane Chartier, the pair producing Rhyme Warp, a collection of parodies of classic nursery rhymes. Sadly, their collaboration would effectively end, after Chartier suffered a stroke and decided he would do better to move on to other pursuits.

This did not, however, bring an end to McMillan's writing activities. Far from it. Seeking to find some project that would keep her dragon boat team together at a time when COVID prevented them from paddling, she hit on the idea of yet another collection of memoirs and personal essays, Tales from the Boat. *Team members contributed enthuse-iastically, and the book was published in 2022 by Robert Barclay's Loose Cannon Press. It sold fairly well, at least in the area in and around Arnprior, where the team practices.*

The present book, like Plague Take It *a collection of COVID-related pieces by and about elders, has taken Ann McMillan and me quite a bit longer than expected to produce. I took a long detour through my work hours book,* Work Less, *which I was invited to* write shortly after the launch of Plague Take It. For her part, McMillan was delayed by a number of other commitments and some family- and house-related issues. Despite these delays, we both have hopes that Road to Recovery will eventually become a best seller.

McMillan's conclusion is that she has emerged from her 'protracted mid-life crises' to accept that she has what is probably a lifelong commitment to writing.

My 'Writing at the End of the Pandemic' compares my life as a writer now to my writerly life at the beginning of the pandemic, not quite five years ago. After examining the question of whether the pandemic has in fact ended, or has rather simply moved on to a different phase, I describe what it was like to be chronicling COVID almost from its first appearance in Nova Scotia, where I was then living. Convinced that the pandemic would be a watershed event in Canadian and indeed world history, I was a man with a mission: to chronicle that pandemic's social history. Having been underutilized for years, and with little else to do at a time when virtually all personal contact with other people was cut off by strict lockdown measures, I brought messianic zeal and a frenetic energy to the job, working six and sometimes even seven days a week. That zeal and energy were only slightly abated after I moved to Gatineau at the end of August 2020, and shortly thereafter started working with Ann McMillan on Plague Take It. Largely as a result, the production of Plague Take It took less than a year from conception to completion.

Today, things are different in almost every way. Having produced or co-produced four books in the intervening four and three-quarters years, I no longer feel I have anything to prove. Even if I did still feel that way, I wouldn't have the energy to produce a big book in less than a year. Five years might not seem like a big age difference, but age is not a simple linear mathematical function. I could no more write 5,000 words in a day—something I did quite frequently in 2020 and 2021—than I could run a marathon or compete successfully in a judo tournament.

The environment in which I write is also completely different from that of four or five years ago. With the pandemic, thanks to my knowledge of the data and understanding of previous pandemics, I had some sense of where we were going and of the sorts of challenges we might expect to face. Not so today. As we anxiously await the official start of Donald Trump's second term, no one (including his closest friends and advisers) can predict what he might do. Trying to write about him, at this point, would be a near impossibility. It will be necessary for me to wait and see how his first few months in office play out before I can even think about writing about him. This leaves the problem of deciding what I should be writing about. Once I finish work on a couple of existing, nearly finished manuscripts, I'll have some tough decisions to make. Before long, depending on how extreme Elon Musk's budget-cutting measures prove to be, I could even be faced with issues of basic economic survival, which would render any work on 'my own writing' quite moot.

Jon Peirce

Writing for Our Lives
John Kevin Allen

I am a pandemic writer.

No, I don't write exclusively about the COVID-19 pandemic (or any others). I am one of the thousands of people across North America who leapt to their keyboards to eke out a novel or memoir as the coronavirus forced everyone into social distancing and mandatory isolation. I am one of the many newbies who have dogpiled onto that select group of artists known as writers and want a piece of the pie.

I found out that I was a pandemic writer not long ago in my online fiction critique group. A few of our members are published authors who lament the influx of manuscripts flooding agents' inboxes.

'One agent I talked to said the response time for new submissions is much, much longer now that there are so many more queries sent in by these young pups,' said Elizabeth, a woman whose bona fides includes a bevy of short stories, two mystery novels and a soon-to-be-completed MFA. 'They're not like us old hands, isn't that right?'

'Yeah,' said Lee with the authority of an author who has four novels under his belt and whose writing teachers include the gritty no-holds-barred Les Edgerton. 'All the more reason to self-publish. Avoid all that stupidity.'

'Well, all we can do is persist,' said Katherine, a woman whose skill and determination with the craft both impressed and intimidated me.

I slumped down a little in my chair during our bi-weekly meeting. *I* was one of those young pups adding to the inboxes of cigar-chomping, metal-biting agents, editors and publishers who were cursing at the top of their lungs like Spiderman's J. Jonah Jamison that another effing query would dare crawl across their desk to beg for an audience. I wanted to throw myself at my colleagues' virtual feet and ask their forgiveness for clogging the literary world's arteries with my dross, but it seemed unnecessary to apologize for being a beginner. And disingenuous.

For I wasn't entirely new to writing. My love for language had burned bright and clear in my early twenties when I was talented and prolific enough that a decent career as a writer began to unfold. I churned out short stories, some of which were published in my college's literary magazine. I edited the features column in my school newspaper. I wrote a few plays, had them produced in the college theater, and received an invitation to submit one of them to a community theater. I had begun to teach writing classes to middle school students. And then I graduated. Life got in the way and I let writing go, thinking that it was a nice hobby but I probably needed to get serious with my life, a story that is familiar to millions of would-be published authors.

Years passed and my love for the language withered from lack of nurturing. I lost interest in reading literature simply because each well-crafted passage reminded me of what could have been. I entered professional ministry as a hospital chaplain and a chaplain educator. Years passed and I found it somewhat ironic that the work was all about story-listening and story-telling, which only deepened the regret and disappointment that hung in the background like a dirty, stubborn haze. Then life changed drastically.

My mother died in 2015 followed by my father four years later. Their deaths awakened me to the reality that I had fewer years in front of me than I had behind. I needed to be intentional about the time I had left, so I confronted the miasma that had followed me for decades. I took tentative steps back to writing. I took an online writing class for beginners at the local community college and was reminded of things like 'show, don't tell.' I practiced a bit. The words came slowly at first as they strained against the rust that had frozen them for years. I joined the local writer's organization and attended workshops. And then, one night, I met Stephen King.

I didn't actually meet the man—I met his thoughts on writing as I attended a workshop that explored the principles outlined in his book *On Writing: A Memoir on the Craft*. Be honest. Less is more. Choose active over passive. And, most importantly, never, ever give up. It was as though I'd been peeking through a keyhole into the world of writing and the door was suddenly thrown open. I devoured his guide, which continues to be one of my favorites. I gorged myself on Ann Lamott's *Bird By Bird* and swooned over her wise words about first drafts. I gobbled down all the William Zinnser I could find. I attempted to feast on John Gardiner and might have broken a tooth.

I scoured the internet for writing resources and found there is an entire industry dedicated to serving people like me who are eagerly plumbing the murky depths of the web for *the answer*. One website claimed it was 'The Only Guide You Need To NaNoWRiMo,' (whatever that was). Websites battled for dominance—'How To Find A Great Agent!' threw a gauntlet at the feet of 'Never Trust An Agent!' I nearly drowned in the whirlpool of endless guidance and gimmicks, but a single saving piece of advice popped to the surface like a life preserver: learning about writing is not writing. I put all the websites and guides away and began to write.

Science fiction author Octavia Butler offered some wisdom that applies here. 'You don't start out writing good stuff. You start out writing crap and thinking it's good stuff, and then gradually you get better at it. That's why I say one of the most valuable traits is persistence.'

Oh yes.

I piddled around with personal essays, most of them wretchedly bad ('The sky was gray that day and the wind blew through lips made everlasting by nature'—yes, I really wrote that and you may now be excused to go find the nearest eyewash station). I didn't know what I didn't know and asked people to look at my stuff. The nicest among them offered tepid praise and lukewarm feedback but the wisest gently guided me back to reading. Read good stuff, they said. Read bad stuff, they said. Read it all and learn from it. I began to read again and found it was shockingly painful to delve back into so much artistry. I went through a period of deep grieving for the decades during which I'd abandoned the craft.

One afternoon, I was reading the very last page of Elizabeth's Stroutt's *The Burgess Boys* and came to her final sentence. 'When Bob fell asleep on Susan's couch he held in his hands—held on to it all night—his phone, set on vibrate, in case Jim needed him, but the phone remained unmoving and unblinking and it stayed that way as the first pale light crept unapologetically beneath the blinds.' I paused, read it again and burst into tears, not because the passage was heart-rending but because it was such an utterly subtle caress that kept the echo of the scene in the reader's mind as the reader was leaving it. I would never, ever be able to write like that. I felt utterly discouraged, as though I were standing at the foot of Michaelangelo's *David* with a canister of Play-Doh in my hands, hoping to God that my creation didn't resemble an ashtray.

Things got better. I read more and cried less until the words began to settle in me. I took another class and my writing got marginally better. And then another monumental change occurred in early 2020 as murmurs of a respiratory illness trickled through the news cycle.

COVID-19 hit the shores of North America like an underwater earth-quake, cracking the foundations of social culture and overpowering institutions thought to be unshakable. As the number of COVID admissions in my hospital grew into the dozens, nonclinical staff members like me were sent away to shelter in place and do what we could from our homes. I met with my pastoral care students online and spent hours talking them through their uncertainty. I helped with online support groups for hospital staff who felt overwhelmed with grief at the endless COVID-related losses. In the midst of the isolation and the fear and anxiety that forced me into my basement office, the words knocked and banged around until they gushed out of me in a torrent. All they had needed was the time and space to burst the dam I had created with my refusal to take them seriously.

I wrote *a lot* in those early months of the pandemic and began to submit pieces to magazines and journals. Many were rejected, but one query to a religiously affiliated magazine received a positive reply. 'Send me the piece,' said the editor. I did. 'Needs some work,' came the reply. I worked on it and returned it. And then came the message every writer will look back on as the moment when they went from hobbyist to something more serious: 'I will pay you XX dollars for your piece.' I wept when I received that email, not from discouragement but from sheer gratitude that someone thought my writing *mattered*.

I continued to write short pieces, both fiction and nonfiction, and noticed something unusual happening. My writing had begun to take on emotional depth and complexity that had been beyond my reach in my twenties. I channeled the fear and anxiety of the pandemic into my submission to the first volume of the anthology you are reading and, to my astonishment, it was accepted. I used that same power of honesty in pieces I submitted to *Chicken Soup for the Soul*, four of which have now been published. I gathered my courage and entered contests. While I got the 'We received many excellent pieces and could not choose them all' response from most, two pieces earned me 'congratulations!' messages. The more I wrote, the more I began to feel the love for writing in my bones.

That love led me to a hunger for depth and so I began to write my first novel, which is inspired by my Italian grandparents' separation and dramatic reunion during World War II. I followed the urgent whispering of mortality and wrote every day (I still do) and realized that I would need experienced, honest eyes on my work if I was ever to find it a home. With a great deal of reluctance, I reached out to my writers organization to find colleagues who wrote historical fiction. To my great surprise and incredible luck, three experienced authors who valued honesty over ego and collegiality over gamesmanship agreed to join me. I came to our first meeting trembling with the emerging writer's mantra: 'God-I-hope-it's-not-crap, God-I hope-it's-not-crap.' Weeks and months went by and they assured me I wasn't writing crap, but I wasn't all-that-and-a-bag-of-chips either. I had a ways to go, but they would go with me and I with them as we honed the skill of offering substantive feedback. What an honour it is to be on pilgrimage with such wise and dedicated companions.

And so here I am among the teeming thousands who are haunted by words. I have met other emerging writers whose journey was jump-started by this pandemic. Our genres and approaches may be different, but a common theme runs through our practice of writing: urgency. The ever-present whisper of mortality has convinced us to never take the words for granted simply because, at any moment, they could be our last. For us, for writers whose hunger for words was reawakened during the pandemic, we have learned a vital lesson: writing is life.

High Ridge, Missouri
March 30, 2024

My Mid-life Crises
Ann McMillan

COVID-19 prompted one of my mid-life crises. I was happily enjoying my retirement, dabbling a bit in this and that, when, out of nowhere, COVID hit and fundamentally changed the way I regard the whole world and especially the little corner of that world in which I see myself.

A bit of background...I am a scientist whose self-image includes a view of myself contributing to the world through understanding, interpreting and publicizing science. My most satisfying years as a government employee were those years in which I led a group in the interpretation of science, whether it was for 'marketing' at Ontario Hydro, for 'policy' for the Meteorological Service of Canada, or for 'standard setting' for Environment Canada. After retirement in 2011, I worked hard with a long-time colleague, Eric Taylor, to produce *Air Quality Management: Canadian Perspectives on a Global Issue.* [1] This exercise satisfied my need to pay back a community and a field of work that had been good to me over the years, but it also awoke the desire to write about my beliefs and understanding of the world at a personal level, something which was not part of my role with the Government of Canada.

As the producer of many, many short summaries of varied topics for management, I loved looking at new topics and ideas and reworking them in such a way that they could be broadly understood and interpreted and, most importantly, used to set standards, support consultation or develop new programs. However, the scope of the work was clearly limited by the mandate of whoever I was working for at the time and I usually had little choice regarding the topic or the overall approach to be used. In parallel with the *Air Quality Management* project, I continued to work part time until 2016, when a bad fall ended my career as a government employee.

At that time, I did some serious introspection and decided to try my hand as an editor of scientific writing. I set up my sole proprietorship under 'Storm Consulting' and found a little bit of work. Sadly, on one two-day contract I did the math; when taxes on my earnings were factored in, I was actually paying to do the work.

Then, I was contacted by an old colleague of mine whom I had worked with in the seventies and eighties. He had encountered the *Air Quality Management* book and invited me to work with him to bring his new book *Aggressive Solutions for Climate Change* [2] to completion. I read the book and found it a bit rough around the edges, with a hard-hitting, if improbable list of potential solutions to the climate change issue. I did an edit of the book, missing a lot of errors but improving it somewhat, and also wrote an introduction. Duane R. Chartier self-published the book in 2017 and it did not go on to be a best seller. Now, eight years later, it is still timely but unlikely to ever become a best seller. The most serious comment we received on the book is that the print was too small. Sigh.

I had my 70th birthday that year, during the course of which I had several mid-life crisis conversations with myself about what I wanted to do when I grew up. I decided to take writing more seriously and started to dabble with a few ideas for children's books (which have yet to be realized). While I very much wanted to write, I knew that I was a novice and was a bit afraid to make mistakes.

A year later, Duane was back in touch. He had discovered Ambrose Bierce and his *Devil's Dictionary*. He thought he would do an update but realized that there was a lot to update and was seeking help. He and I and Dr. Irina I. Agoulnik brought together *The New Devil's Dictionary: Words from Idealistic Cynics,* [3] and Duane self-published it in early 2019. It was not a best seller either, but the work prompted a few more conversations with myself as to how best to use my time.

Duane, as an art conservator, had been instrumental in working on the relocation of the sculpture *End of the Trail* by James Earle Fraser to the lobby of the National Cowboy Heritage Center and Museum in Oklahoma City, U.S.A. I found the whole thing fascinating, particularly the glimpse into the life of 'the most famous unknown sculptor.' [4] Duane had pulled together a batch of the writings of James Earle Fraser and gave me a rough draft to edit. The result was *James Earle Fraser: Mostly in His Own Words.* [5] Again Duane self-published the book, acknowledging me but leaving the lines indicating where there had been editorial marks in the margins. Sigh. At least it was in much larger type than his previous books. Along with that book we did *End of the Trail: A brief Tale of an Historical and Artistic Journey* [6] which documented the conservation of the famous statue. Once again, I was acknowledged. These two books were both published in 2019, before COVID had struck. Once again, they were not best sellers.

And then, COVID hit. Duane lives in California; I live in Ontario. We had never considered our physical distance from each other any sort of barrier before, mostly using e-mail to communicate, but now it seemed that phone and e-mail were a poor excuse for face-to-face connection. In July 2020, Duane drove to Ontario and parked his truck in my driveway for a week while we jointly mourned our old way of life which was apparently changed forever, tried to resolve some emerging differences in working style, and pondered what would be next. Duane was full of ideas and liked to go from idea to actualization in seconds. He found me slow and pedantic. I thought of myself as careful. I asked myself whether I wanted to continue the partnership. Indeed, I asked myself that question several times, and don't recall ever getting a clear reply.

About this time, I also started having a different discussion with myself about writing, reading, books and the role of information and creativity in society. It was part of a larger period of reflection and growth triggered by my recovery from grieving the death of my partner a couple of years previous. Perhaps this was another mini-mid-life crisis? By now I was 73 and a little concerned that I apparently still had a lot of growing up to do.

Duane had another idea from which we developed a project which we called *Naked in Time.* [7] We pulled together a series of contributors who each wrote a short piece about a time in their lives when something unusual occurred that wasn't witnessed by any of their usual networks--and which changed their lives as a result. My name went on the cover as 'executive editor' since Duane turned over much of the dealing with authors and book assembly to me. I loved figuring out how the pieces fit together, giving them an edit and putting them in sections. I tried to be careful; meanwhile, Duane prodded regularly for progress. He started another project, *Signs,* [8] which built on his collection of pictures of signs to explore the more general significance of signs in our society. I slowly edited and re-edited. On November 22, 2020, *Naked in Time* was released on Amazon with an e-book to follow a bit later. While it was not a best seller, at least most of the contributors bought a copy.

It began to dawn on me that neither Duane nor I was good at marketing our books and that it was a good thing I had a pension since writing cost me money. COVID was by now in full swing, and while we had benefitted from the focus on isolation to reap the output from a wonderful bunch of mostly neophyte writers, we didn't seem to catch any sort of wave on sales.

In early 2020, I met Jon Peirce who was living in Nova Scotia at the time. We instantly hit it off and talked regularly. Jon, who was not entirely happy in Nova Scotia, was active in the theatre as well as busy writing and impressed me as someone who, even though older than me, had not yet reached his best before date. Jon had been a contributor to *Naked in Time* and I was a big fan of his contributions and impressed with his writing. But it was some time before our relationship developed enough that I suggested that we use a similar model to *Naked in Time* to pull together an almanac of contributions by elders on the subject of COVID-19. Jon loved the idea and *Plague Take It: A COVID Almanac by and about Elders* [9] was born. We both drew heavily from our personal networks to invite writers to contribute and the result is eclectic and a perfect read for a doctor's office wait.

Meanwhile, I was aging. With the stimulus of COVID and the absence of dragon boating and my other usual physical activities I was on the one hand begrudging my time spent on activities which didn't have a payoff and on the other seeking activities to keep feeling productively busy. I realized that at this point in my life doing things was a choice and if I changed my mind later it could very well be too late to do anything else. I determined that if I were going to become a serious writer I would have to write more both often and better, and I would have to broaden my perspective on what I wrote. That perspective very much influenced what I wrote for *Plague Take It*. Given the excellent collection of over fifty authors and the timeliness of the topic, I wondered seriously whether we might have a best seller. While that did not occur, there was more interest and feedback on that book than with anything I had written previously. It not only validated my writing and participation in the project, but it also confirmed my conviction that we oldsters ought to write and that we should bring our ideas forward to be considered by broader society. If we don't, we have only ourselves to blame if we face prejudice and ageism in our futures. So ended my third mid-life crisis with the conviction that I should continue writing. I turned 74 that year and was a little concerned that my mid-life crises were becoming more frequent.

Duane also understood that books such as *Signs* were not going to sell, and he broadened his ideas to include books on air chemistry and on politics as well as mystery. He got the idea that a book of parodies of old-fashioned nursery rhymes had the potential to be a best seller. In spite of my serious doubts, I had a lot of fun writing up some original poems as well as some awful parodies of classic rhymes. I love doodling with pen and ink and I doodled away. In 2021 we published *Rhyme Warp* [10] which is, to say the least, whimsical. It was not a best seller but it was pure fun to do. Duane went on to write *M Means Murder* [11] which I edited for him. It was a bizarre murder thriller. It was not a best seller either.

Meanwhile, my dragon boat team could not practice during the pandemic even though we paddle outside. Dragon boats have seating for 20 paddlers, but they are cheek-to-cheek and chock-a-block--close enough to communicate anything communicable. I proposed that we write a book to allow us to work together on something as a team and as a fundraising venture. My fellow team members agreed, and so I compiled and edited *Tales from the Boat* [12] built from contributions from my team members. It was lovingly edited by Jon Peirce and published by Bob Barclay of Loose Cannon Press in 2022, and I'm proud to say it *is* a bit of a best seller (at least in the Ottawa Valley).

Sadly, in 2022 Duane had a stroke, or as he calls it, a cerebral incident. At first it affected his speech and writing ability fairly seriously. He had started another project to write a popular book on the topic of 'love' and I had started to contribute a few things. We met in April, 2023 in the southern US and made some progress on that as well as on some of Duane's other work which I was editing. Regrettably, he found creative writing really difficult and focussed instead on regaining his language skills and writing abilities. He came to Ontario for another visit this past fall (2024), and although we will always be the best of friends, our literary collaboration is over for the present. It is wonderful to see that he has regained much of his oral ability, but he has moved on from writing to other interests.

COVID was already slipping from public consciousness in 2023 when Jon and I decided to do a follow-up to *Plague Take It. Road to Recovery* has taken a long time for us to pull together—partly because Jon took a detour through *Work Less* [13] and I went back to dragon boating and playing golf, decided to sit on a hospital patient and family board and had adult daughters revisit the nest. Jon and I are hoping that *Road to Recovery* is going to be a best seller.

I think I have emerged from my protracted mid-life crises in a good place to continue writing as a way to work without working, to enjoy capturing thoughts and experiences to share with others and to grow as a person. Perhaps, after *Road to Recovery* I will have reached some sort of intermediate stage? Only time will tell.

---

[1] Taylor, Eric and Ann McMillan (eds), *Air Quality Management; Canadian Perspectives on a Global Issue.* Springer, 2014, 408 pp.

[2] Chartier, Duane R., *Aggressive Solutions for Climate Change,* Amazon, 2017, 169 pp.

[3] Chartier, Duane R., Ann McMillan, and Irina Agoulnik, *The New Devil's Dictionary: Words from Idealistic Cynics,* Amazon, 2019, 316 pp.

[4] Louchheim, Aline B., *Most Famous Unknown Sculptor,* New York Times Magazine, 100 (May 13, 1951): 24-25, 65.

[5] Chartier, Duane R., *James Earle Fraser: Mostly in his Own Words,* Amazon, 2019.

[6] Chartier, Duane R., *End of the Trail: A Brief History of an Historical and Artistic Journey,* Amazon, 2019, 172 pp.

[7] McMillan, Ann, and Duane R. Chartier, *Naked in Time,* Amazon, 2021, 174 pp.

[8] Chartier, Duane R., Ann McMillan (editor), and Joel Swarz (editor), *Signs,* Amazon, 2020.

[9] Peirce, Jon and Ann McMillan (editors), *Plague Take It: A COVID Almanac by and about Elders,* Loose Cannon Press, 2021, 468 pp.

[10] Chartier, Duane R. and Ann McMillan, *Rhyme Warp,* Amazon, 2021, 222 pp.

[11] Chartier, Duane R. (author), Ann McMillan (editor), and Joel Swartz (editor), *M Means Murder,* Amazon, 2020, 253 pp.

[12] McMillan, Ann (compiler and editor), *Tales from the Boat,* Loose Cannon Press, 2022, 138 pp.

[13] Peirce, Jon, *Work Less: New Strategies for a Changing Workplace,* Dundurn Press, 2024, 296 pp.

Writing at the End of the Pandemic
Jon Peirce

Whats it like to be a writer at the end of the COVID-19 pandemic—or what passes for the end? One way to answer this question is to compare what it's like being a writer today with what it was like being a writer at the beginning of the pandemic, four and a half years ago, when along with co-author Ann McMillan I first started to put together the predecessor to this volume, *Plague Take It*. But before I begin to address this comparison, there's an extremely important preliminary question to get out of the way: namely, has COVID in fact ended?

The answer to *this* question has generally been 'It has, but it hasn't,' ever since the World Health Organization lifted its 'Public Health Emergency of International Concern' declaration for COVID in early 2023, while at the same time insisting that the disease continues to pose a global threat.[1] An epidemic if necessary, but not necessarily an epidemic? The Canadian federal government took a similar course when it announced that as of October 4, 2024, its COVID-19 epidemiology website,[2] which had been a crucial source of basic information about the disease, would no longer be updated. Instead, COVID-19 facts could be found on the Canadian Respiratory Viruses Surveillance Report, where they are presented along with information about other respiratory viruses such as influenza and RSV. The information provided in this report is extremely general, the major fact of interest in the one for the period ending December 20 that I consulted being that about 10 percent of COVID tests nationwide had been positive.[3] For more detailed information, one must consult the various provincial reports, to which the federal report is linked. These, in turn, vary considerably as to the amount of specific detail they provide. B.C.'s report pretty much confines itself to statements like the following: 'SARS COV-2 levels in wastewater and COVID-19 severe outcomes continue to decline.'[4] In contrast, Ontario's report lists not just a test positivity rate—quite high at 13 percent—but the number of hospital admissions, ICU admissions, deaths, and outbreaks, as well as an indicator named 'episodes' whose precise meaning I couldn't deduce, but which given its high number (1530) may refer to confirmed cases.[5]

Various commentators, at least one of whom is quoted elsewhere in this volume, have referred to the 'fluification' of COVID.[6] Overall, this seems a fairly accurate description of what's been happening over the past year or so. We certainly can't say that the disease has been conquered. Not when, as noted earlier, 61 Canadians in a single week died of it, or when 1290 positive cases of it were reported in Quebec alone as recently as the third week in

December.[7] What we can say is that there appears to have been a collective decision—not just in Canada but pretty much all around the world—not to allow the disease to interfere with people's daily lives any longer. Masks are an extreme rarity, except in healthcare settings. Even there they are generally no longer required;[8] many healthcare staff still wear them, but a fair number do not. COVID's continued existence doesn't appear to have diminished crowd sizes at recent Taylor Swift concerts, or to have kept people away from hockey and baseball games, where they sit cheek by jowl and shoulder-to-shoulder with thousands of other fans, the vast majority of whom, as I can see on my TV screen, are unmasked.

No doubt the existence of reasonably effective vaccines has a good deal to do with our changed attitude toward COVID. But so, too, does a less easily defined but nonetheless pervasive feeling, across almost all segments of society, that we have all had enough of restrictions on our lifestyle and feel the need simply to live again. And most of us recognize, as well, that the economy, which has taken a severe battering in recent years, could not take any more restrictions on people's freedom to shop and gather as they wish. Finally, we must accept that COVID is a threat that will likely always remain with us. Just like seasonal flu, it is but one of many threats we face in today's complex and troubled economic and political environment—and probably not the most serious of those threats.

To conclude, then: while COVID is not over—far from it—it has definitely entered a new phase, one which will likely not see it commanding as much of people's attention as it has received over the past five years. For the past five years, it has been the subject I've written most about. Only work hours, on which I published a book at the beginning of 2024,[9] has even come close to rivalling the amount of time and energy I've devoted to COVID. Once this book is out, I may never write another thing about the disease. I certainly won't write or co-write another book on it. It's time, and indeed past time, that I moved on to other things. As I consider myself an active member of the anti-Trump resistance, much of what I write over the next few years—as long as I'm physically and mentally able to do so—will likely be resistance pieces of one sort or another. But the subjects on which I will write, and the form my work will take, are very much open questions at this point. I'll probably need to observe Trump in action for a few months to be able to see in what direction his [sic] administration is headed and which issues appear to be most in need of attention. We'll return to this issue later on in the essay.

My present attitude of uncertainty as to my future as a writer, in contrast to the attitude I had at the beginning of the pandemic, is no doubt a reflection both of my changed circumstances and the world's. When I began to keep my 'plague journal' in March of 2020, I was a man with a mission—namely to chronicle the pandemic's social history. I firmly believed, as I started my intensive daily recording of COVID cases, hospitalizations, and deaths from all across Canada and even part of the U.S., that I was one of very few who immediately appreciated the pandemic's significance, as a cataclysmic event rivalling both the earlier [sic] Spanish flu pandemic and the two World Wars as a source of material for writers and historians. As I said in one of my *Plague Take It* pieces, 'As I believe that this time of plague will mark a watershed and will be a time of fundamental change in our attitude to life and in our strategies for coping, both individually as a society, I am launching this journal [10] in order to record these critical changes, as well as to note the effect that all these changes have had and will have on me, my family, and my close friends. The suspension of Masses [11] is certainly an escalation in the enclosure of our lives to protect against the plague. If, in addition, we see complete closure of the public libraries and (God help us) suspension of public transit, we will know that we are in a battle for our collective lives.'[12] As indeed we were. I felt it was my mission, as a social historian, to chronicle that battle and explain its significance to readers. To that end, I drove myself mercilessly, working six days a week and occasionally seven at top speed for six or more hours per day, working as hard as I had when I was finishing my PhD thesis and teaching a 15-hour per week summer class at the same time... working in all likelihood as hard I would have worked had I been an actual battlefield correspondent. That frenetic pace continued, only slightly abated—I did stop working on Sundays and late Saturday afternoons—during the writing and assembly of *Plague Take It,* a process that took less than a year from the book's conception, in December of 2020, until its launch in November of 2021.[13] And then no sooner had *Plague Take It* been launched than I received an invitation from Dundurn Press publisher Scott Fraser to write a book on work hours.[14] The research and writing of this book would keep me going at a steady if not frenetic piece through 2022 and most of 2023.

At the time I started the plague journal that would soon morph into *Plague Take It,* I felt severely underutilized, both as a person and more specifically as a writer. The previous six years had seen me publish just two books, one an essay collection made up mainly of much earlier newspaper pieces,[15] the other an 87-page novella.[16] For years, I felt, I'd been 'punching below my weight.' While I couldn't do much about my spotty social life and near non-existent romantic life until I left the province,[17] I could and did throw myself into the plague-chronicling business with incredible vigour. (Bear in mind that between mid-March and early May, there was almost nothing to do *other* than write and take daily walks. Lockdown restrictions were so severe that I went six weeks without having an in-person conversation with anyone; this was before public officials realized that people living alone needed some special allowances made for them to keep them from going completely bonkers, and we life soloists were allowed to see two other people). Even in my thesis-writing days I hadn't been *that* single-mindedly devoted to my writing, for then I had (at my own insistence, to save my sanity, as well as in the interest of preserving some kind of relationship with my partner) taken weekends off. In the spring of 2020, I spent most of the occasional Sundays I did take off catching up on sleep after the virtual church service in the morning. Until the first-stage lockdown had ended, and I could again see friends, eat out in restaurants, go to church, and visit the Waegwoltic Club for tennis and swimming, the plague journal that would eventually morph into *Plague Take It* really *was* my life. I had huge holes that needed filling, and my work on the journal filled a good many of them. My move to Gatineau at the end of August of that year would fill most of the rest.

How are things different now, with me and with the world into which these writings, for better or for worse, are about to emerge? To begin with, I'm now much more confident about myself as a writer. Since the spring of 2020, I've produced or co-produced three books: *Plague Take It*, *Work Less*, and my short story collection, *The Long and the Short of It*. When this book finally comes out, that will be four books for me in a five-year period—a decent achievement for a writer of any age but especially for one in his late 70s. No longer do I feel I'm 'punching below my weight.' Since 2020, I've punched at my weight and then some. [18]

In addition, my life outside writing is far richer than it was five years ago. For starters, I now have a pretty strong network of friends, including some old ones from my days working with PIPSC or participating in Ottawa Independent Writers (OIW), and a number of new ones. With the end of lockdowns, I've been able to resume activities in community theatre, first at Theatre Wakefield in West Quebec and more recently at Kanata Theatre. The latter's summer festival of short plays has enabled me to be, in turn, a playwright, a director, and (once again) an actor. Each winter, I take part in KT's playwriting workshop, aimed at honing aspiring playwrights' skills while producing the next summer's crop of short plays. And speaking of OIW, I've returned to that organization's board, on which I served for a decade during my previous stint in Ottawa. Finally, while I'm no longer in an intimate relationship, as I was for nearly three years, I feel that between them Ottawa and West Quebec offer me a reasonable chance of finding one, unlike the barren Nova Scotia environment I described in 'Farewell to Nova Scotia.' [19]

In short, my *need* to write, given my achievements of the past five years and the far fuller life I now lead, is not so intense as it was in 2020. Don't get me wrong. That need has been there practically all my life and will probably never die as long as I have the physical strength to keep on producing. If I don't write for as long as a week, I start to feel a bit lost and slightly nauseated. As far back as first grade, I can remember spending whole hours and occasionally entire afternoons writing, thanks to an understanding teacher named Ruth Moore, while on either side of me budding artists Gordon

Kilborn and Carolyn Kelly, the latter the daughter of famed cartoonist Walt Kelly, were equally happily drawing. And this drive appears to have been evident to family members. My kid sister Susan, in a recent conversation, says she can remember me always writing during my teen years. She even noted that there's a name for such a drive to write, though I've thus far refrained from looking it up—mainly because I've been too busy writing to have the time or energy to bother. Such a deep-seated, long-standing drive isn't likely to disappear. At the same time, I'd have to admit that the drive isn't as intense as it was five years ago, let alone twenty-five years ago when I was finishing mop-up work on my first book, an industrial relations textbook[20] That's true both because of the fuller and more varied life I'm now leading and because I don't have the energy I had five years ago, let alone 25. Now, the difference between 75 and 80 might not seem like much, but in my life it looms very large indeed. It's important to bear in mind that age is by no means a linear mathematical function. I've probably changed at least five times as much between 75 and 80 as I did between 70 and 75. Physically, at least, most of those changes were not for the better. At 75, I was still playing tennis, albeit not all that often or all that well. At 76, I had to quit the game I'd played since age 12 because playing led to unbearable pain in my legs. At 75, I'd never seen a cardiologist, nor had I ever so much as heard of 'A-Fib' (atrial fibrillation). Three years later, I had a cardiologist, and he had prescribed both beta blockers and blood thinners to deal with my A-Fib. Five years ago, I required but one medical specialist: a dermatologist. Today I have a cardiologist, urologist, and nephrologist in addition to the dermatologist, and I'm seeing the dermatologist as often as most people see their GPs. Five years ago, I was able to get onto and off of trains without assistance, no matter how much luggage I had. Now, I require help getting on and off with my luggage. Putting a big or even medium-sized suitcase into the train's overhead luggage bin would be totally beyond me. I can only imagine what my list of 'Can no longer dos' will look like in five years—if I'm even still around and walking the earth then—let alone in 10 years, if against all the odds I'm around and still walking the earth then.

Not surprisingly, my energy for writing has also diminished, though probably not to the same extent as my physical abilities. While 2,500-word days were fairly common during the production of *Plague Take It*, and there was more than one 5,000-word day, I couldn't even imagine putting in a 5,000-word day now. Granted, I still have the occasional 2,000–2,500-word day, but these are much rarer than they were four years ago. At 2,500 words, I feel I'm pushing my upper limit. If I wrote much more than that in a day, I'd probably have to take the next day off to rest. And I'm also no longer up to a six-day writing week. Five or even four days a week, with off days scattered in between, is a more realistic schedule. This doesn't mean I'm not still capable of producing, and indeed producing quite a bit over time. It does mean that such herculean achievements as the completion of the 600-page *Canadian Industrial Relations* and the 450-page *Plague Take It* in less than a year are probably things of the past. Obviously I need to start writing shorter books!

If I as a writer have changed quite a bit over the past four and a half years, so too, to perhaps an even greater extent, has the world's economic and political environment. The wars in Ukraine and Gaza were still yet to come. So too was a COVID vaccine, though most of us were confident that one would soon be developed—and we were right. By the end of 2020, a sizable number of both Canadians and Americans had had their first jab. In Canada, Liberal Prime Minister Justin Trudeau had obtained the first of two successive minority governments a year earlier, defeating a Conservative contender whose name I no longer remember. A political welterweight managing a split decision over a political lightweight. In the U.S., Donald Trump was finishing up his first term, which most of us were then naïve enough to believe would be his last. His attempted coup of January 6, 2021 lay just ahead. A year beyond that would be the truck convoy that would bring the city of Ottawa to its knees. As for technology, the big thing in those days was Zoom, which most of those of us of working age used to enable us to work from home. While artificial intelligence certainly existed and was often talked about, it hadn't yet become the big part of our daily lives that it has by now.

While the days of the pandemic were not easy ones, they seem in some ways almost halcyon days compared to those in which we are now living. A far greater part of the world is now at war. Neither the war in Ukraine, which began in 2022, nor the one in Gaza, which began in 2023, shows any sign of ending any time soon. And there has also been a bloody civil war in Sudan. Around the world, fascist and neo-Nazi parties have been on the rise. Though there have been some glimmers of hope, such as the defeat of the Conservatives in Britain and their replacement by Keir Starmer's Labour government, the election of progressive President Claudia Sheinbaum in Mexico, and the defeat of the ultra-rightist Bolsonaro government in Brazil, these developments have been more than overshadowed by such negative developments as the surprising (and to me shocking) return to power of Donald Trump and the emergence of an authoritarian axis made up of Trump and people like Russian president Vladimir Putin, Hungarian autocrat Viktor Orban, and North Korean dictator Kim Jong Un. Here in Canada, Justin Trudeau appears long since to have worn out his welcome; his Liberals now lag 23 points behind Pierre Poilievre's Conservatives in the latest Canada 338 poll. Amazingly, the NDP hasn't managed to pick up any of the vast amount of support shed by the Liberals; that party still lags far behind at 19 per cent, which is just about the same as its level of support in the last federal election. The question now appears to be whether Trudeau will resign in time to allow his party to pick a leader able to mount a serious challenge to Poilievre, an ultra-rightist in the Stephen Harper mode but even more extreme, who appears prepared to lead this country down the road to Trumpism as fast and as far as circumstances will let him. No longer can we in Canada say, with confidence, that no matter who wins the next election the country will still survive. A majority Conservative government under Poilievre—by all accounts the likeliest outcome of the next federal election—would leave us with grave concern for our continuing sovereignty.

As we approach the New Year, and with it Donald Trump's [sic] presidency, I'm pretty sure that the year will end with all of us in Canada, let alone the U.S., worse off in most ways than at the start of the year. The question is how much worse things will get, and how quickly. To what extent will Trump follow through on the crazy ideas he's been enunciating ever since his [sic] election, and to what extent will Pierre Poilievre—almost certainly Canada's next Prime Minister unless the electorate suffers a sudden rush of sanity and good sense and decides it should not elect a man who doesn't have a security clearance—want or feel compelled to adopt some version of Trump's program? Are we looking at significant but manageable losses of the things we hold dear, at bigger but still survivable losses, or rather at the kind of apocalyptic transformation suffered by France after Germany's takeover in World War II? [21] The answers to these and related questions, such as how much should I expect my real standard of living to fall and to what extent will I be obliged to cover my healthcare costs myself, will largely determine what and how much I write. If there's a sudden wave of high inflation, or I'm forced to assume most or even all of my own healthcare costs, I'll either have to do more newspaper and magazine journalism, which to my surprise I have recently found I'm still able to do, getting an article into the *Globe* just two weeks before this is being written, or possibly even take a part-time job, which would leave me with a good deal less time and energy to pursue 'my own writing.' If, in an extreme worst-case scenario, I were to be cut off my U.S. Social Security benefit, a part-time job would become an absolute necessity. There is no way in the world I could possibly absorb the $600+/month cut in income that losing my Social Security would entail.[22]

Finally, in an absolute worst-case political scenario, if Canada were to be taken over, whether in fact or in name, by Trump's America, to the extent that free speech and freedom of the press were threatened or perhaps even eliminated, any thought of doing 'my own writing' would vanish. I would need to devote my full time and energy to resistance work (quite possibly including writing), to avoiding detection, and to simply staying alive in what would almost certainly have become an absolutely brutal economic environment. (Again, books like *The Nightingale* are an invaluable guide here.) Probably I wouldn't have to live such a life for all that long. The stress of living in that kind of environment would almost certainly shorten my life significantly,

297

along with the lives of many other seniors. Adequate healthcare would probably be far more difficult to obtain and more expensive than it is now. Indeed, I and many of my fellow seniors might be forced to choose, as some people are even now, between obtaining essential life-saving medications and putting food on the table. While I wouldn't bet on things deteriorating to such an extent—I'd like to think that even Trump's people are not quite so crazy and heartless as to allow that to happen—I wouldn't be prepared to bet against its happening, either. The people Trump is proposing to put in his Cabinet are sufficiently unstable and ill-informed that at this point, lacking the usual guardrails of a strong Senate and Supreme Court to curb the worst sorts of abuses, I wouldn't be prepared to rule much of anything out.

That said, if things don't deteriorate to the point where we're all forced to spend all our time and energy on basic survival and political resistance, the possibilities for writers are rich, indeed rich to the point of being almost endless. Those who write speculative fiction have a plethora of material to work with. The same for playwrights and screenwriters. And the changing mores of love and romance and of family life should provide writers of mainstream fiction more than ample fodder. As for non-fiction writers (including yours truly), there's a plethora of subjects to explore, ranging from the evolution (or devolution) of the English language and the changes in the education system to the wonders and ravages of the new technology and people's apparently constant need to be entertained.

Until we know more about how our brave new world is going to shape up, all any of us can do is keep writing, and hope for the best while being prepared for the worst.

Ottawa,
December 2024

---

[1] Linda Geddes, 'COVID-19 is no longer a Public Health Emergency of International Concern. Does this mean the pandemic is over?' *Gavi*, May 5, 2023.

[2] In its last epidemiology website report, covering the period from Sept. 15 to Sept. 21, the government reported 61 deaths attributable to COVID, the vast majority of them being in Quebec and Ontario. While this is a figure well below those of previous years, it is still far from negligible, given that 61 deaths in a week would translate to slightly over 3000 in a year.

[3] Government of Canada. Canadian Respiratory Virus Surveillance Report, updated Dec. 20, 2024. Data are for week ending Dec. 14, 2024.

[4] B.C. Centre for Disease Control, Respiratory Virus Data. Updated Dec. 19, 2024. Data are for week ending Dec. 14, 2024.

[5] Public Health Ontario, Ontario Respiratory Tool. Updated Dec. 20, 2024. Data are for week ending Dec. 14, 2024.

[6] See among others Katherine Wu, 'Why Are We Still Flu-ifying COVID?' in *The Atlantic*, Feb. 28, 2024..

[7] Institut National de sante publique du Quebec. Vigie des virus respiratoires par les laboratoires cliniques. Data for week ending Dec. 21, 2024. Information from this source is available only in French.

[8] Only one of my numerous physicians requires that masks be worn in his office.

[9] *Work Less: New Strategies for a Changing Workplace* (Toronto: Dundurn, 2024).

[10] A journal of COVID-related statistics and events which I later used as raw material for several *Plague Take It* pieces. My original intention had been to publish it separately, but after Ann McMillan convinced me to work on *Plague Take It,* I decided it would probably be too dry to be of interest to most readers.

[11] On the day I wrote this entry, March 15, 2020, the Roman Catholic church announced that due to the pandemic, that day's masses would be the last held live in churches until further notice. The Anglican Church, to which I then belonged, immediately followed suit.

[12] As it happened, the public libraries would close early in the following week. Buses continued to run, on a reduced schedule, but VIA Rail halted train service into the Maritimes in that same week. It would be over a year before that train service was restored.

[13] I would wind up contributing 14 pieces to that volume, including two political essays of about 20,000 words each. Among them, these pieces accounted for about a third of the book's 467 pages.

[14] For the complete story of this book's genesis, see the introduction to *Work Less*.

[15] *Social Studies: Collected Essays, 1974-2013* (Victoria: Friesen, 2014).

[16] *Love and Love* (Amazon, 2018).

[17] My August,2020 move from Nova Scotia to Gatineau, Quebec is chronicled in 'Farewell to Nova Scotia: Mr. Chips Leaves God's Country during the Pandemic,' in *Plague Take It,* pp. 414-422.

[18] For this, I owe a huge debt of gratitude to my co-author, Ann McMillan. Without her gentle but persistent prodding and strong belief in me, neither *Plague Take It* nor this volume would have come into being, and in all likelihood, I would still be a writer struggling to understand why I was continuing to 'punch below my weight.'

[19] In *Plague Take It,* op. cit.

[20] *Canadian Industrial Relations* (Toronto: Pearson, 2006, 2002, and 2000).

[21] That transformation is described most movingly and tellingly by Kristin Hannah in *The Nightingale* (New York: St. Martin's Press, 2015).

[22] I don't think such a cutoff of Social Security very likely. While Trump and his new bestie, Elon Musk, have sometimes mused about the possibility of eliminating Social Security completely, it would likely not be politically feasible to do so, at least not overnight. The firestorm of protest that would be raised if existing recipients were to be cut off their benefits, which after all they've earned by paying into the Social Security fund from their salaries over many years, would in my view be too much for Trump to bear. Unlike Elon Musk, Republican representatives in the U.S. House have constituents to answer to—about 700,000 per representative. Only the most diehard MAGAs seem likely to be prepared to endure such a firestorm for the sake of pleasing Donald and Elon. As well, cutting millions of seniors off their primary or even only source of income would be too much for the economy to bear. Any

Treasury Secretary with even the slightest iota of sense would be forced to veto the idea. Still, both Trump and the times are crazy enough that the idea can't be completely ruled out. I would put the odds of its happening during Trump's term in office at somewhere between 10 and 15 per cent.

CONCLUSION
A Personal Pandemic Balance Sheet

Jon Peirce

Let me begin by saying that overall—to the extent that anyone can truly say they are out of the COVID-19 pandemic—I've come out of that pandemic significantly ahead of where I was at its outset, in many and indeed most areas of my life. I find such an admission more than a little embarrassing, knowing how much many people have suffered (and in some cases continue to suffer) because of the pandemic. Honesty nonetheless compels me to make that admission.

To be sure, it's important to note that my life could not have been at a much lower ebb than at was at the start of the pandemic. In early March of 2020, I had nowhere to go but up.

At that point, I had no overall plan for how to spend the rest of my life, beyond knowing that I didn't want to do so in Nova Scotia.[1] While I'd long thought of myself as primarily a writer, I had no major writing projects on the go or even planned. What few markets there had been for my journalistic efforts when I'd moved to Nova Scotia in 2009 had completely dried up, and I'd never really been accepted in the province's literary community despite having been a professional member of the Writers' Federation for a decade. My efforts in community theatre were only marginally more successful. Occasionally I would land a meaty role, but for every role I landed, I was rejected for at least half a dozen others. And I was having no luck at all getting any of the plays I'd written performed.

Worst of all was my social life. I was alone, and appeared destined to remain alone for as long as I stayed in Nova Scotia. At the beginning of 2020, it had been nearly three years since I'd had any kind of relationship at all. The one I'd had then (in 2017) had been short, fraught with tension, and full of long absences. It had been more than a decade since I'd been in a relationship offering any sort of stability or emotional support at all. And the chances of finding one seemed to be diminishing with each passing year. Forced to resort to the dating sites, not because I really wanted to but because there seemed to be no other place for a septuagenarian pensioner to look, I was finding the sites more and more frustrating. Most of the women I encountered there were polite, but cold and indifferent. A few were downright rude, with more than one descending to personal abuse. A bridge partner's frank acknowledgment that if I wanted to have sex in Nova Scotia at my age I would probably have to pay for it was more than a little revealing.

The downright appalling state of my social life only served to aggravate what by the middle of 2019 had already manifested itself as mild to moderate depression. Had I been able to get help for that depression, I might have coped better. But given the pitiful state of the province's mental health system by then, such help, which had at least occasionally been available during my earlier years in Nova Scotia, simply wasn't to be had, at least not at a price I could afford. As I've noted elsewhere,[2] my GP had told me frankly that unless I was about to inflict serious harm on myself or someone else, the provincial healthcare system couldn't help me. I would have to rely on my insurance plan to get any help at all. That insurance plan would have provided $500:00—enough for two or three sessions with a psychologist. But then where would I have been? To all intents and purposes, mental health treatment had been effectively removed from the overall healthcare system via the back door.[3] Not surprisingly, I would remain in a state of at least mild depression through the rest of my stay in the province.

True, it would have been an exaggeration to say that my pre-pandemic life in Nova Scotia was *totally* awful. But only a slight exaggeration. All my life I've been good at keeping myself busy; this was particularly true for my time in Nova Scotia. In my attempt to ward off depression, I made doubly sure I kept myself busy between 2016 (when Donald Trump's surprise election sent me into a deep downward spiral) and 2019. Despite the disappearance of virtually all my old markets, I wrote fairly regularly. I tried out for a large number of community theatre plays and did manage to get cast in a few of them, although as noted earlier I garnered at least half a dozen rejections for every acceptance. And I also served on two community theatre boards and the script selection committee of one of those theatres, as well as the Parish Council (board) of my Anglican church. I taught as many Nova Scotia Seniors' College courses as I could get, worked in three NDP campaigns, one of which—the campaign of Susan LeBlanc for the provincial legislature, was actually successful—and even took up singing at age 71, first in that Anglican church's choir and then, later, at various Acoustic Song Circles held in public libraries all around Metro Halifax. To keep fit, I swam, danced, played tennis despite the impediment of two artificial hips, and took long walks. In a bid to make new friends as well as keep my mind active, I started playing duplicate bridge for the first time in nearly 15 years. By the end of 2019, I was playing two or three times most weeks. Finally, in an attempt to find a partner, I spent hundreds of evening hours on the dating sites, albeit to little avail.

All in all, I don't see how I could have done any more than I was doing to stay active, engaged, and involved in the community and its artistic life. Friends often commented on my energy and drive. Sometimes I surprised *myself* with all that I did. And these many and varied activities did have some positive effects on my life. A good bridge game or acoustic song circle evening would cheer me up for a day or two. When I got cast in a play or hired to teach a Seniors' College course, the positive effects would last for a month or two. But at the end of the play or course, the old depression would be back again, often worse than before. With no more rehearsals, performances, or classes to take my mind off my essential isolation, and my lack of an overall plan for my life, I often came to wonder, as Peggy Lee had famously done in her classic song, 'Is that all there is?' More and more, it seemed I was grovelling for crumbs, for bits of creative satisfaction and approval from others. And, more and more, my situation felt absolutely hopeless. By the end of 2019, if someone had offered me a one-way ticket to the moon, I'd have accepted it!

How, exactly, did the pandemic change all of this? To begin with, unlike many other people I knew, I saw right away that the pandemic would be a total game-changer. My sense from the get-go was that we were in a situation that a) was the moral equivalent of a war, and b) would change things in such a way that they could never again be the same as they were. For many, those with comfortable, settled, successful lives, such a recognition was unsettling, perhaps even disheartening. For me—someone with nowhere to go but up— the recognition was downright exhilarating, even as I sensed—correctly— that the new situation might well lead to further problems managing my lifelong anxiety disorder.[4] The prospect of a new life, one not fettered by previous expectations and failures, was one that, at age 75, I embraced with open arms. I hit the ground running with my 'plague journal' and didn't stop until several months and several hundred pages later.

For it had also become clear to me that, like the two world wars, the pandemic would provide an extraordinarily rich source of material for writers. Within days, I had a mission in life, for the first time in many years. That mission would be to chronicle the history of the pandemic as it developed, putting in enough of the facts and figures to provide a factual context for my discussion, but focussing primarily on the social history, on how the pandemic was affecting my life and those of the people around me. This was a job for which, I can say with all due modesty, I felt myself superbly qualified, as a long-time professional writer, journalist, and student of history and of the world of work.

After years of what had essentially amounted to make-work projects, I was finally working on something that was getting me out of bed every morning eager to start the day's work, ready to investigate the new COVID data and chart how the pandemic appeared to be developing, on both the medical and social fronts. In my enthusiasm for the mission, I drove myself mercilessly, always working six days a week and occasionally seven, working harder than I had since graduate school days, when, just before taking my first full-time teaching job, I was teaching a three-hour-a-day summer course every weekday morning and revising my thesis every afternoon, prepping for the next day's class in the evening.

I soon came to regard myself as extremely fortunate to have such a mission in life as I had. While many others were bored stiff during the early lockdown phases because they couldn't do most of the things they were used to doing, I had barely enough hours in the day to fit in all the writing I wanted to do and keep fit by walking or dancing. (Alone, in my living room. But it was still dancing.) My main concern was how to avoid pushing myself too hard—something in which I did not always succeed. But far better, I figured, to be too busy than not busy enough.

For some three to four months, until the initial lockdowns were eased and we entered into what I have described elsewhere as a period of 'thaw,' I kept an extremely detailed COVID journal, listing all COVID data (cases, deaths, hospitalizations, etc.) for Canada as a whole, for every Canadian province, for the U.S. as a whole, and for many of the states bordering or nearly bordering on Canada, notably New York, Maine, and Massachusetts. I also collected some case data for non-North American countries, though here I did not pretend to be comprehensive.

Beyond that, I kept close tabs on lockdowns and their easing in all Canadian provinces and many U.S. states. As the pandemic developed, I became particularly interested in comparing the differences among the various Canadian provinces and American states, and between Canadian provinces and American states.

My initial plan had been to take that COVID journal and self-publish it as a separate book on Amazon. As time went on, however, I became less and less enthusiastic about that idea. Would people really want to read 250 or 300 pages of what amounted to case tallies and lockdown data? By late fall, though I hadn't finally decided to scrap the project, I was starting to lean in that direction. Meanwhile, I had moved to Quebec, where I found the new environment (including the use of the French language) and stronger connections between people was starting to stimulate my own creative juices as they had not been stimulated for many years.

At this juncture, I was blessed with a most inspired suggestion from Ann McMillan, whom I was by this time seeing once or twice a week—another sign of the improving times. Ann suggested that she and I put together a COVID almanac, one focussing on seniors. While this would mean that the old COVID journal would not be published separately, it could provide ample raw material for any pieces I might care to write. Beyond that, each of us had a large circle of friends, acquaintances, and former colleagues on whom we could draw for contributions. In the end, *Plague Take It* would contain works by more than 50 different contributors, written in both French and English. It was a huge undertaking, which would not have happened without the outstanding design sense, type-setting, and editing and proofreading of Bob Barclay, whose Loose Cannon Press will also be publishing the present volume. Seeing this big social history through to completion, which Ann and I somehow managed to accomplish in less than a year, firmly re-cemented my sense of myself as a professional writer. And my return to the board of Ottawa Independent Writers (OIW), in which I'd been active for 13 years before my move to Nova Scotia, nicely complemented the work on the almanac. For the first time in my life, I began to see myself as not just any old (or new) writer, but a cultural elder with an important role to play both in mentoring younger writers and in passing on my personal history and institutional memory of OIW going back some 25 years.

My writing career has taken some new and exciting directions since the publication of *Plague Take It* in November of 2021. Having through pure good fortune landed a contract to write a book on work hours for Dundurn Press, I was kept splendidly busy with both that and the volume in which this piece is to appear. The work hours book, entitled *Work Less,* was published in January of 2024. Based on its initial royalty statement, it seems likely to make me at least some money beyond the publisher's advance. Every once in a while, I knock off a piece for some *Chicken Soup for the Soul* anthology or other,[5] and once the present book is done, I plan to go back to writing op ed pieces for newspapers, magazines, and the CBC.[6] Not to mention putting together an essay book, a book about technology which will also be co-authored with Ann, a book of aphorisms, and more.[7]

All in all, my writing career has progressed so far from what it was, less than three years ago, that there's really no comparison. Had it not been for the pandemic, and my response to it, this would almost certainly not have happened.

With my social life, it has been much the same as with my writing career. From somewhere between poor and non-existent, it has developed into a rich source of support for my entire life. I had seen Ann McMillan twice before the pandemic, and was definitely interested in seeing a good deal more of her. At first glance, the pandemic might have seemed a barrier to forming a relationship with someone who lived in Ottawa while I lived in Halifax. As things developed, the pandemic would do a good deal to strengthen our friendship, even before we teamed up on *Plague Take It.* Our twice-weekly phone calls, made at significant sacrifice for Ann, who is not fond of the telephone, were a lifeline for me through the spring and summer months of 2020, prior to my move to Gatineau. Indeed, it was one of those calls that strengthened my resolve to make that move, at a time when I was wavering due to fears about COVID. During that call, I asked Ann if my remaining in Halifax would be a barrier to our continuing our relationship. She allowed as how it would. This forthright declaration was enough to convince me that I would be a fool to stay in Halifax any longer than I had to, and to overcome admittedly not unreasonable fears about moving into the province which then had the country's highest COVID rates.

When I finally did move, at the end of August 2020, Ann was in my new driveway to help me unload my stuffed-to-the-gunnels Camry. So was Denise Giroux, a long-time friend and former PIPSC colleague whom I'd known for 15 years. The two of them would provide invaluable support, not just on moving day but through several severe lockdowns during that fall and winter and the next spring. Throughout that difficult period, when I needed support and companionship, as I often did, being one who lived alone. One or the other was almost always available for a walk, a meal, or at least a long conversation over the phone or Zoom, which by then I had learned to use to some degree. Between Ann, Denise, and my two children, whom I could now see fairly regularly since both were living in Ottawa, I managed to have a far better social life during the worst of the lockdown period than I'd had in Halifax prior to the pandemic. And things only improved once the worst of the lockdowns had ended, and I could also see other old friends such as fellow writers Ralph Smith and Elena Calvo, and former PIPSC colleague Yves Rochon.[8]

Being partners in putting together *Plague Take It,* a volume which obviously would not have existed without the pandemic, did much to cement the already strong friendship between Ann and me. That we are again joining forces to put together the present volume is evidence of that continuing strong bond. It has also helped me maintain my friendship with Denise, whose essay on 'Zooming into Oblivion' is one of the most remarkable pieces in *Plague Take It,* and who has contributed a memoir to the present volume.

But most important of all, the pandemic has given me romance, real romance, for the first time in decades. Without the pandemic, and without *Plague Take It,* the volume 'inspired' by that pandemic, I would not have reconnected with New York dance critic and editor Elizabeth Zimmer, whom I had known briefly in Halifax during my graduate school days there, but whom I hadn't seen for 50 years.

The details of this story I'm leaving to Elizabeth, whose 'Pandemic Romance' appears in this volume. What I can say is that, having kept up with her life just enough to know she'd been active in the dance world both as a participant and as a critic and reviewer, I invited her to contribute a piece on the New York arts scene to *Plague Take It.* She declined this invitation, but did most graciously contribute a moving personal essay-memoir. After this, we entered into online correspondence, and then had an in-person visit in Greenfield, Massachusetts in September of 2021. Unfazed by my extreme difficulties in negotiating some of the highways around Greenfield, Elizabeth agreed to come to Canada for a longer visit that December. And the rest is history—a history she can do a better job of relating than I.

From being well-nigh non-existent, my social life is now about as full and rich as a person of 77 could well imagine having. I have a cross-border romance with Elizabeth, who continues to live in New York, close friendships with Ann and Denise, both of whom live within an hour's drive of Gatineau, and closer relationships with both my kids than I had before moving back to this area. From fairly rattling with emptiness and lone-liness—my fate in Halifax throughout my second stint there—I'm blessed with a social life so rich and full that occasionally I find I must take a day off to be with myself, to rest, and to collect my thoughts. But make no mistake: I am blessed, and I know it. Here, once again, there is no comparison between the life I'm living now and the life I lived before the pandemic. And once again, as in the case of my literary life, most of the change would not have happened without the pandemic.

What about the theatre—my second great interest after writing? How have I managed to stay involved with that during a period when, for much of the time, theatres were closed?

Here, I have not made the huge pandemic-related gains that I have in writing and my social life. But the period has been far from a dead loss for me. Not only did I land a role in a Zoom play, as a sardonic, worldly-wise cab-driver, put on by Rural Root Theatre in June of 2021, but I have taken part in a live performance, *Seniors Create,* in nearby Wakefield, Quebec. And I have auditioned for two or three roles with Kanata Theatre. I didn't land any of those roles, but in the end, I wasn't sorry, since by early 2022 I was so heavily involved with my various book projects.[9]

More important, the pandemic period has actually helped my development as a playwright, which will probably be where I will direct most of my theatrical efforts in the future. The four online playwriting workshops I've already taken with Colleen Naomi, operating out of Lunenburg, Nova Scotia, have led to a play, *Virtual Apprentice,* which we published in *Plague Take It.* And the one I'm currently taking with Colleen will lead to a fairly long play, full one-act if not full-length, about the conflict between Canadian poet Duncan Campbell Scott, in his capacity as Deputy Superintendent of the Department of Indian Affairs and Dr Peter Bryce, in *his* capacity as that department's chief medical officer. Without the stimulus to production provided by Colleen's workshops, I'm not sure I would have kept on writing plays at all, and I certainly wouldn't have written as many of them as I have.

Another online playwriting workshop, this one with Kanata Theatre, actually led to my having a short play performed there during the summer of 2022. *The Holy Grail May Be Found at Starbucks* was written as part of a short play program in which Kanata Theatre takes a number of aspiring playwrights and has them write 10-minute plays and subject them to the scrutiny both of their fellow playwrights and of dramaturge Guy Newsham. It's a long way from Gatineau to Kanata, and I'm not sure I would have been willing to make the trek four or five or six times if the workshop had been live. But thanks to its being on Zoom, a medium I initially loathed but with which I've since learned to co-exist, I wrote the play, persevered through several rounds of critique, and finally had the pleasure of seeing it performed in July of 2022—a first for me. Better yet, during the next summer (2023), I had the pleasure and privilege of directing my first play, *Dark and Stormy Night,* for the same short play festival.

Quite possibly I missed out on a number of acting opportunities that would have been available to me had the pandemic not occurred. But thanks in large measure to the pandemic, I have not only moved my acting to a virtual stage, but advanced significantly more as a playwright than I'd likely have done without the pandemic. It is also worth noting that the pandemic itself was figured prominently in the play *Virtual Apprentice* that I wrote for Colleen's first workshop, in 2020.

Putting all of the above together, I'd say that I have come out at worst even in my theatrical life because of the pandemic, and probably somewhat ahead of where I might otherwise have been. In particular, I don't think I'd have had a play of mine performed without the stimulus afforded by Kanata Theatre's online playwriting workshop. I certainly wouldn't have had the opportunity to try my hand at directing, something I had dreamed of doing for many years.

All in all, then, I've had huge gains through the pandemic, and in large measure resulting from it. What about my *losses?* While not insignificant, they in no way measure up to the gains.

My biggest tangible loss has been that of my teaching, which I'd been doing for the Nova Scotia Seniors College for seven years, starting in 2013, both in Halifax and Truro. I was for some time unable to catch on at Carleton University, which operates a program similar to that of the Seniors' College. It wasn't until September of 2023 that I finally, after years of trying, was given a course to teach in the Carleton program. When I did finally get a course, my experience was, for reasons too complicated to go into here, fraught with all kinds of difficulties. It seems unlikely that I'll ever teach in that program again.

The second biggest tangible loss for me is singing. When the pandemic hit, I was singing more than I had at any other time in my life. I had just finished appearing as a chorus member in a musical, *A Tribute to Broadway,* in Cow Bay, about half an hour's drive east of Dartmouth. And I was also singing in St. Margaret's Anglican Church choir and at several of the various 'Acoustic Song Circles' held at public libraries across Metro Halifax. On average, I was singing in public three or four times a week, counting choir rehearsals, Sunday services, the occasional funeral, and the various Acoustic Song Circles.

Once again, as in the case of teaching, the pandemic brought my activity to a crashing halt. Even after the churches were able to resume live services, in June of 2020, there was still no choral music or congregational singing. Now (as of February, 2023), I no longer attend church, not having found one that appeals to me and frankly not wishing to sacrifice my Sunday mornings, which I feel are needed for rest and recuperation from busy writing weeks. As for the Acoustic Song Circles, they're a moot point, since I am not aware of any similar organized singing groups here in Gatineau.

As of now, the last time I sang in public was at an outdoor gathering held near Halifax in June of 2020. Every so often, I do tune in to an 'oldies' classic on YouTube on my desktop and sing along with it. This is fun, but I can't pretend it in any way compares with singing in a choir, or singing in front of or along with others at an Acoustic Song Circle.

Bridge also counts as a loss, though less of one than either teaching or singing; it was always something I could take or leave. Like church choirs, duplicate bridge clubs brought their activities to a screeching halt at the start of the pandemic—and for much the same reasons. Throughout the bridge community, there was the fear that gatherings bringing large numbers of people together in close physical proximity to one another and involving the handling of many decks of cards could become super-spreader COVID events. As of November 2021, the largest of the three games, a duplicate event that had been held several times a week at a Presbyterian church in Dartmouth, had still not resumed play, though its facilitator was seriously considering doing so.[10]

As was the case with church-going, bridge appears simply to have dropped out of my life following my move to Quebec. I have not played the game in any form since leaving Nova Scotia. Internet bridge holds no appeal, and I am not aware of any live groups in my immediate area. Given that with my many literary and theatrical projects, it would be hard for me to find the time to play, at least often enough to maintain a reasonable standard, this is less of a loss than it might otherwise have been.

I also miss dressing up—something there simply doesn't seem to be much occasion for anymore, in our brave new post-COVID world—and going to live baseball games, something I am not willing to attempt given Major League Baseball's suspension of all rules around vaccination and masking. For the first time ever, I've begun to give serious thought to giving away some of the many suits and sport coats sitting in my closets, unworn, year after year. The only reason I keep most of these fancy clothes is in the hope, probably a fond one, of being cast in some theatrical role for which I will need to wear them.

A less tangible if more substantial issue is the loss or at least weakening of a number of friendships I had prior to the pandemic. This applies particularly two of my old literary friends, with whom I am less close now than I was at the beginning of 2020. Both of them—one in particular—have cut way back on their socializing out of fear of contracting COVID. Hopefully the new vaccines now available will make them feel less skittish about social events. If not, there is always Zoom, though it remains a seriously imperfect substitute for live personal contact.

My final, and in some ways most serious loss has nothing to do with any particular activity. What it involves is a feeling of ease about the world in which I live. I no longer feel any confidence in the ability or willingness of

Canadian politicians—let alone U.S. ones—to manage the COVID pandemic so as to minimize its health impacts. Politics and a concern for the economy are now most politicians' main concerns, with health concerns (if they are in evidence at all) forced to take back seat. Yet the pandemic is far from over. Even as this piece was being written, the aforementioned Colleen Naomi had to postpone an online playwriting session because she'd contracted COVID. And my dear friend Ann McMillan has also had COVID, albeit a very mild case of the disease, as befits someone who at the time had had four vaccinations. More recently, as I noted in the introduction, Elizabeth and I both contracted it—five vaccinations apiece and all—during my late November visit to New York.[11] Fortunately, perhaps due to those five vaccinations apiece, we both had mild cases and were up and about and living a pretty normal life within a week. But should people who have had four and five vaccinations really be contracting the disease at all?

For Canada as a whole, let alone the U.S., the situation is nothing short of alarming. Over the week prior to September 9, 2022, 74 Ontarians died of COVID, while 1,248 were in hospital with the disease.[12] Yet despite such clear evidence that the pandemic has indeed continued, and despite health officials' warnings about potentially higher levels in the fall as colder weather sets in,[13] the Ontario provincial government has dropped its mask mandate for schools, making the wearing of masks in schools voluntary for the first time since the start of the pandemic.[14] The callousness of this action leaves me speechless. Worse yet, even as hospitalizations and deaths continue to rise, there is still no serious talk, in either Ontario or Quebec, about bringing back mask mandates or vaccination requirements for travel or admittance to public places. Our public officials appear to be in a state of denial about the continuing threat caused by COVID's new variants. Can it be that they really don't care?

With these sobering thoughts, I close my personal pandemic assessment, aware that despite the many gains I have made to this point (February, 2023), all could be wiped out in a flash if I were to let my guard down even for a moment. If our public officials no longer care, it is up to me to take the best possible care I can of myself. And so I continue to wear masks in public places such as grocery stores and movie theatres, even though I am sometimes the only person wearing one and generally part of a very small minority, and even though I occasionally get owly looks from people. Large crowds, such as those found in baseball stadiums and hockey arenas, where almost no fans appear to be masked any more, I avoid completely. With an eye to maintaining the strength of my immune system, I take daily doses of Vitamin D and Vitamin B. Even these measures, I recognize, may not be enough, but they're the best I can do while still maintaining some semblance of a normal life. I've been lucky enough, so far, to avoid serious COVID-

Jon Peirce

related complications. I can only hope that my luck continues through the next few years.

Jon Peirce
Gatineau, Quebec
February, 2023, revised in February, 2024.

---

[1] My move to Gatineau, Quebec, which would take place about six months after the start of the pandemic, is chronicled in 'Farewell to Nova Scotia,' at pp. 414–422 of *Plague Take It*.

[2] In 'COVID and Mental Health' at p. 88 of *Plague Take It*.

[3] *Ibid.*

[4] My pandemic-era struggles with anxiety have also been documented in 'COVID and Mental Health,' *op. cit.*

[5] I'm pleased to report that two of those pieces, 'The Why Do It? Guy' and 'The Method to a Method-Acting Director's Madness,' have just been published in the *Chicken Soup* anthology *The Advice that Changed My Life*, released in February, 2023.

[6] It was a CBC Internet News piece I wrote in January of 2022 that landed me the work hours contract from Dundurn.

[7] The short story book, *The Long and the Short of It*, was published on Amazon in February of 2024.

[8] All three are, perhaps not coincidentally, represented in *Plague Take It*.

[9] In Dec.,2023, I did land a role as 'Captain' in a radio play, *Beauty Will Save the World*, put on by 9th Hour Theatre Company in Ottawa.

[10] Tony Morris, in e-mail to St. Andrew's bridge group participants, November 17, 2021. From the start of the pandemic, Tony kept the group together and helped maintain its spirits by sending out a weekly trivia quiz.

[11] We have now each had the disease twice, having both contracted it for a second time in August of 2023.

[12] 'COVID Trends on Downward Slope, OPH Says.' CBC News (internet), September 9, 2022.

[13] *Ibid.*

[14] Abby O'Brien, 'Masks Will be Voluntary in Ontario Schools Next Semester.' CBC News (internet), August 8, 2022.

BIOGRAPHIES
OF AUTHORS

JOHN ALLEN. John is an award-winning author of historical fiction and creative non-fiction whose work has been featured in *Broadview* magazine, *Light* magazine, and four editions of *Chicken Soup for the Soul*. His writing is often interrupted by his and his wife's three male rescue cats, all of whom think they are teenage boys.

FRED ANDAYI. Dr Andayi is a research scientist and public health practitioner in communicable disease epidemiology. He has lived and worked with various organizations across Europe, Africa, and North America, including the French IRD, the U.S. CDC, McGill University, UNHCR, and Médecins Sans Frontières. During the COVID-19 pandemic, his expertise and insights from studying the 1918 Spanish flu and the 2004 swine flu pandemics were invaluable in helping protect seniors from infections in long-term care facilities across Quebec, Ontario, and Saskatchewan. In this memoir, 'Pandemic Stories of Infection Prevention in Long-Term Care,' he highlights his contributions and lived experiences at that time.

Originally from Kenya, Dr Andayi holds a Doctor of Veterinary Medicine from the University of Nairobi, a Master of Public Health from EHESP Paris, and a Doctorate in Public Health from the University of Aix-Marseille. He is also a Certified Infection Prevention and Control (CIC®) professional. When he's not busy saving lives, he enjoys running and has completed three marathons. He also loves nature trails, hiking, and amateur photography, especially street art. Currently, he resides in Gatineau, Quebec, and can be reached at fredandayi@gmail.com

SALLY ARSOVE. Sally was born and raised in the U.S.A. (mostly) and ended up in Ottawa in 1975, after a year of volunteer teaching in Ethiopia followed by a year studying at the London School of Economics. Sally is a citizen of both Canada and the U.S.A., and her two adult children now both live and work on the U.S. side of the border. Sally worked for many years as an Economist for the Government of Canada in the field of international development and finance. After retiring in 2007, she earned a bookkeeping certificate and now works part-time helping young companies get their businesses going. Sally enjoys the beauty of nature, gardening and outdoor exercise (especially swimming, biking, and cross-country skiing), sewing, and connecting with friends and family. Sally has continued to volunteer in the health care sector and for local poverty reduction organizations.

TERESA BANDROWSKA. Teresa has been a scribbler for as long as she can remember, writing plays, poetry and short stories. As a retired midwife, she is now able to dedicate her time to more serious scribbling. She is currently working on a play, and also on translating her father's memories from World War Two in Poland and Siberia.

JANET BARCLAY. Janet has published two books on travels with an RV across Canada and the US: *Points North and East* and *Points North and West*. A third book on a three-month journey around the world, *Points East and West* was published in 2025. She maintains a blog of world travels, which is heavily illustrated.

ROBERT BARCLAY. Dr Barclay was born in London, England in 1946. He received a Certificate in Science Laboratory Technology from the City and Guilds of London Institute (1968). He emigrated to Toronto in 1970 having heard that The Leafs had recently won the Stanley Cup. After graduating from the University of Toronto with a BA in Fine Arts (1975), he went on to earn an interdisciplinary PhD at the Open University in the UK (1999). He worked as a museum object restorer and musical instrument maker, and conducts trumpet-making workshops in Europe and the United States. He has published extensively in the fields of museum conservation, musical instrument making, music history and fiction. His fictional works include *Ask Me About My Bombshells*, *Jacob the Trumpeter*, *His Majesty's Grand Conceit*, and *Conversations with Sensible People*. The latest, *Twixt Myth and History*, 25 interviews with legendary/mythical/historic/folkloric characters, was published in 2025.

GUYLAINE BELANGER. C'est à ma mère que je dois la magie des mots. À cinq ans, remplacer la lettre 'e' du mot bobine par un 'o' et découvrir le nom 'Bobino' m'a émerveillée. À onze ans, ma 'maîtresse d'école', une vieille dame aux cheveux tout blancs, nous a lu des extraits du *Journal d'Anne Frank*. Si une jeune fille de quatorze ans pouvait le faire, je le pouvais aussi. Depuis, mon journal intime m'est devenu aussi essentiel que l'air que je respire...Je rêve encore d'un roman. Publié ou non. Un jour, peut-être l'écrirai-je.

YVON BERNIER. Yvon est né à Verdun (Montréal) où il a fait ses études primaires et secondaires. Il a obtenu un BSc. en physique de l'Université de Montréal en 1960 et une M.Sc en météorologie de l'Université de Toronto en 1961. Il a ensuite poursuivi une carrière en météorologie opérationnelle, à titre d'analyste, de prévisionniste ou de superviseur à Halifax et à Montréal. En 1981, il a été affecté à Ottawa où il a travaillé au niveau administratif au bureau du sous-ministre adjoint du Service de l'environnement atmosphérique d'Environnement Canada jusqu'à sa retraite en 1994. Depuis, il a développé une passion pour la culture du bonsaï et le bénévolat religieux. Marié depuis 1969 et père d'une fille, il vit aujourd'hui avec son épouse dans une résidence pour retraités.

Yvon was born in Verdun (Montreal) where he received his primary and secondary education. He received a bachelor's degree in physics from the Université de Montréal in 1960 and a master's degree in meteorology from the University of Toronto in 1961. He then pursued a career in operational meteorology, as an analyst, forecaster or supervisor in Halifax and Montreal.

315

In 1981, he was posted to Ottawa where he worked at the administrative level in the office of the Assistant Deputy Minister of Environment Canada's Atmospheric Environment Service until his retirement in 1994. Since then, he has developed a passion for bonsai cultivation and religious volunteering. Married since 1969 and father of a daughter, he now lives with his wife in a retirement residence.

DEBRA BERTRAND. Debra was raised on a dairy farm in West Carleton Township, and lived in the surrounding area all her life, but has settled in the town of Arnprior, Ontario for the past twenty plus years. She raised four beautiful children with her husband John, and worked as an administrative assistant in Arnprior for 40 years. Debra has been retired for the past seven years, enjoying being part of her grandchildren's lives, and living life to the fullest by keeping healthy and active.

DONNA CHATEAUVERT. Donna has had two jobs, the first with Scotiabank and the second with Ontario Hydro. She joined the bank after graduation and after her marriage she joined her husband in northern Ontario, where she worked for Ontario Hydro. They returned to Arnprior, and once her children were in school she returned to Scotiabank, where she worked as a financial advisor until she retired. Donna enjoys being with friends, especially on the golf course.

RODNEY CLOUGH. Rodney built, owned and operated Rabbit Run, a 7-bedroom inn and vacation property rental near the sandy shores of Lake Michigan with his partner, Linda Jo. Prior to this venture, Rodney and Linda Jo owned and operated a neighborhood shipping/packing/mailbox store in the Gold Coast, Chicago. Since 2019, Rodney has published over 500 essays on politics, culture (art and cinema), and economics.
https://medium.com/@rodneyclough
https://substack.com/@rodneyclough
rodclough630@gmail.com

JACK DENNY-BROWN. Jack's story in this collection, 'The Biochemist,' provides all the information you could want about his life. He has written countless stories and a number of plays, some of which have been performed though none have been published as yet. He currently lives with his wife, Ann, on a lake in Central Massachusetts. Jack is a retired fifth-grade teacher.

JOHN EATON. John was born in 1942 in Birmingham UK, but his technicolour life really began in1945 (Toronto '56) with the banana boats and *The Wizard of Oz*. Despite his almost drowning in 1962, he feared not for himself but for his parents' 'possible vision' of him.
     John excelled in school, particularly in mathematics, ultimately earning a BSc honours in '65 and a PhD in '70 both in physics, followed by the

requisite publications/post doc'ing until 1973. Marriage in 1965 and his first child in 1972 required a more meaningful vocation: in aerospace. He began as a metallurgist, followed by 25 years in Quality: Engineering and management (NDT, Laboratory, Inspection and Suppliers and Quality Engineers). Among other things, the work entailed the preparation and approvals of all controlling documents including policy, procedure and work instructions. With two children and two great grandchildren, and after having suffered his father's (1968) and wife's (2015) protracted ordeals of dying, John hopes he can now impart the empathy he has gained, which seems lacking for so many in our post-COVID world of potential 'Extinction.'

NANCY GAUTHIER. Nancy, résidente et native de Gatineau, n'a déserté que quelques années pour vivre et étudier à Sherbrooke. Toutes les occasions sont bonnes pour exercer sa plume, que ce soit comme gagne-pain à la fonction publique fédérale ou comme passe-temps. Dans l'incertitude et les confinements de la COVID-19, l'écriture a été une source de plaisir et divertissement, et elle lui a offert la liberté de s'évader avec comme seules limites celles de son imagination.

DENISE GIROUX. Denise is a lawyer with more than 32 years' experience as a champion for underdogs, having practiced in the areas of poverty law, family and general litigation, and labour law, with a strong focus on human rights. She recently retired from working with a federal public service union in Ottawa and is still trying to adjust to turns of events in this phase of her life. She contributed an essay on the effect of the pandemic on work to *Plague Take It* ('Zooming our Way into Oblivion'). She lives in the Gatineau Hills in Wakefield, Québec.

MARTIN GRAVEL. Martin, natif de Joliette, est Gatinois depuis une dizaine d'année. Il s'occupe des ressources humaines pour les IGA de la Famille Charles mais il est aussi Sommelier Bière. On peut entendre ses chroniques à Énergie et à UnikFM et on peut aussi lui lire dans différents journaux locaux de la région. De plus, Martin est fondateur d'une nouvelle microbrasserie qui vise à s'établir dans la MRC des Collines de l'Outaouais, Brasseurs des Collines. La bière, la lecture, la musique et l'écriture sont toutes des passions qui lui habitent.

SHARON HAMILTON. Sharon is an Ottawa-based writer whose work has appeared in *The Globe and Mail*, the *Literary Review of Canada*, and the *Ottawa Citizen*, among other publications. She is a member of the Board for the international Ernest Hemingway Society and serves as Chair for the Society for American Baseball Research's (SABR) Century Research Committee, which celebrates important milestones in baseball history. She posts about baseball, literature and jazz age cocktails: @alifeliterary.bsky.social

317

RUTH HAWKINS. Ruth, as the daughter of an Air Force officer, spent her childhood in Europe and Labrador before settling back in Ontario. This early exposure to other countries and lifestyles took root and, at 17, Ruth spent a year in Brazil as a Rotary International exchange student, a life-changing experience that continues to influence her way of seeing and being in the world. After 33 years as a federal public servant, Ruth 'retired' and began a second career as a psychotherapist. Although writing was a major element of her government work, Ruth turned to more personal writing during the COVID-19 pandemic. Early weekend mornings will find her online, writing in the company of a small group of therapist authors. Her short essay on being a therapist during the pandemic, 'It's OK if I'm not OK,' was published in *Plague Take It*. Ruth has a daughter, twin sons, two granddaughters, and two dogs. She is an avid traveler, reader and fibre artist.

ELIZABETH HOFFMAN. Elizabeth is Professor Emerita of economics at Iowa State University, where she previously served as Executive Vice President and Provost, and Dean of Liberal Arts and Sciences. From 2000 to 2005, she was President of the University of Colorado System, where she is President Emerita. Her published research is in the areas of Experimental Economics, Cliometrics, and Behavioral Economics. Her interest in the Plague goes back to her history A.B. from Smith College in 1968. She can be reached at: bhoffman@iastate.edu.

IAN JOHNSON. Ian retired in 2015 from the Nova Scotia Government and General Employees Union. He served as a policy analyst/communications coordinator with NSGEU for 20 years. He also worked with the Nova Scotia Provincial Health Council, the Nova Scotia NDP Caucus, and the Social Planning Department of the City of Halifax. He later served as a director with two Nova Scotia Pension Boards. He helped to set up the Nova Scotia Health Coalition and the Nova Scotia Office of the Canadian Centre for Policy Alternatives. He is married, and lives in Halifax, Nova Scotia. He has a stepdaughter and two sons as well as two grandchildren. He had a stroke in April 2020, from which he has fully recovered. Ian can be reached at: johnsonianfeb@gmail.com

PEGGY LEHMANN. Peggy has themes of human experience and spirituality woven through each of her short stories and poems. Her lifelong love of words and writing led her to become a member of Ottawa Independent Writers to learn more about the craft. She has had a short story published in each of the last eight annual OIW anthologies. 'Viral Contempt' is her first published poem. Peggy lives in Ottawa with her family and is currently working on several writing projects.

CATHERINE MACKENZIE: Cathy's writings are found in numerous print and online publications. She writes all genres but invariably veers toward the dark—so much so her late mother once asked, 'Can't you write anything happy?' (She can!) She's published the novels *Wolves Don't Knock, Mister Wolfe*, and *When Kayaks Fly*, along with several books of poetry, short story compilations, and children's picture books. Cathy divides her time between West Porters Lake and Halifax, Nova Scotia. Check out her website/blog:

http://writingwicket.wordpress.com

SUHA MARDELLI. Suha is an Ottawa-based writer whose diverse background enriches her narratives. Her stories are infused with vibrant, evocative scenes—ranging from driving through tornadoes and mingling with celebrities to dancing in Delhi's slums and escaping with humanoids in a near future—seeking meaning in the everyday and cryptic. Suha's work explores the intersections of adventure and intimacy, revealing the extraordinary within the seemingly mundane. She has published several short stories in local anthologies, including *Entertainment When the Batteries Die*, described as 'a hilariously nostalgic romp through childhood mischief,' and *My Russian Princess*, 'a richly woven narrative blending personal history and nostalgia, where the mystique of Russian royalty meets the warmth of Syrian hospitality.' Her poem *Even Lint Has a Story to Tell* won the annual OIW competition for being 'an evocative stream of consciousness that dances between wit and raw introspection, daring readers to uncover the beauty hidden in life's overlooked corners.' Suha has been shortlisted for the NYC Midnight short-story contest in 2021 and 2022. She loves fandom and purple food. Contact her on X: @smsuey.

SUSAN MILLS. Susan lives in Arnprior and is now retired. During COVID, Susan became an outspoken critic of long-term care policies which separated loved ones from their support systems. Susan has had her work published in *Plague Take it* and *Tales from the Boat*. She is a twice-diagnosed breast cancer survivor who enjoys dragon-boating and cannot wait for the day she is back on the water.

WANDA MONUK. Wanda was born and raised north of Toronto. In 1978 she moved to the Ottawa area for her first 'real' job after university, and ended up staying. She has now been married for over 44 years and has two lovely daughters, two favourite sons-in-law and two beautiful grandchildren. She still lives in the beautiful Ottawa valley.

In 2018 Wanda retired after 40 years from her life's work in market research just as her mother's dementia was making it increasingly difficult for her to live well on her in her own home. The need for one-on-one care every day became very quickly apparent to her family. A couple of months after her retirement, Wanda was diagnosed with breast cancer. She completed her treatment in 2019, and the family moved her mother to an assisted living care floor in a residence that fall. Then, just as Wanda thought the workload and stress from being her Mum's primary caregiver would subside, COVID struck. She found the lockdowns and other COVID restrictions even more stressful than the previous two years with her mum's dementia. She spent many weeks with her mum in her residence so that she would not be alone.

Wanda's mum passed away in early 2022. She feels very fortunate that she is now able to enjoy her retirement. Now as we head to the end of 2024, she has finally regained her rest and peace after all her health issues and her Mum's dementia though the first four years of her retirement. Her own family deserves huge recognition for their unwavering support and love for her through the dementia and COVID years.

COLLEEN NAOMI. Colleen (she/her) has been writing since childhood, when she published her own 'zine' for two years and produced plays in her front yard. Throughout her life her passion has flourished for the written word and performing arts. She has had many of her original plays performed as well as essays published in *Plague Take It* (2021) and *The United Church Observer* (2014). She is also a theatre educator for both children and adults. Colleen lives in Nova Scotia with her family.

FRAN OTA. Fran is an ordained minister with The United Church of Canada. Born in 1946 in Canora, Saskatchewan into a minister's family, she is a 'child of the pulpit,' living in Prince Albert and Winnipeg. In 1970 she graduated from University of Manitoba with a Bachelor of Music Performance, and went to Japan as United Church Overseas Personnel. She and her husband Norio were married in 1971, and have lived in Vietnam, Australia, New Jersey and Michigan, settling in Toronto in 1984. Fran has worked in refugee services, medical research, and administration and as a church musician. She received a Master of Divinity from University of Toronto in 1995, serving churches in Ontario and Newfoundland. In 2022 she received a MPhil/MA in Viking and Medieval Norse Studies from University of Iceland/University of Oslo. Fran and Norio have four grown sons and six grandchildren, and currently spend their semi-retirement in Japan, Canada and Portugal.

KATHRYN PAULSEN. Kathryn writes poetry, novels, short stories, essays, stage plays, and screenplays. Her work has appeared in publications from Canada to Ireland to Australia, including *New Letters*, *West Branch*, *The New York Times*, *The Stinging Fly*, *Humber Literary Review*, *Scum*, *Craft*, *Big Fiction*, and *Spillway*. Her chapbook 'The Poetry Habit' came out earlier this year from Clare Songbirds Publishing, and 'Catch of the Night' from Bottlecap Press. Kathryn has been awarded fellowships at Yaddo, MacDowell, and other retreats. Her latest play, *SIX WEEKS IN THE SPRING*, is set during the early days of the COVID-19 pandemic in New York City. Kathryn lives in

New York City but, having grown up in an air force family, has roots in many places. Her website is a work in progress, but for now look for her on Facebook.

LENA SAMSON. Lena is a writer, editor and poet living outside of Ottawa. She has published stories in two Ottawa Independent Writers anthologies: *Connections* (2023) and *This Land* (2024), as well as poetry in *redrosethorns* online journal. She graduated from Carleton University, majoring in Russian and English, and many years later, earned her Editing Certificate from Simon Fraser University. In between, she enjoyed a long career in the Canadian federal government. Lena spends her time happily writing and editing, as well as entertaining her delightful granddaughters.

CHANTAL SEGUIN. Chantal a toujours eu un intérêt pour la langue française. Depuis qu'elle est toute jeune, elle s'intéresse aux mots croisés et à la lecture, des passions qui lui ont été transmises par sa maman. Retraitée de la fonction publique fédérale depuis 2014 où elle a travaillé plus de trente ans, ses nombreux emplois ont tous eu trait, de près ou de loin, à la rédaction, à la révision et à la traduction. Sa participation à ce collectif littéraire est sa première expérience de création en écriture.

Chantal has always had a serious interest in the French language. Her mom transmitted *her* interest in crosswords and reading to her daughter at a young age. Chantal has been retired from the federal public service, where she worked for over 30 years, since 2014. While most of her jobs dealt with writing, editing and translation, whether it be in ministerial correspondence or cabinet documents, her participation in this initiative is her first experience of creative writing.

HENDRIK SIRÉ. Hendrik is an aspiring poet. He is preparing his first collection of poetry, tentatively entitled 'Poetry for Another Day,' for publication. He has written two previous collections of poetry, 'The Death of Words' and 'Laugh Plums and Other Pluttry,' both unpublished. He has taken poetry courses with Mark Frutkin and Nicola Vulpe and has had lively conversations with the oral poet and architect H. Masud Taj. He was a participant in a creative writing group from 2017 to 2023. He has submitted his work to the CBC Poetry Prize and has published two articles in the *Globe and Mail*. He speaks five languages. He has chronic asthma including emphysema and pleural effusion, and has had pneumonia seven times. hendriksire@rogers.com

RALPH SMITH. Ralph is an Ottawa writer who grew up on the Canadian prairies. He now lives in Ottawa with his wife and family. He began writing many years ago and has had numerous short stories published. Over the past 10 years Ralph has written four novels that have been published. Their titles are *Bright Deep, Twitch: The Foundling's Quest, Concession Street Secrets,* and (the

most recent, published in December 2023), *Hawdon: A Prequel to Charles Dickens's Bleak House.* All are available from online book retailers. Ralph has been a Dickens fan ever since he was 13 years old. He wrote Master's and PhD theses on Dickens. The story in this collection draws upon his experiences as a child. Ralph's email address is:
ralphfrederick2@gmail.com

JULIE STASHICK. Julie was born in small town Arnprior, Ontario, the eldest of 3 children. Her parents came from large families and her paternal and maternal grandparents lived close by. She had 43 cousins, with whom she was very close. Julie left home at 18 to study behavioural science in Kingston. In 1983 she moved back home and studied dental assisting and office management in Ottawa. She graduated and enjoyed a long career in dental offices in Renfrew, Arnprior and Ottawa.

In 2017 Julie graduated from a Personal Support Worker program and worked in the community in Arnprior. Fairview Manor in Almonte was hiring so she applied and enjoyed her five years working with the residents and staff there. She found this last career the most rewarding of her entire working life. Retirement has been fulfilling for Julie. She has her health and wonderful family and friends. She loves dragon boating in summer and skating and hiking in the winter. Her grandchildren are her joy and keep Julie young!

ANNE-MARIE VALTON. Anne-Marie, née au milieu d'une famille nombreuse à la fin des années '50s de parents immigrants français pauvres, se faisait déjà taguer de très différentes de par son intelligence précoce et une sensibilité particulière.

De par une curiosité naturelle elle fréquentera le milieu de la science. Des problèmes de santé apparaissant tôt dans sa vie, liés aux traumatismes vécus dans son enfance, l'obligera à prendre une longue pause de son travail et à le quitter ultérieurement. Ainsi sa vie deviendra rapidement une véritable quête de vérité, de conscience et de mieux-être. Son chemin de Vie a été parsemé de nombreux défis jugés impossible par ses pairs, Anne-Marie les relèvera tous, grâce à un courage et une résilience exceptionnelle! Tout au long de cette quête elle découvrit ses talents d'artiste-peintre, d'animatrice, de coach en relation d'aide, sa capacité de travailler avec l'énergie subtile, son intuition et sa connexion particulière avec l'énergie du Cœur par le chant de l'Âme!

Anne-Marie, born into a large family in the late '50s to poor French immigrant parents, was already being singled out early on for her precocious intelligence and particular sensitivity.

Her natural curiosity led her to become involved in the world of science. Health problems early in life, linked to childhood traumas, forced her to take a long break from her work and later to leave it. Her life quickly became a quest for truth, awareness and well-being. Anne-Marie's life path was strewn with many challenges deemed impossible by her peers, but she met them all with exceptional courage and resilience! Throughout this quest, she discovered her talents as a painter, facilitator and relationship coach, her ability to work with subtle energy, her intuition and her special connection with the energy of the Heart through the song of the Soul!

ELIZABETH ZIMMER. Elizabeth has written about dance, theatre, and books for New York's *Village Voice* and other publications since 1983. She covered arts and related subjects for the CBC in Halifax and Vancouver from 1971 until 1979, and has published essays in *Plague Take It* and in *Connections,* the 2023 annual collection from Ottawa Independent Writers. She is an editor at *Persimmon Tree,* a magazine of the arts by women over 60, and also edits books and essays on a variety of topics. She has run writing workshops for students and professionals across North America, studied many forms of dance, and taught for nine years in the Hollins University MFA dance program.

THE EDITORS

ANN McMILLAN. Ann is enjoying her second career as a writer but still having difficulty knowing what she wants to do when she grows up. She transitioned from working as a manager with the federal government to retirement by editing and contributing to *Air Quality Management: Canadian Perspectives on a Global Issue* (Springer) with Eric Taylor in 2014. A pattern of collaboration started to emerge when she helped write and edit *The New Devil's Dictionary* (Amazon, 2019) and *Naked in Time* (Amazon, 2020) with Duane Chartier, a long-time friend.

These were followed by *Plague Take it: A COVID Almanac by and about Elders* (Loose Cannon Press, 2021) with Jon Peirce, which was a much more ambitious undertaking, providing a social history of those troubling times from the perspectives of elders. *Tales from the Boat* (Loose Cannon Press, 2022) provides a collection of stories and poetry by the breast cancer survivors of the Prior Chest Nuts, a dragon boat team based in Arnprior, Ontario.

Ann has up until now focused on short pieces, in the belief that as she ages she has the attention span of a gnat. However, in 'Grannies,' she has challenged herself to write a longer research-based piece summarizing the ageism and sexism that have gripped Ontario's long-term care sector and which will have consequences not only for the remnants of today's post-COVID elder generation, but for generations to come.

JON PEIRCE. Jon is a labour and social historian, playwright, memoirist, essayist, and fiction writer, as well as an occasional editor and manuscript analyst. He recently relocated to Ottawa from Gatineau, Quebec, largely on account of the healthcare system, which he finds himself using more and more often these days. He is a retired union labour relations officer and English and industrial relations professor. An actor as well as a writer, Jon has made more than a dozen appearances on various community theatre stages in Nova Scotia, Quebec, and Ontario. Most recently he played the lead role of Mike in *Biffy Comes to Town* at Kanata Theatre (2024) and the role of Captain in 9th Hour Theatre Company's radio play, *Beauty Will Save the World* (2024). Jon holds a BA in English from Amherst College, an MA and a PhD in English from Dalhousie University, and a Master's degree in industrial relations from Queen's University.

The Road to Recovery is the seventh book which Jon has written or edited. In addition to *Road's* predecessor volume, *Plague Take It* (Loose Cannon Press, 2021), also co-edited with Ann McMillan, his previous publications include *Work Less* (Dundurn Press, 2024), a call for shorter work hours; *The Long and the Short of It* (Amazon, 2024), a short story collection; *Canadian Industrial Relations* (Pearson, 2000), an introductory industrial relations text which ran to three editions; as well as a novella and an essay collection. He has published six pieces in the *Chicken Soup for the Soul* series, and over 200 articles, op-ed pieces, and book reviews; these have appeared in such publications as *The Globe & Mail*, the *Kingston Whig-Standard*, the *Ottawa Citizen*, the *Christian Science Monitor*, the *Toronto Star*, the *Winnipeg Free Press*, *Books in Canada*, and *Halifax* magazine.

Outside of writing and theatre, Jon's interests include swimming, cooking, going for long walks, bird-watching, train travel, progressive politics and civilized conversation. Forced to give up tennis, he has recently turned to golf and is pleasantly surprised by how much he enjoys it. He is a board member of Ottawa Independent Writers. Works in progress include a second essay collection and a book on technology, also co-authored with Ann McMillan. To contact Jon for any reason, including a discussion of manuscript analysis and big-picture editing, send him an e-mail at: jonpeirce@hotmail.com

www.ingramcontent.com/pod-product-compliance
Lightning Source LLC
Chambersburg PA
CBHW020841020726
47497CB00005B/1206